Animal Subjects

Cultural Studies Series

ENVIRONMENTAL
HUMANITIES

Animal Subjects
An Ethical Reader in a Posthuman World

edited by
Jodey Castricano

Wilfrid Laurier University Press

We acknowledge the financial support of the Government of Canada through the Book Publishing Industry Development Program for our publishing activities.

Library and Archives Canada Cataloguing in Publication

   Animal subjects : an ethical reader in a posthuman world / Jodey Castricano, editor.

(Environmental humanities series)
(Cultural studies series)
Includes bibliographical references and index.
ISBN 978-0-88920-512-3

   1. Animal rights. 2. Animal welfare. 3. Animal welfare—Moral and ethical aspects. 4. Human–animal relationships. I. Castricano, Jodey, 1947– II. Series. III. Series: Cultural studies series (Waterloo, Ont.)

HV4708.A64 2008   179'.3   C2007-906852-9

© 2008 Wilfrid Laurier University Press
Waterloo, Ontario, Canada
www.wlupress.wlu.ca

Cover design by Blakeley. Cover photo by Eric Isselée. Photo of author by Jacqueline Larson. Text design by Pam Woodland.

∞

This book is printed on Ancient Forest Friendly paper (100% post-consumer recycled).

Printed in Canada

No part of this publication may be reproduced, stored in a retrieval system or transmitted, in any form or by any means, without the prior written consent of the publisher or a licence from The Canadian Copyright Licensing Agency (Access Copyright). For an Access Copyright licence, visit www.accesscopyright.ca or call toll free to 1-800-893-5777.

For Rebekka, whose heart is big

Contents

Acknowledgements ix

1 Introduction: Animal Subjects in a Posthuman World 1
   Jodey Castricano

2 Chicken 33
   Donna Haraway

3 Selfish Genes, Sociobiology and Animal Respect 39
   Rod Preece

4 Anatomy as Speech Act: Vesalius, Descartes, Rembrandt or, The Question of "the animal" in the Early Modern Anatomy Lesson 63
   Dawne McCance

5 A Missed Opportunity: Humanism, Anti-humanism and the Animal Question 97
   Paola Cavalieri

6 Thinking Other-Wise: Cognitive Science, Deconstruction and the (Non)Speaking (Non)Human Animal Subject 125
   Cary Wolfe

7 Animals in Moral Space 145
   Michael Allen Fox and *Lesley McLean*

8 Electric Sheep and the New Argument from Nature 177
   Angus Taylor

9 Monsters: The Case of Marineland 195
   John Sorenson

10 "I sympathize in their pains and pleasures": Women and Animals in Mary Wollstonecraft 223
   Barbara K. Seeber

11 Animals as Persons 241
   David Sztybel

12 Power and Irony: One Tortured Cat and Many Twisted Angles to Our Moral Schizophrenia about Animals 259
   Lesli Bisgould

13 Blame and Shame? How Can We Reduce Unproductive Animal Experimentation? 271
   Anne Innis Dagg

14 On Animal Immortality: An Argument for the Possibility of Animal Immortality in Light of the History of Philosophy 285
   Johanna Tito

   Contributors 301

   Index 305

Acknowledgements

This collection was conceived in Ontario while I was a member of the English and Film Studies Department at Wilfrid Laurier University and came to completion three years and three thousand miles later in British Columbia, my native province, where I returned to become a member of the Critical Studies Department at the University of British Columbia in the Okanagan.

I have always believed in this work and want to extend my gratitude to those who encouraged it and contributed to its making. From this end of the project, I want to thank the dean's office in the Faculty of Creative and Critical Studies at UBCO for financial support in the form of a Book Publication Grant. In the beginning and on the other side of the country was Brian Henderson, the director of Wilfrid Laurier University Press, whose vision and support over the years were invaluable. I also want to thank Lisa Quinn, the acquisitions editor for the Press, who guided the manuscript's journey towards completion over the last year and who gave sound advice while retaining a sense of humour. Similarly, I want to extend my thanks to Beth McAuley for the precision of her copy-editing eye and lastly to Rob Kohlmeier, who took over in the final stages of production and smoothed the way.

Thanks goes, of course, to the contributors to this volume, all of whom responded positively to the call for essays in the first place and who never missed a beat where revisions and deadlines were concerned. Their contributions are the heart of this collection and I am honoured to have worked with such committed scholars, writers, activists and thinkers on a project that seeks a hearing for ethical consideration for nonhuman animals in the field of cultural studies. I especially want to thank my former colleague, contributor to this collection and lunch partner at the vegetarian restaurant in Waterloo, Ontario, Rod Preece, for his encouragement and mentoring in the field of animal studies.

I also want to thank Muriel McMahon for being there to talk to about dreamwork involving empathy and animals, and my colleague, David Jefferess, who knows what this collection means.

I also want to acknowledge Felix, the Alaskan Malamute with whom I live and who has taught me a lot about myself. Thanks also go to Simon, the little terrier who was rescued by the SPCA, who now lives with us and who taught us about learning to trust, and the cats who have their favourite places in the house: Harley, Willie, Suess, Oscar, Puffy and Tom.

At the heart of all of this activity is my partner, Rebekka Augustine, who read through the entire manuscript and generously shared her copyediting skills in addition to her love and encouragement. To her goes my best love.

I

Introduction
Animal Subjects in a Posthuman World

JODEY CASTRICANO

> *The greatness of a nation and its moral progress can be judged by the way its animals are treated.*
> —Mahatma Gandhi

In an interview in *Topia: A Canadian Journal of Cultural Studies*, cultural theorist Cary Wolfe—author of *Animal Rites: American Culture, the Discourse of Species, and Posthumanist Theory* and editor of *Zoontologies: The Question of the Animal*[1]—argues that in spite of the amount of work being done over the last twenty years in field ecology, animal behaviour, cognition and ethology, and in spite of new social movements concerned with animal rights and welfare, "cultural studies and critical theory have really, really lagged behind ... developments in the broader society" in dealing with what Wolfe refers to as the "question of the animal."[2] Following upon the ethical concerns of philosopher Peter Singer, who argued for animal liberation and animal rights in the now-classic *Animal Liberation*,[3] Wolfe maintains that forms of "speciesism"—a term coined in 1970 by Richard D. Ryder, a British psychologist and taken up by Singer[4]—must be given the same critical attention that has been recruited against sexism and racism in critical race studies, feminism and queer theory. In an attempt to address these concerns, *Animal Subjects: An Ethical Reader in a Posthuman World* draws together a diverse group of scholars, writers and activists whose work responds to the social and theoretical lag in cultural studies by calling into question the boundaries that divide the animal kingdom from humanity and by exploring the medical, biological, cultural, philosophical, psychological and ethical *connections* between nonhuman animals and ourselves. The strength of this collection lies in its heterogeneity: while many of the essays constitute significant interventions in their respective fields, others ask sobering questions regarding empathy or the ethical obligations that humans have towards their nonhuman counterparts.

In short, this collection is long overdue in cultural studies where critiques of racism, sexism(s) and classism have radically changed the face of the humanities and social sciences but which have also historically withheld the question of ethical treatment from nonhuman animals. The reasons for this lag amount to a disavowal or a withholding that has, as Cary Wolfe argues, served only to *reproduce* speciesism as an "institution" that would "require… the sacrifice of the 'animal' and the animalistic" to maintain "that fantasy figure called 'the human.'"[5] In *Animal Subjects*, contributors address the question of what it is to be "human" by showing that it cannot be separated from what Paola Cavalieri, a contributor to this volume, calls elsewhere "the animal question," an interrogation of "more than twenty centuries of philosophical tradition aiming at excluding from the ethical domain members of species other than our own."[6]

Launching this interrogation, however, is not as easy as it sounds since the borders of cultural studies have proved almost impervious to the question of the nonhuman animal owing to an internalized paradox that has maintained the very status of the human that cultural studies has sought to critique. As Cary Wolfe points out, "debates in the humanities and social sciences between well-intentioned critics of racism, (hetero)sexism, classism and all other -isms that are the stock-in-trade of cultural studies almost always remain locked within an unexamined framework of *speciesism*," and this lockdown is exacerbated since "most of us [in cultural studies] remain humanists to the core, even as we claim for our work an epistemological break with humanism itself."[7] This lockdown begs the question of the role played by cultural studies in producing new—or, perhaps, all too familiar—forms of hierarchy and exclusion when critiquing essentialist notions of the "human" subject while maintaining the border that enables that subject's privileged position through the marginalizing of the nonhuman. If cultural studies is to make good on its challenge to a humanist tradition that has historically determined its identity and its others by virtue of exclusions based on gender, sexuality, race, ethnicity and class, it must be willing to follow through—as this collection of essays aims to do—on its commitment to destabilizing essentialist notions of the subject that continue to rely on the hegemonic marginalization of the nonhuman. This collection of essays aims to embody the cultural politics behind the idea of hybridity by drawing attention to the nonhuman animal as the figure that sustains the margins of cultural studies to date.[8] In the spirit of hybridizations, therefore, this collection of essays features perspectives often marginalized in the field of cultural studies. The point must be made, however, that the task of giving voice to the margins remains complicated by the fact that what comes under the rubric of "cultural studies" is historically a matter of contention.

CULTURAL STUDIES: WHAT'S IN A NAME?

Originally pioneered by Birmingham University's renowned Centre for Contemporary Cultural Studies in 1964, cultural studies is now a flourishing field aimed at the interdisciplinary study of culture, defined anthropologically as a "way of life," performatively as symbolic practice and ideologically as the collective product of media and cultural industries, usually defined as "popular" culture. The aim of the Birmingham School, headed up by scholars such as Raymond Williams and Stuart Hall, was to examine social change from the point of culture with regards to social life taking into consideration the ideological dimensions of class relations, politics and institutions, as well as values and ideas. Given its breadth, cultural studies has flourished over time through its relation to Western Marxism, feminism, critical race studies and queer studies. Consequently, the definition of the discipline has shifted from its early beginnings in the British New Left to include, according to a recent cultural studies reader, "more analyses of just what it is that constitutes 'value' or the ideological preferred in culture, and how those values got there and got built into us."[9] Although the constituency of the "us" always needs to be considered, it is easy to see that the definition of cultural studies has broadened due to the overlapping of sociology, anthropology, women's studies, literary studies, communication and media studies thus enabling an interdisciplinary study of culture as a viable field. But what's in a name? And what does the interdisciplinary study of culture have to do with nonhuman animals? The latter is a question I hope this collection will address.

In a review-article subtitled "Is Culture Too Important to Be Left to Cultural Studies?" Stefan Collini asserts that rather than attempting a definition of the field, more insight may be gained "by reflecting on the shifting relations among disciplines and on the trajectories of those who have been led to claim the label of Cultural Studies for their own various activities."[10] Those of us in the university who aspire to teach from a cultural studies perspective see it at the most general level as a variable, flexible, critical mode of analysis concerned with inter-, multi- or trans-disciplinary approaches to media and communication studies, ethnography, discourse analysis, studies in visual and musical culture, environmental thought, cultural geography, research on identity politics and literary and film studies. When it comes to mapping the terrain, however, we must invariably struggle at the local level with what we *mean* pedagogically, intellectually and politically by the term *cultural studies* for the simple reason that cultural studies is organized around a set of controversies. In effect, "cultural studies" is notoriously difficult to define succinctly and, according to Norma Schulman, citing Stuart Hall, it has no "doctrine *per se*" or no "'house approved' methodology" even though its aim is to test the limits of conventional disciplines and contribute to the study of a complex network of relations linking knowledge, power and culture.[11] It is too soon to say, however, if the "new" humanities will *replace* disciplines such as English, history and so on or if the new humanities' focus on globalization, cultural policies, gender, ethnicity and sexuality, to take some obvious examples, will change these disciplines from within.

All of this is to say that the field of cultural studies appears to be in constant transition and continues to move away from the limitations of traditional humanities not only in the formation of knowledge but also in the questions it asks of its own relation to power. It seems safe, however, to assume that the study of culture is a pluralistic activity that takes place not inside the narrow parameters of a specific discipline but is, in principle, predicated—like Mikhail Bakhtin's notion of a "dialogic imperative"—upon "a constant interaction between meanings, all of which have the potential of conditioning others."[12] In this regard one might rightfully claim in the analysis of culture that such "interactions" are ubiquitously concerned with the relationship between power and knowledge and, therefore, as Bakhtin says, "at any given time, in any given place, there will be a set of conditions...that will ensure that a word [or, for that matter, a term like 'cultural studies'] uttered in that place and at that time will have a meaning different than it would have under any other conditions."[13] It is to the question of "difference" I would now like to turn because it leads us into a cluster of overlapping questions regarding what is now thought of as "animal studies" whose social and theoretical relevance could hardly be underestimated. In this regard, the essays in this collection aim to revise the contours of the cultural studies map in Canada by seeking to breach the anthropocentric borders of the discipline and in the process trace an intersubjective route to the newly emerging discipline of human–animal relations based on empathy and connectedness. This approach questions the limitations of traditional humanist philosophy that is concerned primarily with the welfare of humankind to the extent that the faith of the humanist in empathy and democracy is steeped in a host of anthropocentrisms. Similarly, the approach to the nonhuman animal question in this collection does not amount to a denial of the differences of the "other"; it does not result, in other words, to the "totalization" initially described by Levinas and glossed by Anthony Beavers as

> limit[ing] the other to a set of rational categories, be they racial, sexual, or otherwise…. Totalization is a denial of the other's difference, the denial of the otherness of the other. That is, it is the inscription of the other in the same. If ethics presupposes the real other person, then such totalization will, in itself, be unethical.[14]

With regard to the notion of ethical responsibility, what is relevant for this collection of essays with regards to Levinas's thought is that empathy and connection can be seen in terms of his concept of "substitution" in which one is made to stand for the other and one has an obligation to respond. In this sense, this collection of essays is tied to Levinas's notion of ethical responsibility of which Levinas writes:

> I speak of responsibility as the essential, primary and fundamental mode of subjectivity. For I describe subjectivity in ethical terms. Ethics, here, does not supplement a preceding existential base; the very node of the subjective is knotted in ethics understood as responsibility.[15]

What this collection of essays seeks to do is to complicate the field of cultural studies by bringing the question of the nonhuman animal into proximity with "the very node of the subjective [which] is knotted in ethics understood as responsibility."

A QUESTION OF THE ANIMAL: THE OBLIGATION TO RESPOND

If cultural studies has been instrumental in achieving a paradigm shift in the humanities since the 1960s, it is due, in part, to the raising of unsettling questions of *difference* with regard to normalized categories of gender, ethnicity, race, class and sexuality. Differences in these areas were not seen as being relevant in the traditional humanities because, as Patrick Fuery and Nick Mansfield point out, humanist culture was/is not only based upon a "model of universal human commonality" but also sees itself as embodying "a transcendent human pluralism and generosity."[16] In this self-determining model, however, humanism is able to make the claim that "certain qualities are more human than others"; thus, leading inexorably to "the evaluation of some people as more or less central (and others more or less marginal) to the human project." However, as many cultural studies scholars have shown, humanism and the "human project" serve "inevitably [to] produce hierarchies of the more or less human." These hierarchies in turn coincide and collude with "the distribution of power along gender and ethnic lines, which have defined Western politics and society since the Renaissance."[17] If the distribution of power has enabled humanism to determine its others, a similar point needs to be made in the case of cultural studies and its ethical framework with regards to its position on "the more or less human" when what is at stake not only involves the ethical treatment of nonhuman animals but also the question of nonhuman subjectivity. In this regard, what would it mean to reopen the relation of the subject and the species?

CULTURAL STUDIES: A NEW TERRAIN

If the traditional humanist with a vested interest in maintaining the boundary between the human and the nonhuman is disturbed by this collection of essays, it might be because contributors map out a new terrain in cultural studies that promises to have a dramatic effect on our critical practices in that the authors all draw humans and nonhuman animals into proximal relationships based on *empathy* and connection. In cultural studies, developments such as these have radical potential for our critical practice because they call into question the anthropocentric hierarchies of identity upon which liberalism historically determined who was human and, more significantly, who was *not* and, thus, rationalized power over the lives of its "others," including the lives of nonhuman animals. As Gayatri Spivak puts it,

> the great doctrines of identity of the ethical universal, in terms of which liberalism thought out its ethical programmes, played history false, because the identity was disengaged in terms of who was and who was not human. That's why all of these projects, the justification of slavery,

as well as the justification of Christianization, seem to be alright; because, after all, these people had not graduated into humanhood, as it were.[18]

Although "the great doctrines of identity" have been dismantled in sociology, political science, postcolonial, feminist literary and cultural studies with regards to gender, race and class, these same fields of study, according to Dana Medoro and Alison Calder, remain "slow to acknowledge the volatility of the human-animal relationship" in spite of advances in studies in animal cognition, behaviour and ethology.[19] In cultural studies the critical lag is called into question by remarks made by Donna Haraway in "A Cyborg Manifesto" where she points out that

> by the late twentieth century in United States scientific culture, the boundary between human and animal is thoroughly breached. The last beachheads of uniqueness have been polluted, if not turned into amusement parks—language, tool use, social behavior, mental events. Nothing really convincingly settles the separation of human and animal.... Movements for animal rights are not irrational denials of human uniqueness; they are clear-sighted recognition of connection across the discredited breach of nature and culture.[20]

In recognition of this connection, this collection seeks to address the ethical and political challenge facing cultural studies with regards to Haraway's observation and, even more to the point, to address what's at stake in Cary Wolfe's more recent provocation in the *Topia* interview: "Why has it taken so long for the academy (and particularly for the ethically and politically-responsive cultural studies departments) to *get it*?"[21] In the spirit of "getting it," this collection of essays is intended to serve as a challenge to cultural studies scholars—particularly in *Canada*—where there is less reference to nonhuman animals in the curriculum than there is in the news.[22] Simply put, the aim of this collection is to include the nonhuman animal question as part of the ethical purview of cultural studies. To this end, this collection seeks to explore the question of the nonhuman animal in interdisciplinary and often *necessarily* eclectic terms: it draws together literary and cultural studies; traces the trajectories of bioethics; poses the question of the animal in relation to public space and "entertainment"; explores the relationship between ecofeminism and nonhuman animal relationships; examines the impact of scientific cynicism on our understanding of, and respect for, both humans and other animals; puts sentience and empathy at the centre of ethics; questions the main tenets of conventional metaphysical humanism that come to a halt before the boundary of the human species; attempts to provide a foothold for a new ethics that adequately embraces nonhuman animals by seeking a radical alteration in our conception of moral reasoning and posits that all living beings primarily feel and intuit rather than merely "think" the world. As mentioned, this collection is necessarily eclectic in that it is meant to give voice to various approaches to the question of the nonhuman animal and to pose the question within wholly different critical frameworks: from eco-feminism to sociobiology and from the history of feminism to literary studies. Thus, the essays cover a broad spectrum of positions drawn from the desks of cultural theorists and activists and extending to the social space of the courtroom and to the scientific, but nevertheless social, space of the laboratory. Not all of these essays fall easily under the rubric of cultural studies as the field has come to be known; but all of these essays serve as touchstones in a widening field of study that seeks to acknowledge diversity by demonstrating that thinking of "animals" or "animal ethics" is *not* by any stretch a stable or even consistent endeavour. To some, this collection will be a welcome addition to the field of cultural studies; to others, it should never speak its name.

THE INTERMINABLE ISSUE OF EQUALITY

According to Peter Singer—a scholar whose appointment in 1999 to the Ira W. DeCamp Professor of Bioethics in the University Center for Human Values at Princeton University was hotly contested for his views on speciesism—the issue of equality lies at the heart of the ethical treatment of nonhuman animals in relation to humans. In the case of the former, Singer contends that

> the appropriate response to those who claim to have found evidence of genetically based differences in ability between the races or sexes is not to stick to the belief that the genetic explanation must be wrong, whatever evidence to the contrary may turn up; instead we should make it quite clear that the claim to equality does not depend on intelligence, moral capacity, physical strength, or similar matters of fact. Equality is a moral ideal, not a simple assertion of fact. There is no logically compelling reason for assuming that a factual difference in ability between two people justifies any difference in the amount of consideration we give to satisfying their needs and interests. The principle of equality of human

beings is not a description of an alleged actual equality among humans: it is a prescription of how we should treat humans.[23]

If the principle of equality is truly a moral ideal then, as Singer argues, "the ethical treatment on which human equality rests requires us to extend equal consideration to animals, too."[24]

As I understand it, Peter Singer's argument to extend ethical treatment to nonhuman animals makes it increasingly possible to see similarities between speciesism and other forms of discrimination, such as racism, in that each of these can be understood to violate the principle of equality by refusing to take the suffering of others into consideration. As Singer puts it, parallels can be found between "racists of European descent [who] typically have not accepted that pain matters as much when it is felt by Africans, for example, as when it is felt by Europeans" and between "human speciesists [who] do not accept that pain is as bad when it is felt by [nonhuman animals] as when it is felt by humans."[25] Of course, in the latter case, many scientists and philosophers still insist that such claims to similarity are specious and, that when it comes right down to it, only humans have the ability to suffer because, as author Stephen Budiansky argues in his behavioural study of animal intelligence, "our ability to have thoughts about our experiences turns emotions into something far greater and sometimes far worse than *mere pain*."[26] As Matthew Scully points out in his critique of this outlook in *Dominion: The Power of Man, the Suffering of Animals, and the Call to Mercy*, Budiansky's views are derived from his observations of the neurophysiological responses of animals to external stimuli through which Budiansky comes to the conclusion that it's just plain *wrong* to ascribe suffering to animals because in their case "pain isn't even pain"—rather, it's all about being "hardwired" and thus "programmed" to the extent that both pain and enjoyment are merely the evidence of "mimicking."[27] In this view, the "mere pain" of animals is simply incommensurate with human suffering because unlike humans, animals lack the "ability" to "reflect" on the "full meaning" of their experience. To see it otherwise—that is, to ascribe consciousness or emotions to animals, to describe their inner lives as being worthy of consideration—is to risk, as Scully observes, "being guilty of 'anthropomorphism,' the attribution of exclusively human characteristics to animals."[28] In this context, it's clear that for some researchers ascribing consciousness or emotions to animals can mean the risk of career-death.

Although the status of nonhuman animals has long been an issue with those concerned with animal welfare and animal rights as well as being a concern of philosophers and scholars working in the field of ethics, the compelling question of nonhuman animals—and their ability to suffer—is conspicuously absent in the new intellectual realm of cultural studies and critical theory. If animal suffering is ignored in these fields of study so, too, is the commensurate issue of animal emotions. As Jeffrey Masson and Susan McCarthy point out,

> very few scientists have acknowledged, researched, or even speculated about animal emotions. So persistent are the forces that militate against even admitting the possibility of emotions in the lives of animals that the topic seems disreputable, almost taboo.... [This, in spite of that fact that] the scholarly literature on animals contains many observations, accounts, and anecdotes that suggest emotions the animals may be experiencing or expressing, or at least call for further research into this possibility. Yet little to none is forthcoming.[29]

The fact that little or no research is forthcoming regarding the possibility of emotions in the lives of animals in the laboratories of animal science departments—where countless animals are subject to every conceivable (and sometimes, inconceivable) experimentation and where opposition, as Matthew Scully points out, is more often than not heard as "an accusation and assault on science itself"[30]—should tell us something of *what is behind* the failure in critical theory or cultural studies to consider either the suffering of animals or the possibility of their emotions being worthy of consideration. In fact, one could argue that contemporary discussions of the question of what it means to be human in a "posthuman" world appear to rely, somewhat ironically, on the exclusion of the question of nonhuman animals from the debate. Similarly, it could be argued that the absence of any sustained attention to the nonhuman animal question in cultural studies and critical theory might serve to warn us that the *politics of exclusion*—which enabled older formations of the humanities to disregard questions of gender, ethnicity, race, sexuality and class—are still operative within the new fields of inquiry that seek to critique the Western, humanist tradition upon which such exclusions have been naturalized and reproduced. One aim of this collection of essays is to rupture the politics of exclusion and to bridge the gap in cultural studies between the nonhuman animal question and a "posthuman" response. In this regard, the collection seeks to draw attention to what Cary Wolfe has called the "imperatives of posthumanist theory" and can be seen as an invitation—or a challenge—to readers "to explore in their own critical practice what it would mean in both intellectual and ethical terms to take seriously the question of the animal—or the *animals*, plural, as Jacques Derrida admonishes us." According to Wolfe—and I strongly agree—posthumanist theory takes seriously the possibility that

> a hundred years from now we will look back on our current mechanized and systematized practices of factory farming, product testing, and much else that undeniably involves animal exploitation and suffering—uses that we earlier saw Derrida compare to the gas chambers of Auschwitz—with much the same horror and disbelief with which we now regard slavery or the genocide of the Second World War.[31]

In this context, one imperative of posthumanist theory and this current collection is to explore the role of *empathy* and *compassion* in the production of knowledge concerning the presence of animals in the moral domain in which "objectivity" and charges of anthropomorphism have traditionally been the roadblock towards progress in discussions of how humans might consider the treatment of nonhuman animals.

THE ISSUES

This collection begins with "Chicken," an essay by Donna Haraway, whose influence is widely felt in cultural studies, women's studies, political theory, primatology, literature and philosophy. Echoing the tone of playful, albeit profoundly serious, experimentation in "A Cyborg Manifesto"—in which Haraway's stated aim is "to build an *ironic* political myth faithful to feminism, socialism, and materialism"—"Chicken" takes up where the "Manifesto" leaves off.[32] Like much of Haraway's writing, the prominent trope of "Chicken" is irony, a strategy Haraway often uses to subvert what she calls "the production of universal, totalizing theory."[33] In Haraway's view, the point of irony is that it is "about humour *and* serious play. It is also a rhetorical strategy and a political method, one I would like to see more honoured within socialist-feminism. At the centre of my ironic faith, my blasphemy, is the image of the cyborg."[34] In the "Manifesto," Haraway's cyborg emerges as a figure of "ironic communication" and serves to critique "'Western' science and politics," which in Haraway's view consists of a "tradition of racist, male-dominant capitalism; the tradition of progress; the tradition of the appropriation of nature as resource for the productions of culture; the tradition of reproduction of the self from the reflections of the other...."[35]

Similar to the cyborg as a figure of ironic communication, "Chicken" in this collection serves as a rhetorical strategy as well as a political method to create an uneasy juxtaposition between fact and fable. Although some readers unfamiliar with Haraway's penchant for irony might find the tone and style of "Chicken" discordant and perhaps incongruous in a collection that aims at a critique of cultural studies regarding the ethical treatment of nonhuman animals, those more familiar with her use of impious metaphor in the cyborg—"a hybrid of machine and organism" used to deconstruct "biological-determinist ideology" as well as the "animal-human (organism) and machine" distinction—will recognize in the-sky-is-falling metaphor of "Chicken" a similar and powerful rhetorical strategy, this time aimed at the economic and political relationships between technoscience and the extensive pollution attributed to factory chicken production in an era witnessing the transnational spread of avian flu.[36]

The placement of the essay in the collection is intended to draw attention to the fact that social and cultural analyses are more often than not the site of multiple contradictions and that irony is a trope that can alert us to theoretical complexities to come. In Haraway's own words, "irony is about contradictions that do not resolve into larger wholes, even dialectically, about the tension of holding incompatible things together because both or all are necessary and true."[37]

It is in this spirit "of holding incompatible things together" that "Chicken" adapts the classical fable of Chicken Little to take an irreverent and highly critical stance towards the *role of technoscience* in the poultry industry in which the factory farming of chickens has reached epic proportions through genetic and chemical manipulations. It also takes relentless aim at ethical issues surrounding factory farming in which chickens, considered by organizations like PETA to be the most abused animals in the world, are not only housed in filthy, crowded conditions but are also genetically manipulated to force their maturation; this to the extent that accelerated weight gain results in a chicken whose legs are no longer able to support its body and who can no longer walk.[38] In this context, Chicken Little can no longer be seen to represent a mistaken or "hysterical" belief that ecological and ethical disaster is imminent. In Haraway's view, it's already happened, especially when it comes to the suffering inflicted on nonhuman animals in factory farming by disenfranchised workers.[39] Significantly, the figure of Chicken Little in Haraway's hands works to undermine the popularized and often comedic representation of nonhuman animals in consumer culture that has enabled and perhaps perpetuated a psychological, emotional and ethical disconnect between animal representation and widespread abuse. In Haraway's essay, instead of being the purveyor of a don't-jump-to-a-ridiculous-conclusion figure, Chicken Little ironically bears witness to the suffering that is all too easily disregarded in the proliferation of animal images used in the media to sell consumer products, such as the steak-sauce commercials that feature computer-generated cows singing rapturously about the product, or the chicken promotion commercial in which three cows stand upright and wear sandwich boards bearing the words "Eat" "Mor" "Chikin." The point is that such "appealing" images of nonhuman animals are ubiquitous in commercial advertising and are associated with consumer products from automobiles to clothing, foods and beverages, pharmaceuticals, life insurance and electronic equipment. Lastly, Haraway's essay forms an indictment against the exploitation of the workers who process chickens—including illegal immigrants, non-unionized women and men, people of colour and even former prisoners—all of whom work in conditions that pose a serious hazard to their health.

Following "Chicken" in the collection is Rod Preece's "Selfish Genes, Sociobiology and Animal Respect." In this essay, Rod Preece—scholar and author of many impeccably researched publications on nonhuman animals, including *Animals and Nature: Cultural Myths, Cultural Realities*; *Brute Souls*; *Happy Beasts and Evolution: The Historical Status of Animals* and *Awe for the Tiger, Love for the Lamb: A Chronicle of Sensibility to Animals*—takes up the topic of genetics in a departure from the deconstructive strategies of Haraway to mount an extended critique of sociobiology and Richard Dawkins's materialist and determinist "selfish gene" theory, which Preece argues has "very negative implications for our understanding of, and respect for, both humans and other animals." As propounded by Dawkins and critiqued by Preece, selfish gene theory contends that both human and nonhuman animals "are all machines created by our genes." In Preece's view, sociobiology and selfish gene theory, the latter an aspect of evolutionary theory, are equally "demeaning of humans and other animals alike" for the simple reason that "human and other animal behaviour cannot be fully understood without also understanding altruism and compassion."

In Dawkins's view, altruism and compassion are laudable in any society but in light of selfish gene theory these are erroneous concepts, like "universal love and the welfare of the species" which, according to Dawkins, "simply do not make evolutionary sense." In opposition to this deterministic view, Rod Preece argues that selfish gene theory is dehumanizing because it inhibits "any genuine consideration of the interests of other species." Likewise, selfish gene theory limits the possibility of considering humans as being anything other than "self-serving" and, therefore, not inclined to care in the slightest about other species, especially the ethical consideration of nonhuman animals. In Preece's view the only way to release sociobiology from the "dehumanizing and materialist prison" of Dawkinism is to come down firmly on the side of an epistemology and ontology that are based in the "recognition of a compassion for others, including other animals."

In philosophical terms, this recognition also comes in the form of an opportunity to question the main tenets of conventional metaphysical humanism which, historically, have relied on the assumption that nonhumans are inferior beings. In the first of three essays concerned with the human/animal division in philosophy, Dawne McCance's "Anatomy as Speech Act: Vesalius, Descartes, Rembrandt or, The Question of 'the animal' in the Early Modern Anatomy Lesson" explores the world of the human anatomy theatre in the years between 1540 and 1640. In this period the division between human and animal life emerged as a "peculiarly modern bio-power" via the anatomy lessons of Andreas Vesalius, the father of modern anatomy, and his reader of a century later, the philosopher René Descartes. Descartes not only studied Vesalius but also practised dissection of animals for purposes of teaching himself to speak on his own authority. McCance, whose academic interests lie in ethics, post-modernism, critical theory and body history, points out that although Descartes attended human anatomies as a spectator, he dissected only animal bodies and was consistent in describing the body—human and animal—as a machine. It was from these lessons, McCance explains, that Descartes was able to move to the argument that the human is distinct from and superior to the animal because animals lack the capacity for speech and, therefore, the capacity for thinking. More specifically, says McCance, for Descartes "real speech" is "what sets the essentially human, *res cogito*, apart" in comparison with "animal" talk. From here, McCance draws upon the work of philosopher Jacques Derrida to explore "the underside of the 'Cartesian' line that marks the human/animal divide and extends into the emerging bio-power of the *res cogito*."

In "A Missed Opportunity: Humanism, Anti-Humanism and the Animal Question," Paola Cavalieri, editor of the international philosophy journal *Etica & Animali* and author of *The Animal Question: Why Nonhuman Animals Deserve Human Rights*, asks why the French strand of thinking, which began in the 1960s and which questioned the conditions of truth in Western metaphysics and the classical metaphysical notions of subjectivity and human "nature," came to a halt before the boundary of the human species. In the context of *Animal Subjects*, Cavalieri's essay critiques the traditional, and particularly the Cartesian, view of human beings that continues to resonate in cultural theory in the form of a bias in favour of human superiority. To this end, Cavalieri draws attention to what she perceives is the failure of highly influential philosophers such as Jacques Derrida, Michel Foucault and Emmanuel Levinas "to rethink the status of nonhuman beings" in spite of the fact that they have launched a "powerful attack on the traditional doctrine regarding 'man's' nature and place in the world that is now known as anti-humanism." If "animals are missing in Foucault's landscape," it is, according to Cavalieri, because Foucault's interest in sexuality as a "history of morals" depends upon his appropriation of the condition of nonhuman animals as "merely a metaphor for, or as a parallel to, the condition of the 'other'—that is, human—beings" and, thus, Foucault's work "goes back to the classical interest in the *human subject*."

Cavalieri also takes Emmanuel Levinas to task in a critique of the well-known story told by Levinas of Bobby, a stray dog who would greet him and his companions when they were being marched back from forced labour while at a concentration camp for Jewish prisoners of war during the Second World War. According to Levinas, Bobby, unlike the camp guards who chased him away, was able to attribute to Levinas and his companions the respect owed to all human beings. In her critique of Levinas, Cavalieri points out that his story not only conveys "the view that to be a good dog means to recognize one's inferiority" but also gives the impression that the issue of vulnerability "remains a *humanism*" because nonhuman animals "remain second-class beings, merely deserving protection against the infliction of wanton suffering, and not covered by the primeval injunction 'do not kill me,'" which attributes special worth to humans. Lastly, Cavalieri calls Derrida's stance on vegetarianism—"the moral question is … not, nor has it ever been whether one should or should not eat animals"—"disappointing" in that, for Cavalieri, Derrida's conclusion seems not only in conflict with deconstruction's "demand for justice" but also ends up reifying hierarchical borders on the basis of suggesting that "nonhuman beings clearly keep counting for less than human beings." In this regard, Cavalieri argues that although deconstruction might be a political weapon against racism, it fails at the border of speciesism and, for this reason, "the ethical centrality of deconstruction loses much of its force."

In "Thinking Other-Wise: Cognitive Science, Deconstruction and the (Non) Speaking (Non) Human Subject," Cary Wolfe, the Bruce and Elizabeth Dunlevie Professor of English at Rice University, argues conversely that deconstruction has been epistemologically and ethically *successful* in setting up a radical "post-ontological" challenge to cognitive science and, thus, to the mechanistic synonyms regarding consciousness and cognition, thought and language that reinforce the divide between humans and nonhuman animals. Taking a pro-deconstructive stance, Wolfe argues compellingly against a "functionalist approach" to consciousness and cognition that has historically guaranteed a certain sort of moral standing based upon representational models of human intentionality and consciousness that privilege the human ability to experience pain based on the capacity for thought or language. In this essay, Wolfe indicts the materialist model of subjectivity promulgated by theorists such as Daniel Dennet whose work in cognitive science, Wolfe argues, reproduces the Cartesian notion that nonhuman animals are incapable of experiencing pain *as* suffering because there is, as Wolfe explains it, "no subject of the *cogito* to do the experiencing; and thus, the pain is not morally relevant."

Wolfe's point is that in Dennet's work both "pain" and "suffering" turn out in philosophical terms to be an *ontological* difference between humans and nonhuman animals that depends upon the view that only human consciousness can *know* what serious suffering entails because of a capacity for thought or language. According to Wolfe, the issue that lies before us is a complicated one in that it is not about "the ethical foregrounding of pain and suffering," nor is it about being in a position to think about "the consciousness, intelligence, and emotional and mental lives of nonhuman animals in terms of their linguistic abilities." Instead, argues Wolfe, what is at stake is the need and even the *responsibility* "to rethink, ever anew and vigilantly so, what we mean by 'person,' 'mind,' 'consciousness'—that entire cluster of terms and the ethical implications that flow from them."

In "Animals in Moral Space," Michael Allen Fox (whose book *Deep Vegetarianism*[40] examines the history, philosophy and environmental dimensions of vegetarianism) and Lesley McLean (whose doctoral research examines the ontological claims made about animals) set out to rethink these terms and their ethical implications by taking the position that what is necessary academically and socially is a *new ethics* that adequately affirms that nonhuman animals deserve to be the subjects of moral concern for their own sake. According to McLean and Fox, traditional, normative, moral theories have been unsuccessful in extending moral status to nonhuman animals because moral arguments have relied upon placing animals in relationship to an "objective" set of considerations to see if they measure up, and only if they do can moral standing be extended to them. In contrast, McLean and Fox argue that assumptions such as these are mistaken and have led animal ethics in the wrong direction. They propose, instead, that "the way into the real world of human/animal interactions is through opening ourselves to *a complex kind of seeing and feeling*" (emphasis mine). Accordingly, they argue that the moral context in which "animals lives are played out has been missed by human observers past and present" because "they have failed to respond *affectively* as well as intellectually" to nonhuman animals. Like many of the contributors to this volume, McLean and Fox take the view that *empathy* is necessarily a key component in any discussion about the presence of animals in the moral domain and the disparity between what we say about animals and how we actually treat them. In this essay, Fox and McLean call for nothing less than a paradigm shift; one that would move away from both institutionalized "forms of domination, exploitation, oppression and violence" and power-based hierarchies with "humans on top" to an ethical model based on "affective perception" as a means of developing a new moral community based on *reciprocity*.

In "Electric Sheep and the New Argument from Nature," Angus Taylor, philosopher, animal rights advocate and author of *Animals and Ethics*,[41] argues that, in spite of the work being done in the last three decades in the field of environmental ethics, one major factor in maintaining the conceptual distinctions between humans and nonhuman animals and upholding the notion of human domination over other species is "the capitalist mode of production [that] militates against viewing the nonhuman world as anything other than a storehouse of exploitable resources." In this context, Taylor demonstrates that arguments against animal liberation take as a given the right to dominate and exploit nonhuman animals based on the Cartesian designation of humans as "masters and possessors of nature" in comparison to Descartes's claim that animals are "literally and simply machines." In other words, this mechanistic view has served to validate the "argument from nature" that resulted in ascribing unique moral worth to human beings and excluding animals from the moral community because "they are by nature radically '*other*,' and therefore legitimate objects of exploitation by us." As Taylor points out, the movement for animal liberation has involved attempts to break down the traditional conceptual boundaries between animals and humans by questioning the opposition between nature and culture, resulting in an overlap between the two that Taylor describes as "the new argument from nature."

In Taylor's view, it is this new argument that sees humans as being responsible for preserving ecological systems but which continues to exclude animals from the moral domain. Taylor takes on this problem in an extended meditation on the fiction of Philip K. Dick, specifically the novel *Do Androids Dream of Electric Sheep?* Dick's work, says Taylor, not only provokes the question, "What does it mean to be authentically human?" but also calls on us with a "moral imperative ... to care for all sentient beings, human or nonhuman, natural or artificial, regardless of their place in the order of things." The point for Taylor, as it is for other contributors to this volume, is that "this imperative is grounded in empathy, not reason," and yet it "confront[s] us urgently with [the] contradiction between our domination of the natural world, a domination driven by triumphant capitalism, and the growing movement to re-establish spiritual values and a sense of harmony with nature." All of this, says Taylor, comes down to the question of "how we choose to be human." This question draws attention to the fact that, "today," as Taylor points out, "a political struggle is being waged over the implications of the intimate relation between humans and nonhumans revealed by ecology and other sciences." This political struggle comes in the form of a *choice* that is the basis for locating the question of the nonhuman animal at the *heart* of not only ecology and other sciences but also of critical theory and cultural studies where it has too long been excluded.

In "Monsters: The Case of Marineland," John Sorenson, professor of sociology and animal rights advocate, puts this ethical perspective to work in a powerful critique of Marineland, a theme park in Niagara Falls, Ontario, that displays both marine and land animals including killer and beluga whales, bear and deer, and prides itself, according to its website, on "keeping our animals happy and healthy."[42] In detailed and provocative opposition to this claim, Sorenson questions the nature and value of what customers experience at Marineland and presents evidence from expert scientists about deplorable conditions for animals held captive there. To this end, Sorenson traces the history of animal display made popular by P.T. Barnum who, in 1861, was the first to put captive whales on public display for profit. Although both whales were dead within a week, Barnum turned their deaths into a marketing strategy whereby the public was encouraged to hurry and view the specimens because, in Barnum's terms "it is very doubtful whether these wonderful creatures can be kept alive for more than a few days."

In his essay Sorenson describes how the display of these "monsters of the deep" was also linked to the public exhibitions of "wild men" from various parts of the colonized world. While today we would view Barnum's displaying of "freaks" as being "repugnant," Sorenson argues that "many of the same cruel and exploitative attitudes persist" in Marineland, which has also been widely criticized by international animal protection groups for keeping animals in "warehouse" conditions that have been likened to those found in Victorian-era zoos where the animals live "with no stimulation, daylight or companions." As Sorensen puts it, "zoos and aquaria are prisons for animals where the public can visit and observe the suffering of the inmates, just as the circus sideshow allowed paying customers the opportunity to derive pleasure from viewing the misfortunes of the disabled." In Sorenson's view, zoos and aquaria function as a sign of the "superiority" of human beings and within these public places animals "are transformed into symbols of power, specimens that demonstrate the imperial power to penetrate and control the world, to collect and to order." For Sorenson, zoos and aquaria are popularized through advertising campaigns that downplay the suffering of animals kept on display for the purpose of public viewing and, instead, promote the view that animals are "cartoon-like creatures who exist to make us laugh and whose interests can be disregarded as long as we derive some amusement from their suffering." In short, Marineland encourages the idea that it's "fun" to watch animals perform tricks for the entertainment of paying customers. As Sorenson argues, "one of the strongest messages that children will derive from a visit to Marineland is that it is ethically acceptable to imprison animals in unacceptable conditions and force them to do pathetic tricks for our entertainment." In this essay, Sorenson's sustained critique of Marineland extends to their website, which promotes a visit to the amusement park as a "unique thrill" in viewing animals who although confined are billed as being "affectionate, as well as incredibly intelligent." As Sorenson points out, the website repeatedly refers to their "playful, friendly" qualities, thus trivializing the extent of their captivity and exploitation. What the public learns from such exploitation is a negative lesson in which imprisonment and domination are normalized through "the guise of fun and family entertainment, presenting domination as entertainment, slavery as fun." Meanwhile, the animals are "turned into mere objects or presented as performing clowns, anxious to please their human masters." As Sorenson notes, Marineland does not take to criticism lightly and has in the past attempted to silence criticism of their operations by suing Niagara Action for Animals, a non-profit, grassroots animal protection group by serving notice of a libel suit claiming $250,000 in punitive damages and seeking an injunction that would stop NAFA from publishing any of the statements made against Marineland. Sorenson argues that in the case of Marineland what we see is "the ability of a commercial institution to draw on the power of ... the legal system ... to silence those who advocate for better treatment of nonhuman animals." In Sorenson's view, what we are left with is a political struggle that is ethically and empathetically determined in that it involves the "decision whether we wish to allow these forms of exploitation to continue or to join those who seek to create a better and more just world, not only for ourselves but for those other living creatures with whom we share it."

The ability to perceive interconnectedness between humans and non-human animals is the focus of Barbara Seeber's essay "'I sympathize in their pains and pleasures': Women and Animals in Mary Wollstonecraft." In this essay, Seeber, whose research focuses on discourses of vegetarianism and animal rights in the eighteenth century, demonstrates that sympathy for the suffering of animals is a recurrent pattern in the work of Mary Wollstonecraft, a first-wave feminist who advocated vegetarianism and animal welfare reform. Seeber argues for Wollstonecraft's place in the history of ecofeminism, pointing out that her concern with the ethical treatment of animals amounts to a political critique of the structures of domination. To this end, Seeber reads Wollstonecraft's texts in the context of eighteenth-century discourses of animal welfare and rights, and demonstrates that Wollstonecraft puts sentience at the centre of ethics. As Seeber claims, in the case of Wollstonecraft, "the treatment of animals is a morally significant and political issue in its own right" in that "animal suffering matters in and of itself and it intersects with other forms of oppression." As Seeber demonstrates in this essay, Mary Wollstonecraft must be considered a central figure in questioning the human/animal divide given that she was writing at a time "when the political struggle to include *women* in the category of the 'human' was far from over" (emphasis mine). Seeber's point is well taken: Wollstonecraft deserves a place in the history of ecofeminism not only because of her advocacy of the rights of women but also because "in all her works, she includes animals in ethical considerations" by calling into question structures of domination that remain familiar to cultural theorists today.

In "Animals as Persons," David Sztybel, a Canadian ethicist who has published widely in animal studies and who is a Fellow at the Oxford Centre for Animal Ethics, takes the issue of ethical consideration one step further by exploring the question of *personhood* by arguing that what makes creatures our fellow beings entitled to moral consideration is not merely rationality but rather "a capacity for conscious experience." Sztybel argues that, although "we cannot confirm directly whether animals have personal experiences by asking them," we can determine that suffering constitutes "personal experience" and that one "need not be human to have a personal experience." In Sztybel's view, personhood cannot be denied to a human being based on intelligence or lack thereof; similarly, in a reversal of the charge of anthropomorphism levelled at ascribing human attributes to nonhuman animals, Sztybel argues that it is "arbitrary to deny personhood ... to nonhuman animals" based on the concept of intelligence since to do so is "to think of personhood in exclusively human terms, projecting human traits onto the concept of 'person.'" What Sztybel calls for in this essay has historical resonance with one of the most famous cases in Canadian legal history—the Persons Case—which resulted in the declaration on 18 October 1929 by the British Privy Council that women are, indeed, persons. In this essay, Sztybel calls for a similar rethinking of the term "person" in order "to overcome speciesist thinking" that has made possible all forms of inequalities if not outright cruelties.

In "Power and Irony: One Tortured Cat and Many Twisted Angles to Our Moral Schizophrenia about Animals," Lesli Bisgould, a Toronto lawyer who worked in civil litigation until leaving to establish her own practice in animal rights law, discusses the "moral schizophrenia" in our relations with nonhuman animals. Bisgould focuses on the profoundly disturbing case of Kensington, the cat whose torture and death (in the Toronto neighbourhood for which the cat was named) were videotaped in the spring of 2001 by Jesse Power, an art student at the Ontario College of Art and Design. The entire film was seventeen minutes long and included footage of the cat being "hung from a noose, beaten, stabbed and thrown against a wall." As described by Bisgould, Kensington's "ear had been removed with pliers, her eye had been removed with dental tools, she was disembowelled. Jesse Power, who had the idea to arrange the film and the event, is seen near the end of the tape, while Kensington still lives, spreading her slit skin and inhaling deeply."

Bisgould's essay is hard to read. It's a visceral and disturbing recounting of a cruel and sadistic act that tests the limits of our comprehension. It also asks us to pay attention to the role of the law when it comes to the ethical treatment of nonhuman animals. The torture and killing of Kensington resulted in the laying of criminal charges: one charge of animal cruelty and one charge of mischief. Bisgould points out that "animal cruelty is an offence against the animal herself" whereas mischief is "a property offence" and is intended to "prohibit people from interfering with other people's things." The irony of this situation becomes apparent when Bisgould demonstrates that the basis for a mischief charge was that it acknowledged that "a crime had been committed, [but] not against Kensington, [it was] against the family who lost its cat"; that is, a loss in the form of "property." And a further irony? Says Bisgould, "We see that Canadian criminal law is much more concerned with protecting one's rights over one's property—generally inanimate things, like sport utility vehicles and lawnmowers—than with the agony of a sentient animal."

The final irony lies in the fact that Power and his partners were exposed to the possibility of greater punishment under the mischief charge than they were under the charge of cruelty. Herein lays the paradox implied in Bisgould's claims regarding "moral schizophrenia," for as she says, "this is a strange situation in which the law finds itself, where we purport to care about other animals, but still hold fast to the idea that if they are not human, they are objects we own and may use for our own purposes." As Bisgould points out, "even an animal cruelty charge—the one that is supposed to be about the animal herself—requires a court to determine whether the suffering inflicted on the animal was 'unnecessary'—meaning some pain and suffering is 'necessary' and perfectly fine."

The story comes full circle not only when the law seems at odds with the public response regarding the torture and killing of Kensington but also when the public's outrage seems to beg the question about the treatment of nonhuman animals in other contexts: (a) when the animal in question is on a factory farm where, as professor of law and philosophy, Gary Francione, points out in *Introduction to Animal Rights: Your Child or the Dog*, "the practices of intensive agriculture follow [from mass transportation to assembly-line slaughter] without any regard for the suffering, distress, or discomfort of animals";[43] and (b) when the nonhuman animal is used in laboratory experiments in biomedical research for the development and testing of surgical procedures, devices, pharmaceutical drugs and consumer products and where many animal experiments, as Francione argues, "can only be described as bizarre and macabre"[44] and yet, lamentably, "the list of what are undeniably trivial uses of animals goes on and on."[45]

Although in more recent years individuals and groups have responded strongly enough to the lives of research animals to force changes in research policy and law, change comes slowly and many researchers are unwilling to change their methods. In recent news, PETA conducted an eleven-month investigation into the methods used in Covance's billion-dollar drug testing labs and went public with its findings—including undercover video footage of workers who are shown "slapping, choking, throwing, threatening, and psychologically tormenting monkeys" (PETA website). As PETA describes, Covance—the organization which bills itself as "one of the world's largest and most comprehensive drug development services companies—[that] has the people, global resources and problem-solving culture to respond to pharmaceutical and biotechnology clients' toughest drug development challenges" (http://www.covance.com/index.php)— had hoped to silence PETA and prevent them from publicizing the videotape footage and other evidence of cruelty in its Vienna, Virginia, laboratory. The same tactics were also used against the PETA Europe organization but, as in the US, a British judge dismissed the lawsuit against PETA and ordered Covance to pay court costs of more than $80,000.

In "Blame and Shame? How Can We Reduce Unproductive Animal Experimentation?" Anne Dagg, author of *Pursuing Giraffe: A 1950s Adventure*, offers a biologist's critique of biomedical experiments that have been shown to have minimal effects in improving human health but during which "many millions of animals suffer and die." As Dagg points out, "some research is carried out without any real theory to guide it." In fact, argues Dagg, what constitutes "scientific worth" when it comes to research "can be roughly measured by the number of citations [a research paper] receives in the years following its publication." In this essay, Dagg describes her analyses of animal research findings published in scientific psychology, neurology and cancer journals, and by the staff at the Hospital for Sick Children in Toronto. She argues that when research articles describing animal experimentation receive few or no citations, this indicates the animals suffered pain and usually death for no possibly good reason. Dagg's essay points to the fact that scientists seem largely unwilling to give up their right to carry out whatever research they wish, no matter how pointless and wasteful. Her essay concludes with an appeal to researchers to be more mindful of the unnecessary pain and death of millions of nonhuman animals and in this regard illuminates an issue not generally seen on the radar of cultural studies.

The last essay in this volume is concerned with another dimension of animal studies relevant to cultural analysis: the exclusion of nonhuman animals from *spiritual* considerations; in this case, the withholding of the possibility of immortality. In "On Animal Immortality: An Argument for the Possibility of Animal Immortality in Light of the History of Philosophy," Johanna Tito, author of *Logic in the Husserlian Context*, argues that mainstream philosophical thought, running from Plato through Descartes, has tended to deny the possibility of immortality to nonhuman animals on the basis that only the rational soul is immortal and only humans are capable of rationality. Tito points out that the question of immortality was central to Christian thinkers such as St. Augustine and St. Thomas and that their views on immortality, coupled with those of Plato, contributed to a division between conceptions of the rational soul and the animal. Tito, however, wants to call this division into question by drawing upon another strain of thought in both the philosophical and Christian tradition that "values aspects of the soul other than its rational prowess." It is this strain of thought, argues Tito, "that, in principle, at least, gives animals a chance at immortality" and thus contributes to the changing definition of what it is to be "human" in that it maintains that what is important is love and passion, both of which are, in part, irrational. Tito puts it this way: "Both the shift to love and passion (Augustine, Tertullian, Kierkegaard) and to the living, bodily and irrational aspect of rationality (Husserl, Maritain, Bataille) levels the playing field for human and nonhuman animals, for in inter-defining mind and body, mental and material, rational and irrational, the human/animal divide is bridged." Finally, Tito's essay is a call to "move away from human chauvinism to embrace our common bond with animals." In Tito's view and, arguably, in the collective view of the contributors to this volume, this move requires nothing less than "the transformation of a scientific psychology into a phenomenological psychology in which the *subject* is treated, not by number and abstraction, but by empathy," a paradigm shift which brings us closer to understanding our relationship with nonhuman animals through our capacity to *love*.

IN PERSON

In putting together this collection, I am encouraged that there are many serious and determined people who are concerned with the lives of nonhuman animals, their right not to be treated as property and particularly with the fact of their pain and suffering. On some days, the battles waged in the name of animal rights seem insurmountable, especially when one is confronted with images of and stories about the vast numbers of nonhuman animals who suffer individually and die in laboratories, on factory farms, in amusement parks, rodeos and zoos. If it matters to you, even one example becomes too many.

While writing this introduction, I happened upon an image in a book by Daniel Francione called *Introduction to Animal Rights: Your Child or the Dog?* The image is captioned "Modern mechanized slaughter unquestionably causes terror to animals, such as this cow, who is riding up in a restrainer to be stunned before she is shackled, hoisted, and slaughtered. This process complies with the requirements of the Humane Slaughter Act" (91). The image shows the desperate struggle of a cow caught in the restrainer, the mechanism closing upon her like a vise grip. Her mouth is open and her eyes are wide with terror, the distress visible for anyone who has eyes to see. I can only imagine the sounds she is making. I cannot look upon this image for long because what it stirs up in me is unspeakable.

Although as a child I was always concerned with the welfare of animals, the first time I registered this experience in my academic life was years ago when I was a second-year undergraduate student and had occasion to see a documentary film on factory farming and animal experimentation that was being screened by the sparsely attended Animal Rights Club. Called *The Animals*, the film documented the electrocution of an elephant; experiments performed in psychology labs, which drove primates insane either through deprivation, pain infliction or drug administration, including hallucinogens; radiation burn and gunshot experiments performed by the military on tethered sheep and dogs; and the terrible lives of animals with the advent of factory farming. About the same time, I saw a video of experiments done at the Medical School of Penn State University that had been made by the researchers, in which nonhuman primates were inflicted with brain damage using the most violent methods and without using any anesthesia. On film, researchers were shown teasing and mocking the injured animals. The videotapes were taken from the labs by animal rights activists and released to the media starting a controversy in the United States and

Great Britain (the experiments were funded by the National Institutes of Health and conducted jointly between Penn State and the University of Glasgow). Gary Francione, professor of law and currently Distinguished Scholar of Law and Philosophy at Rutgers University School of Law in Newark, New Jersey, argued that the experiments violated federal laws that required the use of anesthesia and, as a result, the US government, according to an interview with Francione, closed the head injury lab at Penn State to conduct a full investigation and, by the fall of 1985, suspended funding and fined the university.

During this time, I was enrolled in a second-year biology course that required students to perform a dissection on a rat that had been "prepared" (read: raised, killed and preserved) for our use. After seeing the documentaries and after hearing one teaching assistant claim that laboratory rats were not "real" animals—because they had been raised and bred in cages and their feet had never touched the ground—my lab partner and I went to the professor and, although it was the end of the course and time for the final exam—and the mandatory dissection—we announced we were not going to do it. In the wake of a two-hour discussion, I recall the professor saying that although he didn't agree with us he would respect our position because we had shown initiative in challenging the status quo. He allowed us to answer the final exam questions on anatomical structures by making available to us the body of a small rabbit that had been killed on the road. We were grateful for having our views acknowledged because during these times there was little or no support for students who felt strongly about animal rights, especially the right of animals not to be treated as the property of others. As I mentioned, attendance at the Animal Rights Club meetings in the early 1980s was dismal. There were only four of us: two being the president and vice-president and the other members of the club my lab partner and me. Needless to say this was not a group that people were clamoring to join. Viewing those documentaries was hard: in the face of such suffering, there were choices to be made.

But things *have* changed since then. PETA now features a highly informative website for students to learn about alternatives to dissection and advises students of their rights in refusing to perform dissections based on ethical concerns. If such action is possible for high school students and university undergraduates it would seem that in cultural studies and critical theory we ought to be able to follow. In fact, I think we are now more than ever poised to ask about the role of empathy in relation to teaching, research and knowledge production and to do so with conviction, especially where it comes to the right of sentient beings not to be treated as the property of others. For me, the road to editing this collection began with the viewing of the documentary films and the refusal to participate in the dissection of an animal killed for the classroom; this path led me to bringing together in a Canadian context writers and thinkers whose concern for nonhuman animals is *both* rigorously intellectual and unapologetically empathetic. In an era of posthumanism and in the spirit of compassion, this collection of essays is intended to participate in changes to our field of study and, hopefully, to open debates where previously there were none. Assuredly, some will continue to argue that many of the essays do not fall under the rubric of cultural studies or that they are too diverse or even that in being heterogeneous the collection lacks unity. To these readers I would say that this collection provides the opportunity to examine what is at stake with regards to the aporia in cultural studies and like early feminist scholarship to give voice to diversity in hope of addressing ethical questions whose social and theoretical relevance based upon compassion can hardly be underestimated.

NOTES

1 Carry Wolfe, *Animal Rites: American Culture, the Discourse of Species, and Posthumanist Theory* (Chicago: University of Chicago Press, 2003).
2 See Dana Medero and Alison Calder, "Ethics, Activism, and the Rise of Interdisciplinary Animal Studies: An Interview with Cary Wolfe," *Topia: A Canadian Journal of Cultural Studies* 10 (Fall 2003): 40.
3 Peter Singer, *Animal Liberation*, 2nd ed. (New York: Avon Books, 1990).
4 Speciesism is a term attributed to British psychologist, ethicist, and historian Richard Ryder, author of *Victims of Science: The Use of Animals in Research* (London: David Poynter, 1975). After doing experiments on laboratory animals Ryder began to speak out against the practice and became one of the pioneers of animal liberation and animal rights. The term was taken up by Australian philosopher Singer in *Animal Liberation*. The term is understood to describe a doctrine that certain species are innately superior to others and is used to describe the exploitation by humans of "lower" species. See Tom Regan and Peter Singer, *Animal Rights and Human Obligations* (Englewood Cliffs, NJ: Prentice Hall, 1976).
5 Wolfe, *Animal Rites*, 6.
6 Paola Cavalieri, *The Animal Question: Why Nonhuman Animals Deserve Human Rights*, trans. Catherine Woolard (New York: Oxford University Press, 2004), 3.

7 Wolf, *Animal Rites*, 1.
8 In light of continuing opposition to the inclusion of animal studies within cultural studies, the idea of hybridity as a primary concept within the discipline has seemed ironic since hybridity or hybridization is concerned with *margins* as being the zone of conflict and difference. See David Macey's recently published—and in the field of Cultural Studies frequently referenced—*The Penguin Dictionary of Critical Theory* (New York: Penguin Books, 2000).
9 See Allan J. Gedalof, Jonathan Boulter, Joel Faflak, and Cameron McFarlane, eds., *Cultural Subjects: A Popular Culture Reader* (Toronto: Thomson Nelson, 2005), viii.
10 See Stefan Collini, "Escape from DWEMsville: Is Culture Too Important to Be Left to Cultural Studies?" *Times Literary Supplement*, 27 May 1994: 3-4.
11 See Norma Schulman's "Conditions of Their Own Making: An Intellectual History of the Centre for Contemporary Cultural Studies at the University of Birmingham," *Canadian Journal of Communications* 18, no. 1 (1993), retrieved 15 August 2005 from www.cjc-online.ca/viewarticle.php?id=140.
12 See Mikhail Bakhtin's discussion of heteroglossia and the relationship between language and ideology in *The Dialogic Imagination: Four Essays*, ed. Michael Holquist, trans. Caryl Emerson and Michael Holquist (Austin: University of Texas Press, 1981), 426.
13 Ibid., 428.
14 See Anthony F. Beavers, "Researching Levinas," retrieved 4 November 2006 from http://faculty.evansville.edu/tb2/trip/levinas_intro.htm.
15 See Emmanuel Levinas, *Ethics and Infinity: Conversations with Phillippe Nemo*, trans. Richard A. Cohen (Pittsburgh: Duquesne University Press, 1985), 97.
16 In *Cultural Studies and Cultural Theory* (Toronto: Oxford University Press, 2000), Patrick Fuery and Nick Mansfield write, "One of the things that most clearly defines the break that the new humanities represent is the attitude to humanism. Put simply, many contemporary intellectuals and theorists no longer see themselves fulfilling the cultural project that arose in the Renaissance, which saw the study and fulfillment of human nature as its purpose ... [Moreover,] the general attack on humanism has denied its fundamental premise that there is such a thing as a universal human nature" (4-5).
17 Ibid., 10-11.
18 See Gayatri Chakravorty Spivak, "Remembering the Limits: Difference, Identity and Practice," in Peter Osborne, ed., *Socialism and the Limits of Liberalism* (London: Verso, 1991), 229.
19 Medora and Calder, "Ethics, Activism, and the Rise of Interdisciplinary Animal Studies," 40.
20 Donna J. Haraway, "A Cyborg Manifesto: Science, Technology, and Socialist-Feminism in the Late Twentieth Century," in *Simians, Cyborgs, and Women:*

The Reinvention of Nature (New York: Routledge, 1991), 151–52. Emphasis added.
21 Medora and Calder, "Ethics, Activism, and the Rise of Interdisciplinary Animal Studies," 41. Emphasis in original.
22 A recent exception to this in Canada was a two-day conference held at Brock University on 24–25 February 2005 that was dedicated to "two days of thinking about animals." The conference was a joint effort of the Canadian Studies Association and Brock University's "Thinking about Animals" project. Similarly, at the 2005 Canadian Association for Cultural Studies Conference (CACS) "Insides, Outsides, and Elsewheres" held 20–23 October 2005 in Edmonton at the University of Alberta, I put together the first panel of its kind in the history of the association based on this question. Entitled, "The Question of the Animal, Why Now?" this panel featured papers by scholars (including Roxanne Harde, Dawne McCance and Marian Scholtmeijer) who were concerned to critique the division between humans and nonhuman animals and to address the human–animal relationship in the context of posthumanist cultural studies. Lastly, an email (21 October 2006) from John Sorenson of Brock University (and a contributor to this volume) recently announced the creation of a new Concentration and Minor in Critical Animals Studies by the Department of Sociology as part of a "commitment to engaged scholarship directed towards social justice." In celebration of this initiative, a conference entitled "Thinking about Animals: Dominance, Captivity and Liberation" was held at Brock University in St. Catherine's Ontario on 15-16 March 2007 and was co-sponsored by the Niagara Action for Animals, a local non-profit, all-volunteer charity "devoted to ending all forms of animal cruelty through education, direct action and legitimate protest." At the time of this writing the "Nature Matters: Materiality and the More-Than-Human in Cultural Studies of the Environment" (at which I will be presenting) is planned for 25–28 October 2007 and will be hosted by the Faculty of Environmental Studies at York University in Toronto. It will feature a number of panels on nonhuman animal issues signals a breakthrough in the field of Cultural Studies in Canada.
23 Singer, *Animal Liberation*, 5.
24 Ibid., 1.
25 Peter Singer, *Practical Ethics* (London: Cambridge University Press, 1993), 34.
26 Qouted in Matthew Scully, *Dominion: The Power of Man, the Sufffering of Animals, and the Call to Mercy* (New York: St. Martin's Press, 2002), 6. Emphasis added.
27 Ibid.
28 Ibid.
29 Jeffrey Masson and Susan McCarthy, *When Elephants Weep: The Emotional Lives of Animals* (New York: Delacorte Press, 1995), 2–3.

30 Scully, *Dominion*, 377.
31 Wolfe, *Animal Rites*, 190.
32 Haraway, "A Cyborg Manifesto," 149. Emphasis added. Of this style, Haraway writes: "Perhaps more faithful as blasphemy is faithful, than as reverent worship and identification. Blasphemy has always seemed to require taking things very seriously. I know no better stance to adopt from within the secular-religious, evangelical traditions of United States politics, including the politics of socialist feminism. Blasphemy protects one from the moral majority within, while still insisting on the need for community. Blasphemy is not apostasy.... Irony is about humour and serious play. It is also a rhetorical strategy and a political method, one I would like to see more honoured within socialist-feminism. At the centre of my ironic faith, my blasphemy, is the image of the cyborg" (149).
33 Ibid., 181.
34 Ibid., 149. Emphasis added.
35 Ibid., 150.
36 See People for the Ethical Treatment of Animals (PETA), "The Chicken Flesh Industry," retrieved 3 September 2005 from www.peta.org. "According to a report from the USDA, 98 percent of chicken carcasses are contaminated with *E. coli* bacteria by the time they reach the market, largely because of the filthy conditions in the sheds where they are raised."
37 Harraway, "A Cyborg Manifesto," 149.
38 See People for the Ethical Treatment of Animals (PETA), "Kentucky Fried Cruelty," retrieved 12 August 2007 from www.kentuckyfriedcruelty.com. According to PETA, an extensive and ongoing campaign against Kentucky Fried Chicken, officially begun in 2001 after a successful campaign against McDonald's to improve the welfare of the animals killed for its restaurants, reveals that KFC suppliers continue to "cram birds [850 million per year] into huge waste-filled factories, breed and drug them to grow so large that they can't even walk, and often break their wings and legs. At slaughter, the birds' throats are slit and they are dropped into tanks of scalding-hot water—often while they are still conscious."
38 According to PETA's undercover investigations, "every time undercover investigators enter the facilities of KFC's suppliers, they find hideous abuse and suffering. At one KFC 'Supplier of the Year' slaughterhouse in West Virginia, workers were caught tearing birds' heads off, ripping them apart, spitting tobacco into their eyes, spray-painting their faces, and throwing them against walls—all while the birds were still conscious and able to feel pain." Retrieved 13 August 2007 from www.kentuckyfriedcruelty.com/u-undercover.asp.
39 Michael Fox, *Deep Vegetarianism* (Philadelphia: Temple University Press, 1999).
40 Angus Taylor, *Animals and Ethics* (Peterborough, ON: Broadview Press, 2003).

41 Marineland Canada, "Behind the Scenes" an "Introduction to Marineland," retrieved 5 August 2005 from www.marinelandcanada.com/educational/introduction/behindthescenes.

42 Gary Francione, *Introduction to Animal Rights: Your Child or the Dog?* (Philadelphia: Temple University Press, 2000), 12.

43 Ibid., 38.

44 Ibid., 42. The list, indeed, does go "on and on" and Francione's book is just one of hundreds giving detailed examples of the pain and distress caused to millions of nonhuman animals in countless laboratory experiments every year.

45 See People for the Ethical Treatment of Animals (PETA) new website at http://dir.salon.com/story/tech/feature/2002/10/21/peta/index.htm that "tutors teenage animal-rights warriors how to resist dissection in biology class and mystery meat in the cafeteria." The website provides details on laws based on the Canadian Charter of Rights and Freedoms and student choice policies in Nova Scotia's South Shore, Vancouver, British Columbia, Toronto, Ontario and on school board policies in Kelowna and Westbank, British Columbia, that allow students to chose "humane alternatives." PETA provides students with a sample letter to send to their instructors stating they will not participate in an assignment involving dissection and a request that the instructor " provide ... an alternative that will not involve my direct or indirect participation in the dissection of any animal that has been killed for the purpose of a classroom dissection or at a slaughterhouse." Retrieved 15 October 2006 from www.peta2.com/TAKECHARGE/t-dissection2.asp.

BIBLIOGRAPHY

Bakhtin, Mikhail M. *The Dialogic Imagination: Four Essays*. Edited by Michael Holquist and translated by Caryl Emerson and Michael Holquist. Austin: University of Texas Press, 1981.

Beavers, Anthony F. "Researching Levinas." Retrieved 5 November 2006 from http://faculty.evansville.edu/tb2/trip/levinas_intro.htm.

Cavalieri, Paola. *The Animal Question: Why Nonhuman Animals Deserve Human Rights*. Trans. Catherine Woolard. New York: Oxford University Press, 2004.

Collini, Stefan. "Escape from DWEMsville: Is Culture Too Important to Be Left to Cultural Studies?" *Times Literary Supplement*, 27 May 1994: 3-4.

Fox, Michael. *Deep Vegetarianism*. Philadelphia: Temple University Press, 1999.

Francione, Gary. *Introduction to Animal Rights: Your Child or the Dog?* Philadelphia: Temple University Press, 2006.

Fuery, Patrick, and Nick Mansfield. *Cultural Studies and Cultural Theory.* Toronto: Oxford University Press, 2000.

Gedalof, Allan J., Jonathan Boulter, Joel Faflak, and Cameron McFarlane, eds. *Cultural Subjects: A Popular Culture Reader.* Toronto: Thomson Nelson, 2005.

Haraway, Donna J. "A Cyborg Manifesto: Science, Technology, and Socialist-Feminism in the Late Twentieth Century." In *Simians, Cyborgs, and Women: The Reinvention of Nature.* New York: Routledge, 1991.

Levinas, Emmanuel. *Ethics and Infinity: Conversations with Phillippe Nemo.* Translated by Richard A. Cohen. Pittsburgh: Duquesne University Press, 1985.

Macey, David. *The Penguin Dictionary of Critical Theory.* New York: Penguin Books, 2000.

Masson, Jeffrey, and Susan McCarthy. *When Elephants Weep: The Emotional Lives of Animals.* New York: Delacorte Press, 1995.

Medora, Dana, and Alison Calder. "Ethics, Activism, and the Rise of Interdisciplinary Animal Studies: An Interview with Cary Wolfe." *Topia: A Canadian Journal of Cultural Studies* 10 (Fall 2003): 39–52.

Regan, Tom, and Peter Singer. *Animal Rights and Human Obligations.* Englewood Cliffs, NJ: Prentice Hall, 1976.

Schulman, Norma. "Conditions of Their Own Making: An Intellectual History of the Centre for Contemporary Cultural Studies at the University of Birmingham." *Canadian Journal of Communication* 18, no. 1 (1993). Retrieved 15 August 2005 from www.cjc-online.ca/viewarticle.php?id=140.

Scully, Matthew. *Dominion: The Power of Man, the Suffering of Animals, and the Call to Mercy.* New York: St. Martin's Press, 2002.

Singer, Peter. *Animal Liberation.* 2nd ed. New York: Avon Books, 1990.

———. *Practical Ethics.* London: Cambridge University Press, 1993.

Spivak, Gayatri Chakravorty. "Remembering the Limits: Difference, Identity and Practice." In Peter Osborne, ed., *Socialism and the Limits of Liberalism.* London: Verso, 1991.

Taylor, Angus. *Animals and Ethics.* Peterborough, ON: Broadview Press, 2003.

Wolfe, Cary. *Animal Rites: American Culture, the Discourse of Species, and Posthumanist Theory.* Chicago: University of Chicago Press, 2003.

———, ed. *Zoontologies: The Question of the Animal.* Minneapolis: University of Minnesota Press, 2003.

2

Chicken

DONNA HARAWAY

PART I: CHICKEN

Chicken is no coward. Indeed, this warrior bird has plied his trade as a fighting cock around the world since the earliest days such fowl consented to work for people, somewhere in south and southeast Asia.

Anxious if brave, Chicken Little has long worried that the sky is falling. He has a good vantage point from which to assess this matter; for Chicken, right along with his over-reaching companion, *Homo sapiens*, has been witness and participant in all the big events of Civilization. Chicken laboured on the Egyptian pyramids, when barley-pinching Pharaohs got the world's first mass egg industry going to feed the avians' co-conscripted human workers. Much later—a bit after the Egyptians replaced their barley exchange system with proper coins, thus acting like the progressive capitalists their exchange partners always seem to want in that part of the world—Julius Caesar brought the Pax Romana, along with the "ancient English" chicken breed, the Dorking, to Britain. Chicken Little knows all about the shock and awe of History, and he is a master at tracking the routes of Globalizations, old and new. Technoscience is no stranger either. Add to that, Chicken knows a lot about Biodiversity and Cultural Diversity, whether one thinks about the startling variety of chicken-kind for the 5,000 years of their domestic arrangements with humanity, or considers

---

From B. Eekelen, J. Gonzalez, B. Stötzer and A. Tsing, eds., *Shock and Awe: War on Words* (Santa Cruz, CA: New Pacific Press, 2004), 23–30.

the "improved breeds" accompanying capitalist class formations from the nineteenth century to now. No county fair is complete without its gorgeous "purebred" chickens, who know a lot about the history of eugenics. It is hard to sort out shock from awe in chicken-land. Whether the firmament takes a calamitous tumble or not, Chicken holds up a good half of the sky.

In 2004 CE, Chicken Little donned his spurs once more and entered the war on words thrust on him by Current Events. Ever a gender bender, Chicken joined the GLBT Brigade and outdid himself as a postcolonial, transnational, pissed-off spent hen and mad feminist. Chicken admitted that s/he was inspired by the all (human) girl underground fight clubs that s/he found out about on www.extremechickfights.com. Ignoring the sexism of "chick"—extreme or not—and the porn industry and pedophilic scene that vilifies the name of chicken, our Bird raptured those fighting girls right out of History and into his trannie sf world, fit to confront the Eagles of War and the Captains of Industry. S/he felt this rapturous power because s/he recalled not just the exploits of Cousin Phoenix, but also the years when s/he was a figure of Jesus Resurrected, promising the faithful that they would rise from the ashes of History's barbecues.

Barbecue. An unkind reminder of where Chicken Little had best concentrate her attention. For, at the end of a millennium, in 2000, 10 billion chickens were slaughtered in the US alone. Worldwide, 5 billion hens—75 percent in cramped, multi-occupancy quarters called battery cages—were laying eggs, with Chinese flocks leading the way, followed by those in the United States and Europe. Thai chicken exports topped $1.5 billion in value in an industry supplying Japanese and EU markets and employing hundreds of thousands of Thai citizens. World chicken production was 65.6 million tons, and the whole operation was growing at 4 percent per year. Captains of Industry, indeed. Chicken could conclude that her/his major vocation seems to be breakfast and dinner while the world burns.[1]

Contrary to the views of her pesky friends in the transnational animal rights movement, our Opportunistic Bird is not against surrendering a pound of flesh in exchange for pecking rights in the naturalcultural contractual arrangements that domesticated both bipedal hominids and winged gallinaceous avians. But there's something seriously foul in current versions of multi-species global contract theory.

One way to tell the trouble—one detail among myriads—is that a three-year study in Tulsa, Oklahoma—a centre of factory chicken production—showed that half the water supply was dangerously polluted by poultry waste. Go ahead, microwave sponges in your kitchens as often as the clean food cops advise; inventive bacteria will outwit you with their fowl alliances.

Well, one more detail. Manipulated genetically since the 1950s to rapidly grow mega breasts, chickens given a choice choose food laced with pain killers. "Unsustainable growth rates" are supposed to be about dot-com fantasies and inflationary stock markets. In Chicken's world, however, that term designates the daily immolation of forced maturation and disproportionate tissue development that produces tasty (enough) young birds unable to walk, flap their wings or even stand up. Muscles linked in evolutionary history and religious symbolism to flight, sexual display and transcendence instead pump iron for transnational growth industries. Not satisfied, some agribusiness scientists look to post genomics research for even more buffed white meat.[2]

The first farm animals to be permanently confined indoors and made to labour in automated systems based on Technoscience's finest genetic technologies, feed-conversion efficiency research, and miracle drugs (not pain killers, but antibiotics and hormones), Chicken might be excused for being unimpressed by the McDonald Corporation's grudging agreement in 2000 to require that its suppliers give 50 percent more space per bird destined to be Chicken McNuggets and Eggs McMuffin. Still, McDonald's was the first corporation in the world to admit that pain and suffering are concepts familiar to under-rated bird brains. Chicken's ingratitude is no wonder, when no humane slaughter law in the US or Canada to this day applies to chickens.

In 1999 the EU did manage to ban battery cages—beginning in 2012. That should allow for a smooth transition. Perhaps more sensitized to ever-ready holocaust analogies, the Germans will make those cages illegal in 2007. In the market-besotted US, Chicken's hope seems to be in designer eggs for the omega-3 fatty acid-conscious and free-range certified organic chickens for the conscience-stricken and pure of diet. The up-to-the-minute ethically fastidious might procure their chicken fix like the citizens in Margaret Atwood's sf novel, *Oryx and Crake* (2003). There, chicken knobs—tasty organs without organisms, especially without annoying heads that register pain and perhaps have ideas about what constitutes a proper domestic bird's life—are on the menu. Genetically engineered muscles-without-animals illustrate exactly what Sarah Franklin means by designer ethics, which aim to bypass cultural struggle with just-in-time, "high technology" breakthroughs.[3] Design away the controversy, and all those free-range anarchists will have to go home. But remember, Chicken squawks even when his head has been cut off.

The law cannot be counted on. After all, even human labourers in the chicken industry are super-exploited. Thinking of battery cages for laying hens reminds Chicken Little how many illegal immigrants, ununionized women and men, people of colour and former prisoners process chickens in Georgia, Arkansas and Ohio. It's no wonder that at least one US soldier who tortured Iraqi prisoners was a chicken processor in her civilian life.

PART II: **SICK**

It's enough to make a sensitive Bird sick, as much from the virus of transnational politics as from the other kind. An avian flu outbreak in seven Asian nations shocked the world in the winter of 2004. Luckily, only a few humans died, unlike the tens of millions who succumbed in 1918-19. But before the 2004 fears abated, about 20 million chickens were prophylactically slaughtered in Thailand alone. Global TV news showed unprotected human workers stuffing innumerable birds into sacks, tossing them undead into mass graves, and sprinkling on lime. In Thailand, 99 percent of chicken operations are, in Global Speak, "small" (fewer than 1,000 birds, since it takes more than 80,000 to be "large") and could not afford biosecurity—for people or birds. Newscasters waxed eloquent about a threatened transnational industry, but spoke nary a word about farmers' and chickens' lives. Meanwhile, Indonesian government spokespeople in 2003 denied any avian flu in those salubrious quarters, even while Indonesian veterinary associations argued that millions of birds showed signs of avian flu as early as October.

Perhaps the Bangkok *Post* on 27 January 2004 got the war of worlds, words and images right with a cartoon showing migratory birds from the north dropping bombs—bird shit full of avian flu strain H5N1—on the geobody of the Thai nation.

This postcolonial joke on trans-border bioterrorism is a nice reversal of US and European fears of immigrants of all species from the global south. After all, prototypes for technoscientific, export-oriented, epidemic friendly chicken industries were big on the Peace Corps agenda (a theme picked up later by GATT), right along with artificial milk for infants. Proud progenitor of such meaty progress, the US had high hopes for winning the Cold War in Asia with standardized broilers and layers carrying democratic values. In Eugene Burdick and William J. Lederer's 1958 novel, *The Ugly American*, set in a fictional southeast Asian nation called Sarkan, Iowa chicken farmer and agricultural teacher Tom Knox was about the only decent US guy. Neither Knox nor subsequent Development Experts seem to have cared much for the varied chicken-human livelihoods thriving for a long time throughout Asia.

Chicken Little is, of course, no virgin to debates about political orders. The darling of savants' disputes about the nature of mind and instincts, the "philosopher's chick" was a staple of nineteenth-century learned idioms. Famous experiments in comparative psychology gave the world the term "pecking order" in the 1920s. Chicken Little remembers that this research by the Norwegian Thorleif Schjelderup-Ebbe, a serious lover and student of chickens, described complex social arrangements worthy of fowl, not the wooden dominance hierarchies in biopolitics that gained such a hold on cultural imaginations. Behavioural sciences of both human and nonhuman varieties continue to find anything but dominance and subordination hard to think about. Chicken knows that getting better accounts of animal doings, with each other and with humans, can play an important role in reclaiming livable politics.

Laying hens and fertile eggs dominate Chicken Little's closing thoughts. Perversely, s/he finds there the stuff of freedom projects and renewed awe. The British claymation animation film *Chicken Run* (2000) stars 1950s Yorkshire hens facing a life of forced toil. The appearance of Rocky, the Rhode Island Red, catalyzes a liberation drama that gives no comfort either to "deep animal rights" imaginations of a time before co-species domestication nor to millennial free traders in chicken flesh. Pecking hens have other biopolitical tricks tucked under their wings.

Chicken Little returns in the end to the egg—fertile eggs in school biology labs that once gave millions of young hominids the privilege to see the shocking beauty of the developing chick embryo, with its dynamic architectural intricacies. These cracked-open eggs did not offer an innocent beauty, but they also gave no warrant to colonial or postcolonial arrogances about Development. They can renew the meaning of awe in a world in which laying hens know more about the alliances it will take to survive and flourish in multi-species, multi-cultural, multi-ordered associations than do all the secondary Bushes in Florida and Washington. Follow the chicken and find the world.

The sky has not fallen, not yet.

NOTES

1. Figures are from United Poultry Concerns, available from www.upc-online.org.
2. Myostatin regulates muscle development, and its gene is under intense scrutiny. Commercial interest relates to the world's number-one genetic disease (muscular dystrophies), wasting disorders (including aging and AIDS-related muscle loss), space flight-induced muscle atrophy, sports (watch out, steroid purveyors!) and bigger chicken muscles.
3. Sarah Franklin, "Stem Cells R Us," in A. Ong and S. Collier, eds., *Global Assemblages* (London: Blackwell, 2004), 59–78.

BIBLIOGRAPHY

Franklin, Sarah. "Stem Cells R Us." In A. Ong and S. Collier, eds., *Global Assemblages*. London: Blackwell, 2004.

3

Selfish Genes, Sociobiology and Animal Respect

ROD PREECE

> *We, and all other animals, are machines created by our genes... a predominant quality to be expected in a selfish gene is ruthless selfishness. This gene selfishness will usually give rise to selfishness in individual behaviour. However, there are special circumstances in which a gene can achieve its own selfish goals best by fostering a limited form of altruism at the level of individual animals. "Special" and "limited" are important words in the last sentence. Much as we might wish to believe otherwise, universal love and the welfare of the species as a whole are concepts which simply do not make evolutionary sense.*
>
> *... if you wish, as I do, to build a society in which individuals cooperate generously and unselfishly toward a common good, you can expect little help from biological nature. Let us try to teach generosity and altruism, because we are born selfish. Let us understand what our own selfish genes are up to, because we may then at least have the chance to upset their designs, something which no other species has ever aspired to.*
>
> —Richard Dawkins, *The Selfish Gene*

> *The economy of nature is competitive from beginning to end.... No hint of charity ameliorates our vision of society, once sentimentalism has been laid aside. What passes for cooperation turns out to be a mixture of opportunism and exploitation.... Given a full chance to act for his interest, nothing but expediency will restrain [an animal or human], from brutalizing, from maiming, from murdering....*
>
> —Michael T. Ghiselin, *The Economy of Nature and the Evolution of Sex*

Selfish gene theory is perhaps currently the most popular general theory in the life sciences. It constitutes the philosophical postulates of, and justification for, the gene's-eye view of animal behaviour as expounded by the devotees of sociobiology. "We are survival machines," proclaims Richard Dawkins, "robot vehicles blindly programmed to preserve the selfish molecules known as genes." This he wrote in his 1976 *The Selfish Gene*. In his 1995 *River Out of Eden: A Darwinian View of Life*, Dawkins reiterated and furthered this conception of the nature of human and nonhuman animal. There has been much criticism of this theory, most incisively by Stephen Jay Gould,[1] apparently without withering its popularity unduly. Most of the criticism, however, has been of the theory as science, or of its conception of human nature, rather than, as I consider in this essay, its relationship to long-rejected themes of Western thought, and the ethical implications for our attitudes towards animals.

As Dawkins acknowledges, selfish gene theory is a materialist and determinist theory. It is the kind of theory that provoked Michael Oakeshott to exclaim in caustic despair:

> When a geneticist tells us that "all social behaviour and historical events are the inescapable consequences of the genetic individuality of the persons concerned" we have no difficulty in recognizing this theorem as a brilliant illumination of the writings of Aristotle, the fall of Constantinople, the deliberations of the House of Commons on Home Rule for Ireland, and the death of Barbarossa; but this brilliance is, perhaps, somewhat dimmed when it becomes clear that he can have nothing more revealing to say about his science of genetics than that also is all done by genes, and that this theorem is itself his genes speaking.[2]

Richard Dawkins's selfish gene theory is, on the basis of selfish gene theory itself, the consequence not of Dawkins's perceptive insights but of Dawkins's genes! Not only is selfish gene theory reductionist, but, when confronted, Edmund O. Wilson, the author of *Sociobiology*[3] and advocate of the theory of kin selection, proudly proclaimed himself a reductionist.[4] Reductionism is not, however, the failing of theories of naturalist determinism alone. It is equally a failing of their primary opponents, the advocates of environmental determinism. Neither Nature nor Nurture theory in their radical forms allows the animal (or human) to be an individual, spontaneous, creative, independently choosing, caring, feeling being in and of itself. It is only such insofar as its genes or environmental conditions require it. And, if that is so, what is there about the intrinsic animal for us to respect or be considerate of? If either theory is correct, the animal is indeed a machine and there are no adequate grounds for denying Descartes's treatment of animals as automata, whereby we have no obligations towards them. It is a conclusion which the sociobiologists decry. But they never offer us an escape from the contradiction.

The evidence for Richard Dawkins's selfish genes thesis becomes much more complex and sophisticated as his studies progress. As with most such theories, however, the complexity and sophistication serve not to illuminate but to blur the premises on which the theory is founded. And it is at the level of these fundamental conceptions of the nature of the animal that the validity of selfish gene theory must be judged, for the sophistication is founded on the quicksand of these materialist and determinist conceptions. If these are false, not only is the theory false, it also denies us a ready appreciation of the animal realm.

Determinist and materialist explanations of social phenomena have played a significant and, in scientific circles, a preponderant role in Western intellectual history since the seventeenth century when scientists began to concentrate their attention on matter and its relations. "Matter in motion" was their defining perception of reality. Humans and animals were viewed as a part of nature in the same way that trees, rocks and planets were a part of nature. It was not evidence that persuaded such theorists as Thomas Hobbes to analyze humans and animals in these terms, but a desire to replicate the successes of the natural sciences. If the rest of the universe was explicable by reducing everything to its simplest parts, then so too must be the animal realm. If the rest of nature was explicable in universal laws, then so too must be the animal realm. Thus, it was not that animals and humans actually behaved like trees, rocks and planets that persuaded Hobbes to espouse his theories. Rather, it was that animals and humans had defied ready explanation. If they were to be understood fully, they must be treated as though they were like planets. The stimulus was the desire to have a theory that could be made to work, whether or not it provided an adequate explanation.

Those who pride themselves on their materialistic "realism" might care to ponder why Aboriginals and Asians have always recognized animals as possessors of an essence anything but material. Prima facie, this might encourage us to deliberate whether it is not "reality" that encourages our materialist conceptions, but a particular world view. We were persuaded, we might hypothesize, to regard animals in the scientific way we do because it accorded, not with facts, but with the ideational underpinnings of the myth, the culture, of science itself.

We can recognize an early precursor of modern materialism at the beginnings of the rationalist tradition in Greece during the fourth century BC. Democritus espoused an atomism he apparently derived from his mentor, Leucippus, avowing that "the nature of eternal things consists in small substances infinite in quantity."[5] Likewise, Epicurus saw ultimate reality as material in nature. While their views remained in a decided minority and then were eclipsed by Platonic idealism, their interpretations remained dormant—despite an unsuccessful attempt at resuscitation by Lucretius in the first century BC—waiting to be revived in a more propitious era.

In the mid-seventeenth century, consequent upon the rapid developments in the experimental sciences and in light of the new understanding of matter, Pierre Gassendi resurrected and revised the atomic theory of Democritus and Epicurus in his *De vita, moribus et doctrina Epicurii* (The Life, Modes and Doctrines of Epicurus) of 1647, and *Syntagma philosophiae Epicurii* (Corpus of the Philosophy of Epicurus) of 1649. Materialist conceptions had already informed the work of Caluccio Salutati, Francesco Guiccardini and Niccolo Machiavelli in fifteenth- and sixteenth-century Italy, though without receiving any explicitly theoretical analysis, and were popularized in Britain by Thomas Hobbes in his *De cive* of 1642 (English language edition 1645) and, more dramatically, in the *Leviathan* of 1651. This revival culminated in the thoroughgoing materialism, determinism and skepticism of Baron d'Holbach's *Systeme de la Nature* of 1770 which, in turn, proved a stimulus via Ludwig Feuerbach to the dialectical materialism of Karl Marx, whose doctoral thesis was on the materialism of Democritus. Thence arose the positivism of Auguste Comte, which proved a natural parent of the "behaviourism" of B.F. Skinner.

Despite the significant diversity in all these theories, they share a common central viewpoint, summarized by George H. Sabine in his discussion of the Epicurean notion of nature: "So far as the world at large is concerned ... nature means simply physics, the atoms out of which all things are made. So far as human beings are concerned nature means self-interest, the desire of every man for his own individual happiness."[6] And, one might add, as far as animals are concerned in such a scheme, nature means no more than self-interest, the satisfaction of biological needs. Materialism and egoism are essentially associated concepts and all the theories that embrace them are subject to the same kind of critique. Selfish gene theory replaces unsophisticated atoms with sophisticated genes, yet subscribes to the same general conception of materialist "reality." For both human and animal, the gene rather than the individual becomes the actor. Dawkins is a worthy successor to Democritus and Epicurus, and those they influenced. And his theory is just as vulnerable to the ready refutation advanced against such theories from Plato in the *Gorgias* and the *Republic* (where Callicles and Glaucon respectively play Dawkins's role) to G.E. Moore in *Principia Ethica*, from the fourth century BC to the twentieth century AD.

The prime problem encountered by all materialist, determinist and self-interest theories, including selfish gene theories, is one of explaining, or even acknowledging, apparent instances of spontaneity, creativity and altruism. The moment they are encountered, they are whisked away, transubstantiated into some other phenomenon than that which our senses witnessed and our minds judged them to be. They are translated from what our experience says they are into something consistent with materialist preconceptions. The unfathomably complex is reduced to the readily comprehensible. And if what we wish to understand is, as yet, unfathomable, we resort to a myth to explain it. Sometimes, as in Marx's case, the determinism is asserted as a dictate of the laws of history, and spontaneity is applauded as the appropriate human condition, without ever appearing to recognize the contradiction. Gassendi espoused an Epicurean determinism, yet, almost in the same breath, denounced Descartes with vitriol for treating animals as automata.[7] They suffer from the eternal determinist's paradox: how to have a scientific (hence, as the myth has it, irrefutable!) explanation and at the same time retain our concern for other beings because it is morally right to do so. Dawkins sits uncomfortably on the same horns. He asserts the necessity of "ruthless selfishness" yet applauds generous co-operation and a society based unselfishly on a common good—

all of which is denied to him on the premises of the theory he espouses. Animal welfare scientists who espouse sociobiology must be equally perplexed. They respect the animals they study but are compelled to recognize this respect as no more than a symptom of their genetic promptings. Even more, their theory requires them to acknowledge that the animal has no qualities that are worthy of their affection and their respect. One cannot escape the contradiction by asserting one's ideals and then insisting that because they have been acknowledged they must be compatible with the theory. One must abandon the claims of morality and worthiness or modify, if not abandon, the theory.

Many classical utilitarians recognized the tension between the assertion of universally self-interested behaviour as the defining aspect of the human (and animal) condition and the apparent incompatibility, yet desirability, of altruism. In Hobbes's *Leviathan* the altruism is explained as a chimera that masks the reality of our self-interest. In the later versions there emerges the doctrine of "enlightened" self-interest, as propagated in the classical liberal doctrines of David Hume, Jeremy Bentham, James Mill and Herbert Spencer.[8] As a matter of biological fact, they insisted, being determined to make their theories "scientific," all humans (all animals) pursue their individual self-interest. They are, though they did not employ the term, self-interested machines. The "enlightened" aspect involves the recognition that the rational pursuit of our self-interest requires that our permanent interests are best served by behaviour that acknowledges the rights and interests of others, and permits others to pursue their interests unhindered to the extent that they do not impinge harmfully on our own long-term interests. This does not, however, add a new motive to human action. Human behaviour does not become altruistic, whatever may be claimed for it. It becomes, in fact, more sophisticatedly egotistical. It acknowledges the rights of others only to the extent that our own interests are neither harmed nor threatened, and indeed are effectively furthered, by it. And it requires that others come to acknowledge the benefits to themselves of behaving likewise. What should be clear is that such a doctrine is of little help with regard to our appropriate attitude towards animals. Our short- and long-term interests are, at least sometimes, quite incompatible with theirs. Except with our companion animals, we rarely enter into a contract with them, explicit or implicit. Moreover, a case can be made that we have a greater responsibility towards them in precisely those circumstances where their and our interests are at odds. Nothing in early utilitarian theory allows us to deal with such circumstances.

Famously, the classical liberal utilitarian Jeremy Bentham included animals in the doctrine, "the question is not, can they *reason*? nor can they *talk*? but, can they *suffer*?"[9] Of course, the maximization of pleasure and minimization of pain is both the central motor and desideratum of utilitarianism, though it cannot be derived from the theory. It is a postulate of the theory. Moreover, when Bentham adds "each [is] to count as one and no more than one," he postulates an ethic which is equally underivable from the theory. It is predicated on the increasingly individualistic language of the Enlightenment, but its estimation of the equal inherent value of all is derived from some prior predilection of the mind, accommodated to the premises of utilitarian and "scientific" thought. It arose, at least in part, from Bentham's authentic concern to devise a just and effective moral and legal system, beneficial to both humans and animals. Why, then, did Bentham not recognize the possibility of a similar concern in others? If Bentham was aware that "suffering" was a relevant criterion, whence did he come to that recognition if not by some principle prior to utility in his mind, which prompted him to posit the significance of utility?

Recognizing the reality, if not commonality, of genuinely altruistic behaviour, the later utilitarian John Stuart Mill argued, paradoxically, that over time enlightened self-interest can turn into authentic altruism—towards both fellow humans and fellow animals,[10] a proposition which Dawkins repeats in a new language.[11] Old wine in new bottles, but no less leaky than before. If people become accustomed to doing good out of rational self-interest, Mill claimed, they will continue to do so even if they do not expect any particular reward. It should be patently clear, however, that if all behaviour is initially self-interested, enlightened or otherwise, the acquisition of altruism through habit would be an impossibility. One would have a compelling motive, or causal agent—self-interest—for not acquiring such a habit. And if one does acquire such a habit, if one does come to act altruistically because one has learnt not to be selfish, that fact does not extend the utilitarian theory, it confounds it. The existence of a motive other than, and inconsistent with, self-interest refutes the theory that all behaviour is self-interested, whether pleasure or gene driven. The fact of altruism is predicated not only on our common sense experiences but also on the failure of self-interest theory at every turn to explain satisfactorily the complex reality of human behaviour.

Selfish gene theory and sociobiology are to be understood as intrinsic elements of utilitarian, determinist, and materialist theory. When Edward O. Wilson tells us that "Mechanophilia, the love of machines, is but a special case of biophilia,"[12] he acknowledges, unwittingly, that sociobiology is nothing other than Cartesianism with a sprinkling of awe. On the foundations of sociobiology, there can be no spontaneity, no creativity in the animal (or for that matter, the human) world. The animal is blindly following pre-ordained rules. All "will," other than that directed to genetic interests, is expunged from the animal. If the animal is truly a living machine—"bête machine" was Descartes' phrase, and Wilson tells us the machine is "in key respects quasi-alive"—on what basis may we respect the animal in a manner different from the bizarre idea of respecting a machine in and for itself? How may we treat the animal "machine" as an end in itself, as an object of moral consideration, when we treat a machine—a watch, say, or a locomotive—entirely as a means to an end?

For the sociobiologists, instead of individuals acting selfishly as a matter of biological necessity—as machines—it is genes which do so. The advantage of treating genes rather than individuals as the self-interested "actors" is that it allows one a ready explanation of apparently altruistic behaviour, though only in favour of the interests of our genetic relatives. "Altruism" is posited as consistent with self-interested behaviour in that genes engage in "kin selection." Thus, Robert Wright in *Three Scientists and Their Gods* writes:

> Fortunately for the theory of natural selection, it turns out that there is a way altruism can get off the ground without relying on group selection. It is called "kin selection." The idea behind kin selection is that the gene, not the individual, is the unit of natural selection, and the interests of the gene and the interests of the individual don't always coincide.
>
> If you are a prairie dog (or are just yourself, for that matter) and you have a recently invented gene—synthesized, say, by your great-grandparents—so do roughly half of your siblings and one-eighth of your cousins. Now, suppose this gene is a warning-call gene, and suppose some siblings and cousins are in your vicinity when a predator appears. You can get up on your hind legs and tip everyone off to the impending danger, in the process tipping the predator off to your location and getting eaten. This may seem like a very valiant thing for you, and your warning-call gene to do. But, in fact, the "sacrifice" made by your warning-call gene is no such thing.
>
> Sure, the gene perishes along with its "altruistic" possessor (you) but meanwhile in the bodies of a dozen siblings and cousins, two or three or four or five carbon copies of the gene are carried off safely to be

transmitted to future generations. Such a gene will do better in the evolutionary market place than a "coward" gene, which would save itself only to see its several replicas plucked from the gene pool. The theory of kin selection is very much in the spirit of Samuel Butler's observation that "a hen is only an egg's way of making another egg."[13]

Wright might have thought to add another line from Butler which is equally apposite: "Life is the art of drawing sufficient conclusions from insufficient premises." Selfish gene theory becomes quite compelling in its artistry, in its subtleties and sophistication. It is very much less compelling when one examines its premises and their consistency with at least some of the empirical examples offered in confirmation. The prairie dog has usually sacrificed itself to save only one other animal, not from two to five. The capacity of the predator to hunt and feed is limited. Rarely is more than one hunted at a time, even though they weigh only three pounds and even though coyotes hunt them in pairs. Prairie dogs used to be the favoured prey of black-footed ferrets, which are now rare, but, like badgers, the ferrets excavate them from, and take over, their burrows. Self-sacrifice does not appear to be an issue. Their other predators are rattlesnakes, burrowing owls, eagles and hawks, none of which offers much of a self-sacrificing opportunity, since they hunt singly and only one would be taken at a time. Coyotes would appear to be the only predator which offers the prairie dog an opportunity for self-sacrifice. Even in this instance, customarily, the prairie dog ensures that it rather than one other prairie dog is killed. It is simply an exaggeration to imagine that as a consequence of the self-sacrifice "in the bodies of a dozen siblings and cousins, two or three or four or five carbon copies of the gene are carried off safely to be transmitted to future generations." Moreover, in the case of human preference for kin, is the preference increased when we are aware that it is our cousins we are acting in favour of, or does it remain the same if we are ignorant of the relationship? If awareness of the relationship is relevant, the gene alone cannot be the agent of selection, for it must act the same whether the relationship is known or not.

Selfish gene theory is modernity's version of earlier cynicism. It is a restatement in contemporary genetic prose of Machiavelli's view, in *The Prince* (1513), that "love is held by a chain of obligation which men [read 'genes'] being selfish, is broken whenever it serves their purpose," and of Spinoza's assertion in *Ethics* (1677) that the "endeavour wherewith each thing [read 'gene'] endeavours to persist in its own being is nothing more than the actual essence of the thing itself."[14] Similarly, we read in La Rochefoucauld's *Maxims* (1655), "Interest speaks all sorts of tongues, including that of disinterestedness."[15] Scientific materialism spawned a psychology of misanthropy, now rekindled in the minds of the selfish gene theorists.

In *A Passage to India*, E.M. Forster has college principal Fielding say to Dr. Aziz, "I'd far rather leave a thought behind than a child." That would be an implausible sentiment to possess if selfish gene theory were valid. In Victor Hugo's *Les Miserables*, the plot is set by the preferential treatment of the innkeeper Thenardier and his wife in favour of their daughter Eponine and against their ward Cosette. On the basis of selfish gene theory, the Thenardiers could have behaved in no other way. There would be no point in condemning them. Nor would there be any logical or ethical grounds for doing so. If selfish gene theory were correct, the altruistic efforts of Jean Valjean to right the wrong would have been of necessity in vain, if not impossible—after all, to recall Dawkins, "universal love" (Valjean does not know Cosette before he rescues her) "simply [does] not make evolutionary sense." If selfish gene theory is correct, almost all literature is based on a misconception of what it is to be human. Dante tells us in *Paradise*: "My will and my desire were turned by love, / The love that makes the sun and other stars."[16] If Dawkins is right, Dante's asexual love of Beatrice is a fraud. While few would wish to deny that the spring of love lies in our genetic inheritance, those who have loved either humans or animals know that Dante speaks the truth. Love is quite different from self-interest. Indeed, love for another being, human or animal, is precisely the willingness to act in the interest of that other when that interest counters our own self-interest, genetic or individual. On sociobiology and selfish gene premises, such "love" is only possible if there is an immediate genetic relationship with the object of one's affections—which makes it not love at all, or even respect.

To escape the problem, the selfish gene theorist will simply have to insist that the humanitarian Jean Valjean, and the besotted Dante, were less well adapted evolutionarily than the greedy Thenardiers. Two points need to be made. First, since, according to Wright, the more selfish "gene will do much better in the evolutionary market place," then humanity must of necessity have been becoming throughout its history, and will continue to become, more selfish. W.E.H. Lecky's and Charles Darwin's thesis that our respect for humans and other animals has been developing over time will have to be rejected as incompatible with evolutionary theory.[17] The

Thenardiers are the *necessary* products of evolutionary success. Valjean is a Neanderthal. Secondly, there is absolutely no point in our attempting to intervene to make the world a more humanitarian place. It is the genes, not we, who will decide. Moreover, there is no basis for us to desire a less selfish world. We could have no genetically produced desire to applaud altruism.

Yet it is a remarkable fact, and one itself entirely inconsistent with selfish gene theory, that we all do side with Valjean and Cosette against the Thenardiers. If selfish gene theory were correct we would be more likely to root for the Thenardiers over Valjean if we happened to have more genes in common with them. We could not embrace the acts of Valjean because his behaviour was admirable. Indeed, we would not find it admirable. We could have no genetic grounds for admiring Valjean, and many genetic grounds for rejecting his behaviour. Nor could we delight in Victor Hugo's pronounced animal sensibilities throughout his novels—the role of the goat Djali in *Notre Dame de Paris* is especially moving. Nor could we admire Hugo's role as president of the French Anti-Vivisection Society.

We should not, of course, deny the merit of selfish gene theory as a plausible explanation of why we tend to prefer the interests of our kin to those of strangers, of our fellow humans to those of other species. Indeed, we should applaud it. It is a useful, and probably valid, theory of a very significant aspect of human and other animal behaviour. Yet the task is to understand not merely the self-interested aspects of behaviour but the complexities of moral decision-making, especially towards other species, which involve a balancing of our individual self-interests and special kin relationships combined with our awareness, derived from some decidedly different source from our genes, that each is entitled to some, if not necessarily equal, moral consideration. The difficulties of selfish gene theory explode when it attempts to become the overarching explanation of behaviour. It is then no more successful than the materialism of Epicurus, Gassendi, and Hobbes, and somewhat less successful than John Stuart Mill in his acknowledgement that the ethical *quality* of an action—rather than a calculation of the *amount* of pleasure it gave—determined its merit. As Mill failed to recognize, however, such an assertion destroys not only the felicific calculus of Bentham, but all determinist, materialist, and classical utilitarian theory.

When we return to the premises of selfish gene theory we can recognize that they involve an outright and unsynthesizable contradiction. "We are survival machines, robot vehicles," says Richard Dawkins, "blindly programmed to preserve the selfish molecules known as genes." If we are machines, we are determined matter. If we are robots, we do not make any meaningful choices. Apparent choices are what are programmed into us by our genes. "Altruism" is a misnomer. It is merely a synonym for the peculiar selfishness which occurs in what Dawkins calls "those special circumstances in which a gene can achieve its own selfish goals best by fostering a limited form of altruism at the level of individual animals." Let us be clear about it. When Dawkins uses the word "altruism" in this way, it is entirely misleading. The behaviour described as altruistic is anything but. It is merely genetically selfish behaviour which promotes the interests of others who share similar genes. It is the enlightened self-interest of the utilitarians occurring at the level of genes rather than individuals. As Rousseau pointed out, with perhaps a degree of exaggeration, "for every two men whose interests converge, there are perhaps one hundred thousand who are adversaries."[18] And, if that is in *any* degree accurate, what price the compatibility of human and animal interests?

However much the statements of selfish gene theorists may counter the everyday observances of ordinary people, at least they are self-consistent, as long as they remain at the level of genetic theory alone. The consistency problem—the unsynthesizable contradiction—becomes immediately apparent, however, when Dawkins continues: "… if you wish, as I do, to build a society in which individuals cooperate generously and unselfishly toward a common good, you can expect little help from biological nature." Yet, surely, if Dawkins does possess such a wish there must be a great deal more to being human than one's biological nature, and, unless one can discover some compelling category of distinction that has so far eluded natural history,[19] a great deal more to being animal, too. At best, on Dawkins's own terms, biology and genetic theory permit only enlightened self-interest. Dawkins debars himself from possessing the cooperative, generous, and unselfish desires he claims to possess. They are simply not allowed to him on the view he has of the human genetic *machine*. Moreover, whence might Dawkins derive the idea of a common good? Whence does he acquire his belief in the morality of co-operation, generosity, and selflessness? They cannot come from the dictates of his genetically driven self-interested machine, for such values are inherently opposed to the notion of self-interest, whether genetic or individual. Either Dawkins is mistaken about his values, or his view of the human as a genetically powered robot is hopelessly inadequate—at best unidimensional in a multi-dimensional world.

Renowned evolutionary theorist John Maynard Smith insists emphatically that Richard Dawkins's *The Selfish Gene* "is a book about the evolutionary process—it is not about morals, or about politics, or about the human sciences."[20] Why, one wonders, if that is so, does Dawkins write about morals in the book? Maynard Smith is emphatically wrong. Moral and political consequences follow of necessity from the view of the human or animal as a machine, as both the Cartesians and the anti-Cartesians fully understood. Dawkins acknowledges the relevance of the moral issues by raising them explicitly—and his inconsistencies allow us to see how incomplete selfish gene theory is as an explanation of the human phenomenon, let alone the human condition, as well as the animal phenomenon and condition.

A self-interest theorist could argue, quite consistently, that Dawkins's values are beliefs to which he has been socialized by those whose interests it is in for Dawkins to hold the values he does. But that would only demonstrate that socialization was able to override the dictates of Dawkins's genes. Moreover, and more importantly, one could not then claim those values to be worthwhile in themselves. One would be required to conclude that those characteristics which Dawkins cherishes are not worth cherishing—or, at least, that Dawkins has no adequate grounds for maintaining his values. The fact that he would, rightly, steadfastly refuse to renounce those values and to deny that he had somehow been compelled to maintain them suggests prima facie that those values are not merely the products of socialization, that generosity, and co-operation, and selflessness are worthwhile in themselves. Yet, if they are, they cannot be the product of our selfish genes. The "common good" on Dawkins's scientific terms can at best—and that would be a logical stretch—be the greatest happiness of the greatest number, which, as J.S. Mill acknowledged, permits the most heinous oppression of minorities and less powerful beings. Nazism is fully justifiable on the greatest happiness principle. The fact that sociobiologists genuinely care for animals indicates not the poverty of their ethics but the poverty of the philosophical foundations of their science.

If we are "survival machines," as Dawkins imagines, generosity, co-operation, and unselfishness are impossible unless they also contribute to the genetic self-interest of the individual subscribing to such values. Dawkins's theory can permit him to hold the values he does only if, *mirabile dictu*, selfish behaviour promotes necessarily the interests of others, and we are led back to the long-rejected inadequacies of the enlightened utilitarians and their belief in the providential hand of a marketplace selfishness. If selfish gene theory is offered as the underlying explanation of human behaviour, then either it is at best only a partial explanation of what happens in some instances (i.e., it is wrong in its universalist claims) or it is the kind of behaviour that Dawkins promotes is impossible.

Is it not wiser and reflective of a far closer awareness of reality to understand, as Rousseau did, that there are two *natural* aspects of our primordial animality: what he called "self-love" (involving both our selfishness *and* self-respect or individual dignity) and what he called "pity" (natural compassion, sympathy, ultimately empathy)? As he queried in *Emile*, "How do we let ourselves be moved by pity if not by transporting ourselves outside of ourselves and identifying with the suffering animal, by leaving as it were our own being, to take on its being?"[21] If that is the height of empathy, and a rare occurrence, the fact that it happens at all is enough to demonstrate compassion and to deny utilitarian premises. Moreover, we all witness lesser instances every day. Has modern incremental science not ignored a significant part of human, and concomitantly animal, nature? If we are to be hard-nosed realists, must we not reject the unidimensional view of the utilitarian and the selfish gene theorist, and inquire more fully into the sources of our natural compassion?

If, for Bentham, only material individuals are real,[22] for modern sociobiologists and selfish gene theorists, too, only individuals are real, and their reality exists through their genes. Utilitarians and their modern counterparts are wedded to materialism—a world consisting of individual bodies in the tradition of Democritus and Epicurus. And it is this subscription that informs their conclusions. When they encounter altruistic behaviour they are constrained to cram it into their materialist conceptual boxes, for it is their preconceptions rather than evidence that persuade them that altruism is inconsistent with material bodies operating as machines. It is no accident that materialist conceptions of reality were revived at the time of the development of the experimental sciences. The materialist mentality is predicated on the successes of the early science of mechanics, which postulates, but does not demonstrate, a materialistic determinism. If, as Francis Bacon understood, such conceptions work for explaining part of nature, it does not follow that their principles can be extended to the animal and human world.

Western science has produced an understanding of the behaviour and relations of bodies far superior to that of other civilizations. But the cost has been the underestimation of the will and the spirit. Let us not imagine, however, that the West has produced only a scientific materialism and philosophical determinism. The world of literature, in Shelley, in Byron, in Swift, in Wordsworth, in Hugo, indeed among most literary figures from the classic period to the present, has managed to keep alive the world of the spirit, the will, and the higher emotions; and most of them have recognized animals as worthy beings in themselves, deserving of our ethical consideration.[23] Even some of those philosophers who proclaimed an Epicurean reality, Gassendi, for example, nonetheless proclaimed an inconsistent but genuine dismissal of self-interest: "There is no pretence for saying that any right has been granted to us to kill any of those animals which are not destructive or pernicious to the human race."[24] Even those who deny the possibility of an authentic altruism by the use of a determinist framework paradoxically still possess it.

How, we must ask, do we interpret (example one) the prairie dog's behaviour when he senses the predator approaching and departs into his burrow as swiftly as he might while his brother alerts the group? Can selfish gene theory permit these individual differences without coercing the evidence into meaninglessness? What if (example two) a father desires, as fathers often do, that his daughter remains a virgin, thereby denying his genes an increase in their carbon copies? What if (example three) a husband feels more protective of the interests of his wife than those of his own siblings, to whom he is more closely related genetically? Do not such feelings counter genetic self-interest? What if (example four) a parent consciously attempts to treat her adopted offspring in precisely the same manner as the child she has borne? And what if she achieves it without any conscious effort? What if (example five) on seeing some person, or some animal, in peril, I risk my own life to save that person or animal, though I lack a close genetic relationship to that other being, and although I know I risk not only depriving my offspring of a parent but also hindering my chance of having further offspring? Is such behaviour impossible because Dawkins tells us that a concern with "the welfare of the species as a whole" and "universal love" are "concepts which do not make evolutionary sense"? If all these occurrences are deemed consistent with selfish gene theory, can selfish gene theory be telling us very much at all? And, if they are not, since such events occur frequently, would their occurrences not refute the universality, or even generality, of the theory? Selfish gene theory is reminiscent of the discussion of the attempt to derive too much from a concept in Lewis Carroll's (i.e., Charles Dodgson's) *Through the Looking Glass*: "When I make a word do a lot of extra work like that," said Humpty

Dumpty, "I always pay it extra."[25] "Selfish genes" are underpaid—and overvalued.

One can, and selfish gene theorists often do, contort and contrive such instances to fit into preconceived selfish gene boxes, but when one does so one is distorting the reality. The first of the above examples reflects the fact that sometimes the individual prairie dog ignores his own genetic interests and the interests of his siblings in favour of his own individual self-interest—he prefers the Hobbesian account of reality to that of Dawkins. The second example is rather more complex but is certainly reflective of the fact that our dispositions may move us frequently towards the very opposite of what may appear to be the interests of our genes. The third example reflects the fact that upon marriage the individual's sense of self may, at least in some instances, cease to be entirely that of an individual as one fuses one's identity with that of the spouse, a fusion later extended to include the offspring. The fourth example is an indication that love and responsibility are stimulated by far more than genes. And the fifth signifies that sometimes our behaviour is quite simply altruistic—acting for another being, fellow human or fellow animal, because we are the kind of person who acts for another, who possesses a natural compassion which arises from within. Compassion is raising to the level of consciousness what we know in our genes, and debating with ourselves the relative strengths of the competing interests in play. On the basis of logic and evidence, this final example is the foundation, if only occasionally encountered in this extreme form, of our authentic respect, consideration, and concern for other species.

The need for the selfish gene theorists to explain these examples as something other than what they appear to be, and are, follows from their conception that only individual bodies are real, and bodies must have self-interests that relate to those material entities and determine their behaviour. Seen from the perspective of humans as bodies—rather than, in addition, minds, spirits, energies or souls—it may well be "unnatural" to be altruistic, to be compassionate, but that is because in Western materialism the concept of "nature" is wedded to the idea of animals as biological machines. And if machines have interests, they can only be self-interests—if they can be interests at all.

A major difficulty with selfish gene theory is that it is insufficiently clear what is allowed to count as evidence against the theory. For a scientific theory to be meaningful, one needs to know in advance precisely what kind of occurrences will be deemed to constitute a refutation of the theory. If spouses will commonly prefer the interests of their partners to those of closer genetic relatives, if wives will treat a criticism of their husbands as equivalent to a criticism of themselves, if fathers desire the "purity" of their daughters, if a humanitarian rescues an animal in distress, are they acting consistently with the theory? Prima facie, promiscuity and familial proliferation are more readily consistent with the theory. If promiscuity and loving faithfulness, virginity and the maximization of genetic copies are all deemed consistent with the theory, then it would appear to be vacuous.

One must readily acknowledge—indeed, who has ever denied?—that genetic (familial) and social relationships encourage a mother to give preference to her natural offspring, a son to have a greater loyalty to parents than to humanity at large. It would, however, be churlish, and would reflect a willful negligence of the evidence, to ignore the fact that our sense of morality offers us an awareness that the consanguinity preference should, at least on occasion, be mitigated by other considerations. That awareness is not itself derived from our *selfish* genes but from something deeper within us. It cannot come from socialization alone, for it would be the essential interest of our selfish genes to reject the lessons of the socialization—and little reason for the socializers to instruct us in moral behaviour towards anyone but themselves and their closest relatives. There would be an overriding motive to ignore that to which we are being socialized. Altruism is not, logically cannot be, an extension of self-interest.

The customary response of utilitarians to such complaints is to claim that I performed my altruistic act in order to feel better about myself, to make myself happy with my generosity. But that is to confuse the consequences of actions with their motives. It is quite probable that I will achieve a measure of satisfaction by bringing about the happiness of another, but to the degree that my own happiness is the motive for the action, that happiness is less likely to be the consequence. Again though, the important question to ask is, if we are selfish by our natures, as Ghiselin writes, or by the nature of our genes, why should I be rendered happy through my generosity, through precisely that behaviour which is at odds with my supposed nature? Selfish genes could only instruct me to abhor generosity in myself beyond that suitable for gene replication. Altruism and compassion would thus appear to be as natural aspects of humanity as self-interest. Indeed, if, as Dawkins asserts, "we can expect little help from biology" in our quest for a world of compassion and justice, does not the fact that some people, at least some times, including Dawkins on his own admission, seek justice, display compassion, indicate that our biology, our selfish genes, are but a part of us, and that which our very human essence strives to overcome? Therein lies the human reality as much as in the selfish genes.

In a series of empirical studies, Stephen R. Kellert has demonstrated that "ecologistic, moralistic, and naturalistic values" are absent in young children, which only begin to develop slowly between the ages of six and nine with "an appreciation of the autonomy and independence of other creatures" and a recognition "of animals as possessing interests and feelings unrelated to themselves." Between thirteen and seventeen, we "witness a sharp increase in abstract, conceptual and ethical reasoning about the natural world."[26] Consequently, so many are persuaded to conclude, our consideration for other species is a learned, an acquired characteristic, and not a part of our inherent nature. There is no natural compassion, no innate moral sense. This, it seems to me, is like arguing that the sex drive is an acquired characteristic, since it is not present in young children. As the psychologist Jean Piaget demonstrated long ago, there are distinct developmental stages in the emergence of human intellectual and emotional thinking.[27] The fact that a sense of compassion arises only after a period of self-serving egocentrism should not for one moment persuade us it is not a natural part of our intrinsic nature. As the heroine went tumbling down the rabbit hole in *Alice's Adventures in Wonderland*, her first thought after the miles she had fallen and her anticipation of arriving in the "Antipathies" was of her cat Dinah. "I hope they'll remember her saucer of milk at tea-time."[28] No big deal, of course. But it was a perfectly natural sentiment. Alice was in the developmental stage of recognizing "animals as possessing interests and feelings unrelated to" herself.

One is entitled to wonder how the narrowly conceived "survival machine," the molecule-preserving "blindly programmed...robot vehicle" postulated by Dawkins could have written "The Rime of the Ancient Mariner," or *Faust*, or even *The Selfish Gene*; could have composed the "Pathétique Sonata," sung the *Marseillaise*; set out on the heroic adventures of a Magellan; or undertaken the compassionate ethological work of a Jane Goodall. How could I marvel at the sunrise this morning, become bewitched by the antics of a companion cat, be struck with awe by the majesty of a mountain lion, or marvel at the opening of a rosebud, if I am but a machine? Just as a sense of the sublime must be added to the sense of beauty to understand our aesthetic sense, so compassion must be added to selfish genes to understand our moral sense. What chance could there ever be of an epiphany in Dawkins's limited terms?

The world of the selfish gene, as a world without authentic sacrifice, is a world without heroes, and, indeed, without humanity or animality. It is a world in which the Thenardiers are no worse than Valjean and are the prospect of an ever-gloomier future. It is a world which denies the compassion of our experience, not because of the evidence, but because it is conceptually convenient to do so. Altruism is a fact, one which makes the world a wonder, and one which needs to be investigated more thoroughly by scientists than selfish-gene theory permits.

It would, of course, be inappropriate to suggest that nonhuman species share the creative and speculative capacities or the general sentiments of humans. But if we take the theory of evolution seriously we must assume that human and nonhuman species are inherently homologous until, and to the extent that, differences are demonstrated. That is, the theory requires us to assume, prima facie, the very opposite of that assumed by those who complain of the anthropomorphism among, for example, the more adventurous of the ethologists. And if we allow ourselves the assumption of similarities between humans and nonhumans, unless and until demonstrated otherwise, it is not unreasonable to postulate that human intelligence is little more than the addition of language to the cognitive powers possessed by the more complex nonhuman creatures.[29] Thus, we are entitled to consider it probable that the most complex of nonhuman species possess a measure of spontaneity and creativity. And, of course, our experience of our companion animals, a day spent watching sea lions, or a reading of *Through a Window: My Thirty Years with the Chimpanzees of Gombe* strengthens the conviction. Doubting Thomases might wish to provide an explanation of the behaviour of courageous crows, risking their lives provocatively to remain by the roadkill, even when sated. Who could deny the performance has an element of a high-risk game?

In the final analysis, selfish gene theory is not only controverted by our experience of other humans and other species, it is also demeaning of them. As mere replicators of their genes' interests, neither human nor beast is worthy of the ethical consideration we know both intuitively and by our life experience is required of us, not least towards our nonhuman kin, both the nearer and the genetically distant. If selfish gene theory reflects empirical reality, a genuine consideration of the interests of other species is an impossibility. On the basis of Dawkins's theory, it is neither possible nor desirable to concern ourselves with the interests of other species unless it is concomitantly self-serving. Yet Dawkins acknowledges that to be false. Dawkins is, indeed, in his evaluation of co-operation, generosity, and unselfishness, an admirable human being whose very theories contradict his own existence.

Sympathetic to the altruistic aims and purposes of Jeremy Bentham and his fellow utilitarians—despite their denials of altruism's authenticity in their theories—Thomas Hill Green resolved to provide a compatible theory that allowed for the reality of spontaneity, creativity, and self-improvement he found in the writings of Hegel and in his own experience. His *Lectures on the Principles of Political Obligation* (1895) rescued classical liberalism from its dehumanizing materialist and determinist prison. Classical Dawkinsism is in need of a similar deliverance. Dawkins requires his Green. Until then we will continue to care for the nonhuman realm, but animal welfare scientists will have no adequate biological theory capable either of encouraging, explaining, or legitimating animal welfare goals. The answer lies in a recognition of a compassion for others, including other animals, as a natural part of the psyche. In his *Mutual Aid: A Factor of Evolution*,[30] Peter Kropotkin argued persuasively that Darwin and Wallace had underestimated the degree to which co-operation was of evolutionary benefit. Yet it is more than that, too. It is to be admired the more precisely when no benefit to the actor is intended. Animal welfare scientists would do well to address it in their hypotheses, asking to what degree natural compassion is in conflict with those other driving aspects of behaviour that diminish the degree to which compassion can have its way.

NOTES

1. Gould wrote, "When sociobiology is injudicious and trades in speculative genetic arguments about specific human behaviors, it speaks nonsense. When it is judicious and implicates genetics only in setting the capacity for broad spectra of culturally conditioned behaviors, then it is not very enlightening. To me, such an irresolvable dilemma only indicates that this latest attempt to reduce the human sciences will have very limited utility." Quoted from *Bioscience*, 26 (March 1976): 182-83, in Connie Barlow, ed., *From Gaia to Selfish Genes: Selected Writings in the Life Sciences* (Cambridge: MIT Press, 1991), 191.
2. Michael Oakeshott, *On Human Conduct* (London: Oxford University Press, 1975), 15n1.

4 Edward O. Wilson, *Sociobiology: The New Synthesis* (Harvard University Press, 1975).

4 See Robert Wright, *Three Scientists and Their Gods* (New York: Times Books, 1988), 117.

5 Simplicius stated Democritus's view, as explained by Aristotle in his long lost essay "On Democritus," in his *Commentary on the Heavens*, excerpted in Jonathan Barnes, ed. and trans., *Early Greek Philosophy* (London: Penguin, 1987), 247. Of course, the views of the Pre-Socratics are known almost entirely via their later commentators.

6 George H. Sabine, *A History of Political Theory*, 4th edition, rev. by Thomas Landon Thorson (Hinsdale: Dryden Press, 1973), 133.

7 Pierre Gassendi, "Metaphysical Colloquy, or Doubts and Rebuttals Concerning the Metaphysics of Rene Descartes with his Replies" (1641), rebuttal to Meditation 2, Doubt 7, in *The Selected Works of Pierre Gassendi*, trans. Craig B. Brush (New York: Johnson Reprint Corporation, 1972), 197-98.

8 Modern utilitarians distinguish between act, rule and preference utilitarianism, thus making the general theory less subject to its ready criticisms. Whether they succeed is outside the scope of this paper. What is here relevant is that selfish gene theory commits the same errors as classical utilitarianism. The modern variants of utilitarianism are not relevant to the issue for they offer no avenue of escape for the selfish gene theorist.

9 Jeremy Benthan, *An Introduction to the Principles of Morals and Legislation*, ed. J.H. Burns and H.L.A. Hart (1789; reprint, London: Methuen, 1982), 17, 4, b, 282. Contrary to conventional wisdom, Bentham was far from the first to indicate pain and suffering as the relevant criteria. The idea is present in Bernard Mandeville's *The Grumbling Hive* of 1705 and is taken further in *The Fable of the Bees* of 1714. It finds an honourable place in Lord Shaftesbury's *Characteristics* (1711) and David Hartley's *Observations on Man* (1749). It pervades Jean Jacques Rousseau's *Emile* (1762), forms the underpinning of the Rev. Richard Dean's *An Essay on the Future Life of Brutes* (1767), and dominates the Rev. Humphry Primatt's *The Duty of Mercy and the Sin of Cruelty to Brute Animals* (1776): "Pain is pain, whether it be inflicted on man or on beast."

10 See John Stuart Mill, "Three Essays on Religion" (1874), in *Works of John Stuart Mill*, vol. 10, *Essays on Ethics, Religion and Society* (Toronto: University of Toronto Press, 1965), 185-87.

11 Richard Dawkins, *The Selfish Gene*, 2nd ed. (Oxford: Oxford University Press, 1989), 3.

12 Edward O. Wilson, *Biophilia: The Human Bond with Other Species* (Cambridge: Harvard University Press, 1984), 116.

13 Wright, *Three Scientists and Their Gods*, 132-33.

14 Niccolò Machiavelli, *The Prince* (1513), chap. 7; Baruch Spinoza, *Ethics*, Part 1, XVI (1677).

15 La Rochefoucauld, *Maxims* (1655), Maxim 39.
16 Dante, *Paradise* (XXXIII), 142f.
17 W.E.H. Lecky, *History of European Morals from Augustus to Charlemagne*, vol. 1 (New York: D. Appleton and Company, 1869), 102-103; Charles Darwin, *The Descent of Man, and Selection in Relation to Sex* (1874; reprint, New York: A.L. Burt, n.d.), 139. Darwin was apparently following Lecky's outline.
18 Jean Jacques Rousseau, "A Preface to *Narcisse*," trans. Benjamin Barber and James Forman, *Political Theory* 6, no. 4 (1978): 549.
19 As early as 1747, Carl Linneaus wrote to the German naturalist Johann Gmelin: "[I demand] that you show me a generic character ... by which to distinguish between Man and Ape. I myself assuredly know of none." Quoted in Carl Sagan and Ann Druyen, *Shadows of Forgotten Ancestors: A Search for Who We Are* (New York: Random House, 1992), 274.
20 Quoted in Barlow, ed., *From Gaia to Selfish Genes*, 195.
21 Jean Jacques Rousseau, *Emile, or On Education*, ed. and trans. Allan Bloom, Book 4 (New York: Basic Books, 1984), 223.
22 See James L. Wiser, *Political Philosophy: A History of the Search for Order* (Englewood Cliffs, NJ: Prentice Hall, 1983), 296.
23 See, for example, Rod Preece, *Animals and Nature: Cultural Myths, Cultural Realities* (Vancouver: UBC Press, 1999), as indexed.
24 Quoted in Colin Spencer, *The Heretic's Feast* (London: Fourth Estate, 1993), 204.
25 Lewis Carroll, *Through the Looking Glass* (1872; reprint, London: Penguin, 1974), 101. Dodgson was an Oxford mathematician and logician, and his Alice books were, in part, treatises on logic.
26 Stephen R. Kellert, *The Value of Life: Biological Diversity and Human Society* (Washington, DC: Island Press, 1997), 47, 49.
27 See Jean Piaget, *Judgment and Reasoning in the Child* (New York: Littlefield, Adams, 1928) and *The Moral Judgment of the Child* (New York: Free Press, 1965). Lawrence Kohlberg has refined this approach to the understanding of learning development in his *Essays on Moral Development* (San Francisco: Harper and Row, 1984).
28 Lewis Carroll, *Alice's Adventures in Wonderland* (1865; reprint, London: Penguin, 1994), 14.
29 See Derek Bickerton, *Language and Species* (Chicago: University of Chicago Press, 1990), especially chap. 1, "The Continuity Paradox."
30 Peter Kropotkin, *Mutual Aid: A Factor of Evolution* (1914; reprint, Boston: Extending Horizon Books, n.d.). In *The Descent of Man*, Darwin acknowledged that "in the earlier editions of my *Origin of Species* I perhaps attributed too much to the action of natural selection or the survival of the fittest" (68). Apparently, Kropotkin thought Darwin's concession still did not go anywhere near far enough.

BIBLIOGRAPHY

Barnes, Jonathan, ed. and trans. "On Democritus." In *Early Greek Philosophy*. London: Penguin, 1987.

Benthan, Jeremy. *An Introduction to the Principles of Morals and Legislation*. Edited by J.H. Burns and H.L.A. Hart. 1789 Reprint, London: Methuen, 1982.

Bickerton, Derek. *Language and Species*. Chicago: University of Chicago Press, 1990.

Burns, J.H., and Hart, H.L.A., eds. *An Introduction to the Principles of Morals and Legislation*. London: Methuen, 1982.

Carroll, Lewis. *Alice's Adventures in Wonderland*. London: Penguin, 1994.

———. *Through the Looking Glass*. London: Penguin, 1974.

Darwin, Charles. *The Descent of Man, and Selection in Relation to Sex*. 1874. Reprint; New York: A.L. Burt, n.d.

Dawkins, Richard. *The Selfish Gene*. 2nd ed. Oxford: Oxford University Press, 1989.

Gassendi, Pierre. "Metaphysical Colloquy, or Doubts and Rebuttals Concerning the Metaphysics of Rene Descartes with his Replies." In *The Selected Works of Pierre Gassendi*. Translated by Craig B. Brush. New York: Johnson Reprint Corporation, 1972.

Ghiselin, Michael T. *The Economy of Nature and the Evolution of Sex*. Berkeley: University of California Press, 1974.

Gould, Stephen Jay. "Bioscience." In Connie Barlow, ed., *From Gaia to Selfish Genes: Selected Writings in the Life Sciences*. Cambridge: MIT Press, 1991.

Kellert, Stephen R. *The Value of Life: Biological Diversity and Human Society*. Washington, DC: Island Press, 1997.

Kohlberg, Lawrence. *Essays on Moral Development*. San Francisco: Harper and Row, 1984.

Kropotkin, Peter. *Mutual Aid: A Factor of Evolution*. 1914. Reprint, Boston: Extending Horizon Books, n.d.

Lecky, W.E.H. *History of European Morals from Augustus to Charlemagne*. Vol. 1. New York: D. Appleton and Company, 1869.

Mill, John Stuart. "Three Essays on Religion" (1874). *Works of John Stuart Mill*. Vol. 10, *Essays on Ethics, Religion and Society*. Toronto: University of Toronto Press, 1965.

Oakeshott, Michael. *On Human Conduct*. London: Oxford University Press, 1975.

Piaget, Jean. *The Moral Judgment of the Child*. New York: Free Press, 1965.

———. *Judgment and Reasoning in the Child*. New York: Littlefield, Adams, 1928.
Preece, Rod. *Animals and Nature: Cultural Myths, Cultural Realities*. Vancouver: UBC Press, 1999.
Rousseau, Jean Jacques. *Emile, or On Education*. Edited and translated by Allan Bloom. Book 4. New York: Basic Books, 1984.
———. "A Preface to *Narcisse*." Translated by Benjamin Barber and James Forman. *Political Theory* 6, no. 4 (1978): 549.
Sabine, George H. *A History of Political Theory*. 4th ed. Revised by Thomas Landon Thorson. Hinsdale: Dryden Press, 1973.
Sagan, Carl, and Druyen, Ann. *Shadows of Forgotten Ancestors: A Search for Who We Are*. New York: Random House, 1992.
Spencer, Colin. *The Heretic's Feast*. London: Fourth Estate, 1993.
Wilson, Edward O. *Biophilia: The Human Bond with Other Species*. Cambridge: Harvard University Press, 1984.
———. *Sociobiology: The New Synthesis*. Cambridge: Harvard University Press, 1975.
Wiser, James L. *Political Philosophy: A History of the Search for Order*. Englewood Cliffs, NJ: Prentice Hall, 1983.
Wright, Robert. *Three Scientists and Their Gods*. New York: Times Books, 1988.

4

Anatomy as Speech Act
Vesalius, Descartes, Rembrandt or, The Question of "the animal" in the Early Modern Anatomy Lesson

DAWNE McCANCE

EXPLICATOR CHIRURGIAE

Since, in early modern Europe, dissections are affairs of the night, our story opens under cover of darkness: late in the evening, long into January 1544, as, through rain now turning to sleet, two figures edge down an unlit Arno River embankment. Despite the cumbersomeness of their cargo and the precariousness of foothold on the slick riverbank, our figures descend noiselessly to an awaiting barge, hurriedly setting a makeshift coffin down on its planks. The vessel's departure is swift, also silent, for by order of Secretary Marzio de Marzii, acting on behalf of the Duke of Tuscany himself, its journey from Florence to Pisa must be covert in every sense. What calls for such secrecy, what the crude chest contains, is nothing more than a nameless human cadaver, procured stealthily from the Hospital of Santa Maria Nuova in Florence and now on its clandestine way to the Pisan Monastery of San Francesco. In his letter of instruction, written from Pisa on 22 January 1544 to the trusted intermediary Pier Francesco Ricci, Secretary Marzio de Marzii actually ordered two corpses, "persons young rather than old" would be preferred: "...let them be enclosed in two cases and sent as quickly as possible down the Arno by barge or boat. This matter ought to be handled by you secretly, both the procurement of those bodies and their dispatch, and let them be delivered to the convent of San Francesco of the conventual friars where everything will be arranged."[1] Curiously, what is handled surreptitiously one day calls, on another day, for the attention of all onlookers, for the lone cadaver now passing silently under the Ponte Vecchio—the only corpse that could be had, and a defective one at that, without all its ribs intact—will soon be at the centre stage of a theatrical performance: the first public anatomical demonstration to be given at the University of Pisa by the renowned visiting professor, Andreas Vesalius of Brussels.

Such is the paradox of early modern anatomy. On the one hand, in the years between 1540 and 1640, "the period of the *discovery* of the Vesalian body,"[2] the opening of the human corpse for dissection and the mapping of its interior terrain were heralded as new modes of scientific investigation offering extraordinary possibilities, equal to "the triumphant discoveries of the explorers, cartographers, navigators, and early colonialists." It was a project "conducted with boundless optimism."[3] On the other hand, although the dissection of human cadavers was introduced to the Christian West by 1400, with a post-mortem dissection recorded as early as 1286,[4] two centuries had to pass before the practice could be freed from religious and Galenic teachings that prompted revulsion at the display and dismemberment of a corpse. The unease persisted into the period of the so-called discovery of the Vesalian body, when "the procurement and cutting open of cadavers for scientific (thus profane) purposes, and the inevitable delay in burial of the dead that followed, were [still] considered religiously and anthropologically dangerous acts."[5] The university—then as now, a strange nexus of ecclesiastical, political and juridical forces—positioned itself shrewdly on both sides of the issue at once. As the place where dissection was carried out and controlled, the university maintained an official and visible deference to traditional authority and public sensibility—properly discreet in its procurement of corpses, ostensibly upholding a kind of repression of human anatomies. At the same time, as a complex system of strategies and spaces through which the human body was being transformed into a new object of knowledge, the university was functioning as what Foucault called a *body politic*, "a set of material elements and techniques that serve as weapons, relays, communication routes and supports"[6] for the exercise of an emerging, peculiarly modern, bio-power. As distinct from interdiction or prohibition, this bio-power "displays itself most" when it "hides itself best,"[7] precisely by working through discursive fields and institutional architectures that we tend to think of as exempt from power's domain. In the late-night scene of the furtive passing of a body under a bridge, we open onto the story of bio-power as among modernity's "most hidden things."[8]

Central to this story is the father of modern anatomy, Andreas Vesalius, who was deft at negotiating both sides of the dissection issue. On one side, Vesalius aligned himself, illustriously, with institutional and prudential authority, working within the university's mechanism of checks and controls: in 1537 at age twenty-three, for instance, and only the day after completing his doctoral exams at the University of Padua, then the world's most renowned medical faculty, Vesalius assumed the Paduan chair of surgery and anatomy, becoming its *Explicator Chirurgiae* (surgeon F *chirurgien*; surgery OF *cirurgie*, L *chirurgia*, G *kheirourgia*, literally "a working [*ourgia*] with the hands [*kheir*, hand]"). His reputation as Europe's leading anatomist was already established by 1543 when the *Fabrica* was published—dedicated to Charles V, "the divine Charles, Great and Invincible Emperor," who, upon receipt of the book, quickly appointed its author as physician to the imperial household, "our *medicus familiaris ordinarius*."[9] Yet, even while so well serving the official machine, Vesalius was introducing practices that would transform things altogether. Since the changes brought to dissection by the *Explicator Chirurgiae*—and unmistakably, these were *works of the hand*—make for a defining moment in the genealogy of modern bio-power, they will be my concern here. My contention is that, as Giorgio Agamben suggests in *The Open*, where in modernity the hand holds power over life, where power is bio-power, the human/animal division is always at stake.[10] In the Vesalian anatomy theatre, and paradoxically in the process by which the human body is being cut open and thus "profaned," a distinctively modern and hierarchical human/animal difference is put in place. Simultaneous with the introduction of this difference, and constitutive of it, I will argue below, the anatomist-physician, for the first time, claims the authority to speak for himself. In my analysis, with the emergence of this authoritative first-person speech-and-hearing-act situation, the difference Vesalius marks out between human and animal is made to pass "as a mobile border within living man,"[11] so as to oppose not only human and animal but also the human and the animal in man.[12] Let us proceed to Pisa, then, where my case will be made.

ACCORDING TO C.D. O'MALLEY, Vesalius arrived in Pisa to take up his teaching engagement at the university there sometime between the 20 and 22 January 1544.[13] En route to Pisa from Padua, he stopped in Bologna, where he agreed to present an anatomical demonstration before a large group of spectators gathered at the medical school. The dissection extended far into the December 1543 night until, still incomplete, it was halted for reason of the cold winter weather, to be resumed the following day. Great was the annoyance of the spectators, O'Malley reports,[14] when in the morning they learned that Vesalius had departed at dawn for Pisa, no doubt to avoid the debates that inevitably followed a dissection's conclusion and that incited voices of opposition to human dismemberment. Even as a student in Paris where he learned grave-robbing to cope with the shortage of corpses, Vesalius was adept at circumventing roadblocks put in the way of his progress in human dissection. He was not deterred, then, when on arriving in Pisa to conduct his first anatomical demonstration there, he found not two cadavers but one, and without all the ribs needed to make a complete skeleton. "When I began to demonstrate anatomy at Pisa there were not enough bones," Vesalius recalls in his *Letter on the China Root*; Duke Cosimo came to the rescue again: "the cadaver of a nun from some burial vault in Florence was sent on a fast barge for the preparation of a skeleton." As another way round the obstacle of the shortage of bones, Vesalius notes in his *Letter* that, acting on his instructions, "some of [my] students made keys for the beautiful cemetery of San Pisano so that they might investigate the many burial monuments, built like warehouses, in search of bones suitable for study," a notable find in one raid being "a hunchback girl of seventeen."[15]

About the dissection of these particular cadavers, the nun and the hunchback girl of seventeen, we will consult Vesalius again. For now, however, let us foreground a point that, although obvious, is, for the genealogy of bio-power, anything but an insignificant detail: *the cadavers in question are human*. Vesalius dissected *human cadavers*, using animals solely for comparative purposes. Moreover, as he became more skillful in procuring human specimens for dissection, so was he increasingly emboldened in making the case for their use. Vesalius rested this case on the fundamental difference that he said pertained between the human and the animal, a difference that Galen had failed to recognize. Indeed, for Vesalius, it was his "recognition" of a fundamental human/animal difference that set him apart from his predecessor, whose anatomy, he claimed, was error-filled for the reason that it was constructed without access to human cadavers. In the "Preface" to the *Fabrica*, Vesalius underlines this point: Galen worked only with animals; he never cut open a human body.[16] He was "deceived" by his monkeys, Vesalius writes; not only was Galen frequently wrong, "even about his apes," he also failed to acknowledge "the infinite multiplicity of differences between the organs of the human and simian bodies."[17] Vesalius worked with human cadavers, and of equal importance to that, he performed dissections himself; he obtained his knowledge *first-hand*.

In the history of medicine, nothing was more deleterious, he said, than the relegation of dissection to barber-surgeons, "ordinary persons wholly untrained in the disciplines subserving the art of medicine."[18] Barbers were known to badly hack up bodies.[19] Moreover, Vesalius claimed, "when the use of the hands was wholly entrusted to the barbers, not only was true knowledge of the viscera lost to the physicians, but also the practice of dissection soon died away, because they did not undertake it, and those to whom the manual skills had been entrusted were so unlearned that they did not understand the writings of the professors of dissection."[20] The practice introduced in the Vesalian anatomy theatre, with no less than revolutionary implications, had the physician himself, with his own hands, undertaking human dissection. With recovery of the hand came a newfound entitlement: no longer simply a mouthpiece of the ancients, the physician-surgeon could now speak for himself—and hear his own words as authoritative for the emerging anatomical science. With Vesalius, I suggest, an entirely new speech and hearing situation is introduced to the West, one that entails a wholesale reorganization of subjects and spaces and that pre-inscribes the Cartesian subject/object division by representing bodies as objects of knowledge. To appreciate why this is the case, we need to enter the Vesalian theatre, paying heed to what Andrea Carlino calls the "iconography" of the anatomy lesson[21] that is enacted there. Before that, however, and to gain a better sense of the changes he introduced, we will consider the iconography that prevailed in anatomy before Vesalius came on the scene.

A MODEL OF PRE-VESALIAN dissection practice is given by the *Anatomia*, an influential treatise on anatomy written in Latin in 1316 by Mondino de Luzzi (1270–1326), professor of medicine at Bologna, and first printed in 1474. Although Mondino performed human dissections and is considered to have taught anatomy from a human cadaver, his *Anatomia* is anything but a modern anatomy manual: a "heavily Galenic" text, it "is wholly inspired by the *De juvamentis membrorum*, a sort of compendium of Galen's anatomy that began to circulate in the Christian West at the end of the twelfth century."[22] Importantly for our purposes, woodcuts that were done to accompany the *Anatomia*'s various editions provide illustrations of the pre-Vesalian anatomy lesson.[23] (See fig. 1.) None of these illustrations shows the anatomist-physician applying his hands to the dissection of the body. Rather, as Andrea Carlino notes in his discussion of the 1493 *Anatomia* frontispiece, the professor-in-charge, dressed in formal academic garb, plays the role of a *lector*: some distance removed from the dissection table and seated on a *cathedra*, an elevated structure provided with stairs and much resembling a pulpit, he is shown reading or reciting a text, "usually one inspired by Galen."[24] Below, and removed from the *lector*, in the foreground of the image, a cadaver is laid out horizontally on a board, under which is a basket for the detritus of the dissection. Leaning over the cadaver, shown with knife in hand, is a *sector*, the one who actually performs the dissection; usually a barber, he is, Carlino observes, the only figure not in academic gown. A person standing to the right holds a pointer. He is the *demonstrator* or *ostensor* who "indicates to the *sector* the parts of the body that are to be dissected or displayed."[25] Often, the *ostensor* also translates the text being read from Latin into the vernacular, since the *sector* would almost certainly know no Latin. The other six bystanders portrayed in this woodcut, all dressed in academic robes, "who seem little interested in what is taking place before their eyes, are deep in conversation."[26]

In Carlino's reading, all seven extant title page representations of Mondino's *Anatomia* suggest that the pre-Vesalian anatomy lesson centred on the *lector*. It is the *lector* who dominates the lesson and who, as "orchestrator of the entire performance," has pre-eminent position in organizing the iconography of the Mondino anatomy scene.[27] This is not to say that the *lector* is shown as either knowledge source or locus of authority. Rather, his position, "in a space defined by the professorial pulpit and clearly distinguished from the opposite space for dissection, makes evident the scission between the theoretical activity of the physician-anatomist and the practical example directed toward an empirical examination of the cadaver."[28] In the pre-Vesalian anatomy lesson, theoretical knowledge is derived solely from such authors as Galen and Avicenna, whose words the *lector* reads and recites from his *cathedra*, on high and removed. For all his pre-eminence, then, the *lector* plays only a mediating role in this scene; he serves as but a relay, an "academic conduit,"[29] for the words of classical authors, words whose authority is attested to iconographically by the large size and high placement of the volume being read. The *ostensor*, in turn, mediates again, translating the words transmitted by the *lector*, serving as a conduit "between the *lector* and the *sector*" or "between word and deed,"[30] where the (spoken and written) word belongs unquestionably to

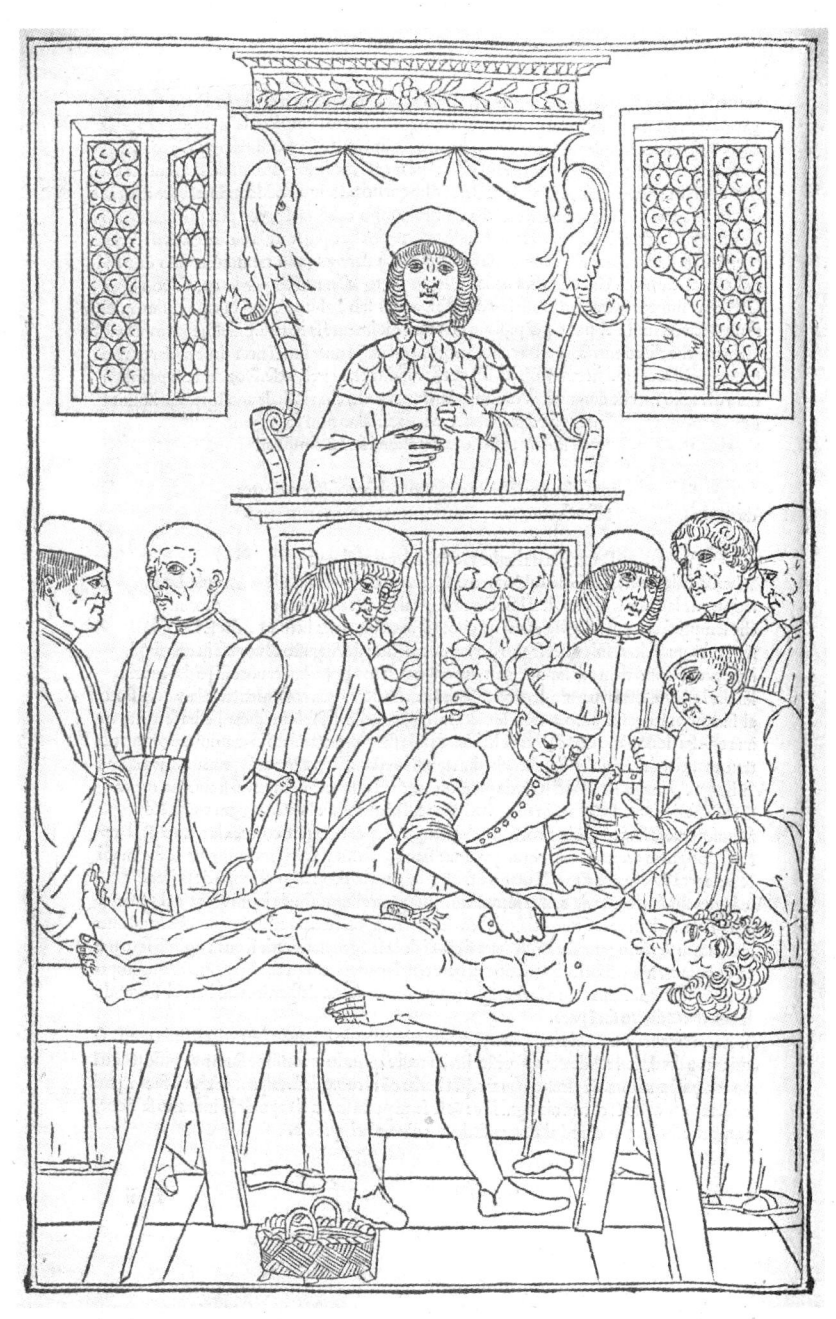

FIGURE 1 From *Anatomia*, Mondino de Luzzi, 1316.

authoritative traditional sources. The anatomy lesson provides an occasion for transmission of these sources: it "turns out to be little more than a ritual to celebrate the ancient classical authorities on the subject through a reading of their texts."[31] We should note, then, that while one woodcut from 1509 shows the *lector* holding a pen, the detail only underlines further "his removal from the practical act of dissection"[32]—and from the act of writing. In the pre-modern, pre-Vesalian, Mondino model, the anatomist-physician has not written the book he recites: he has not yet taken quill or scalpel—or speech—*into his own hands.*

It is just this long-standing "neglect of that primary instrument, the hand" that Vesalius targets in his "Preface" to the *Fabrica*, where he bemoans the "deplorable division" in dissection practice of the *sector* from the *lector*, "the latter like jackdaws aloft in their high chair, with egregious arrogance croaking things they have never investigated but merely committed to memory from the books of others, or reading what has already been described."[33] With his dismissal of this practice whereby physicians "haughtily govern the ship from a manual" and his opting instead to "put his own hands to the matter,"[34] Vesalius sets the transition to modernity on its way. For a fuller sense of how this happens, let us follow Vesalius and our three corpses—the male with the missing ribs, the nun, and the hunchback girl of seventeen—to Pisa and attend to the visiting professor's inaugural demonstration there.

AS IT TURNED OUT, when Vesalius arrived for the occasion in January 1544, he found a university newly refurbished by Duke Cosimo, but with an anatomy theatre not yet constructed. Exactly where in Pisa Vesalius conducted his first public dissection is thus uncertain.[35] We can still observe the event, however, by studying the *Fabrica* frontispiece, for what this illustration represents is not an actual anatomy taking place, Jonathan Sawday reminds us, so much as an "idealization"[36] of the dissection scene that Vesalius introduced in Padua, Bologna, Pisa and elsewhere—a scene that shows the *structure* of the theatre, and the lesson, to be radically transformed. (See fig. 2.) It belongs to the genius of Vesalius that he knew how to use pictorial representation as a powerful vehicle for change: a talented draughtsman himself, he also worked with a team of illustrators to produce for the *Fabrica* images that continue to be reprinted and celebrated[37]— and, importantly, that show cut-open human cadavers as sculptural artifacts or objects, rather than as *bodies* being violated.[38] In part, it is through

FIGURE 2 From *Fabrica*, Andreas Vesalius, 1543, frontispiece. Image source: Wikimedia Commons.

these representations of human body parts as artifacts that Vesalius makes the human/animal division pass between the human and the animal in man, so as to separate internal, living speech from the dead body–object being dissected. It was also his genius to recognize that the *Fabrica* images were being made for a *book*, the first, we might say, of its kind: *De humani corporis fabrica libri septem* "marked a turning point in the history of anatomy," Carlino observes, not only because of the revision of human morphology it proposed but also because of its achievement as a publishing venture.[39] Issued in 1543 from the Basel printing shop of Johannes Oporinus, the *Fabrica* became "one of the most important and astute successes of the first century of printing,"[40] and not the least because it made the pen as much a feature of Vesalian anatomy as was the scalpel, thereby helping to establish the novel status of the anatomist as author, one who speaks on his own authority. That the two, quill and scalpel, belong inextricably together is much the point of the Vesalian self-portrait (see fig. 3) included in the *Fabrica*, where the anatomist is shown dissecting a forearm: on a table beside the foregrounded hand of the cadaver (which is held by the prominently portrayed hand of the anatomist), surgical instruments are arranged—along with inkwell, paper and pen. The image underscores the authority of Vesalius as both anatomist and writer, joining body and book together, both as works of the hand.[41]

In the dissection portrayed in the *Fabrica* frontispiece, the newly claimed authority of the physician-anatomist is apparent from his relocation to beside the corpse. No longer, as in the Mondino model, is the presiding physician set apart from the body being dissected. No *cathedra* is in view. Where the latter opened the pre-Vesalian anatomy lesson to tradition's transcendence and teleology, the chair's removal cuts that dimension off, in somewhat the same way as, in Julia Kristeva's reading of Hans Holbein the Younger's 1521 painting of the *Body of the Dead Christ in the Tomb*, the low stone ceiling suggests the collapse of transcendency that is now underway in the culture.[42] Granted, the *Fabrica* title page represents the theatre as a vault, a platform or stage that is surrounded by what Sawday calls a "basilica" or "open air arcade" equipped with massive architectural supports and concentric rings of benches,[43] yet the fact remains that the image centres at its base on a corpse (a human corpse, laid out beneath a skeleton) and—on the same horizontal plane and immediately beside the dissection table, *with his hand on the cadaver*—on the figure of the physician-anatomist, Andreas Vesalius himself. The anatomist's relocation from the *cathedra* to beside the corpse belongs to what Kristeva describes as the

ANATOMY AS SPEECH ACT 73

FIGURE 3 From *Fabrica*, Andreas Vesalius, 1543.
Image source: Wikimedia Commons.

passage from symbol to sign, where the symbol's transcendent or otherworldly casing gives way to a transcendentalizing of the signifying subject himself, in this case a physician-anatomist, who now claims his own authority before the body he is investigating first-hand. Kristeva says that the passage from symbol to sign introduces a new *objectivity* and with that, a subject/object dichotomy that relegates the body to the other, object, side of the line.[44] As I suggest above, this move is already evident in the *Fabrica* illustrations that depict viscera, musculature, circulatory and skeletal systems as sculptural fragments, rather than as parts of a "natural body" (being violated by the anatomist's knife).[45] Such reconstituting of the body as object calls for an all-out challenge to traditional authority, as is indicated by several iconographic details of the *Fabrica* title-page scene. For instance: two barbers demoted to the foot of the dissection table are reduced to the role of sharpening knives; a figure, frequently associated with Galen—who as we have noted did anatomies on animals only, who, Vesalius says in the *Fabrica*, "never dissected a human body"[46]—is shown with a barking dog; and, as another anti-Galenic feature and one that codes the new human/animal divide, a monkey, "as if to demonstrate is own essential feral qualities," is shown biting the hand of a bystander.[47]

No detail more decisively demarcates the human/animal separation taking place, however, than the anatomist's relocation from *cathedra* to beside the corpse, and with that, his reclaiming of the hand, for with Vesalius, anatomy bases itself on first-hand knowledge and "solely upon investigation of the human cadaver,"[48] ceasing to take the animal as a substitute for the human, save early on for comparative purposes. Now, the differentiation of human from animal becomes a "scientific" imperative. Simultaneous with this, and I suggest of key importance for the genealogy of bio-power and its subject, Vesalius, not content to recite the words of his predecessors, announces the arrival of autonomous first-person speech, anticipating what Descartes, one hundred years later, calls "real speech," the kind that only humans have and that, for all subsequent modernity, determines the human/animal divide. Between the *Anatomia* and *Fabrica* anatomy lessons, no change is more significant than this: the physician-anatomist, for the first time, has the experience of *hearing himself speak*. In my reading, it is this authoritative, first-person speech-and-hearing act situation that the *Fabrica* frontispiece represents and that Vesalius foregrounds in his "Preface." Here, *hearing oneself speak* emerges together with, and is inseparable from, the reclaimed hand, both as forms of "seizure." To make this case is necessarily to counter the ocularcentric master narrative, according to which the shift into modernity constitutes the death of speech and the overtaking of the ear by the eye.[49] Critics are so persuaded by the ocularcentric account that even studies engaging speech act theory and its relation to bio-power, such as Mieke Bal's *Double Exposures: The Subject of Cultural Analysis*, are confined to analyses of sight and of looking.

My point is not to diminish the significance of the ocular, but rather to suggest that the oral and aural are crucial to modernity as well: to bypass speech and hearing is to obscure (to contribute to the "hiding" of) the workings of bio-power.

WE ARE IN PISA, among the spectators gathered in the *Fabrica* frontispiece anatomy theatre. As an attempt to elaborate on the above point and to open speech act theory beyond the eye to the ear, let us briefly consider the Vesalian dissection scene as an early instance of what Bal in *Double Exposures* calls Western modernity's discourse of "exposition or *exposé*."[50] In such discourse, Bal says, a "first-person" expository agent exposes a "third-person" object for "us," the "second-person" spectators. Exposition, for Bal, is about showing and seeing, about making something visible, putting an object on display—as is surely the case in the *Fabrica* theatre, where Vesalius, his hand raised in a gesture of pointing, exposes the cut-open corpse (not incidentally, a *female* corpse, about which we will have more to say). But this gesture of showing, never a matter for eyes alone, is always also, as Bal notes, an act of *speaking* and of seeming to say, "Look! That's how it is!" The "Look!" aspect of exposition "involves the visual availability of the exposed object," while the "That's how it is!" aspect "involves the authority of the person who knows."[51] Gestures of exposing connect these two aspects: the object, laid bare for looking, and the subject who, in exposition, speaks with "the authority of the person who knows,"[52] and for this reason, Bal contends, exposure is "double," as much a putting on display of the knowing subject as of the exposed object; as much a performance—a performative speech act, an act of producing the subject and meaning—as a discourse that is "constative," and that tells us "how it is." But exposure is double in another way that Bal does not consider: in joining display with "first-person" speech (and hearing), exposition necessarily involves both eye and ear. Never simply about kinds of looking, the rhetoric behind every subject/object constitution is always about speech and hearing as well.[53]

What is on display does not speak. Bal reminds us of this: what is put on display by a "first-person" speaker for a "second-person" spectator occupies a "third-person" position that is "silenced by the discursive situation."[54] In the dissection scene portrayed in the *Fabrica* frontispiece, the severed female body is of course speechless in death. If this body recalls the mythical Medusa who, though her mouth is open, is unable to scream, speechless in death, it may be not only because the displayed corpse, like Medusa, occupies a silenced "third-person" position but also because this particular cadaver, in Vesalian literature, has acquired "monstrous" associations. These stem in part from the fact that the woman being dissected in the frontispiece scene is, as Vesalius puts it, "fat."[55] The corpulent corpse of the frontispiece is the same one that appears in the *Fabrica* portrait of Vesalius dissecting a forearm, although in the latter image, as O'Malley and others have noted, the female body is shown even larger still, disproportionately "large and stout,"[56] particularly in relation to the size of the woman's head. "In the 1555 edition of the *Fabrica* we are told that the body was that of an unusually large woman," O'Malley comments, "but certainly Vesalius does not describe the body as that of a giant."[57] A few sentences later, however, O'Malley refers to "the gigantic figure's forearm,"[58] suggesting that, for him at least, there *is* something monstrous about this female corpse. Monstrous, perhaps, and for all assembled in the anatomy theatre, malignant as well: for according to Vesalius's dissection notes, the female cadaver in question was obtained from the gallows; and not only that, before her execution, in fear of being hanged, the woman had falsely declared herself to be pregnant. Although midwives, after interrogating her, disputed the pregnancy claim, it remained for Vesalius to open her dead body and, before the assembled crowd, to demonstrate the object itself.[59] Only an anatomical *exposé* could disprove the claim, or prove the lie, absolutely.[60] It was in service of truth, then, that, Vesalius tells us, he took great care when slicing open the woman's body not to "disturb the uterus in any way," and to ensure that "none of the uterine membranes has been destroyed. Everything is seen intact just as it appears to the dissector immediately upon moving the intestines to one side in a moderately fat woman."[61] It is striking that in this signature *exposé*, caught in an image that continues, almost timelessly, to captivate, the laid-out corpse is elevated slightly and rotated 90 degrees from the positioning of a cadaver in the Mondino model, so that to look at the image is to view the female body not horizontally but from the genitals up. "Look! That's how it is!" Vesalius says. At least as Freud has it in his "Fetishism" essay, the male viewer of this inaugural exposition can only recoil from the sight of the dead woman's genitals, and must now remain forever traumatized by the terror of his own castration.[62]

We must leave these peculiar preoccupations with wombs and uterine membranes and with female bodies sliced open in the service of truth, but as we do so, let us underline this point: it is a truth claim that is at stake in the new Vesalian speech and hearing situation, a claim made possible when, in joining theory to practice, the anatomist vacates the Mondino high chair, takes scalpel and pen in hand and, with all theatrical flourish, speaks and hears himself constate, "Look! This is how it is!"[63] No less than truth was on the line in every anatomy lesson, the truth of Vesalian anatomical science—and of its knowing subject. Such was the stake of the public dissections Vesalius performed in Pisa of two other cadavers we have already mentioned, both of them female and monstrous at once, and in their "monstrosity," both of them closer to the animal than to the human side of the line: the nun delivered from Florence on a fast barge, and the hunchback girl of seventeen, stolen from her beautiful San Pisano burial place. Both died of lung failure, Vesalius notes in passing, the girl's resulting from "an impediment to respiration caused by her malformation," and the nun's from pleurisy.[64] But what really interests Vesalius about these two corpses is what needs demonstration in order to be proven true: whereas for the woman in the *Fabrica* frontispiece, this was the (empty) womb, for these two cadavers Vesalius dissected the uterus, he says, "solely for the sake of the hymen,"[65] which, prior to Pisa, he had not yet had the opportunity to display. "I examined the uterus of the girl since I expected her to be a virgin because very likely [since she was a hunchback] nobody ever wanted her. I found a hymen in her as well as in the nun, at least thirty-six years old, whose ovaries, however, were shrunken as happens to organs that are not used," Vesalius explains, and with some satisfaction, since "I had never dissected a virgin, except for a child of perhaps six years, dead of a wasting disease, which I had obtained in Padua—for the preparation of a skeleton—from a student who had secretly removed it from a tomb."[66] With these cadavers, the nun and the hunchback girl, the hymen's exposition would seem to be done. Vesalius, however, a real man of the hand, draws his conclusions "not from a single instance, and so a possible anomaly, but from repeated investigations and observations."[67] For reason of the inseparability of theory and practice, then, the very principle on which his anatomical authority depends, he hesitates to state the truth just yet, explaining that "I am not accustomed to saying anything with certainty after only one or two observations."[68]

HANDS ON

When, in 1629, René Descartes relocated from France to the Netherlands, his move coincided with the transfer of the centre of anatomy from southern to northern Europe, from Padua to Leiden, and then to Amsterdam. In Amsterdam, Descartes thought he could live and work unnoticed; just as importantly, having given up his study of mathematics in the wake of the Galileo affair, he could pursue his study of anatomy, daily visiting the butcher stalls in the Kalverstraat quarter to witness animal slaughters and to procure specimens and organs to take back to his dwelling for dissection. According to his biographer Adrien Baillet, Descartes studied Vesalius and other notable anatomists—but, aspiring himself to become a first-hand man and to speak on his own authority, Descartes "taught himself in a much surer way by personally dissecting animals of different species; and he discovered directly many things more detailed than all those authors had reported in their books."[69]

This resolve to teach and speak for himself was acquired early on, Descartes tells us in his *Discourse on Method*, and not the least at the college of La Flèche in Anjou, where classrooms were structured like Mondino dissection theatres, and where learning, the Jesuit *lectio* in classical authorities, took place as "jackdaw" recitation.[70] No doubt, as Descartes passed to and from the butcher stalls, he crossed paths with Rembrandt van Rijn, who at the time also lived in the Kalverstraat quarter and who also regularly visited the butchers to obtain carcasses for dissection. Perhaps Descartes and Rembrandt stood together at the gallows to witness the hanging of Adriaan Adriaanszoon, also known as Aris Kint, who after his execution for stealing a coat, became the corpse painted in Rembrandt's *Anatomy Lesson of Dr. Nicolaas Tulp* (the arm in this painting may have been anatomized by Vesalius himself).[71] Francis Barker[72] suggests that Descartes may even have attended the 31 January 1632 Tulp dissection. Rembrandt's painting of the dissection, portraying Tulp in so magisterial a way, brought immediate fame to the doctor (who, in another claim to notoriety, provided the first description of an orangutan in 1641). Rembrandt's painting also became perhaps the best-known emblem of what Jonathan Sawday calls "the culture of dissection."[73]

Frequently a spectator at human anatomies, Descartes dissected only animal bodies himself, which is consistent with his view of the body, either animal or human, as a machine, every function and behaviour of which can be explained in micro-mechanical terms.[74] Only by joining theory and practice, by first taking scalpel in hand and providing a mechanistic science of the animal body derived from his own anatomy lessons, could Descartes then move to the argument for another kind of substance that is completely incongruous with the machine, that "cannot be explained by the powers of matter," and that, as it is peculiar to the human alone, separates man from brute and makes the human, as distinct from the animal, a mind-body composite.[75] Although we take the Cartesian moment to be decisive for the emergence of modern bio-power, little attention is given this moment as a dissection scene: how significant is it that Descartes, in providing modernity with its philosophical meta-text, held both pen and scalpel? And why have critics attended almost solely to the role of the visual in Descartes, bypassing the importance of the speech act in his work, the decisive role that speech and hearing have in determining the Cartesian human/animal divide?[76] I suggest that if the ocularcentric account of the death of speech, the overtaking of the oral-aural by the "Cartesian" perspectival eye, anywhere receives a challenge, it is from Descartes himself, for whom speech is not simply one indicator among others of what distinguishes a human from a dog, but rather the "best and most certain evidence that there is a significant difference between humans and beasts."[77] According to Descartes, as Lilli Alanen notes, because animals lack the capacity for speech, they lack the capacity for thinking: the two, thought and speech, are inseparable for him; they "overlap," as Alanen puts it, a matter to which I will return below. For now, and in keeping with the emphasis Alanen gives it, the surest sign, for Descartes, that something is thinking, indeed for the most part "the *only* certain sign of thinking,"[78] is the capacity of using speech or language. More specifically, "real speech" is what sets the essentially human, *res cogito*, apart:

> The evidence that a thing is thinking is not only that it talks—parrots can talk—but that it has "real speech" of the kind humans have, which involves the capacity "of indicating by word or sign something pertaining to pure thought and not natural impulse." The mere expression of their "natural impulses of anger, fear, hunger and so on" that even dumb animals can communicate by their voices or bodily movements is not sufficient. It is the capacity of using and understanding conventional signs that is the decisive evidence of thought or reason.[79]

Yet, to appreciate the crucial role that speech and hearing play at this, another founding, moment, an additional feature of Cartesian thought must be considered. In my view, this feature is all-important and deserves a fuller analysis than I can provide here. Put briefly, Descartes not only privileges "real speech" (and therefore, the capacity to *hear* and discriminate, to differentiate this from "animal" talk), he also holds that the speech-thought capacity is innate, that pure ideas come first, are understood ("heard") on the inside before being exhibited through *res extensa*.[80] I have been reading Vesalius, insofar as he introduces authoritative first-person speech, as anticipating the distinctiveness granted to human ("real") speech by Descartes: Vesalius is first to hear his own words as authoritative, as having precedence over the recited voices of tradition. But in this legacy of filiation or handing down, Descartes, pupil-son of the master Vesalius, becomes father of the master, the son before the father, when he grants priority to *inner speech*, taking pure thought-speech to be prior, on the inside, to the spoken or written sign—as if "real speech" were "heard" before, as Derrida puts it in *Speech and Phenomena*, it needs to risk death in the body of a signifier given over to the world.[81] This is what Derrida calls *phonocentrism*: an operation of "hearing oneself speak" in "the interiority of self-present life," an operation that joins the pure idea to phonetic speech and that makes "absolutely pure auto-affection"[82] modernity's philosophical and ethical point of departure—the "origin" from which its bio-power is set loose.

WE ARE NOW in the Cartesian anatomy theatre, where Descartes, once unable to account for it mechanistically through first-hand dissection of animal bodies, must needs postulate a thinking substance that is utterly distinctive in the human and that manifests itself in "real speech."[83] By and large, we have taken this Cartesian division of *res cogito* and *res extensa*, human and animal, to be a dualism of the absolute sort. What I will suggest here, however, in the interests of uncovering some elements that remain all-but hidden, is that Descartes's internal/external, "ghost in the machine," dualism is not so stable a binary after all. I take this point in part from Lilli Alanen's contention that, in Descartes, the internal and external—thought and speech—"overlap" and are essentially interconnected, in that "real speech" is the external sign that something is thinking (*hearing itself speak*) on the inside.[84] I argue above that this thought-speech connection is inseparable for Descartes, whose inward thinking involves a double idealizing of the "real speech" that it is heard and understood in the sphere of pure auto-affection before it is let out into the world. But let us stay with the "overlap," an impossible problem for Cartesian dualism: the folding of the outside in, the notion that language and thought are related, and that even their priority might be reversed by Descartes. Alanen suggests as much. For Descartes, she says, it is as if, from the start, thinking, the *res cogito*, needs the bodily supplement of speech,[85] which, even as inner speech, implies a kind of writing, what Véronique Fóti calls a "cryptography" of some sort.[86] In Descartes's work, the most significant locus of this folding of inner and outer, of one in the other, is the cornarium or pineal gland which, in its own movements and in its role in dispersing the subtle blood particles called "animal spirits" to the brain, governs the interactions of the body with the immaterial soul. We might conclude this section with a brief discussion of how, in his writing on this innocuous gland, so persistent a topic in his correspondence, Descartes performs something that is "deconstructive" of his own dualism, and through this "performativity" shows us how to undercut "Cartesian" bio-power.[87]

This little gland, Descartes writes to Meyssonnier on 29 January 1640, is "the principal seat of the soul, and the place in which all our thoughts are formed. The reason I believe this is that I cannot find any part of the brain, except this, which is not double."[88] As seat of the soul, and thus, we must say, of "real speech," the cornarium is already problematic for Descartes: for it is material, part of the "animal" body, and yet, at the same time, is the locus of the immaterial, incongruous element that divides human from animal and the human from the animal in man. In his descriptions of this gland that so fascinates him, Descartes betrays this overlap, betrays what David Farrell Krell calls the gland's—the Cartesian system's—*differential structure and function.*"[89] Consider, for example, just the location of the gland: appropriate to its function as the seat of intellection, the cornarium is found at the centre, "in the middle of the concavities."[90] Since, however, the gland, as Descartes describes it in his *Treatise of Man*, "is composed of matter which is very soft," matter which, we might say, is almost immaterial, the cornarium is "not completely joined and united to the substance of the brain but only attached to certain little arteries whose membranes are rather lax and pliant."[91] Its location, then, is actually off-centre, or often off-centre, for "very little [force] is required to cause it to incline and to lean, now more or less, now to this side now to that."[92] As to what causes the gland to agitate, to lean this way and that "like a flame dancing on its candlewick,"[93] Descartes cites three kinds of forces: the first of these is interior and immaterial, "the force of the soul"; the second is interior and material, "differences found among the particles of the [animal] spirits" that leave the gland on their way to different regions of the brain;[94] the third is exterior and material, "the action of objects that impinge on the senses."[95] My summary is sorely abbreviated, but it is safe to say, nevertheless, that even in his description of the location of the pineal gland, Descartes falls far short of a radical, clear-and-distinct dualism.

Rather than dualism, *difference* would more adequately describe his discourse on the pineal gland, with its references to "the differences found among the particles of the spirits that leave" the cornarium; the "different" particles that act "differently" against the gland; and the animal spirits "always differing among themselves in some way."[96]

No less do such differences prevail where the size of the cornarium is concerned. Not only very soft, this flickering flame-shaped gland is also very small, smaller in humans than it is in animals—and volatile, so much so that, like the soul, it departs the body soon after death. For this reason, Descartes explains to Mersenne, unless the cadaver be that of a dumb animal or a dull-witted human, the cornarium is unlikely to be found during dissection. "Three years ago at Leiden, when I wanted to see it in a woman who was being autopsied, I found it impossible to recognize it, even though I looked very thoroughly and knew well where it should be, being accustomed to find it without any difficulty in freshly killed animals," Descartes tells Mersenne. "An old professor who was performing the autopsy, named Valcher, admitted to me that he had never been able to see it in any human body. I think this is because they usually spend some days looking at the intestines and other parts before opening the head."[97]

Perhaps Rembrandt's 1656 painting of *The Anatomy Lesson of Dr. Jan Deyman*, where the brain is being dissected and the abdominal cavity bypassed, captures something of the incongruity, and overlap, involved in Descartes's discourse on the pineal gland: "digging for [the convict's] soul in a brain brought fresh from the scaffold."[98] The "differential" elements of this discourse cannot be escaped. Indeed, as David Farrell Krell puts it, "difference—and I am tempted to write the word as *différance*, with a pineal *a*, as it were—dominates the system."[99]

A PAINTER OF HANDS

In the Glasgow Art Gallery, there is an early painting by Rembrandt, *Slaughtered Ox*, dating to around 1640. It seems odd to refer to this painting as a "still life" (*nature morte*), for what it portrays ("displays") is the massive carcass of a butchered ox, strapped to and suspended from a crossbeam. In the background, behind and to the side of the eviscerated animal, a stooped woman appears to be mopping the floor. The woman, a maid, "is represented at work, turning away from us as well as from the corpse, as if her presence in the represented space were just a coincidence," Mieke Bal observes in *Reading "Rembrandt": Beyond the Word–Image Opposition*.

"She seems to be there merely as an effect of the real, as a token of 'life' within the scene of death." The maid is but a "figurant" in what Bal calls this "representational, realistic" rendering that remains free of all "narratorial intrusion." Similarly, the heap of clothing in the right-hand corner of the painting is "meaningless" and "empty" of narrative content. And in the dead body, here "clearly circumscribed," we see death as so much "a given" that "we can overlook it."[100]

The relation of this painting to the 1655 *Slaughtered Ox* that hangs in the Louvre has been much debated (see fig. 4). The content of the second painting is similar to the first: the opened and emptied body of a butchered ox hangs from a gibbet, while in the background, a woman, the maid, looks out from behind a Dutch door. To continue with Bal's analysis, while the first painting, as realistic, secures boundaries—the dead body clearly circumscribed, the distinctiveness of the maid from the ox, the absence of self-reflexivity in the work—in the Louvre painting, inside and outside, as it were, overlap; one is folded into or fused with the other. In the second *Slaughtered Ox*, Bal says, "The opened body is openness itself. It is literally the body turned inside out; there is no outside left; all we see is inside. Instead of being inside a butcher shop, we are within a body."[101] The position of the maid in the second work, "the seamless contiguity between the two bodies in the Louvre painting," partakes of this same challenge to human/animal, inside/outside oppositions. This maid, rather than a figurant is a "character" whose "intrusion on the scene is a narrative event." Bal notes that "where her body ends, that of the ox begins," and "where the outer representation of her body recedes, the gigantic inner body seems to take over," so much so that the opened animal body here replaces the woman's body, "the emptiness of the ox's body representing the womb."[102]

With this return to the womb and to uterine membranes on display, we must abbreviate Bal's reading of these Rembrandt paintings and move quickly to a conclusion. Bal is no doubt right to align the boundaries being put in place at this pivotal, early-modern moment with "masculinity" and "clarity" (the Cartesian "clear and distinct"), whereas "femininity tends to be related to fusion, transgression, and connectiveness,"[103] to what, following Krell, I have called "differential" elements of the kind Bal finds in the second painting, as distinct from the first. She is also astute in noting the proximity Rembrandt gives in the second painting to the animal and female bodies, the one merging into the other, both on the underside of the "Cartesian" line. Aside from the question of what prompts Rembrandt by the 1650s to undertake his particular challenge to emerging binaries—

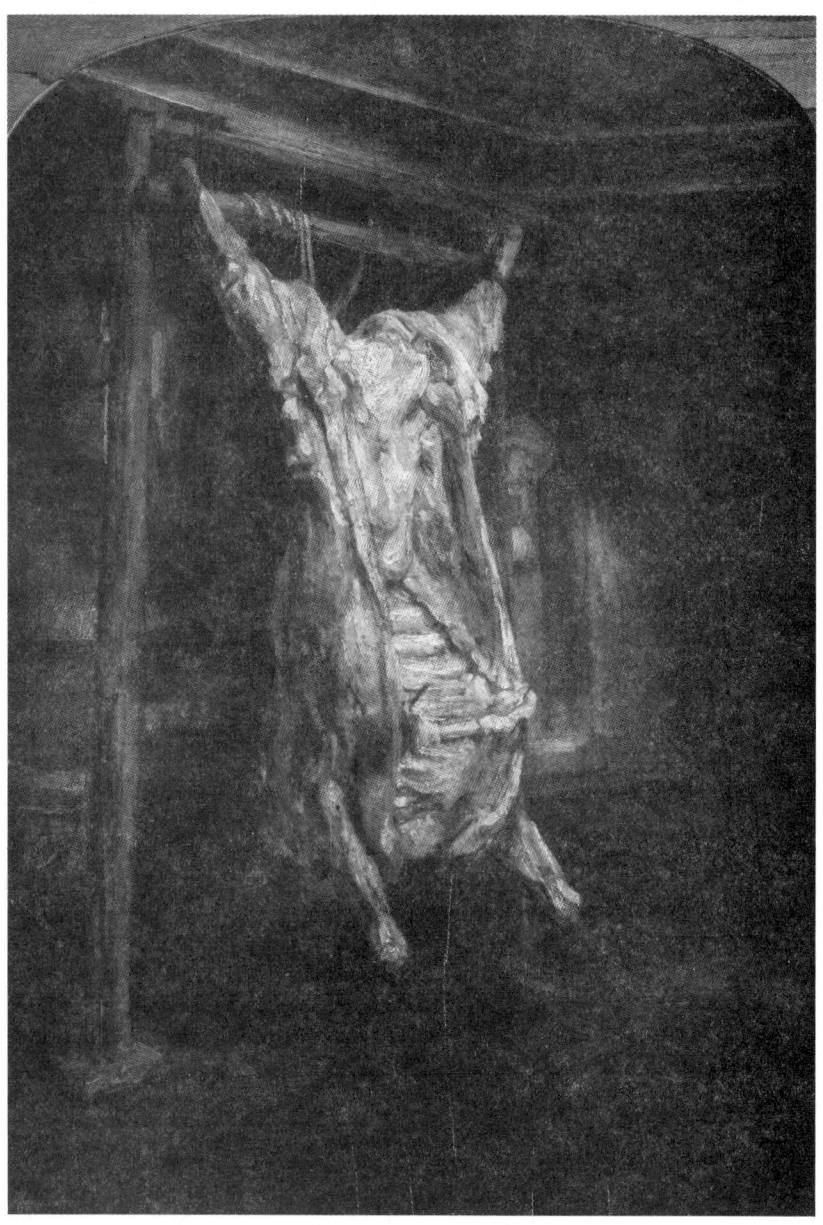

FIGURE 4 *Slaughtered Ox*, Rembrandt, 1655. The Louvre, Paris. Image source: ibiblio.org.

a question that is also much debated and that is bound up with issues of authorship—what interests me about the second painting and what is particularly relevant for my undertaking in this chapter, is Rembrandt's *performative* strategy—his *work of the hands*—in the Louvre painting and in several other of his works. I have suggested above that, for all his theatricality, Vesalius introduces to modernity the kind of constative speech act that, to sustain its own authority, must needs mask the performativity of language. Generally, we take Descartes to be the "father" of such constative speech, although as I have argued, his own writing (as *writing*, it already corporealizes the idealized hand) might be read as performing a displacement of "Cartesian" inside/outside, human/animal oppositions. With Rembrandt, it seems to me, performativity is radicalized through *hand-work*, through "a hand" that is unmistakably material, embodied, and so that blurs the either/or divide.

With Bal, then, I am taken by the difference in the paint-handling between the two *Slaughtered Ox* works. Whereas, in the first painting, "the substance of the paint does not strike the eye, nor does the work of painting draw attention to itself," in the Louvre painting, "the daring roughness of the handling of the paint"[104] is no less than astonishing. It seems to me that this paint-handling is not unrelated to what Svetlana Alpers refers to as Rembrandt's "fascination with the hand."[105] Not only in *The Anatomy Lesson of Dr. Nicolaas Tulp*, but over and over again, Rembrandt painted hands and gave prominence to the hands that feature in his works, a matter to which Alpers has given careful consideration in her reading of such paintings as *Bathsheba*, *The Return of the Prodigal Son*, *Jacob Blessing the Children of Joseph* and *Aristotle Contemplating the Bust of Homer*. Moreover, and of some significance for my work here, the hands to which Rembrandt gives prominence gesture towards connection rather than separation. His hands are not instruments of seizure; they reach out to the other, offer comfort, welcome and forgiveness. In *Aristotle Contemplating the Bust of Homer*, for instance, "Rembrandt makes the philosopher's relationship to that great writer he so admired a matter of touch. While one oversized hand rests on his hip, fingering his heavy gold chain, the other rests on, in order to feel and thus to know, the marble bust."[106] In *An Old Woman*, similarly, the woman "does not look at the book in front of her as much as she absorbs it through her touch."[107] Where the issue of paint-handling is concerned, the hands to which Rembrandt gives prominence are those of the painter, Rembrandt himself. Rembrandt's laborious working of his paint, "the remarkable substantiality of his paint and painted surfaces,"[108] is what undercuts realism and its subject/object separations, so much so, that when we look at a Rembrandt painting, what we see performed is the activity of painting, the "furiously energetic"[109] work of the painter's own hands, "the performance of his brush."[110]

"Why," Jonathan Sawday asks, "should Rembrandt have wished to identify himself with dead creatures? Why the interest in showing animals as if they had, somehow, been the victims of an execution?"[111] If, as Bal in contemplating the Louvre *Slaughtered Ox* contends, the substance of the paint in this particular dissection scene "is also the substance of death. And the substance of death is dead, stinking flesh. What we have to deal with—what the work does not spare us from—is the effect of the putrifying smell of paint."[112] Quite apart from the sculpted poses of the reified bodies represented in the *Fabrica* illustrations, what we have to deal with in the Louvre *Slaughtered Ox* is the "killing power"[113] of the new regime. Rembrandt's refusal of the referential either/or must then be read as a gesture of confrontation with the "hidden" workings of an emerging bio-power.

NOTES

1. Marzio di Girolamo Marzi Medici, "Letter to Majordomo Pier Francesco Ricci" (1543). Archivio di Stato di Firenze, Mediceo del Principato 1171, Insert 6, fol. 286, 1–2. Retrieved 27 January 2007 from *The Medici Archive Project*, www.medici.org. See also D.D. O'Malley, *Andreas Vesalius of Brussels: 1514–1564* (Berkeley: University of California Press, 1964), 200.
2. Jonathan Sawday, *The Body Emblazoned: Dissection and the Human Body in Renaissance Culture* (London: Routledge, 1995), 23.
3. Ibid., 24, 25.
4. O'Malley, *Andreas Vesalius of Brussels*, 12.
5. Andrea Carlino, *Books of the Body: Anatomical Ritual and Renaissance Learning*, trans. John Tedeschi and Anne C. Tedeschi (Chicago: University of Chicago Press, 1999), 3.
6. Michel Foucault, *Discipline and Punish: The Birth of the Prison*, trans. Alan Sheridan (New York: Vintage, 1977), 28.
7. Michel Foucault, *Foucault Live: Collected Interviews 1961–1984*, ed. Sylvère Lotringer (New York: Semiotext(e), 1989), 220.
8. Ibid.
9. O'Malley, *Andreas Vesalius of Brussels*, 189.
10. In *The Open: Man and Animal*, trans. Kevin Attell (Stanford: Stanford University Press, 2004), Giorgio Agamben suggests: "In our culture, the decisive political conflict, which governs every other conflict, is that between

the animality and the humanity of man. That is to say, in its origin Western politics is also biopolitics" (80).
11 Ibid., 15.
12 The reason I use "man" rather than a more "inclusive" term is that "woman" is not the "human" side of the binary at this stage in European history. Woman is not a speaking subject at this point or in the early modern anatomy theatre; she is understood to receive male speech and seed and to lack active, living speech herself. The division I track between the "human" and the "animal" in "man" is not a division that passes through the woman.
13 O'Malley, *Andreas Vesalius of Brussels*, 199.
14 Ibid., 198.
15 Ibid., 201.
16 Vesalius makes his point without, he says, wishing to give an impression of "impiety" or to appear "insubordinate to [Galen's] authority." Andreas Vesalius, *On the Fabric of the Human Body* (*De Humani Corporis Fabrica Libri Septem*) translated by William Frank Richardson and John Burd Carman (San Francisco: Norman Publishing, 1998), liv. See also O'Malley, *Andreas Vesalius of Brussels*, 321. This is an important ploy, one that Descartes repeats in his *Discourse on Method*. See Francis Barker, *The Tremulous Private Body: Essays on Subjection* (London: Methuen, 1984) on the importance of such posture for the "unseen" workings of bio-power.
17 Vesalius, *On the Fabric of the Human Body*, liv; O'Malley, *Andreas Vesalius of Brussels*, 321.
18 O'Malley, *Andreas Vesalius of Brussels*, 317.
19 Vesalius, *On the Fabric of the Human Body*, lii.
20 Ibid., 319.
21 Carlino, *Books of the Body*.
22 Ibid., 10.
23 In *Books of the Body*, Carlino explains that a printing of Mondino's *Anatomia* was included in John Ketham's influential *Fasciculus Medicinae*, a collection of medical texts issued for the first time in Latin in 1491. The *Fasciculus*, with Mondino's treatise intact, "was highly successful and it circulated widely, serving as one of the founding texts of academic medical and anatomical science at least until the mid-sixteenth century. It was a manual intended for medical students and barbers as well as for surgeons and physicians" (9). Carlino notes further that "[we] know of seven different pictorial representations of Mondino's anatomy lesson that have appeared in the many reprintings of the *Fasciculus* and of the *Anatomia*" (10), all of which, though they differ from each other in certain significant details, use the same "basic framework" to display the anatomy scene (13).
24 Carlino, *Books of the Body*, 12.
25 Ibid., 11.

26 Ibid.
27 Ibid., 13.
28 Ibid., 18-19.
29 Ibid., 20.
30 Ibid., 12.
31 Ibid., 20.
32 Ibid., 16.
33 O'Malley, *Andreas Vesalius of Brussels*, 317, 319.
34 Ibid., 320.
35 In *Andreas Vesalius of Brussels*, O'Malley writes of the site in Pisa of Vesalius's anatomy lessons: "At one time it was proposed that they had been held in the Accademia Cesalpiniana in the Via della Sapienza, and in 1901 an inscription to that effect was engraved in stone and affixed to the building. More recently it has been asserted that, on the basis of new documents, the anatomy was held in the 'Palatio Veteri Domini Commissarii Pisani,' which corresponds to the present Palazzo del Governo situated in Lung' Arno Galileo Galilei. Thereafter still another student declared that Vesalius taught in that region of Pisa where the Palazzo dell' Ordine de Santo Stefano was built in 1562" (200).
36 Sawday, *The Body Emblazoned: Dissection and the Human Body in Renaissance Culture*, 66, 69.
37 For a discussion of the identity of the artist or artists responsible for the Vesalian illustrations, see J.D. de C.M. Saunders and Charles D. O'Malley, eds. *The Illustrations from the Works of Andreas Vesalius of Brussels* (New York: Dover Publications, 1950), 25-29. Saunders and O'Malley conclude that Vesalius himself was responsible for at least some of the *Fabrica* plates.
38 See Glenn Harcourt, "Andreas Vesalius and the Anatomy of Antique Sculpture," *Representations* 17 (Winter 1987): 28-61. This illustration strategy provided Vesalius with a way of "bracketing *in representation* the simple fact that anatomical knowledge is constituted through the violation and destruction of its proper object in practice," Harcourt points out. "The idealized, classical forms of the figures, the fact that they do not read as actual cadavers, sets up a foil within the structure of the illustrations that mitigates the deadening, objectifying force of the accompanying narrative: 'With a very sharp razor make a circular incision around the umbilicus, deep enough to penetrate the skin, then from the middle of the pectoral bone make a straight, lengthwise incision to the umbilicus'" (34-35).
39 Carlino, *Books of the Body*, 1.
40 Ibid., 39.
41 See Jonathan Goldberg, *Writing Matter: From the Hands of the English Renaissance* (Stanford: Stanford University Press, 1990), 86-88. Later in this chapter, I turn to Rembrandt's ties to the scalpel and to what Jonathan Sawday

calls the "culture of dissection" (2). At this juncture, however, it is interesting to note that many Renaissance artists, including Michelangelo, Raphael and Leonardo, took the scalpel in hand and performed their own dissections. This they did "to improve their art," Linden Edwards suggests. Many of these artists left behind drawings of their dissections. "The anatomy notebooks of Leonardo are of special interest in that they contain over 750 red-chalk drawings of his own dissections, which are marvels of observation and insight." See Linden F. Edwards, *The History of Human Dissection* (Fort Wayne, IN: Fort Wayne and Allen Country Public Library Publication, 1955), 10.

42 See Julia Kristeva, "Holbein's Dead Christ," in *Black Sun: Depression and Melancholia*, trans. Leon S. Roudiez (New York: Columbia University Press, 1989).

43 Sawday, *The Body Emblazoned: Dissection and the Human Body in Renaissance Culture*, 67.

44 Julia Kristeva, *Desire In Language: A Semiotic Approach to Literature and Art*, ed. Leon S. Roudiez, trans. Thomas Gora, Alice Jardine, and Leon S. Roudiez (New York: Columbia University Press, 1980), 36-63. In Kristeva's words, the semiotic practice of the sign "assimilates the metaphysics of the symbol and projects it onto the 'immediately perceptible.' The 'immediately perceptible,' valorized in this way, is then transformed into an *objectivity*—the reigning law of discourse in the civilization of the sign" (40).

45 To cite again Glenn Harcourt's "Andreas Vesalius and the Anatomy of Antique Sculpture," the tactic employed consistently by Vesalius and his draftsmen in the *Fabrica* is to dissociate dissection images from the physical body being dissected: "there is a distinct dissociation of the 'natural' body (i.e., the actual, dissected corpse employed as the draftsman's model) from its anatomized image. But in this case, that body is itself transformed in and through the process of its representation. It is in essence pictorially reconstructed as a carefully crafted, albeit fragmented, artifact" (29).

46 O'Malley, *Andreas Vesalius of Brussels*, 321.

47 Carlino, *Books of the Body*, 49; see also 45-50.

48 O'Malley, *Andreas Vesalius of Brussels*, 165.

49 See, for example, Martin Jay, *Downcast Eyes: The Denigration of Vision in Twentieth-Century French Thought* (Berkeley: University of California Press, 1994).

50 Mieke Bal, Double Exposures: The Subject of Cultural Analysis (London: Routledge, 1996), 1-2.

51 Ibid., 2.

52 Ibid.

53 Bal says in *Double Exposures* that she chooses not to privilege one kind of vision but rather to "differentiate modes, if not kinds of vision" in the interest of "multiplying perspectives" and "proliferating points of view" (9). What

she does not consider, however, is the link between the *speech* of speech act situations and (any kind of) *hearing.*

54 Ibid., 4.
55 O'Malley, *Andreas Vesalius of Brussels*, 143.
56 Ibid.
57 Ibid., 148.
58 Ibid., 149.
59 In the *Fabrica* title page dissection scene, we must be struck by "the sudden eruption of a crowd into the anatomy theatre": a throng of some seventy or eighty people, where previous dissections were characterized by "the relative absence of the onlooker" (Sawday, *The Body Emblazoned: Dissection and the Human Body in Renaissance Culture*, 66).
60 O'Malley, *Andreas Vesalius of Brussels*, 143.
61 Ibid.
62 See Freud's essay on "Medusa's Head," where this castration drama is also set out. "Medusa's Head" (1940), trans. James Strachey, in *The Standard Edition of the Complete Psychological Works of Sigmund Freud*, vol. 7 (London: Hogarth Press, 1953).
63 In the *Fabrica* title page dissection scene, performative elements are hard to miss: they include stage, audience, props, embellished cartouche, and of course Vesalius himself in theatrical costume, his left hand raised in a gesture of pointing.
64 O'Malley, *Andreas Vesalius of Brussels*, 201.
65 Ibid.
66 Ibid.
67 Ibid., 154.
68 Ibid., 201.
69 Adrien Baillet, *La vie de Monsieur Des-Cartes* (Genève: Slatkine Reprints, 1970), 197. My translation.
70 "That is why, as soon as I was old enough to emerge from the control of my teachers, I entirely abandoned the study of letters. Resolving to seek no knowledge other than that which could be found in myself or else in the great book of the world, I spent the rest of my youth traveling." René Descartes, *The Philosophical Writings of Descartes*, vol. 1, ed. and trans. John Cottingham, Robert Stoothoff, and Dugald Murdoch (Cambridge: Cambridge University Press, 1985), 115.
71 According to Simon Schama, among the items found in Rembrandt's studio after his death were "four flayed arms and legs anatomized by Vesalius," one of which may have been used as he model for the forearm being dissected by Dr. Tulp. Simon Schama, *Rembrandt's Eyes* (New York: Alfred A. Knopf, 1999), 342.
72 Barker, *The Tremulous Private Body*, 77.

73 Sawday, *The Body Emblazoned: Dissection and the Human Body in Renaissance Culture*, 2.
74 See Stephen Gaukroger, *Descartes' System of Natural Philosophy* (Cambridge: Cambridge University Press, 2002), 22–23.
75 Lilli Alanen, *Descartes's Concept of Mind* (Cambridge, MA: Harvard University Press, 2003), 80–81.
76 In *Descartes's Concept of Mind*, Alanen for one, recognizes that one of the important features of Cartesian thought that has been neglected is its connection with speech (82).
77 Ibid., 85.
78 Ibid., 83.
79 Ibid., 84.
80 For one example only, see Descartes, *The Philosophical Writings of Descartes*, vol. 1, 44–47.
81 Jacques Derrida, *Speech and Phenomena and Other Essays on Husserl's Theory of Signs*, trans. David B. Allison (Evanston, IL: Northwestern University Press, 1973), 77. In *Descartes's Concept of Mind*, Alanen notes that "Descartes takes thought to be causally and logically prior to speech and considers the latter to be the instrument or medium for expressing the former" (84). She then goes on to ask: "Does this mean that the structure of language or speech reflects the structure of the thoughts that it is used to convey? Both involve representation, but in different ways: thought represents immediately, speech by means of external, public signs or symbols. It is difficult to account for what it is to think of something without using the analogue of speech and language" (84). This is precisely my point in turning to Derrida's analysis in *Speech and Phenomena* of the way in which, in the phonocentric tradition, if "thought represents immediately," it does so by of the operation of "hearing oneself speak."
82 Derrida, *Speech and Phenomena*, 78, 79.
83 See Alanen, *Descartes's Concept of Mind*, 94.
84 Ibid., 83.
85 Ibid.
86 In "Presence and Memory: Derrida, Freud, Plato, Descartes," *The Graduate Faculty Journal of the New School for Social Research* 11 (1986), Véronique M. Fóti uses the term "cryptopgraphy" in a discussion of Descartes's work on the pineal gland in its relation to memory. She notes that there are two kinds of memory in Descartes, one bodily and dependent and one purely intellectual, and she interprets the latter "as the power to summon the innate ideas from their crypto-inscription to explicit presence" (75). Here, again, Descartes's dualism is, from the start, threatened by a certain "overlap" of outer and inner, an instability brought by graphing—imprinting or writing—of embodied speech.

87 For my notion of performativity, I am indebted to Michael Naas's fine reading of the preformativity of Derrida's texts in *Taking on the Tradition Jacques Derrida and the Legacies of Deconstruction* (Stanford: Stanford University Press, 2003).
88 René Descartes, *The Philosophical Writings of Descartes*, vol. 3, *The Correspondence*, trans. John Cottingham, Robert Stoothoff, Dugald Murdoch, and Anthony Kenny (Cambridge: Cambridge University Press, 1991), 14.
89 David Farrell Krell, "Paradoxes of the Pineal: From Descartes to Georges Bataille," *Contemporary French Philosophy*, ed. A. Phillips Griffiths. Special Issue of *Philosophy* 21 (1998): 216.
90 Descartes, *The Philosophical Writings of Descartes*, vol. 3, 143.
91 René Descartes, *Treatise of Man*, trans. Thomas Steele Hall (Amherst, NY: Prometheus Books, 2003), 91.
92 Ibid.
93 Krell, "Paradoxes of the Pineal: From Descartes to Georges Bataille," 219.
94 Descartes, *Treatise of Man*, 91. Descartes's animal spirits, themselves differential in structure and function, are "terrestrial particles that are infused with subtle matter" (Descartes, *The Philosophical Writings of Descartes*, vol. 3, 225).
95 Descartes, *Treatise of Man*, 96.
96 Ibid., 91.
97 Descartes, *The Philosophical Writings of Descartes*, vol. 3, 146.
98 Sawday, *The Body Emblazoned: Dissection and the Human Body in Renaissance Culture*, 157.
99 Krell, "Paradoxes of the Pineal: From Descartes to Georges Bataille," 219.
100 Mieke Bal, *Reading "Rembrandt": Beyond the Word–Image Opposition* (Cambridge: Cambridge University Press, 1991), 384–85.
101 Ibid., 387.
102 Ibid., 358.
103 Ibid., 387.
104 Ibid., 384, 385.
105 Alpers 1988, 29.
106 Ibid., 25.
107 Ibid., 24. Alpers reads these hands as challenging the visual dominance of the Cartesian I/eye, but she does not consider Rembrandt's hands, or handwork, as opening the interiority of hearing-oneself-speak. To her argument, then, I would add the ear: Rembrandt's hands are not only necessary supplements to the eye; by reaching out, by figuring a human understanding dependent on physical contact, by their materiality and movement, they already gesture to an outside of "Cartesian" interiority and they "space," open the auto-affective enclosure. See Svetlana Alpers, *Rembrandt's Enterprise: The Studio and the Market* (Chicago: University of Chicago Press, 1988).

108 Ibid., 8.
109 Schama, *Rembrandt's Eyes*, 598.
110 Alpers, *Rembrandt's Enterprise*, 39. What also interests me in Descartes' work on the pineal gland and in Rembrandt, and what I am not able to explore here, are questions of memory and melancholia.
111 Sawday, *The Body Emblazoned: Dissection and the Human Body in Renaissance Culture*, 149.
112 Bal, *Reading "Rembrandt,"* 386.
113 Ibid., 382.

BIBLIOGRAPHY

Agamben, Giorgio. *The Open: Man and Animal*. Translated by Kevin Attell. Stanford: Stanford University Press, 2004.
Alanen, Lilli. *Descartes's Concept of Mind*. Cambridge, MA: Harvard University Press, 2003.
Alpers, Svetlana. *Rembrandt's Enterprise: The Studio and the Market*. Chicago: University of Chicago Press, 1988.
Baillet, Adrien. *La vie de Monsieur Des-Cartes*. Genève: Slatkine Reprints, 1970.
Bal, Mieke. *Double Exposures: The Subject of Cultural Analysis*. London: Routledge, 1996.
———. *Reading "Rembrandt": Beyond the Word–Image Opposition*. Cambridge: Cambridge University Press, 1991.
Barker, Francis. *The Tremulous Private Body: Essays on Subjection*. London: Methuen, 1984.
Carlino, Andrea. *Books of the Body: Anatomical Ritual and Renaissance Learning*. Translated by John Tedeschi and Anne C. Tedeschi. Chicago: University of Chicago Press, 1999.
Derrida, Jacques. *Memoirs of the Blind: The Self-Portrait and Other Ruins*. Translated by Pascale-Anne Brault and Michael Naas. Chicago: University of Chicago Press, 1993.
———. *Speech and Phenomena and Other Essays on Husserl's Theory of Signs*. Translated by David B. Allison. Evanston, IL: Northwestern University Press, 1973.
Descartes, René. *Treatise of Man*. Translated by Thomas Steele Hall. Amherst, NY: Prometheus Books, 2003.
———. *The Philosophical Writings of Descartes*. Vol. 3, *The Correspondence*. Translated by John Cottingham, Robert Stoothoff, Dugald Murdoch, and Anthony Kenny. Cambridge: Cambridge University Press, 1991.
———. *The Philosophical Writings of Descartes*. Vol. 1. Edited and translated

by John Cottingham, Robert Stoothoff, and Dugald Murdoch. Cambridge: Cambridge University Press, 1985.

———. *The Philosophical Writings of Descartes*. Vol. 2. Edited and translated by John Cottingham, Robert Stoothoff, and Dugald Murdoch. Cambridge: Cambridge University Press, 1984.

Edwards, Linden F. *The History of Human Dissection*. Fort Wayne, IN: Fort Wayne and Allen Country Public Library Publication, 1955.

Fóti, Véronique M. "Presence and Memory: Derrida, Freud, Plato, Descartes." *The Graduate Faculty Journal of the New School for Social Research* 11 (1986): 67–81.

Foucault, Michel. *Foucault Live: Collected Interviews 1961–1984*. Edited by Sylvère Lotringer. New York: Semiotext(e), 1989.

———. *Discipline and Punish: The Birth of the Prison*. Translated by Alan Sheridan. New York: Vintage, 1977.

Freud, Sigmund. "Fetishism" (1927). Translated by James Strachey. In *The Standard Edition of the Complete Psychological Works of Sigmund Freud*. Vol. 21. London: Hogarth Press, 1961.

———. "Medusa's Head" (1940). Translated by James Strachey. In *The Standard Edition of the Complete Psychological Works of Sigmund Freud*. Vol. 7. London: Hogarth Press, 1953.

Gaukroger, Stephen. *Descartes' System of Natural Philosophy*. Cambridge: Cambridge University Press, 2002.

Goldberg, Jonathan. *Writing Matter: From the Hands of the English Renaissance*. Stanford: Stanford University Press, 1990.

Harcourt, Glenn. "Andreas Vesalius and the Anatomy of Antique Sculpture." *Representations* 17 (Winter 1987): 28–61.

Jay, Martin. *Downcast Eyes: The Denigration of Vision in Twentieth-Century French Thought*. Berkeley: University of California Press, 1994.

Krell, David Farrell. "Paradoxes of the Pineal: From Descartes to Georges Bataille." *Contemporary French Philosophy*, ed. A. Phillips Griffiths. Special Issue of *Philosophy* 21 (1998).

Kristeva, Julia. "Holbein's Dead Christ." In *Black Sun: Depression and Melancholia*. Translated by Leon S. Roudiez. New York: Columbia University Press, 1989.

———. *Desire in Language: A Semiotic Approach to Literature and Art*. Edited by Leon S. Roudiez. Translated by Thomas Gora, Alice Jardine, and Leon S. Roudiez. New York: Columbia University Press, 1980.

Medici, Marzio di Girolamo Marzi. "Letter to Majordomo Pier Francesco Ricci" (1543). Archivio di Stato di Firenze, Mediceo del Principato 1171, Insert 6, fol. 286. Retrieved from *The Medici Archive Project*, www.medici.org.

Naas, Michael. *Taking on the Tradition: Jacques Derrida and the Legacies of Deconstruction.* Stanford: Stanford University Press, 2003.

O'Malley, C.D. *Andreas Vesalius of Brussels: 1514–1564.* Berkeley: University of California Press, 1964.

Saunders, J.D. de C.M., and Charles D. O'Malley, eds. *The Illustrations from the Works of Andreas Vesalius of Brussels.* New York: Dover Publications, 1950.

Sawday, Jonathan. *The Body Emblazoned: Dissection and the Human Body in Renaissance Culture.* London: Routledge, 1995.

Schama, Simon. *Rembrandt's Eyes.* New York: Alfred A. Knopf, 1999.

Vesalius, Andreas. *On the Fabric of the Human Body (De Humani Corporis Fabrica Libri Septem).* Translated by William Frank Richardson and John Burd Carman. San Francisco: Norman Publishing, 1998.

5

A Missed Opportunity
Humanism, Anti-humanism and the Animal Question

PAOLA CAVALIERI

THE PROBLEM

In 1993, in a book entitled *The Great Ape Project*,[1] many authors from different disciplines argued for the extension of basic human rights to the nonhuman great apes, gaining substantial support in many countries, but not in France—that is, in the country which has recently generated, within the strand of postmodern thought, the powerful attack on the traditional doctrine regarding "man's" nature and place in the world that is now known as anti-humanism. Recently, moreover, philosopher Jacques Derrida—the initiator of that deconstructionist approach whose aim is to challenge the traditional assumptions providing the foundation for most Western discourses—openly attacked the proposal, claiming that the arguments of the authors engaged in animal liberation ethics are often "badly articulated or philosophically inconsequential."[2]

In general, one would feel entitled to suppose that the cultural attitude that, starting from the 1960s, put into question the main tenets of traditional metaphysical humanism, might positively predispose French thinkers towards any attempt to rethink the status of nonhuman beings. And, in particular, one might entertain this idea with reference to Jacques Derrida, who repeatedly declared that the *discourse of animality* was for him "a very old anxiety, a still lively suspicion."[3] Why, then, such a persistent lack of interest in the animal question from French philosophical circles?[4] And why such a negative reaction from Derrida?

It is to these questions that I shall try to give here an answer, albeit synthetic and preliminary. Together with Derrida, I shall consider Michel

Foucault and Emmanuel Levinas, that is, two authors who not only strongly shaped the recent French cultural landscape but who are also representative—by incorporating the influences of such prominent German philosophers as Friedrich Nietzsche and Martin Heidegger—of a more general continental climate. I shall argue that, apart from any specific problems with their views, all three authors fail to deal adequately with the question of nonhumans because, like most other postmodern philosophers, they cannot escape two legacies of the traditional doctrines they challenge. The first one is that bias in favour of the intellectual who, by causing a selective focus on moral agents—the beings whose *behaviour* is morally evaluable—to the detriment of mere moral patients—the beings whose *treatment* is morally evaluable—produces perfectionist doctrines that are hardly compatible with the theoretical basis of contemporary egalitarianism. The second one is the more or less explicit acceptance of an old theoretical approach that on the one hand makes global philosophical systems too disconnected from scientific investigation, and on the other makes ethics too dependent on global philosophical systems. The order in which I shall examine the authors in question is inversely connected to the attention they pay to the animal question—null in the case of Foucault, minimal in the case of Levinas and gradually growing for Derrida.

MAN NEVER DIES

The philosopher and historian of ideas, Michel Foucault, can be plausibly regarded as the most authoritative French heir to the Nietzschean tradition. The statement that, by immediately attracting general attention, turned Foucault into one of the leading figures of anti-humanism—"Man is dead"—clearly echoes Nietzsche's claim that "God is Dead," and Foucault himself openly declares that he tries, as far as possible, to see what can be done in specific historical domains "with the help of Nietzsche's texts."[5]

This detailed work on sectorial histories, with a focus on the attendant exercises of power that gradually develops into a global analytics of power, can probably be seen as the most influential aspect of Foucault's work, in spite of the parallel, continued presence of typically epistemological interests. Thus, though the very idea of "man's death" has an epistemological component—the claim, that is, that the concept of "man" lately shaped by the so-called human sciences was soon dissolved by new disciplines essentially focusing on systems and structures—what concerns us here is its theoretical component aimed at challenging the traditional, and particularly Cartesian, view of human beings.

In this respect, Foucault's basic claim is that humanist essentialism is wrong in maintaining that human beings are governed by autonomous will or reason. For on the one hand, autonomy of the individual is mostly an illusion, as specific techniques of power shape the individual's life, and coercive knowledge systems shape the individual's world view. And, on the other, reason is merely one among the features of human beings—there also exist different forces, generically covered under the notion of "unreason," which, though devaluated or suppressed, always tend to re-emerge in the form of resistance to the prevailing rationalist constructions. With regard to this picture, Foucault tends to present himself as a detached analyst, observing and explaining the persistent interplay of power and resistance. Despite claims to the contrary, however, his stance is not always that of the impartial spectator. As German philosopher Jürgen Habermas has stressed, with a shift from a model of dominion borrowed from a structuralistic interpretation, where no value judgement can be advanced, to a model of dominion borrowed from Marxism, which elicits resistance,[6] Foucault shows a strong normative tendency to uncover, and to recover, the voice of those who are oppressed by the prevailing practices. In fact, he even develops the notion of the "specific intellectual" who, through a work of unmasking the subjugating practices that reveals their origin and roots, helps the various groups of oppressed with their specific struggles.[7]

Clearly, as has been observed,[8] such interest in resistance to power reveals once again Nietzschean influences—Nietzsche's will to power is also the will to resist constraints imposed by others. There is, however, an important difference between Nietzsche and Foucault, one which has to do with the conceptualization of humans and nonhumans. For, though in both authors animals are peripheral subjects, Foucault, as Clare Palmer aptly notices,[9] makes the radical gesture of severing Nietzsche's analytics of power from its animal roots, and of applying it only to intrahuman relations. Totally lacking in Foucault is that, as it were, sociobiological leaning that puts Nietzsche's analysis of human behaviour so much in consonance with modern scientific thinking, as contrasted to traditional ontological approaches. Nietzsche repeatedly stresses that human beings are animals, and often develops his arguments starting from this perspective—suffice it to think of his radical claim that "the beginnings of justice, as of prudence, moderation, bravery—in short, of all we designate as the *Socratic virtues*, are *animal*."[10] Also, the will to power, far from being a uniquely human prerogative, is for Nietzsche obviously an animal, or even biologic, heritage. In other words, even in the absence of any explicitly focused treatment, for Nietzsche oppression is patently something that nonhumans can endure too, as it is confirmed by his interspecific treatment of the question of domestication.[11] None of this is to be found in Foucault. When it comes to the problem of oppressive systems involving nonhumans, what we find in his "anti-humanist" approach is absolute amnesia.

Such acts of erasure are not uncommon in French philosophy. To make just one example, Jean-Paul Sartre explains his view of humans by contrasting them with paper knives. While the paper knife, he argues, "serves a definite purpose, so that its essence precedes its existence, there is one being whose existence precedes its essence, a being which exists before it can be defined—man [*sic*]."[12] Thus, the alleged uniqueness of human beings is surreptitiously built on the absurd contrast between a complex organic being and a simple inorganic object, and on the mere erasure of the other animals. Something similar happens with Foucault, on different levels.

On the level of historical reconstruction, Foucault misses the issue of nonhumans even when a parallel naturally arises from his very analysis. So, when he claims that Descartes irrevocably excludes all that is "unreason" from the newly arising world view, he fails to notice that Descartes's gesture decrees not only the exclusion of the mad, but also the much more radical exclusion of the "brutes."[13] Again, when considering the role played by positivism in objectifying the mad, the sick, the criminal, he utterly forgets how the work of objectification had started with the treatment of animals in experimental sciences.[14]

Animals are missing in Foucault's landscape also on the level of interpretive analysis. According to his most widely known approach, power, previously essentially consisting of a right of seizure, and being chiefly power of life or death, in the eighteenth century started to focus on the conduct of conduct, aiming not at submitting to but at generating forces.[15] Clearly, animals are wholly out of sight here, as obviously the power exercised over them is quite the same now as it was in the past. But Foucault subsequently expanded his views. Confronted with the objection that his approach was unable to account for structural power relations, he distinguished power relations in general from relationships of domination, specifying that, while the former are unstable, so that resistance may yield a reversal of roles, the latter—which include racism and sexism and which can involve violence or physical restraint—are stable and hardly reversible.[16] It may seem that, against this new background, there is room for at least a cursory reference to human relationships with animals. Not so—nonhuman beings are nowhere to be found in the new schema either. More: in one of his latest returns to the issue, Foucault distinguishes what he calls *capacities*—which are exerted over things and give the ability to modify, use or destroy them—from *power relations* proper, relations between human individuals or groups.[17] With this, it is evident that the traditional Kantian distinction between things and persons has totally occupied the antihumanist scene.

At this point, one might think that animals are never mentioned by Foucault. But the reverse is true. Nonhumans, though never directly invested by ethical considerations, are frequently referred to in Foucault's work. They are present as examples, reference points, explaining notions in a wide range of occasions, many of which have to do with subjugation and violence. This particular feature, which is clearly detectable in Nietzsche too,[18] can be best explained by reference to feminist philosopher Carol Adams's notion of the "absent referent."[19] The notion refers to a paradoxical use of language in which something is both present and absent. The absent referent enters into play when the literal treatment of one individual or group is obscured and is appropriated as a metaphor for the treatment of another individual or group. For example, when a raped woman says she feels "like a piece of meat," the absent referents are animals since their death experience (being killed for meat) now describes a life experience of a human (being raped).

This is just what happens with the presence/absence of animals within Foucault's discourse on power. When describing situations in which some humans, depending on the historical periods and on the specific institutions in which they are involved (asylums, prisons, etc.), are imprisoned, killed or disciplined by training and beating, more often than not Foucault compares their condition to that of animals, while at the same time nowhere showing any interest in the condition and treatment of animals per se.[20] Moreover, though interpreting, and employing, "animality"—just like "madness" or "unreason"—as a constructed and variable category, nowhere does he attempt at deconstructing it, thoroughly forgetting his normative tendency to stand with the oppressed.[21] In other words, Foucault morally removes nonhuman beings, and appropriates their condition merely as a metaphor for, or as a parallel to, the condition of other—that is, human—beings.

In the light of all this, it comes as no surprise that, after a long detour, Foucault goes back to the classical interest in the *human subject*, even claiming that one of his long-term objectives had always been a history of the different modes by which human beings are made subjects.[22] To such a history, focused on sexuality and proceeding backwards in the centuries, Foucault devotes studies which, in spite of the innovative methodology, are dominated by the conventional problems of mainstream Western philosophy.[23] Moreover, defining his work on sexuality as a "history of morals," he declares that he aims at overcoming modern universal normative systems in favour of the recovery of individualized forms of virtue ethics centred on the cultivation of the self—the ancient "art of life."[24] Quite apart from the clear humanist bias, this apparently new interest in the moral agent is a revealing move, because it sheds light on all of Foucalt's theoretical path. For, against this background, it is plausible to claim that the mad were not for Foucault mere moral patients deprived of cognitive skills—they were somehow different subjects, bearing, so to speak, the reasons of unreason. This is most clearly apparent when, in *Madness and Civilization*, Foucault renders his impressive homage not only to Nietzsche but also to figures such as Van Gogh and Artaud, by pointing to them as the geniuses whose work fed on its close connection with a madness *so wise* as to summon the world to judgement.[25]

All considered, given this construal of the mad—or better, more generally, of the abnormal[26]—as *another sort* of moral agent, and in light of the recovery of the traditional focus on the identification of a worthy form of life, to the detriment of that "modern" aspect of ethics whose task is to protect the interests of individuals other than the agent, the absence in Foucault's anti-humanism of any consideration of the nonhuman question is far less surprising than one might think.

THE OTHER IS THE SAME

In a short article of 1975, the French-naturalized philosopher Emmanuel Levinas tells the story of Bobby.[27] Bobby was a stray dog who for a short time, before being chased by the camp guards, greeted him and his companions every time that—because of their daily forced work—they were taken from, and brought back to, the concentration camp for Jewish prisoners of war where they had been confined during the Second World War.

In the article, Levinas states that Bobby was "the last Kantian in Nazi Germany."[28] With this, he means that Bobby, unlike the camp guards, was able to attribute to him and his companions the respect owed to all human beings. Ironically, however, Levinas's definition of Bobby derogates Bobby himself: for a nonhuman animal to be a Kantian means to accept one's status as a thing. In other words, Levinas's idea somehow conveys the view that to be a good dog means to recognize one's inferiority. This is an old story. Like slave virtue, nonhuman virtue lies in self-denial.

Though Levinas is known as one of the authors who most resolutely attempted to reformulate humanism, he deserves inclusion in this context in light of the fact that he takes the anti-humanist arguments so seriously that what he produces could be paradoxically seen as a form of anti-humanist humanism,[29] clearly influenced by the Heideggerian preoccupations with a consciousness that may precede objectifying knowledge and with a critique of Western instrumental reason. Such preoccupations are made particularly apparent by his shift in the approach to the human subject.

Confronted with the innumerable historical horrors produced by the modern construal of "man" as an appropriating and consuming entity, Levinas makes in fact the innovative gesture of bringing to the forefront the passivity, rather than activity, of the human self. Setting aside the traditional focus on that side of human beings that is connected with characteristics like rationality and freedom and is prone to see the Other as something to be consumed by an all-powerful Same, Levinas brings his philosophical attention to bear on that different level at which humans can be seen as marked by a basic form of passivity. At such a level—which he sometimes links to pre-reflective consciousness or "sensibility" and sometimes refers, in a more religious vein, to an absolutely removed and "an-archical" past—the Other prevails over the Same.[30]

How can this happen? Because in this original moment, Levinas claims, the subject is exposed, before harbouring either knowledge or freedom, and without any rational mediation, to a naked vulnerability which resists assimilation and consumption.[31] Such exposition—which is also an abandonment—makes the subject passive to the powerlessness of the Other and acquiescent to the order that comes from the Other's mute face: "do not kill me."[32] Given that it is just the aspect of vulnerability that obliges and prevents from doing harm, the subject turns out to be *passive to the passivity* of the Other. And since what the Other elicits from the subject is a response to vulnerability, Levinas maintains that the primary mode of subjectivity is responsibility, or the ability to respond. All the more so: since the subject is bound to respond both for the wrongs that the Other suffers and for the wrongs that the Other commits, what we find here is,

Levinas specifies, *responsibility for responsibility*.[33] We shall return to these points.

In view of the fact that he connects passivity to what he calls the ethical—the relation to the Other—and activity to what he calls the ontological—the relation to the world—Levinas maintains that in his perspective ethics, in contrast with its traditional, and even Heideggerian, subordination, is "first philosophy."[34] Though this claim might be disputed, as the search for a solid ethical foundation seems sometimes to fulfill Levinas's ontological need for a univocal meaning of being,[35] such proposed axiology is in fact innovative. Even more innovative is, needless to say, the avowed centrality of passivity against the long-standing obsession with knowledge and power. Why, then, do not these shifts in perspective make room for a rethinking of the status of nonhuman beings—a rethinking that may allow for a different consideration for Bobby?

Of course Bobby is vulnerable and mute, and of course he is devoid of any power over us. Yet, as we have seen, for Levinas he matters only as the *unaware* upholder of respect for humans. This stance is confirmed, on a more general level, by Levinas's view that, though the ethical extends to all living entities, animals remain second-class beings, merely deserving protection against the infliction of wanton suffering, and not covered by the primeval injunction "do not kill me."[36] And while it can be objected that this approach, though revolving around vulnerability, avowedly remains a *humanism*, the objection begs the question, for the problem is just whether an ethical doctrine attributing special worth to humans is defensible.

What are, then, Levinas's grounds for selectively focusing on human beings? Due to the repeated claims that the response to vulnerability "knows nothing about biology,"[37] one can exclude any reference to species membership. The grounds most frequently advanced seem to be variations of traditional appeals. Among them, the claim that animals cannot anticipate the future and are thus deprived of that fear that urges humans to provide for future needs by making tools or building homes; and, with more emphasis, the claim that, lacking language, animals cannot attain universality on the theoretical level and universalization on the ethical level.[38] There is, however, a different argument that is more in tune with Levinas's approach and that gives a particular twist to the traditional appeals as well. It is the idea that "with the appearance of the human there is something more important than one's life, and that is the life of the other."[39]

It is because of this idea that Levinas, implicitly rejecting contemporary evolutionary theory, states that humans are an entirely new phenomenon in relation to animals, and again because of it that he painfully and counter-intuitively maintains that animals lack that "pure" face which would earn them the attention due to the vulnerable.[40] What, then, does he exactly mean? Beyond any rhetoric of style, what he means is simply that humans are more worthy beings because they can act in a way that can be morally evaluated—in other words, because humans are moral agents.

As we have remarked in Foucault's case, such perspective is a quite traditional one—most Western philosophy revolves around the question of the existence conditions of morality, issuing in the development of various theories of the agent. Isn't it surprising, however, to find such a stress on agency in an author who apparently vindicates a theory of patiency, centring on vulnerability and passivity?[41] Arguably, the key to this contradiction has to do with a deep motive in Levinas's approach, revolving around the contrast between nature and "culture." A long-standing preoccupation with French philosophy, this contrast is connected to the disvalue attached to whatever is natural and to the idea that "man's" worth is proportionate to the degree of his *release* (*arrachement*) from nature's bonds.[42] Against this background, in which ethical freedom has long been seen as the quintessential form of *release*, Levinas not surprisingly sees humans as the bearers of an ethics that is "against-nature, against the naturality of nature," and animals as instead entrapped in pure being—a being which is "a struggle for life without ethics."[43]

But apart from the fact that such a view rests on the shaky ground of the empirically false assumption that *all and only* humans have a degree of freedom, this is merely an explanation of, not a justification for, Levinas's views. For the fact remains that Levinas's normative conclusions can be reached only thanks to his unquestioned reliance on the postulate that only moral agency entitles to full moral patiency. Such a perfectionist postulate, however—apart from having dangerous implications for human equality, as we shall see more closely while discussing Derrida—has been seriously undermined by the recent charge of failing to distinguish between the *what* and the *how* of ethics, that is, between the goal that is to be achieved by ethics and the way in which that goal is to be achieved.[44]

In view of all this, one can plausibly infer that what re-emerges as the *main character* on Levinas's stage is just that Same that he has so strongly challenged. The Same—that is, just that consciousness that knowledge and freedom allow to subjugate the Other. The Same—that is, just that rational, linguistic being who allegedly should come much later—both chronologically and axiologically—than the passive subject open to the Other.

A confirmation of this inference comes from a closer inspection of the two points we temporarily set aside—the idea of passivity to passivity and the notion of responsibility for responsibility. For, on the one hand, the idea of "passivity to passivity" epitomizes in the most effective way the fact that Levinas does not place passivity only on the side of the patient but also on the side of the subject encountering the Other—that is, of the agent. And, on the other hand, since in order to be responsible it is necessary to be morally answerable, the notion of "responsibility for responsibility" makes it clear that Levinas does not place activity merely on the side of the agent but also on the side of the encountered Other—that is, of the patient.

Taken together, these points cannot but mean that the passivity Levinas has in mind is *temporary and reversible* and *interchangeable with activity*—that it is, in other words, only the obvious vulnerable side of the moral agent. Thus, when all the dust is settled, what remains is only a further avatar of the traditional theory of the agent.[45] On the face of this, one is at a loss to see how the theoretical ambiguity which licenses Levinas's attempt to exclude nonhumans as mere moral patients from the category of the Other does not cause the collapse of his whole enterprise of putting passivity at the centre of his doctrine.

DECONSTRUCTION OR RESTORATION?

If Foucault appears to be, all considered, more conservative than his source of inspiration, and Levinas remains rooted, despite claims to the contrary, in the metaphysical tradition of human superiority, it might seem that a different situation holds in the case of Jacques Derrida's relationship with his intellectual background. Heidegger's thought has been a reference point for most French philosophy in the last fifty years, and Jacques Derrida is no exception. But, though acknowledging his debt to the German philosopher, Derrida—unlike Levinas—often declared that he disagreed with him on the question of "animality," charging him with humanistic bias.[46]

Derrida's interest in animals goes back to the 1970s, just when a revolution in thought about nonhumans was spreading in English-speaking countries. Initially, such interest was sporadic and confined to a few scattered words on the obscurantism of the traditional metaphysical discourse on animality.[47] Starting from the end of the following decade, however, Derrida launches a series of attacks on Heidegger, criticizing the dogmatism and the authoritarian rhetoric he shows when dealing with nonhumans.[48] Finally, the criticisms give way to a more creative phase, in which Derrida directly engages in a deconstructive approach to the nonhuman question.

It is to this latest phase that we owe his most radical claims, apparently challenging the foundations of all animal exploitation. While recasting the question of the subject after deconstruction, Derrida detects in the traditional notion of subjectivity a sacrificial schema implying the possibility of a "non-criminal putting to death" of animals.[49] Furthermore, after emphasizing the unprecedented proportions of the contemporary subjection of nonhumans, he goes as far as to suggest an analogy between our industrialized and systematized use of animals in factory farming, biomedical research, and much else and "the worst cases of genocide."[50]

In the face of this, it would seem natural to infer that Derrida may finally take the anti-humanist stance to its logical consequences, and may introduce into continental philosophy, though with different theoretical tools, a position similar to those defended by many analytic moral philosophers. But, as the remarks presented in the opening paragraph show, this is not so. In the very context in which he criticizes the sacrificial schema of what he calls "the carno-phallogocentric structure," Derrida does not hesitate to dismiss philosophical vegetarianism, thus erasing at one stroke the entire problem of the value of animal life.[51] His postulate is that, when we introject corpses, the operation is symbolic in the case of humans, and both real and symbolic in the case of animals. From this, he draws two inferences. On the one hand, owing to the difficulty of actually delimiting the symbolic, the task of determining our responsibility is too "enormous" to be undertaken. On the other, due to the presence of the symbolic aspect, vegetarians merely practise a different mode of denegation—they too "partake of animals, even of men [sic]." Thus, Derrida's conclusion is that it is not enough to forbid oneself to eat meat in order to become non-carnivore, and that "the moral question is ... not, nor has it ever been" whether one should or should not eat animals.[52]

Even though in Derrida's style of philosophy, as has been noticed, logic tends to lose its traditional supremacy on rhetoric,[53] this apparent lack of consistency is disappointing. How can one speak of animal slaughter in terms of *genocide*, and at the same time put the actual killing of animals on the same plane with the symbolic consumption of humans? But Derrida's stance is even more disappointing in light of his more general perspective. For on the one hand, after claiming that the metaphysical premises of Western discourses are characterized by binary oppositions based on implicit hierarchies, he has identified in deconstruction a practise that, by disclosing such hierarchies and calling into question their elements, causes the implosion of the discourses.[54] And on the other, while illustrating deconstruction's engagement in the demand for justice, he has included the human-animal boundary among the binary oppositions that, being constructed, can therefore be deconstructed.[55] Why, then, such a conservatism in his conclusions? Why is it that, for Derrida, despite any first impression, nonhuman beings clearly keep counting for less than human beings?

The answer lies, I think, in an implicit argument which can be articulated as follows. On the one hand, stating that it would be "asinine" (in French, *bête*, the adjective which condenses, as has been stressed, idiocy and animality into one crassly anthropocentric expression) to think otherwise, Derrida repeatedly speaks of an *abyssal rupture* between humans and animals, including our closest relatives, the nonhuman great apes.[56] This can be seen as the first premise—all nonhumans, while more intelligent than authors like Descartes or Lacan might think,[57] are less cognitively endowed than all human beings. On the other hand, like Levinas, Derrida, though taking into consideration what he calls "passivity" or "inability," clearly sticks to the priority of agency, giving central ethical stage to *responsibility*—that is, to a feature requiring specific cognitive skills.[58] This is the second premise—cognitive endowment is decisive for moral status. Finally, whenever concretely tackling normative questions regarding animals, Derrida merely demands the elimination of *excessive* suffering, but not of exploitation and killing, openly avowing compassion, that is, a lesser form of moral consideration.[59] This is the foreseeable conclusion of the unexpressed argument—nonhuman animals, while counting directly, have vastly inferior moral status with respect to human beings.

Read as such, Derrida's position, far from being innovative, reflects a quite common stance. In fact, Derrida seems to differ from Kant only in defending direct, rather than indirect, duties of benevolence to nonhumans, and is quite close to Levinas, according to whom we certainly "do not want to make an animal suffer needlessly."[60] I shall not deal here with the factual question of the abyssal rupture—whose defence is certainly more consonant with religious than with post-Darwinian thought—in order to focus on the ethical question of the alleged relevance of cognitive endowment for moral status. Derrida has to confront here the question we briefly hinted at with reference to Levinas, that is, the problem of the position with respect to normative equality of those non-paradigmatic humans who aren't normally cognitively endowed—the severely intellectually disabled, the brain-damaged, the senile.

When employed by philosophical critics of the doctrine of human superiority, such problem is referred to as the argument from marginal cases.[61] In its general form, the argument stresses the inconsistency of any position that defends a perfectionist view according to which cognitive endowment is morally relevant when dealing with nonhumans, and abandons such a view when it comes to humans at the same, or at a lower, cognitive level. Though the overall position could be made consistent both by the inclusion of some nonhumans in the privileged sphere, and by the exclusion of some humans from such a sphere, the fact that the argument is usually addressed to egalitarian authors rules out the exclusive stance, making moral extensionism hardly avoidable. This seems to be the case with Derrida. How, then, can he stick to the perfectionism that allows him to grant nonhumans inferior status without at the same time jeopardizing the status of non-paradigmatic humans?

In continental philosophy, where the naturalistic constraint that science sets the limits of ontology is easily disregarded, most authors defend the view that all humans can be equally included in the privileged moral category because they remain ontologically equal whatever their empirical differences. Derrida, however, cannot even attempt such escape route—due to his attacks on metaphysical humanism, he cannot try to shift from the notion of (cognitively endowed) responsible agent to the notion of human being through the idea of a persisting, essential human nature. Is there any other path he can follow to prevent his intellectual bias from implying that non-paradigmatic humans do not deserve the same consideration as normal humans?

While discussing the *Great Ape Project*'s proposal, Derrida does briefly touch on the argument from marginal cases.[62] However, misled by his perfectionist inclinations, he misunderstands it. Not being able to conceive of an egalitarian hypothesis represented by an extended moral community including *both* marginal humans *and* some animals, he almost instinctively opts for the hierarchical and dilemmatic interpretation according to which the admission of some nonhuman beings is obtained at the price of the exclusion of marginal humans. His conclusion is that the argument has dangerous implications and is characterized by "geneticist" and "racial" attitudes.[63]

Does all this enable Derrida to escape from the cogency of the argument? Apparently not. For his somewhat implicit line of reasoning is circular. To say that the argument is dangerous because it (allegedly) imperils the status of some humans, without even considering the possible advantages for some nonhumans, is question begging—if what is in question is the assessment of the value of certain beings on a mentalistic basis, one cannot introduce a preliminary assessment of value based on species membership. But circularity is not the only problem with Derrida's rejoinder.

As we have seen, the "dangerousness" of the argument is partly explained by reference to geneticism and racialism. The introduction of such notions—parts of a chain also including biologism and "continuism," or the "naïve misapprehension of [the] abyssal rupture" between humans and nonhumans[64]—points to a perspective which can be traced back to the Heideggerian idea that, since the end of traditional philosophy is linked to the triumph of science, philosophy's new vocation can have nothing to do with naturalism. It is within this perspective, where the aversion to "scientism"—the attempt to extend the scientific approach to other disciplines—easily turns into the view that whatever has a scientific ring to it is to be regarded suspiciously in philosophy, that Derrida's charges to the "Darwinian" proposal of the *Great Ape Project* must be placed.[65] Due to his revulsion for any possible lapse of philosophical discourse into the scientific realm Derrida fails to grasp the distinction between: (a) a descriptive recourse to science in relevant empirical matters, such as the possession by some beings of specific cognitive characteristics that are usually seen as morally relevant; and (b) the normative use of biological categories, such as the direct introduction of membership in a genetic group as a morally relevant characteristic. It is not surprising, then, that he ends up equating a morally progressive demand with forms of biologistic discrimination.

Rather surprising is, instead, another facet of Derrida's reasoning. For, in light of the fact that his rejection of racism makes clear his acceptance of the idea that membership in a particular biological group is not in itself morally relevant, one wonders how Derrida might obstinately defend a moral barrier between humans and nonhumans with analogous cognitive endowment.[66] Does this not amount to a blatant instance of biologism—more specifically, of biologistic discrimination based, rather than on race membership, on species membership? If so, the presence of such an obvious contradiction is difficult to understand even in a perspective where the requirement of consistency tends to yield its supremacy. Difficult, at least, unless one harbours the suspicion that what is obscurely at work here is the traditional idea that animals, in contrast with humans, are "mere beings of nature," with the consequence that the much despised naturalistic approach is not entirely out of place in their case.

Arguably, all this goes a long way towards explaining why deconstructionism may be "a political weapon against racism,"[67] but certainly is not a political weapon against *speciesism*. Nonetheless, this is not the whole story. Though it can be claimed that at the basis of Derrida's unsatisfying position regarding the animal issue there is a mixture of concealed perfectionism, undeclared pro-human bias and confused rejection of naturalism, something more deserves to be considered.

A CONCLUSION ABOUT ETHICS

In the period when the anti-humanist wave was swelling, a phenomenon was spreading in Western countries that quintessentially embodied the form of domination through control and manipulation which anti-humanist doctrines impute to modern science. The rise of factory farming marked a new turn in our power relationships with animals, both because of the dreadful mechanized procedures it introduced and because of the number of the individuals involved. If, for traditional metaphysical strands in continental philosophy, such a shift could go unnoticed, to authors challenging power's ubiquity, conventional humanism's tendency to reification and traditional hierarchies, it could have offered the opportunity to radically reconsider, well beyond any reference to "needless suffering" or any call for compassion, the moral status of nonhumans. As we have seen, this did not happen, and the negative reception given even to the limited moral extensionism of the *Great Ape Project* is only a further confirmation of such general inability to deduce all the consequences of a general stance. Prominent among the traditional hindrances at work was, as it has been suggested, a selective focus on moral agency—a focus made possible by the unexamined acceptance of two ideas: the agent-patient parity principle, according to which the class of (full) moral patients coincides with the class of moral agents; and the humanistic assumption according to which all and only members of the species *Homo sapiens* are moral agents.

Of the three exemplary positions we have considered, Foucault's view is the one whose faults are most visible and, in a sense, least convoluted. As we have seen, in Foucault's treatment of the Other—for him, firstly and avowedly, the mad[68]—the perfectionist inclination which his latest production brings fully into light has simply the effect of effacing the problem of nonhuman animals. As a result, his perspective, however flawed, does not need convoluted distinctions and inconsistent applications of arguments. As is paradigmatically shown by his famous description of Velazquez's painting *Las meninas*, where the presence of a nonhuman subject in the scene is simply erased,[69] Foucault's anti-humanism fails for blatant blindness.

The picture becomes more complex when it comes to Levinas and Derrida, who, apart from the centrality of moral agency, share a further aspect they inherited from mainstream continental philosophy. I am referring to their view of ethics. For neither author sees ethics as an autonomous field of inquiry, endowed with internal standards of justification and critique. Rather, both still regard ethics as closely intertwined with general explanations of the universe and as dependent on specific conceptions of being. It might be said that such an approach, which is heir to the religious aspiration to integrated interpretations of things already embodying normative aspects, is better represented by those metaphysical doctrines to which anti-humanism objects. The problem, however, affects post-modern authors as well.

As far as Levinas in concerned, I have already suggested how his persisting search for a univocal sense of being points to a prevalence of ontology over ethics. One can now add that in Levinas's entire work one can see the production of a system *within which only* his specific construal of the ethical relation with the Other can make sense. For what can his stress on the "an-archy" of the call from the Other mean when extrapolated from his view of the relation between time and activity?[70] And what particular ethical meaning can one grant, for example, to the difference Levinas draws between the *Said*—a statement whose truth or falsity can be ascertained—and the *Saying*—the performative position of oneself facing the Other—outside his particular framework?[71] All in all it seems that, once again, Levinas does not leave the traditional onto-theological landscape he criticizes.

The situation is analogous if we turn to Derrida's thinking. Derrida attacks the metaphysics of subjectivity and, following Heidegger, criticizes all Western metaphysical tradition[72]—but this merely to offer, again following Heidegger, a "philosophy of the originary" that makes sense of the universe in an even deeper and more comprehensive way.[73] Since it is to this global view that Derrida's ethical stances are connected, they tend to stand or fall together with it. If, instead of sticking to the idiosyncratic substantive notion of subject that can be charged with an inherent will to master and sacrifice,[74] one gives prominence to the formal notion of agent, construed as a rational intentional being that logically identifies in mere intentionality the relevant similarity between itself and its recipients, the ethical centrality of deconstruction loses much of its force. And if one does not think that hierarchical dichotomies are the central problem in ethics, the replacement of the binary opposition between humans and nonhumans with "multiple and heterogeneous" hierarchical borders[75] does not turn out to be a main theoretical achievement. Even more to the point, for those who do not share Derrida's anti-scientific stance, there is no reason to opt for an ethics that discounts the rational application of general criteria with respect to "the ordeal of the undecidable."[76]

Ethical theories of the kind just described have obvious difficulties in overcoming ingrained perspectives such as the view that nonhuman animals are inferior beings with respect to human animals—indeed, they cannot even make room for the notion of "nonhuman animals." On the other hand, it can plausibly be claimed that they also have difficulties in producing a *universally acceptable*, though minimal, ethical doctrine that might protect the least among us. Luckily, we already have such a doctrine—contemporary human rights theory—which is the most refined product of that analytic style in ethics that has actually, and for quite some time, given up any metaphysical commitment. The doctrine's simple reliance on the idea that the basic interests—to life, freedom and well-being—of individuals, whatever their group membership and whatever their cognitive level, have a direct normative force imposing an equal prima facie duty of noninterference; its independence from any preconceived and undemonstrable philosophical world view; and, finally, its focus, through the notion, not of ontologically loaded "natural rights" but of moral rights carrying legal overtones, on the beings who suffer the injury, are the result of a long work in rational, argumentative ethics. And, not incidentally, it is just the logic of this doctrine that entails now the rejection of speciesism together with racism and sexism, and which, thanks to the abandonment of the traditional intellectual bias, points to the inclusion of many nonhuman animals into the privileged moral category till now confined to human beings.[77] If seen in this light, French anti-humanism's inability to produce any radical result on the animal question is only one among the shortcomings of an unsatisfactory approach to ethics.[78]

NOTES

1. Paola Cavalieri and Peter Singer, eds., *The Great Ape Project. Equality beyond Humanity* (London: Fourth Estate, 1993). The American edition was published in 1994 (St. Martin's Press), and the French edition, *Le Projet Grands Singes*, in 2003 (One Voice).
2. Jacques Derrida and Elisabeth Roudinesco, *De quoi demain... Dialogue* (Paris: Fayard/Galilée, 2001), 108.
3. Jacques Derrida, *Of Spirit: Heidegger and the Question*, trans. Geoffrey Bennington and Rachel Bowlby (Chicago: University of Chicago Press, 1989), chap. 2.
4. A notable exception is represented by the journal of theoretical politics *Le débat*, which devoted a dossier to the issue. See Paola Cavalieri, Luc Ferry, Marie-Angèle Hermitte, and Joëlle Proust, "Droits de l'homme, droits du singe, droits de l'animal," *Le débat* 108(2000): 155–92; and Paola Cavalieri and Élisabeth de Fontenay, "Droits de l'homme, droits du singe, droits de l'animal (suite)," *Le débat* 109 (2000): 137–60.
5. For the statement on man's death, see Michel Foucault, *The Order of Things: An Archaeology of the Human Sciences* (New York: Vintage Books, 1994), part 2, chap. 9, sec. 8. For the reference to Nietzsche, see the Foucault interview "Le retour de la morale," *Les Nouvelles Littéraires* (June 28–July 5, 1984): 36–41.
6. See Jürgen Habermas, *The Philosophical Discourse of Modernity: Twelve Lectures*, trans. Frederick Lawrence (Cambridge, MA: MIT Press, 1987), chap. 5, sec. 4.
7. Michel Foucault, *Truth and Power*, in Colin Gordon, ed., *Power/Knowledge: Selected Interviews and Other Writings 1972–1977* (New York: Pantheon Books, 1980), 81–83. Brian Hindess, in *Discourses of Power: From Hobbes to Foucault* (Oxford: Blackwell, 1996), 155–56, aptly stresses Foucault's inconsistency in criticizing the "utopian" critique of power while at the same time often condemning domination in the name of liberty.
8. See Hindess, *Discourses of Power*, 151.
9. Clare Palmer, "'Taming the Wild Profusion of Existing Things'? A Study of Foucault, Power and Human/Animal Relationships," *Environmental Ethics* 23, no. 4 (2001): 339–58.
10. Friedrich Nietzsche, *Daybreak*, trans. R.J. Hollingdale (Cambridge: Cambridge University Press, 1997), aphorism 215. Incidentally, this points to a question I shall not deal with here because of space constraints, that is, to the application to nonhumans of the notion of "virtuous agent." A virtuous agent is a being whose conduct can be guided, if not by general rational principles,

by an immediate perception of the interests of others, by empathy with those who suffer, by courageous impulses.

11 See for example, Friedrich Nietzsche, *On the Genealogy of Morals*, trans. Walter Kaufmann (New York: Vintage, 1969), chap. 2, sec. 2-6, or Nietzsche, *The Gay Science*, trans. Walter Kaufmann (New York: Vintage, 1974), aphorism 352.

12 Jean-Paul Sartre, *Existentialism and Humanism*, trans. Philip Mairet (London: Methuen, 1973), 26-27.

13 Michel Foucault, *Histoire de la folie à l'âge classique* (Paris: Plon, 1961), part 1, chap. 2.

14 Ibid., part 3, chap. 4.

15 See, for example, Michel Foucault, "Right of Death and Power Over Life," in Paul Rabinow, ed., *The Foucault Reader* (New York: Pantheon, 1984). For a discussion, see Hindess, *Discourses of Power*, 143ff.

16 Michel Foucault, "L'éthique du souci de soi comme pratique de la liberté," in *Dits et Écrits: 1954-1988*, vol. 4 (Paris: Editions Gallimard, 1994), 728. On this point see the analysis by Clare Palmer in her "'Taming the Wild Profusion of Existing Things'?"

17 Michel Foucault, "The Subject and Power," in Hubert Dreyfus and Paul Rabinow, eds., *Michel Foucault: Beyond Structuralism and Hermeneutics* (Chicago: University of Chicago Press, 1982), 217. Actually, this dichotomic framework was already detectable in earlier works. See, for example, Foucault, *The Order of Things*, part 2, chap. 9, sec. 6.

18 Suffice it here to think of the frequent metaphorical use of the notion of "vivisection," as for example in aphorisms 198, 218 or 244 of Friedrich Nietzsche, *Beyond Good and Evil*, trans. Walter Kaufmann (New York: Vintage Books, 1989). On Nietzsche's unquestioning view of animals, see Monika Langer, "The Role and Status of Animals in Nietzsche's Philosophy," in H. Peter Steeves, ed., *Animal Others: Ethics, Ontology, and Animal Life* (New York: SUNY Press, 1999).

19 See Carol Adams, *The Sexual Politics of Meat: A Feminist-Vegetarian Critical Theory* (New York: Continuum, 1991), part 1.

20 See for example in Foucault, *Histoire de la folie*, part 1, chap. 5, the description of how the "model of animality" shapes the asylums till the end of the Eighteenth century causing the use of cages and chains; or ibid., part 3, chap. 5, the reference to the dawning idea of the "bestiality" of those who treated the mad as "beasts."

21 For an attempt to utilize Foucault's critical tools to uncover a genealogy of "animality," see Palmer, "'Taming the Wild Profusion of Existing Things'?" 339-58.

22 Foucault, "The Subject and Power," 208.

23 Curiously, nonhumans sometimes appear without appearing in such new context as well—for instance, when "human" sexuality is compared to "animal"

sexuality by specific historical sources. See, for example, Michel Foucault, *The History of Sexuality*, vol. 3, *The Care of the Self*, trans. Robert Hurley (New York: Pantheon, 1986), part 6, chaps. 1 and 2.

24 Michel Foucault, "On the Genealogy of Ethics: An Overview of Work in Progress," in Dreyfus and Rabinow, eds., *Michel Foucault: Beyond Structuralism and Hermeneutics*, 232–37.

25 Foucault, *Histoire de la folie à l'âge classique*, final words of chap. 4. It might be noted in passing that Antonin Artaud has been the quintessential focus of the French discussion of intellectual madness; see on this, Jacques Derrida, "La parole soufflé," in *Writing and Difference*, trans. Alan Bass (Chicago: University of Chicago Press, 1978).

26 This is the term Foucault ended up employing to collectively denominate the objects of his main concern—the psychologically, legally and sexually deviant. See Michel Foucault, *Abnormal: Lectures at the Collège de France 1974–1975* (London: Verso, 2003).

27 Emmanuel Levinas, "The Name of a Dog, or Natural Rights," in *Difficult Freedom: Essays on Judaism*, trans. Seán Hand (Baltimore: Johns Hopkins University Press, 1990), 151–53.

28 Ibid., 153.

29 See, for example, Emmanuel Levinas, "Humanism and An-archy" and "No Identity," in *Collected Philosophical Papers*, trans. A. Lingis (The Hague: Martinus Nijhoff, 1987). With reference to the first essay, in his interesting article "Levinas's Skeptical Critique of Metaphysics and Anti-Humanism," *Philosophy Today* 41, no. 4 (1997), Peter Atterton clearly speaks of Levinas's problem of "providing an ethical justification for anti-humanist critique" (498).

30 On sensibility see in particular Emmanuel Levinas, *Totality and Infinity: An Essay on Exteriority*, trans. Alphonso Lingis (Pittsburgh: Duquesne University Press, 1969), II: B: 4. For a synthesis of the argument see, for example, Emmanuel Levinas, "Transcendence and Height," in R. Bernasconi, S. Critchley, and A. Peperzak, eds., *Emmanuel Levinas: Basic Philosophical Writings* (Bloomington: Indiana University Press, 1996), 11–31.

31 See Levinas, *Totality and Infinity*, III: B: 1.

32 See ibid., III: B: 1, 2.

33 See Emmanuel Levinas, *Otherwise Than Being or Beyond Essence*, trans. Alphonso Lingis (The Hague: Martinus Nijhoff, 1981), IV: 4; see also IV: 3 and III: 6: b.

34 See among others, Emmanuel Levinas, "Ethics as First Philosophy," trans. Seán Hand and Michael Temple, in Seán Hand, ed., *The Levinas Reader* (Oxford: Blackwell, 1989).

35 Emmanuel Levinas, "Meaning and Sense," in Bernasconi, Critchley, and Peperzak, eds., *Emmanuel Levinas: Basic Philosophical Writings*, sec. 5.

36 Emmanuel Levinas, "The Paradox of Morality," trans. Andrew Benjamin and Tamra Wright, in Robert Bernasconi and David Wood, eds., *The Provocation*

of Levinas: Rethinking the Other (London: Routledge, 1988), 169–72. On the view that the extermination of living beings has to do with work and with needs, while murder concerns only the human Other, see, for example, Levinas, *Totality and Infinity*, III: A: 2.

37 See Levinas, *Otherwise Than Being or Beyond Essence*, III: 6: C.

38 See, for example, Emmanuel Levinas, "Language and Proximity," in *Collected Philosophical Writings*, trans. Alphonso Lingis (The Hague: Martinus Nijhoff, 1987), 122; Levinas, *Totality and Infinity*, II: D. Another conservative feature of Levinas's references to nonhumans is, as Carrie Rohman noticed, their tendency to sustain the privileging of human consciousness "by abjecting the animal"; see C. Rohman, "Reading the Face: Ethics and the Species Barrier in Levinas and Derrida," paper presented at the Society for the Study of Ethics & Animals in January 2003. Levinas's conservatism, however, does not appear only with regard to animals—see, for example, the connection he establishes between the "home" and the feminine, and his selective focus on "paternity" when discussing fecundity. See Levinas, *Totality and Infinity*, II: D: 2; IV: C–F.

39 Levinas, "The Paradox of Morality," 172.

40 Ibid., 169.

41 Actually, Levinas goes so far as to suggest that his approach overcomes the strictures of reciprocity: see his "Meaning and Sense" in Bernasconi, Critchley and Peperzak, eds., *Emmanuel Levinas: Basic Philosophical Writings*, sec. 6; some critics credit him with this achievement: see Zygmunt Bauman, *Postmodern Ethics* (Oxford: Blackwell, 1993), 220.

42 For a recent instance see, for example, Luc Ferry, *The New Ecological Order*, trans. Carol Volk (Chicago: University of Chicago Press, 1995), 32, 36.

43 See Emmanuel Levinas, *Of God Who Comes to Mind*, trans. Bettina Bergo (Stanford: Stanford University Press, 1998), part 3, "Notes on Meaning," sec. 8; and Levinas, "The Paradox of Morality," 172. Of course, for Levinas, who claims that pure passivity precedes freedom within the ethical, freedom is to be construed not as freedom of choice, but as the possibility to overcome the "biological" constraints. But on this, see Atterton, "Levinas's Skeptical Critique." By the way, it is worth noticing that it is especially repugnant to appeal to the capacity to take other beings' interests into consideration in order to exclude some beings' interests from consideration.

44 The distinction is quite common now in analytic moral philosophy, and can be probably traced back to Geoffrey J. Warnock, *The Object of Morality* (London: Methuen, 1971).

45 For an analysis of the weight of the Kantian legacy in Levinas's perspective see John Llewelyn, "Am I Obsessed by Bobby?" in Robert Bernasconi and Simon Critchley, eds., *Re-Reading Levinas* (Bloomington: Indiana University Press, 1991), 234–46.

46 See for instance the critique advanced in Jacques Derrida, "*Geschlecht* II: Heidegger's Hand," trans. John P. Leavey, in John Sallis, ed., *Deconstruction and Philosophy* (Chicago: University of Chicago Press, 1987), 173ff.
47 See Jacques Derrida, *Glas*, trans. John P. Leavey Jr. and Richard Rand (Lincoln: University of Nebraska Press, 1986), 37; and Jacques Derrida, *The Post Card: From Socrates to Freud and Beyond*, trans. Alan Bass (Chicago: University of Chicago Press, 1987), part 3, n. 20.
48 See for example Derrida, *Of Spirit*, chap. 2.
49 Jacques Derrida (with Jean-Luc Nancy), "'Eating Well,' or the Calculation of the Subject: An Interview with Jacques Derrida," in Eduardo Cadava, Peter Connor, and Jean-Luc Nancy, eds., *Who Comes After the Subject* (New York: Routledge, 1991), 112.
50 Jacques Derrida, "The Animal that therefore I Am (More to Follow)," trans. David Wills, *Critical Inquiry* 28, no. 2 (2002): 394-95.
51 Derrida (with Jean-Luc Nancy), "'Eating Well,'" 113.
52 Ibid., 115. See also Derrida and Roudinesco, *De quoi demain*, 113-114. Were not the question at issue so tragic, such claims could, as Christian Vandendorpe suggests, evoke the "amused smile" often stirred by Derrida's recourse to rhetorical figures as the oxymoron and the paradox. See Christian Vandendorpe, "Rhétorique de Derrida," *Littératures* 19 (Winter 1999): 169-93. On Derrida's conclusion on vegetarianism, see also David Wood, "*Comment ne pas manger*—Deconstruction and Vegetarianism," in Steeves, ed., *Animal Others*, and the reply from Matthew Calarco in "Deconstruction Is Not Vegetarianism: Humanism, Subjectivity, and Animal Ethics," *Continental Philosophy Review* 37 (2004): 175-201.
53 See Habermas, *The Philosophical Discourse of Modernity*, chap. 7, Excursus, sec. 1. Derrida himself speaks of "another consistency" which is no longer logico-metaphysical; see the quotation in Luc Ferry and Alain Renaut, *French Philosophy of the Sixties: An Essay on Antihumanism*, trans. Mary H.S. Cattani (Amherst: University of Massachusetts Press, 1990), chap. 1, sec. 3, point 1.
54 For a synthesis, see Jacques Derrida, "Positions," in *Positions*, trans. Alan Bass (London: Athlone Press, 1981).
55 Jacques Derrida, "Force of Law: The 'Mystical Foundation of Authority,'" trans. Mary Quaintance, in Drucilla Cornell, Michael Rosenfeld, and David Gray Carlson, eds., *Deconstruction and the Possibility of Justice* (London: Routledge 1992), 19.
56 For the comment on the use of "asinine," see David L. Clark, "On Being 'the Last Kantian in Nazi Germany': Dwelling with Animals after Levinas," in Jennifer Ham and Matthew Senior, eds., *Animal Acts: Configuring the Human in Western History* (New York: Routledge, 1997), 188. For the abyssal rupture see, for example, Derrida, "The Animal that therefore I Am," 398-99; Derrida and Roudinesco, *De quoi demain*, 12, 121.

57 See, for example, Jacques Derrida, "And Say the Animal Responded?" trans. David Wills, in Cary Wolfe, ed., *Zoontologies: The Question of the Animal* (Minneapolis: University of Minnesota Press, 2003).
58 For passivity, see Derrida, "The Animal that therefore I Am," 396. For responsibility, see, for example, Derrida (with Jean-Luc Nancy), "'Eating Well,'" 112-113, 117; see also Derrida and Roudinesco, *De quoi demain*, 18.
59 See Derrida, "The Animal that therefore I Am," 395.
60 Levinas, "The Paradox of Morality," 172.
61 For a comprehensive survey, see Daniel A. Dombrowski, *Babies and Beasts: The Argument from Marginal Cases* (Chicago: University of Illinois Press, 1997).
62 Derrida and Roudinesco, *De quoi demain*, 113-114.
63 Ibid., 114.
64 Derrida, "The Animal that therefore I Am," 398. In *Of Spirit*, chap. 2, Derrida goes so far as to praise Heidegger's approach to nonhumans since it avoids anthropocentrism while at the same time doing away with the "difference in degree."
65 Actually, the idea is Roudinesco's, but Derrida does not object. See Derrida and Roudinesco, *De quoi demain*, 105.
66 "Et bien sure ... je juge aussi ridicule que détestable la nouvelle hiérarchie qui placerait tels ou tels animaux au-dessus [sic] des handicapés humains." Ibid., 113.
67 See the report of a conference held by Derrida at the University of York in May 2002 in Will Shaw, "Deconstruction Is a Political Weapon," *York Vision* 139 (18 June 2002): 10.
68 See Foucault, *The Order of Things*, preface.
69 The powerful dog sitting on the right is excluded from the number of the painted figures and merely described as a bulky mass. See Foucault, *The Order of Things*, part 1, chap. 1, sec. 2. Another revealing example is the title—"Du gouvernement des vivants"—that Foucault chose for the description of a course devoted to the techniques and procedures aimed at guiding the conduct of "men." See *Annuaire du Collège de France, Histoire des systèmes de pensée, année 1979-1980* (1980), 449-52.
70 See for example Levinas, *Otherwise Than Being or Beyond Essence*, IV: 1, V: 5.
71 See, for example, ibid., 1: 3, V: 3. The same holds, of course, for all the religious overtones, for the connection between Otherness, Infinity and God, and so on.
72 For a direct engagement with Heidegger's thought on this topic see Derrida, *Of Spirit*, chap. 5, point 3.
73 See on this point Habermas, *The Philosophical Discourse of Modernity*, chap. 7, sec. 4.
74 See, for example, Derrida (with Jean-Luc Nancy), "'Eating Well,'" 114; Derrida, "Force of Law," 18-19; and Derrida and Roudinesco, *De quoi demain*, 110.

75 See Derrida, "The Animal that Therefore I Am," 399. See also Derrida (with Jean-Luc Nancy), "'Eating Well,'" 116.
76 Derrida, "Force of Law," 24.
77 On this, see Paola Cavalieri, *The Animal Question. Why Nonhuman Animals Deserve Human Rights* (New York: Oxford University Press, 2001); and Paola Cavalieri, "The Animal Debate: A Reexamination," in Peter Singer, ed., *In Defense of Animals: The Second Wave* (Oxford: Blackwell, 2005). See also Sue Donaldson and Will Kymlicka, "The Moral Ark," *Queen's Quarterly* 114, no. 2 (Summer 2007): 3–21.
78 I am grateful to Raymond Corbey, Harlan B. Miller, Piercarlo Necchi, Krzysztof Pomian and Franco Salanga for their helpful comments on drafts of this paper.

BIBLIOGRAPHY

Adams, Carol. *The Sexual Politics of Meat: A Feminist-Vegetarian Critical Theory*. New York: Continuum, 1991.
Atterton, Peter. "Levinas's Skeptical Critique of Metaphysics and Anti-Humanism." *Philosophy Today* 41, no. 4 (1997): 491–506.
Bauman, Zygmunt. *Postmodern Ethics*. Oxford: Blackwell, 1993.
Bernasconi, R., S. Critchley, and A. Peperzak, eds. *Emmanuel Levinas: Basic Philosophical Writings*. Bloomington: Indiana University Press, 1996.
Calarco, Matthew. "Deconstruction Is Not Vegetarianism: Humanism, Subjectivity, and Animal Ethics." *Continental Philosophy Review* 37 (2004): 175–201.
Cavalieri, Paola. "The Animal Debate: A Reexamination." In Peter Singer, ed., *In Defense of Animals*, 2nd ed. Oxford: Blackwell, 2005.
———. *The Animal Question. Why Nonhuman Animals Deserve Human Rights*. New York: Oxford University Press, 2001.
Cavalieri, Paola, Luc Ferry, Marie-Angèle Hermitte, and Joëlle Proust. "Droits de l'homme, droits du singe, droits de l'animal." *Le débat* 108 (2000): 155–92.
Cavalieri, Paola, and Élisabeth de Fontenay. "Droits de l'homme, droits du singe, droits de l'animal (suite)." *Le débat* 109 (2000): 137–60.
Cavaileri, Paola, and Peter Singer, eds. *The Great Ape Project: Equality beyond Humanity*. London: Fourth Estate, 1993.
Clark, David. L. "On Being 'the Last Kantian in Nazi Germany': Dwelling with Animals after Levinas." In Jennifer Ham and Matthew Senior, eds., *Animal Acts: Configuring the Human in Western History*. New York: Routledge, 1997.

Derrida, Jacques. "And Say the Animal Responded?" Translated by David Wills. In Cary Wolfe, ed., *Zoontologies: The Question of the Animal*. Minneapolis: University of Minnesota Press, 2003.
———. "The Animal that therefore I Am (More to Follow)." Translated by David Wills. *Critical Inquiry* 28, no. 2 (2002): 394-95.
———. "Force of Law: The 'Mystical Foundation of Authority.'" Translated by Mary Quaintance. In Drucilla Cornell, Michael Rosenfeld, and David Gray Carlson, eds., *Deconstruction and the Possibility of Justice*. London: Routledge, 1992.
———, with Jean-Luc Nancy. "'Eating Well,' or the Calculation of the Subject: An Interview with Jacques Derrida." In Eduardo Cadava, Peter Connor, and Jean-Luc Nancy, eds., *Who Comes After the Subject*. New York: Routledge, 1991.
———. *Of Spirit: Heidegger and the Question*. Translated by Geoffrey Bennington and Rachel Bowlby. Chicago: University of Chicago Press, 1989.
———. *The Post Card: From Socrates to Freud and Beyond*. Translated by Alan Bass. Chicago: University of Chicago Press, 1987.
———. "Geschlecht II: Heidegger's Hand." Translated by John P. Leavey. In John Sallis, ed., *Deconstruction and Philosophy*. Chicago: University of Chicago Press, 1987.
———. *Glas*. Translated by John P. Leavey Jr. and Richard Rand. Lincoln: University of Nebraska Press, 1986.
———. "Positions." In *Positions*. Translated by Alan Bass. London: Athlone Press, 1981.
———. "La parole soufflé." In *Writing and Difference*. Translated by Alan Bass. Chicago: University of Chicago Press, 1978.
Derrida, Jacques, and Elisabeth Roudinesco. *De quoi demain ... Dialogue*. Paris: Fayard/Galilée, 2001.
Dombrowski, Daniel A. *Babies and Beasts: The Argument from Marginal Cases*. Chicago: University of Illinois Press, 1997.
Donaldson, Sue, and Will Kymlicka. "The Moral Ark." *Queen's Quarterly* 114, no. 2 (Summer 2007): 3-21.
Dreyfus, Hubert, and Paul Rabinow, eds. *Michel Foucault: Beyond Structuralism and Hermeneutics*. Chicago: University of Chicago Press, 1982.
Ferry, Luc. *The New Ecological Order*. Translated by Carol Volk. Chicago: University of Chicago Press, 1995.
Ferry, Luc, and Alain Renaut. *French Philosophy of the Sixties: An Essay on Antihumanism*. Translated by Mary H.S. Cattani. Amherst: University of Massachusetts Press, 1990.

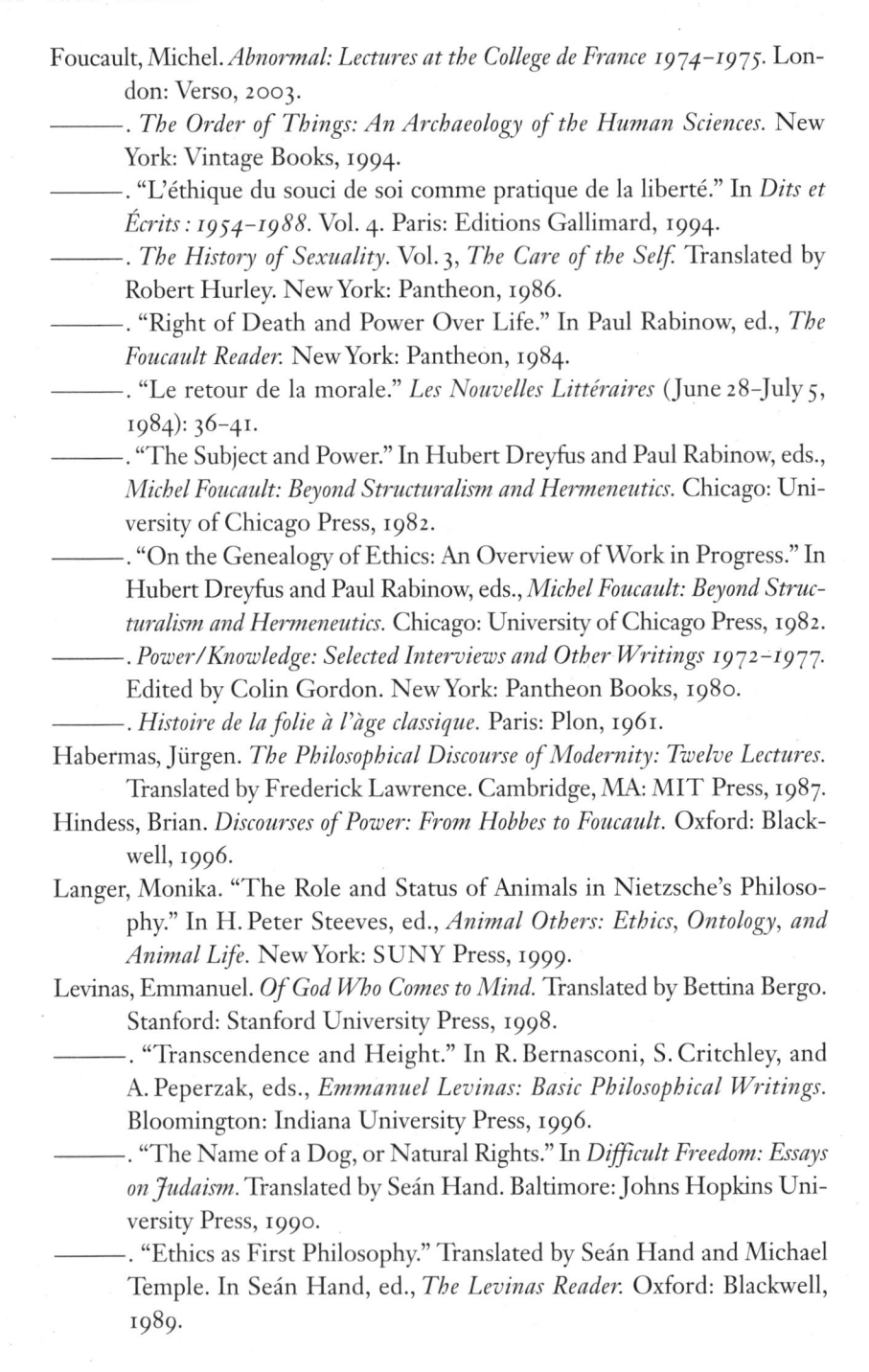

Foucault, Michel. *Abnormal: Lectures at the College de France 1974-1975.* London: Verso, 2003.

———. *The Order of Things: An Archaeology of the Human Sciences.* New York: Vintage Books, 1994.

———. "L'éthique du souci de soi comme pratique de la liberté." In *Dits et Écrits: 1954-1988.* Vol. 4. Paris: Editions Gallimard, 1994.

———. *The History of Sexuality.* Vol. 3, *The Care of the Self.* Translated by Robert Hurley. New York: Pantheon, 1986.

———. "Right of Death and Power Over Life." In Paul Rabinow, ed., *The Foucault Reader.* New York: Pantheon, 1984.

———. "Le retour de la morale." *Les Nouvelles Littéraires* (June 28–July 5, 1984): 36-41.

———. "The Subject and Power." In Hubert Dreyfus and Paul Rabinow, eds., *Michel Foucault: Beyond Structuralism and Hermeneutics.* Chicago: University of Chicago Press, 1982.

———. "On the Genealogy of Ethics: An Overview of Work in Progress." In Hubert Dreyfus and Paul Rabinow, eds., *Michel Foucault: Beyond Structuralism and Hermeneutics.* Chicago: University of Chicago Press, 1982.

———. *Power/Knowledge: Selected Interviews and Other Writings 1972-1977.* Edited by Colin Gordon. New York: Pantheon Books, 1980.

———. *Histoire de la folie à l'âge classique.* Paris: Plon, 1961.

Habermas, Jürgen. *The Philosophical Discourse of Modernity: Twelve Lectures.* Translated by Frederick Lawrence. Cambridge, MA: MIT Press, 1987.

Hindess, Brian. *Discourses of Power: From Hobbes to Foucault.* Oxford: Blackwell, 1996.

Langer, Monika. "The Role and Status of Animals in Nietzsche's Philosophy." In H. Peter Steeves, ed., *Animal Others: Ethics, Ontology, and Animal Life.* New York: SUNY Press, 1999.

Levinas, Emmanuel. *Of God Who Comes to Mind.* Translated by Bettina Bergo. Stanford: Stanford University Press, 1998.

———. "Transcendence and Height." In R. Bernasconi, S. Critchley, and A. Peperzak, eds., *Emmanuel Levinas: Basic Philosophical Writings.* Bloomington: Indiana University Press, 1996.

———. "The Name of a Dog, or Natural Rights." In *Difficult Freedom: Essays on Judaism.* Translated by Seán Hand. Baltimore: Johns Hopkins University Press, 1990.

———. "Ethics as First Philosophy." Translated by Seán Hand and Michael Temple. In Seán Hand, ed., *The Levinas Reader.* Oxford: Blackwell, 1989.

———. "The Paradox of Morality." Translated by Andrew Benjamin and Tamra Wright. In Robert Bernasconi and David Wood, eds., *The Provocation of Levinas: Rethinking the Other*. London: Routledge, 1988.
———. *Collected Philosophical Papers*. Translated by A. Lingis. The Hague: Martinus Nijhoff, 1987.
———. *Otherwise Than Being or Beyond Essence*. Translated by Alphonso Lingis. The Hague: Martinus Nijhoff, 1981.
———. *Totality and Infinity: An Essay on Exteriority*. Translated by Alphonso Lingis. Pittsburgh: Duquesne University Press, 1969.
Llewelyn, John. "Am I Obsessed by Bobby?" In Robert Bernasconi and Simon Critchley, eds., *Re-Reading Levinas*. Bloomington: Indiana University Press, 1991.
Nietzsche, Friedrich. *Daybreak*. Translated by R.J. Hollingdale. Cambridge: Cambridge University Press, 1997.
———. *Beyond Good and Evil*. Translated by Walter Kaufmann. New York: Vintage, 1989.
———. *The Gay Science*. Translated by Walter Kaufmann. New York: Vintage, 1974.
———. *On the Genealogy of Morals*. Translated by Walter Kaufmann. New York: Vintage, 1969.
Palmer, Clare. "'Taming the Wild Profusion of Existing Things'? A Study of Foucault, Power and Human/Animal Relationships." *Environmental Ethics* 23, no. 4 (2001): 339–58.
Sartre, Jean-Paul. *Existentialism and Humanism*. Translated by Philip Mairet. London: Methuen, 1973.
Vandendorpe, Christian. "Rhétorique de Derrida." *Littératures* 19 (Winter 1999): 169–93.
Warnock, Geoffrey J. *The Object of Morality*. London: Methuen, 1971.
Wood, David. "*Comment ne pas manger*—Deconstruction and Vegetarianism." H. Peter Steeves, ed., *Animal Others: Ethics, Ontology, and Animal Life*. New York: SUNY Press, 1999.

6

Thinking Other-Wise
Cognitive Science, Deconstruction and the (Non)Speaking (Non)Human Subject

CARY WOLFE

I want to begin with a story—a dog story, in fact.

It's a story about a recent experiment on a canine's signifying abilities that appeared on 11 June 2004 in my hometown newspaper, *The Houston Chronicle*, which was a reprint of an article that appeared that same day in *The Washington Post*, which in turn was courtesy of the Associated Press, which in turn was about the lead article in the magazine *Science* for the 11 June 2004 issue. The *Post* story carried the title "Common Collie or Überpooch: German Pet's Vocabulary Stuns Scientists." But I prefer my hometown headline, "Dogs May Be as Smart as Owners Think They Are,"[1] because it unwittingly directs us towards a question that I will insist is essential to addressing these kinds of issues, one that definitively separates how cognitive science (represented here by Daniel Dennett) and deconstruction (in the person, here, of Jacques Derrida) understand what language is and how it is related to the question of subjectivity—both of which depend upon very different assumptions about what *knowledge* is and the kinds of knowledge we can have of ourselves and of others—in this case (the hardest case, perhaps) nonhuman others (represented here by the taxonomy *canis familiaris*).

It is tempting to call that question that divides cognitive science and deconstruction simply "Theory," but in the current, supposedly "post-theoretical" climate that would only invite a reified understanding (which would also be a "strategy of containment," to use Fredric Jameson's well-known phrase) of "Theory" as a specialized set of epistemological obsessions carried out in a second-order, cosmetic operation, after the real work of cultural studies and historicism (whether new or old) and the sociology of knowledge is over with, and we have nothing better to do than sit around and ask, what do we *really* mean when we say "dog"? So let me be more specific: the issue that separates cognitive science and deconstruction is, as we shall see, one that goes all the way down, both epistemologically and ethically: whether or not knowledge—including knowledge of our own subjectivity and that of others—is *representational* (Dennett) and, within that, how we are to construe the relationship between epistemological and ontological questions.

This might sound at first blush like an overly complicated way of marking the difference between what is traditionally called "realism" (associated, so the story would go, with cognitive science) and "idealism" (with deconstruction), but as Richard Rorty has pointed out with characteristic economy and clarity, "the representationalism-vs.-antirepresentationalism issue is distinct from the realism-vs.-antirealism one, because the latter issue arises only for representationalists.... For representationalists," Rorty continues, "'making true' and 'representing' are reciprocal relations: the nonlinguistic item which makes S true is the one represented by S. But antirepresentationalists see both notions as equally unfortunate and dispensable."[2] He concludes,

> Antirepresentationalists need to insist "determinacy" is not what is in question—that neither does thought determine reality nor, in the sense intended by the realist, does reality determine thought. More precisely, it is no truer that "atoms" are what they are because we use "atom" as we do than that we use "atom" as we do because atoms are as they are. *Both* of these claims, the antirepresentationalist says, are entirely empty.[3]

Part of what I will be trying to bring out in what follows is that this apparently purely epistemological quibble is far from purely epistemological; indeed, I want to suggest that understanding its full implications is crucial to our ability to think about nonhuman subjects in a rigorous and clear-headed way—a contention whose irony will emerge here in due course, I trust, because cognitive science typically reserves for itself the mantel, precisely, of rigour and clear-headedness (as scientific discourses are wont to do), while the charge of paradoxical incoherence and/or conceptual static is typically laid at the feet of deconstruction (with John Searle's response to Derrida's critique of J.L. Austin in "Signature Event Context" being only the most well-known example). To put it telegraphically, then:

paradoxically, the only way to represent nonhuman subjectivity (or *any* subjectivity) is to be antirepresentational, and (a corollary) the only way to address the ontology of nonhuman beings is to be post-ontological.

The sort of intervention I am attempting here is of a particular moment, I think, because Dennett's work is often regarded as a more philosophically referenced version of what is taken to be a core feature of cognitive science generally: that it is thought to be, in its "functionalism," resolutely post-ontological and post-representational in precisely this way. In this light, Dennett's work presents itself as a less reductive and more nuanced version of what Terrence Deacon, in *The Symbolic Species*, characterizes as "materialistic reductionism," which offers in theories of mind and consciousness "the dominant alternative to the Cartesian perspective." It is "exemplified," he writes, "by the theoretical claim that the mind is like the sort of 'computation' that takes place in electronic computers. In simpler terms, minds are software (programs) run on the hardware (neural circuits) of the brain." The "strong" version of this claim (or the weakest) is called "eliminative materialism," which holds that

> notions such as mind, intention, belief, thought, representation, and so on will eventually be eliminated in discussions of cognitive processes in favor of more mechanistic synonyms that refer to chemical-electrical signaling processes of the brain. Mentalistic terms, it is suggested, are merely glosses for more complex brain processes that we at present do not understand.[4]

With those contexts in mind, let us return to the story of Rico the Überpooch, if he is one. According to the various reports, a nine-year-old Border Collie living in Germany with his human companions has recently been shown in "a series of careful studies" carried out by Julia Fischer, a biologist at the Max Planck Institute for Evolutionary Anthropology in Leipzig (a good pedigree, I'd say!), to have "a stunningly large vocabulary of about 200 words" that correspond to a collection of toys, balls and the like, a range comparable to that of great apes, dolphins and parrots who have undergone extensive training in language experiments.[5] In the experiments, Rico and his owner were placed in one room, while ten of the dog's toys were placed in another. The dog was then instructed by his owner to retrieve two randomly selected objects named by the owner, while the owner remained secluded in the separate room to avoid any chance of Clever Hans activity. In forty tests, Rico was accurate thirty-seven times. Even more impressively, in the next phase of the study, the researchers put seven of his toys in the room along with one he had never seen before. The owner then called out the unfamiliar name of the new toy, and Rico was correct in seven out of ten tries. Finally, in the last phase, researchers tested Rico a month later, and he still remembered the name of the new toy three out of six times without having seen it since the first test—a rate equivalent to that of a human three-year-old.[6]

The key finding of the study, we are told, is that Rico is apparently capable of a process called "fast mapping"—an ability to instantly assign a meaning to a new word, a strategy human toddlers use to learn language at a prodigious rate, and a skill thought to be exclusively the province of humans. Rico apparently "can do something scientists thought only humans could do: figure out by process of elimination that a sound he has never heard before must be the name of a toy he has never seen before."[7] According to the authors of the study, all of this suggests "that mammals developed abilities to understand sounds before humans learned to speak,"[8] and Rico's remarkable learning abilities "may indicate that some parts of speech comprehension developed separately from human speech." "You don't have to be able to talk to understand," Dr. Fischer observes. And Sue Savage-Rumbaugh—whose language acquisition work at Georgia State University with the Bonobo Kanzi is well known—goes even further in a commentary published in the same issue of *Science*, suggesting that "if Rico had a human vocal tract, one would presume that he should be able to say the names of the items as well, or at least try to do so."[9]

Of course, we might well add to this appendix of scientific commentary that appears alongside the publication of the study in *Science* the remarks of Daniel Dennett (the director of the Center for Cognitive Studies at Tufts University), whose books *Consciousness Explained* and *Kinds of Minds: Toward an Understanding of Consciousness* would seem to shed light not only on what we have discovered here about the cognitive abilities and mental life of our Überpooch but also on the ethical implications thereof. Indeed, from Dennett's point of view, it is hard to overstate how much it matters, in ethical terms, that we are able to be as specific as possible about the cognition and consciousness of particular beings. "What makes a mind powerful," he writes, "indeed, what makes a mind conscious—is not what it is made of, or how big it is, but what it can do. Can it concentrate? Can it be distracted? Can it recall earlier events?...When such questions as these are answered, we will know everything we need to know about those minds in order to answer the morally important questions."[10] As he puts it, "Membership in the class of things that have minds provides an all-important guarantee: the guarantee of a certain sort of moral standing. Only mind-havers can care; only mind-havers can mind what happens."[11]

As I have already suggested, Dennett's functionalist approach to questions such as "what is a mind-haver?"—not "what is it?" but "what can it do?"—is perhaps what he is best known for, but what I want to argue now is that Dennett's apparent functionalism and materialism are unable to escape the spell of the very philosophical tradition—whose most extreme expression is Cartesian idealism—that he supposedly rejects. In *Kinds of Minds* and throughout his work, Dennett rightly rejects the idea that "some central Agent or Boss or Audience"[12]—what he also sometimes calls a "Cartesian puppeteer"[13]—takes in and "*appreciates*" the information produced by the neural networks and uses it to "steer the ship" of subjectivity.[14] In what he debunks as "the Myth of Double Transduction," the nervous system first transduces input from its environment (light, sound, temperature, etc.) into neural signals, and then, in a second moment, "in some special central place, it transduces these trains of impulses into some *other* medium, the medium of consciousness!... The idea that the network *itself* could assume the role of the inner Boss and thus harbor consciousness seems preposterous," he continues, but that is exactly what happens, he argues, in the distributed networks in both brain and body from which consciousness arises.[15] To ask for something more—to assume that "what *you* are is something *else*, some Cartesian *res cogitans* in addition to all this brain-and-body activity"—is to "betray a deep confusion," because what you are "just *is* this organization of all the competitive activity between a host of competences that your body has developed."[16] To ask for more is to remain captive to what he calls "the Cartesian theater," the specter of a disembodied, free-floating "central knower" or "self" who stands aside from and above these processes, at once the product and appreciator of them.

Dennett's apparently robust, materialist account of embodied consciousness and mentation, buttressed by an impressive understanding of neural networks, evolutionary processes, perceptual mechanisms and the like, would seem to find an apt accompaniment in an understanding of language within the context of a larger prosthetics of signifying systems in all their technicity and exteriority, one that would seem quite consonant with contemporary theorists in the humanities and social sciences from Derrida and Kittler to Bateson and Luhmann.[17] The source of our greater intelligence when compared to our mammalian relatives, he argues, is not the size of our brains but rather "our habit of *off-loading* as much as possible of our cognitive tasks into the environment itself—extruding our minds (that is, our mental projects and activities) into the surrounding world, where a host of peripheral devices we construct can store, process, and re-present our meanings, streamlining, enhancing, and protecting the processes of transformation that *are* our thinking"—a process that "releases us from the limitations of our animal brains."[18] And "thanks to our prosthetically enhanced imaginations," he continues, "we can formulate otherwise imponderable, unnoticeable metaphysical possibilities."[19]

This seems perfectly correct, of course, as far as it goes. Few would argue with Dennett's observation that "there is no step more uplifting, more explosive, more momentous in the history of mind design that the invention of language," through which *Homo sapiens* "stepped into a slingshot that has launched it far beyond all other earthly species in the power to look ahead and reflect."[20] But the problem is that Dennett's notion of language—even while it appears to understand language as prosthesis and as tool that not only "requires intelligence" but "*confers* intelligence"[21]— is a fundamentally representationalist one that reinstalls the disembodied Cartesian subject at the very heart of his supposedly embodied, materialist functionalism. "The free-floating rationales that explain rudimentary higher-order intentionality of birds and hares—and even chimpanzees—are honored," he writes, "in the designs of their nervous systems, but we are looking for something more: we are looking for rationales that are *represented* in those nervous systems."[22]

The problem here is not—as he argues in an essay contemporaneous with *Kinds of Minds*, entitled "Animal Consciousness: What Matters and Why"—his insistence that we should be "analyzing patterns of behavior (external and internal—but not 'private'), and attempting to interpret them in the light of evolutionary hypotheses regarding their past or current functions."[23] The problem is that this "something more" turns out to be another version of the very "user-illusion" that Dennett wants to reject, and it becomes more and more fatefully tethered to a particular notion of language. Dennett argues that "the sort of informational unification that is the most important prerequisite for *our* kind of consciousness is not anything we are born with, not part of our innate 'hard-wiring,' but in surprisingly large measure is an artifact of our immersion in human culture." So far, so good. But then Dennett's formulation takes a bizarre turn indeed:

> What that early education produces in us is a sort of benign "user-illusion"—I call it the Cartesian Theater: the illusion that there is a place

in our brains where the show goes on, towards which all perceptual "input" streams, whence flow all "conscious intentions" to act and speak. I claim that other species—and human beings when they are newborn—simply *are not beset* by the illusion of the Cartesian Theater. Until the organization is formed, there is simply no user in there to be fooled.[24]

Here again, the problem is not the contention, familiar from earlier texts such as *Consciousness Explained*, that "in order to be conscious—in order to be the sort of thing it is like something to be—it is necessary to have a certain sort of informational organization that endows that thing with a wide set of cognitive powers"; nor is it even his contention that "this sort of internal organization does not come automatically with so-called 'sentience.'"[25] The problem is rather the simultaneous insistence upon and disavowal of the central importance of the "user-illusion" that (illusory though it may be) definitively and, for all practical purposes, ontologically and ethically separates "us" from "them." But how, one might ask, is this insistence really any different from the Cartesianism Dennett rejects, particularly when we remember his insistence above on the difference between "the free-floating rationales that explain rudimentary higher-order intentionality of birds and hares" that are a product of "the designs of their nervous systems" and the "something more" of human intentionality and consciousness, "rationales that are *represented* in those nervous systems" and are indeed *anchored* (to stay with Dennett's metaphor) by those representations. This problem is only made more acute in *Kinds of Minds*, in other words, because the production of that illusion is tethered more and more tightly to a representationalist understanding of language and how it bears upon questions of phenomenology, which in turn leads Dennett down the blind alleys of the very metaphysical tradition he had hoped to surpass.

Take, for example, the tortured trajectory of the following argument: "Many animals hide but don't think they are hiding. Many animals flock but don't think they are flocking,"[26] Dennett argues. They have "know-how," as he puts it, but not "represented knowledge."[27] Eventually, some creatures began

> off-loading problems into the world, and just into other parts of their brains. They began making and using representations, but they didn't know they were doing so. They didn't need to know. Should we call this sort of unwitting use of representations "thinking"? If so, then we would have to say that these creatures were thinking, but didn't know they were thinking! Unconscious thinking—those with a taste for "paradox-

ical" formulations might favor this way of speaking, but we could less misleadingly say that this was *intelligent but unthinking* behavior, because it was not just not reflective but also not reflectable-upon.[28]

As an example of such "intelligent but unthinking behavior," Dennett offers the "distraction display" among some species of low-nesting birds, who, when predators approach their nest, put on an ostentatious show of feigned injury, captivating the predator's attention and promising an easy kill that the predator, now drawn away from the vulnerable eggs, is never quite able to make.[29] Such behaviours among nonhuman animals are quite abundant and well-known, but none of them, Dennett argues, manifests what he calls the workings of a "third-order intentional system":

> An important step toward becoming a person was the step up from a *first-order* intentional system to a *second-order* intentional system. A first-order intentional system has beliefs and desires about many things, but *not* about beliefs and desires. A second-order intentional system has beliefs and desires about beliefs and desires, its own or those of others. A third-order intentional system would be capable of such feats as *wanting* you to believe that it *wanted* something.[30]

If this has a familiar ring to it, it should, because it is exactly the strategy that Jacques Lacan famously uses—in his essay of 1960, "The Subversion of the Subject and the Dialectic of Desire in the Freudian Unconscious"[31]—to juridically separate the human from the animal as that being, alone among the living, who can *lie by telling the truth*. The animal, in Lacan's terms, can pretend, but not *pretend to pretend*—only the human, as "subject of the signifier," can do that. As Jacques Derrida summarizes Lacan's position in a recent essay—and here the distance between Dennett's discourse and Lacan's will become absolutely minimal:

> There is, according to Lacan, a clear distinction between what the animal is capable of, namely, strategic pretense ... and what it is incapable of and incapable of witnessing to, namely, the deception of speech [*la tromperie de la parole*] within the order of the signifier and of Truth. The deception of speech ... involves lying to the extent that, in promising what is true, it includes the supplementary possibility of telling the truth in order to lead the other astray, on order to have him believe something other than what is true (we know the Jewish story recounted by Freud and so often quoted by Lacan: "Why do you tell me that you are going to X in order to have me believe you are going to Y whereas

you are indeed going to X?"). According to Lacan, the animal would be incapable of this type of lie, of this deceit, of this pretense in the second degree, whereas the "subject of the signifier," within the human order, would possess such a power and, better still, would emerge as subject, instituting itself and coming to itself as subject *by virtue of this power*, a second-degree reflexive power, a power that is *conscious* of being able to deceive by pretending to pretend.[32]

As I have already suggested, one of the ironies of Dennett's discourse is that even as it promises a rigorous, clear-headed view of these complexities—"Don't confuse ontological questions (about what exists) with epistemological questions (about how we know about it)!" as we are admonished in the opening pages of *Kinds of Minds*—it reproduces *in detail* the Cartesian position it claims to move beyond, and does so, moreover, precisely because it is unwilling or unable to pursue the full implications of the "'paradoxical' formulations" (such as "intelligent but unthinking behavior") that it indulges but doesn't think through.

As Derrida's later work makes clear, that Cartesianism rests on two fundamental points: (1) the assertion that animals, however sophisticated they may be, can only "react" but not "respond" to what goes on around them. And this is so because (2) the capacity to "respond" depends upon the ability to wield concepts or representations, which is in turn possible only on the basis of language—and this, very precisely in the sense voiced by Dennett when he writes, "No matter how close a dog's 'concept' of cat is to yours extensionally (you and the dog discriminate the same sets of entities as cats and noncats), it differs radically in one way: the dog cannot consider its concept.... [N]o language-less mammal can have a concept of snow in the way we can, because a language-less mammal has no way of considering snow 'in general' or 'in itself.'"[33]

And on this point, of course, Dennett's putatively materialist account of embodied consciousness falls in line not just with the work of Descartes but even more conspicuously with that most *disembodied* of philosophical humanisms, the work of Martin Heidegger, whose characterization of the animal as that which "has a world in the mode of not-having" depends, as Derrida argues in *Of Spirit*, on the inability of the animal to "have access to entities *as such* and in their Being" because of a lack of language which is "not primarily or simply linguistic," but rather, as Derrida puts it, "derives from the properly *phenomenological* impossibility of speaking the phenomenon."[34] In light of Derrida's critique, then, Dennett's discourse takes its place in a long line of philosophers from Aristotle to Lacan, Kant, Heidegger and Levinas, all of whom "say the same thing: the animal is without language. Or more precisely unable to respond, to respond with a response that could be precisely and rigorously distinguished from a reaction.... Even those who, from Descartes to Lacan, have conceded to the said animal some aptitude for signs and for communication," Derrida continues, "have always denied it the power to *respond*—to *pretend*, to *lie*, to *cover its tracks* or *erase* its own traces"[35]—hence the fallback position we find here in Dennett and Lacan, when more explicitly metaphysical versions of humanism are no longer available: the difference between communication and metacommunication, signifying and signifying *about* signifying, thinking and *knowing* you're thinking, and so on.

But the problem with this position, as Derrida points out, is that "it seems difficult in the first place to identify or determine a limit, that is to say an indivisible threshold between pretense and pretense of pretense.... How could one distinguish," he continues,

> for example in the most elementary sexual parade or mating game, between a feint and a feint of a feint? If it is impossible to provide the criterion for such a distinction, one can conclude that every pretense of pretense remains a simple pretense (animal or imaginary, in Lacan's terms), or else, on the contrary, and just as likely, that every pretense, however simple it may be, gets repeated and reposited undecidably, in its possibility, as pretense of pretense (human or symbolic in Lacan's terms).... Pretense presupposes taking the other into account; it therefore supposes, simultaneously, the pretense of pretense—a simple supplementary move by the other within the strategy of the game. That supplementarity is at work from the moment of the first pretense.[36]

And the distinction between the inscription of the trace and its erasure as the means by which to juridically separate the human from animal fares no better. As Derrida argues in that same essay

> *and this is why so long ago I substituted the concept of trace for that of signifier*, the structure of the trace presupposes that to trace amounts to erasing a trace as much as to imprinting it.... How can it be denied that the simple substitution of one trace for another, the marking of their diacritical difference in the most elementary inscription—which capacity Lacan concedes to the animal—involves erasure as much as it involves the imprint? It is as difficult to assign a frontier between pretense and pretense of pretense, to have an indivisible line pass through

the middle of a feigned feint, as it is to assign one between inscription and erasure of the trace.[37]

The point here, as Derrida argues, is

> less a matter of asking whether one has the right to refuse the animal such and such a power ... than of asking whether what calls itself human has the right to rigorously attribute to man ... what he refuses the animal, and whether he can ever possess the *pure, rigorous, indivisible* concept, as such, of that attribution. Thus, were we even to suppose—something I am not ready to concede—that the "animal" were incapable of covering its tracks, by what right could one concede that power to the human, to the "subject of the signifier"?[38]

What Derrida helps us to see—and we can *only* see it if we have the "taste for 'paradoxical' formulations" typically associated with deconstruction, the sort that Dennett's analytical style blithely suggests we ignore—is that just because a particular discourse operates within parameters and conventions that we think of as "scientific," or presents itself as a materialist rendering of the problem of consciousness in relation to embodiment, *does not mean that that discourse is not metaphysical.* In the terms sketched by Rorty at the outset of this essay, the problem with such a discourse is that its apparently scientific, materialist surpassing of metaphysical idealism (whose extreme form is positivism or, in the more contemporary terms used by Deacon, "eliminative materialism") actually shares a deeper identity with that very idealism, because *both* are framed by a prior, more fundamental commitment to *representationalism*. As a methodological and theoretical consideration for such discourse, language appears as a rather unimportant, second-order phenomenon whose job is to be as transparent as possible to the concepts (and beyond that, the objects) they represent (which is why the eventual goal for "materialistic reductionism" can be to eliminate it all together). At the same time, paradoxically, this apparently insubstantial thing called language constitutes the phenomenological and indeed ethical divide between human and nonhuman subjectivity, but precisely because it *is* rendered insubstantial; paradoxically, it constitutes the phenomenological specificity of the very being who then, in an idealist abstraction if ever there was one, rises above it to deploy it literally at will—or, in Dennett's terms, by "intention."

Indeed, what Derrida writes about Austin and speech act theory in "Signature Event Context" applies even more pointedly to the recovery and maintenance of the humanist subject in Dennett, as what Derrida there calls "a free consciousness present to the totality of the operation, and of absolutely meaningful speech [*vouloir-dire*] master of itself: the teleological jurisdiction of an entire field whose organizing center remains *intention*"—an intention that expresses itself, for instance, in the difference between pretending and pretending to pretend, thinking and knowing you're thinking, and so on.[39] And this, as I've already suggested, has far-reaching consequences for the "rigour" and "objectivity" of the knowledge that we think we can have of ourselves and of other nonhuman beings, a rigour and objectivity that analytical philosophy and cognitive science have typically reserved for themselves over and against the "merely epistemological" quandaries of poststructuralist philosophy. For as Derrida points out, "it is not certain that what we call language or speech acts can ever be exhaustively determined by an objective science or theory"; indeed, "it is more 'scientific' to take this limit ... into account and to treat it as a point of departure for rethinking this or that received concept of 'science' and of 'objectivity.'"[40] Now all of this might be viewed as "merely theoretical," if you like, were it not for the fact that Dennett himself insists that the ethical stakes of determining which creatures have minds—a determination that depends, in turn, on a quite specific relation to language—are dire indeed. On the one hand, Dennett argues that "the ethical course is to err on the side overattribution, just to be safe" when considering the possibility of nonhuman minds, because the ethical consequences of being niggardly and then later being found wrong could be grave.[41] At the same time, however, he writes: "'It may not be able to talk, but surely it thinks!'—one of the main aims of this book has been to shake your confidence in this familiar reaction."[42] But because a deeply flawed theory of "talking" is central to a representationalist notion of "thinking" in Dennett's work, and because only things that think (that is to say, both think *and know* they are thinking) have minds, and because only things that have minds (and, we might add, *know* they have minds!) merit ethical consideration, Dennett is forced to embrace ethical implications that, despite his generous gestures to the contrary, would seem to run directly counter to the supposed point of his entire project, which is, of course, to take seriously the status—epistemologically and ethically—of different "kinds of minds."

Take, for example, Dennett's rendering of the difference between pain and suffering, which unwittingly reproduces the very Cartesianism that Dennett has time and again declared the enemy. Dennett writes that "we might well think that the capacity for suffering counts for more, in any moral calculations, than the capacity for abstruse and sophisticated reasoning."[43] But on this point, Dennett follows Descartes almost to the letter. Descartes—who is often misunderstood on this point—insisted *not* that animals do not feel those sensations we call "pain," but only that they do not *experience* them as suffering because there is "no one home," no subject of the *cogito* to do the experiencing; and thus, the pain is not morally relevant.[44] Similarly, Dennett argues that "for such states to matter—whether or not we call them pains, or conscious states, or experiences—there must be an enduring subject *to whom* they matter because they are a source of suffering."[45]

My point here, of course, is not that human and nonhuman animals all experience the same kinds or levels of suffering; even the most ardent animal rights philosophers, such as Peter Singer, agree that they do not.[46] My point is that the difference between "pain" and "suffering" in Dennett turns out to be not just a difference in degree but a difference in *kind*, an *ontological* difference, and one that simply reproduces on another level the difference between thinking and knowing you're thinking, having thoughts and having represented thoughts, and so on.[47] The problem, in other words, is with the unwitting Cartesianism of Dennett's "enduring subject," which in turn leads him (not surprisingly) to embrace some ethical conclusions that should, I think, give us pause. For example, when Dennett attempts to draw out the ethical consequences of his contention that "human consciousness ... is a necessary condition for serious suffering,"[48] he ends up suggesting that "a dissociated child does not suffer as much as a non-dissociated child."[49] And just as different forms of being *human* in the world are rewritten, as they are here, in terms of a homogeneous Cartesian ideal, *nonhuman* beings, in all their diversity, are now rendered not as fully complete forms of life that are radically irreducible to such a thin, idealized account of what counts as "subjectivity," but rather as diminished or crippled versions of that fantasy figure called "the human"—the Cartesian *cogito* now rewritten as the "user-illusion" *qua* "enduring subject." Nonhuman animals are now seen as "creatures that are *naturally* dissociated—that never achieve, or even attempt to achieve, the sort of complex internal organization that is standard in a normal child and disrupted in a dissociated child."[50]

The problem here is not the ethical foregrounding of pain and suffering. The problem is that Dennett's ontological distinction between pain and suffering is based upon a set of phantom abilities, anchored by but not limited to language and its imagined representational capacities in relation to the world of things, that *no subject, either nonhuman or human, possesses in truth*. We can get an even sharper sense of this by reference to Derrida's very different approach to the question of nonhuman suffering, which takes place, ironically enough, by way of utilitarian philosopher Jeremy Bentham, who anchors the animal rights philosophy of Peter Singer. The relevant question here, Bentham asserts, is not "can they talk," or "can they reason," but "can they *suffer*?" For Derrida, putting the question in this way "changes everything," because "from Aristotle to Descartes, from Descartes, especially, to Heidegger, Levinas and Lacan"—and, we might add, to Dennett—posing the question of the animal in terms of either the capacity for thought or language "determines so many others concerning *power* or *capability* [*pouvoirs*], and *attributes* [*avoirs*]: being able, having the power to give, to die, to bury one's dead, to dress, to work, to invent a technique."[51] What makes Bentham's reframing of the problem so powerful is that now "the question is disturbed by a certain *passivity* ... a not-being-able.... What of the vulnerability felt on the basis of this inability?" he continues, "what is this non-power at the heart of power?... What right should be accorded it? To what extent does it concern us?" It concerns us very directly, in fact, for "mortality resides there, as the most radical means of thinking the finitude that we share with animals, the mortality that belongs to the very finitude of life, to the experience of compassion, to the possibility of sharing the possibility of this non-power."[52]

From this vantage—to return now to the story with which we began—we can derive from the exploits of Rico the Überpooch an unexpected lesson whose ethical as well as epistemological resonance we are now in a position to appreciate: that even though thinking about the consciousness, intelligence and emotional and mental lives of nonhuman animals in terms of their linguistic abilities has historically been a crucial means for getting such questions on the table *at all*,[53] it may not be the best way, and it is certainly not the only way, of approaching these questions. From this vantage, Rico's prodigious signifying abilities may be only one sign among many others—and only the one most readily legible to *us*, as language-dependent creatures—of a thinking (if that's what we want to call it) that we ought to be interested in not because it is a diminished or dim approximation of ours, but because it is part of a very different way of being in the world that calls upon us to rethink, ever anew and vigilantly so, what we mean by "person," "mind," "consciousness"—that entire cluster of terms and the ethical implications that flow from them. In this light, as Derrida suggests, "it would not be a matter of 'giving speech back' to animals, but perhaps of acceding to a thinking, however fabulous and chimerical it might be, that thinks the absence of the name and of the word otherwise, as something other than a privation."[54]

NOTES

1. Rob Stein, "Common Collie or Überpooch? German Pet's Vocabulary Stuns Scientists," *The Washington Post*, 11 June 2004, A1; and Rob Stein, "Dogs May Be as Smart as Owners Think They Are," *Houston Chronicle*, 11 June 2004: A1, A14.
2. Richard Rorty, *Objectivity, Relativism, and Truth: Philosophical Papers*, vol. 1 (Cambridge: Cambridge University Press, 1991), 2–4. Emphasis in original.
3. Ibid., 5.
4. Terrence W. Deacon, *The Symbolic Species: The Co-Evolution of Language and the Brain* (New York: Norton, 1997), 442. Though I cannot make the argument within the confines of this essay, of course, I would suggest that Deacon's work is, if anything, more Cartesian than Dennett's. This becomes clear in the final chapter of the text which, even as it attempts to argue for a substantial continuity between the mental lives of human and nonhuman animals, reinstates, via the terms "representation" and "experience," the quintessentially Cartesian distinction we will see Dennett run aground on below—namely, the distinction between sensations and the *experience* of sensations (possibly only for beings who operate with symbolic representations) that anchors Descartes infamous position on the ethical irrelevance of pain in nonhuman animals. See in particular Deacon, *The Symbolic Species*, 448–50, where we find such question-begging formulations as the following: "We live most of our concrete lives in the subjective realm that is also shared with other species, but our experience of this world is embedded in the vastly more extensive symbolic world."
5. Stein, "Common Collie or Überpooch?"
6. Tony Czuczka, "Study Shows Dogs Can Remember Words," *Associated Press Wire Report*, 10 June 2004, 2. Available online at http://customwire.ap.org.
7. Stein, "Common Collie or Überpooch?" A1.
8. Czuczka, "Study Shows Dogs Can Remember Words."
8. Stein, "Common Collie or Überpooch?" A1.
10. Daniel C. Dennett, *Kinds of Minds: Toward an Understanding of Consciousness* (New York: Basic Books, 1996), 158.
11. Ibid., 4.
12. Ibid., 73.
13. Ibid., 80.
14. Ibid., 73.
15. Ibid., 72–73.

16 Ibid., 155-56.
17 Relevant texts here would be, for example, Jacques Derrida, *Archive Fever*, trans. Eric Prenowitz (Chicago: University of Chicago Press, 1996); Gregory Bateson, *Steps to an Ecology of Mind* (New York: Ballantine Books, 1972); Niklas Luhmann, *Social Systems*, trans. John Bednarz Jr. with Dirk Baecker (Stanford: Stanford University Press, 1995); Friedrich Kittler, *Essays: Literature, Media, Information Systems*, ed. John Johnston (Amsterdam: OPA, 1997).
18 Dennet, *Kinds of Minds*, 134-35.
19 Ibid., 146.
20 Ibid., 147.
21 Ibid., 99.
22 Ibid., 131.
23 Daniel C. Dennett, "Animal Consciousness: What Matters and Why," in Arien Mack, ed., *Humans and Other Animals* (Columbus: Ohio State University Press, 1999), 296.
24 Ibid., 292. Emphasis in original.
25 Ibid., 293.
26 Dennett, *Kinds of Minds*, 119.
27 Ibid., 154.
28 Ibid. Emphasis in original.
29 Ibid., 121-22.
30 Ibid., 120. Emphasis in original.
31 In *Écrits: A Selection*, trans. Alan Sheridan (New York: Norton, 1977).
32 Jacques Derrida, "And Say the Animal Responded?" trans. David Wills, in Cary Wolfe, ed., *Zoontologies: The Question of the Animal* (Minneapolis: University of Minnesota Press, 2003), 130. Emphasis in original.
33 Ibid., 159.
34 Jacques Derrida, *Of Spirit: Heidegger and the Question*, trans. Geoffrey Bennington and Rachel Bowlby (Chicago: University of Chicago Press, 1989), 53. See also my discussion of these questions in Derrida's work in "In the Shadow of Wittgenstein's Lion: Language, Ethics, and the Question of the Animal" in *Zoontologies*, 1-57.
35 Jacques Derrida, "The Animal that therefore I Am (More to Follow)," trans. David Wills, *Critical Inquiry* 28, no. 2 (2002), 48-49. Emphasis in original.
36 Derrida, "And Say the Animal Responded?" 135-36.
37 Ibid., 137. First emphasis added.
38 Ibid., 137-38. Emphasis in original.
39 It is the "intentional stance" that gives one of Dennett's most well-known books its title. See Daniel C. Dennett, *The Intentional Stance* (Cambridge, MA: MIT Press, 1987), the contours of which are summarized in chap. 2 of *Kind of Minds*.

40 Jacques Derrida, *Limited Inc.*, trans. Samuel Weber et al., ed. Gerald Graff (Evanston, IL: Northwestern University Press, 1988), 118.
41 Dennett, *Kinds of Minds*, 6.
42 Ibid., 159.
43 Ibid., 162. This approach is central, of course, to the argument of animal rights philosophy, whose articulation I take up in detail in *Animal Rites: American Culture, the Discourse of Species, and Posthumanist Theory* (Chicago: University of Chicago Press, 2003). See especially chap. 1 and the conclusion.
44 See Tom Regan's clarification of this point in his discussion of Descartes in *The Case for Animal Rights* (Berkeley: University of California Press, 1985). See also in this connection a footnote by Derrida that makes clear the connection of this point in Descartes to the capacity for language, in Derrida's "And Say the Animal Responded?" 143n1.
45 Dennett, *Kinds of Minds*, 161.
46 See my discussion of this body of work in *Animal Rites*, chap. 1.
47 See in this connection the self-disintegration of the distinction between "pain" and "suffering" at the end of Dennett's essay "Animal Consciousness," which evinces quite well an understanding of language that hamstrings his every move: "When I step on your toe...the pain, though intense, is too brief to matter, and I have done no long-term damage to your foot. The idea that you 'suffer' for a second or two is a risible misapplication of that important notion, and even when we grant that my causing you a few seconds pain may irritate you a few seconds or even minutes—especially if you think I did it deliberately—the pain itself, as a brief, negatively-signed experience, is of vanishing moral significance" (298).
48 Dennett, *Kinds of Minds*, 165.
49 Ibid., 164.
50 Ibid.
51 Derrida, "The Animal that therefore I Am...," 396, 395.
52 Ibid., 396.
53 As in the well-known work with the great apes Washoe, Kanzi, Koko and others, but also with birds, as in Irene Pepperberg's research. The literature at this point is extensive, but for an overview, one might consult the section "Conversations with Apes," in Peter Singer and Paola Cavalieri, ed., *The Great Ape Project* (New York: St. Martin's Press, 1993), 27–79; the essays by Duane Rumbaugh and Colin McGinn in Mack, ed., *Humans and Other Animals*; and the section "Language" in Robert W. Mitchell, Nicholas S. Thompson, and H. Lyn Miles, eds., *Anthropomorphism, Anecdotes, and Animals*, ed. (Albany, NY: SUNY Press, 1997).
54 Derrida, "The Animal that therefore I Am," 416.

Bibliography

Bateson, Gregory. *Steps to an Ecology of Mind*. New York: Ballantine Books, 1972.

Cavalieri, Paola, and Peter Singer, eds. *The Great Ape Project*. New York: St. Martin's Press, 1993.

Czuczka, Tony. "Study Shows Dogs Can Remember Words." *Associated Press Wire Report*, 10 June 2004.

Deacon, Terrence W. *The Symbolic Species: The Co-Evolution of Language and the Brain*. New York: Norton, 1997.

Dennett, Daniel C. "Animal Consciousness: What Matters and Why." In Arien Mack, ed., *Humans and Other Animals*. Columbus: Ohio State University Press, 1999.

———. *Kinds of Minds: Toward an Understanding of Consciousness*. New York: Basic Books, 1996.

———. *The Intentional Stance*. Cambridge, MA: MIT Press, 1987.

Derrida, Jacques. "And Say the Animal Responded?" Translated by David Wills. In Cary Wolfe, ed., *Zoontologies: The Question of the Animal*. Minneapolis: University of Minnesota Press, 2003.

———. "The Animal that therefore I Am (More to Follow)." Translated by David Wills. *Critical Inquiry* 28, no. 2 (2002): 369–418.

———. *Archive Fever*. Translated by Eric Prenowitz. Chicago: University of Chicago Press, 1996.

———. *Of Spirit: Heidegger and the Question*. Translated by Geoffrey Bennington and Rachel Bowlby. Chicago: University of Chicago Press, 1989.

Kittler, Friedrich. *Essays: Literature, Media, Information Systems*. Edited by John Johnston. Amsterdam: OPA, 1997.

Lacan, Jacques. "The Subversion of the Subject and the Dialectic of Desire in the Freudian Unconscious." In *Écrits: A Selection*. Translated by Alan Sheridan. New York: Norton, 1977.

Luhmann, Niklas. *Social Systems*. Translated by John Bednarz Jr. with Dirk Baecker. Stanford: Stanford University Press, 1995.

Mack, Arien, ed. *Humans and Other Animals*. Columbus: Ohio State University Press, 1999.

Mitchell, Robert W., Nicholas S. Thompson, and H. Lyn Miles, eds. *Anthropomorphism, Anecdotes, and Animals*. Albany, NY: SUNY Press, 1997.

Regan, Tom. *The Case for Animal Rights*. Berkeley: University of California Press, 1985.

Rorty, Richard. *Objectivity, Relativism, and Truth: Philosophical Papers*. Vol. 1. Cambridge: Cambridge University Press, 1991.

Stein, Rob. "Common Collie or Überpooch? German Pet's Vocabulary Stuns Scientists." *Washington Post*, 11 June 2004: A1.
Wolfe, Cary. *Animal Rites: American Culture, the Discourse of Species, and Posthumanist Theory*. Chicago: University of Chicago Press, 2003.

7

Animals in Moral Space

MICHAEL ALLEN FOX
LESLEY McLEAN

THE NEED TO RESITUATE ANIMALS IN ETHICS

The idea that nonhuman animals have some kind of moral status has hovered on the fringes of philosophical discourse for quite some time. Since the beginnings of both Western and Eastern thought, there have been voices willing to affirm that animals are unique beings that should be treated with decency and respect. Apart from the edicts of emperors and selective scriptural injunctions, however, such precepts were kept alive by only a few eccentric thinkers until the enactment of the first humane (or anti-cruelty) statutes in various constituencies during the seventeenth century and those following. These regulations made minor inroads into human beings' consciousness of their abusive, exploitative and oppressive treatment of animals. But recently, some scholars have argued that even anti-cruelty laws regard animals for the most part as property, as things or, at best, as expendable resources that merely require some special handling in order to prevent what's designated as "unnecessary suffering" (i.e., suffering in excess of what is required in order to fulfill particular human goals). A growing number of people believe that this is not good enough: *animals deserve to be the subjects of moral concern for their own sake.* Consequently, in the past few decades there has been a variety of attempts to find a way to integrate nonhuman animals into the moral sphere.

The dominant strategy for achieving this objective has been to re-examine the criteria for moral considerability that are implicit in traditional normative moral theories, then see whether animals measure up to these and, if they do, significant moral standing can legitimately be extended to them. A classical utilitarian approach, for example, looks for evidence of pain and suffering in members of other species and, if identified, these indicators qualify such creatures as sentient beings whose experiences count, morally speaking, and should be factored into our determination of which outcomes we should pursue or avoid. A rights approach, on the other hand, tries to discern signs of mental life that go beyond sentience, perhaps even as far as personhood. Nonhuman animals that exhibit such signs have earned a degree of moral status that compels us to bestow certain fundamental moral and/or legal rights upon them. These approaches are of value to the extent that they do not just seek to figure nonhumans as being, or being like, failed, marginal or second-rate humans, but instead give due recognition to the basic needs of organisms that, while different in their welfare (or quality of life) requirements, are nonetheless constituted in many respects like ourselves. All such ethical approaches must be regarded as preliminary, however, for the reason that we do not yet know very much about the mental lives of animals, nor have we learned to decipher much about their systems of communication. A moral outlook that is adequate to the complex behaviour and experiences of animals, and that stands a chance of being durable and gaining widespread acceptance, is still very far in the future.

A NEW DIRECTION

The viewpoint advanced in this essay is that humans must develop a new image of what nonhuman animals are like, and correspondingly develop new ideas about how we ought to relate to them. But in order to provide a foothold for a new ethics that adequately embraces animals, a radical alteration in our conception of moral reasoning is needed. All too often and too predictably, moral arguments are treated as if there is some "objective" set of considerations that, ideally at least, will settle a dispute or resolve a dilemma. It may be difficult to locate, but that is nonetheless the point and purpose of ethical problem-solving, according to the received opinion. We believe this assumption is mistaken in general, and that it has led animal ethics in the wrong direction in particular. This is not the place to conduct a full-scale critique of ethical theorizing, however; we are concerned here only with how we ought to reflect on our relationship with members of other species. A different standard of relevance has to be adopted. We propose that the way into the real world of human/animal interactions is through opening ourselves to a complex kind of seeing and feeling. Most of the moral context in which animals' lives are played out has been missed by human observers both past and present, because they have failed to look in order to see. And they have failed to respond affectively as well as intellectually to significant forms of animal behaviour and expression because they have brought rigid abstract concepts and unilluminating ways of observing to bear on what is similar to, and yet very different from, the familiar.

There are many ways of arguing in ethics: logical reasoning, dramatization, the use of examples or vignettes, anecdotes, parables, metaphorical comparisons, psychological sketches, storytelling—all of these devices and more have been used to forward conclusions. Philosophers are now beginning to appreciate that no single device, such as the first of these, exhausts the field, and that all are quite fruitful. Those that are not objective in the customary sense, do not lack anything to be respectable or valid; rather, their forcefulness comes from the impact they exercise upon imagination, intuition and feeling—those aspects of a full person that have been traditionally neglected, even reviled, by self-appointed defenders of "rationality." As we shall argue, the kind of ethical scheme that is suitable for humans and animals is a function of cognition in the broadest sense.

We present below a two-part exploration of this problem. The sections "Moral Space" and "How to Think about Moral Space" below focus on the need to conceive of the physical space on this planet as moral space. Physical space is essential to the realization of the moral life, for whatever organism we have in mind. This notion is easiest to grasp within the human context; but we suggest that *for any type of moral existence to be meaningful, it must be translated into spatial terms and played out in the real world*. This applies to the moral existence of animals as well as to the shared moral life with them that we may one day develop. Moral theorizing about animals is all well and good, but realizing the ideal of animal liberation is more of a practical and concrete enterprise than it is an abstract and theoretical one.

In the section "Perceiving Other Animals in Moral Space," we argue for the need to open up a phenomenological and conceptual space within which to establish a human/nonhuman world of interaction. More specifically, this section delineates an opening that allows animals to guide us in how we should interpret and understand what they are telling us—by means of their expressions, behaviour and psychological abilities. Animals doubtless have a sophisticated mental life. However, when we talk about "animal minds," to what are we referring? Only by reflecting carefully on this question, we believe, will humans be able to take the quantum leap forward that a new, genuinely inter-species ethic signifies. The space thus created allows for the construction of a moral life that embraces non-human animals and in which we can wholeheartedly participate. We hope to contribute something here that will clarify the nature of this enterprise and help advance it.

MORAL SPACE: PRELIMINARIES

Humans must learn—or rather discover—what it means to live a moral life, in the face of the challenge other species now present. The challenge is unprecedented, because for the first time in history, a significant change in consciousness makes it begin to be possible to view animals in a new light—as morally important beings. We are not yet at the stage where this change is universally understood and endorsed. Nonetheless, discussions of the nature of morality, of where animals fit into the picture and of the scientific evidence of animals' amazing capacities have gone some way towards undermining speciesist attitudes as well as old distinctions that prevent animals from being acknowledged as "subjects-of-a-life"[1] and as possessing moral worth in their own right. Important though it is to re-examine the criteria of moral considerability, something more is needed in order to accelerate the evolution of humans' moral outlook in regard to animals. This is a fresh attempt to define and depict moral space.

To begin with, we express our agreement with those who argue that the space in which we live and move and have our being is a space of valuing. Human action is always imbued with reasons for its occurrence, and among these are the desired and valorized ends that each of us seeks to realize, and that we often jointly cherish. As James D. Proctor suggests, "we inhabit a moral earth. It is moral precisely because we inhabit it. The values we have woven into our existence on earth are not necessarily the best ones possible, nor certainly are they self-evident, but there is never some value vacuum we must fill; the earth is already a moral place."[2] Perception is infused with value from as early as we are able to have preferences and make value discriminations. And as an animal of culture, each human being, developing a complex awareness of the world, already finds him- or herself immersed in a value-field, as phenomenologists have demonstrated. The point is reinforced by Michael R. Curry, who writes that "places..., the basic sites of human activities, are intrinsically normative."[3] That is, the space in which human life, culture and history unfold does not just have valuational potential, it presents itself to us as an arena that is already value-laden. (To say that "places ... are intrinsically normative" does not entail any thesis about the intrinsic value, or value-apart-from-human-interests, that may reside in nature; rather, it simply refers to the union of value judgements and human behaviours that take place in the real world.) Each individual takes on this value-laden world, and the challenge of the moral life is, quite literally, one of how to "change ... his [or her] piece of the world to make it better."[4]

The idea of moral space has inspired ethical theories of various sorts, but has been especially useful to those whose interest is in proposing new directions for morality. Within the more traditional theoretical framework of ethics, Alan Goldman has suggested that the function of rights is to "carve out a moral space in which persons can develop as distinct individuals free from the constant intrusion of demands from others."[5] In a similar vein, Nicholas Low and Brendan Gleeson urge that "the discourse of human rights has emerged from the spatially situated struggle against injustice.... Rights embody the need for protection of the human person in nature.... Rights ... make space for people to behave in the way they want in accordance with their desires and needs."[6] This way of speaking has great strength in that it attaches a spatial representation to the notion of personal inviolability that lies at the heart of respect for persons, and hence, of rights discourse itself. We all understand the need for personal space, whether or not we've ever articulated it to ourselves. We share the sense that others should give us room to be active, to express ourselves in a unique manner, to move freely about, and that the minimal condition for all of this is that our bodies may not be liberally touched, manipulated, controlled or abused by others. If exceptions are to be made to any of these conditions, they must either be justified by appeal to shared moral principles or laws, or else allowed by oneself.

There are other interesting applications of the idea of moral space as well. Some of these, although arising from the preoccupations of diverse disciplines, help point us in the right direction. Margaret Urban Walker, for example, criticizes a standard view of the "moral expert" as one who applies codified principles to specific cases in a disinterested manner, and argues instead for a new model of ethics consulting which sees it as

> a kind of interaction that invites and enables something to happen, something that renders authority more self-conscious and responsibil-

ity clearer. It is also about the role of maintaining a certain kind of reflective space (literal and figurative) within an institution, within its culture and its daily life, for just these sorts of occasions.[7]

For Walker, then, moral space refers to both an openness of mind and an environment for working out new relationships, as, for instance, between patient and physician.

In a different, but related context, B.R. Tilghman, discussing how certain painters render human life, defines moral space as "a pictorial space designed to represent human beings in the fullness of their psychological nature and in their dramatic interactions with one another."[8] Tilghman stresses that "the movements of the body that are in question are ... the doings of people," and then adds, "as elements of human action we are not dealing simply with 'movements,' but with gestures, postures, facial expressions, and the like that are already replete with the human character, intention, and purpose."[9] Finally, Tilghman draws attention to a comment made by Ludwig Wittgenstein in his *Philosophical Investigations*:

> I see a picture which represents a smiling face. What do I do if I take the smile now as a kind one, now as malicious? Don't I often imagine it with a spatial and temporal context which is one either of kindness or malice? Thus I might supply the picture with the fancy that the smiler was smiling down on a child at play, or again on the suffering of an enemy.[10]

Pictorial space, then, according to Tilghman and Wittgenstein, is the space of portrayal in the sense in which agency and moral character may be revealed in and through it. While both authors restrict their descriptions to representations of human life, we wish to go further with the idea of moral space, as will become evident.

Visionary environmental philosophers have employed the concept of moral space as well, but in a way that is more revolutionary and revisionist. For example, speaking of the need to develop an ethics for the future that is both ecological and bioregional, Jim Cheney observes that such an outlook must "*locate* us in a *moral* space which is at the same time the space we live in physically."[11] Meanwhile, Anthony Weston concludes that an evolving environmental ethics will affirm values that "open up the possibility of reciprocity *between* humans and the rest of nature." By doing so, he affirms, it will lead to an "opening of the 'space' for interaction, for the reemergence of a larger world."[12] This comes much closer to the notion we wish to develop, namely, the conception of moral space as a place both physical and phenomenological wherein our ideas about animals and the precepts that guide our interactions with them receive expression. What we mean to suggest here is not just a mapping of ideas onto the environment, but is more like a process of creating a new moral community through bringing into being, by means of the reorganization of physical space, a shared moral life in the real world.

There is much talk today of "expanding the moral community" and of a "larger circle of moral concern." These spatial images have become prominent within contemporary ethical discourse and literature. An augmented moral terrain is meant to include nonhumans, if not all of the rest of nature. However, if we look at the chronic forms of abuse, exclusion, dehumanization and violence prevalent in the world today—a great many of them institutionally enshrined—it becomes clear that humans have not been especially successful in establishing a true moral community among themselves, let alone beyond their own species perimeter. As one philosopher-colleague provocatively observed to me a few years ago, "We have not even gotten to anthropocentrism yet."[13] So what hope is there for a moral community that includes animals, whether an expanded one or a differently conceived one? As is the case with so many issues that have ethical, social and political dimensions, the problems can seem intractable and the lure of an alienating cynicism, undeniable. However, negativism helps no one and extinguishes hope. We may be far from treating fellow human beings as true equals, but this shouldn't deter us from investigating the bonds that might be developed across species boundaries. Some would even say that it is essential to do so, for several reasons.

First, as feminists and social ecologists have shown, various forms of domination, exploitation, oppression and violence are interconnected. We may think that it is necessary to resolve these problems within the human sphere before moving on to another; but perhaps this is merely an illusion brought about by compartmentalizing certain dynamics of interaction occurring in different contexts that are in fact similar or identical, or at least that are better understood as stemming from a common source. Hence, while it may be tempting to believe that if everyone were to concentrate on the same set of human problems, they'd soon be solved, this is not realistic. If we confront a range of interconnected problems, some purely human, some of a broader sort, then addressing them from a variety of perspectives and individual commitments can only be beneficial for the overall project of ameliorating or eliminating them.

Second, proponents of a non-violent way of life often suggest that the way we treat animals is a measure of the moral worth of a society. When the least powerful beings, who have no voice to speak on their own behalf, are constantly the victims of uncaring cruelty, it reflects extremely poorly on all of us. The abuse of animals is nothing new, but it has reached epidemic proportions. Species diversity is under threat nearly everywhere on the globe. More and more animals are becoming mere tools to be manipulated: as laboratory preparations, victims of factory farming and industrialized slaughter, malleable life-forms to be re-engineered and in order to become suppliers of raw materials (such as organs and cells for transplantation).[14] They continue to pay the high price of both human folly and human progress. Animal exploitation is systemic and institutionalized. But no society can call itself just if its daily operations and the quality of life it promotes depend upon such practices.

Third, we need imaginative horizons to inspire us to think ahead, to seek fulfilment of our ideals. This is true not only in relation to venerable human ideals like freedom, autonomy and self-realization, but also—if we care enough—to other ideals such as animal liberation, interspecies justice, world peace, environmental sustainability and the like. Human consciousness is very blinkered and needs to be re-energized and indeed dramatically reoriented if we are to deal effectively with the most serious problems that now confront us. To a large extent, we lack the concepts and outlooks that are required in order to do this. Perhaps only a paradigm or Gestalt shift—or several—can help us break through the repetitive cycle of self-destructive behaviours into which humanity seems locked.

Fourth, for both prudential and ethical reasons, we must prepare for the likelihood of contact with extraterrestrials that scientists increasingly predict. We can best accommodate this eventuality by coming to terms with terrestrial creatures of all kinds. Indeed, as has recently been reported in the *New Scientist*, "animal research has given us the most unequivocal way of detecting intelligent life yet devised."[15] Whereas efforts to break the code of nonhuman communication systems have failed thus far, new applications of information theory to them look like providing a means of evaluating signals received from beyond the earth.

HOW TO THINK ABOUT MORAL SPACE

We believe that *the concept of moral space plays a crucial role in the process of developing fresh perspectives on how we ought to live on the earth*. It also helps frame new ideas about animals and how we can fruitfully coexist with them. By implication, the concept of moral space tells us a great deal about what it is to be human and what the possibilities are for our species' ethical evolution. Stephen S. Birdsall has remarked, "Our choices are, in effect, guided by a map of moral alternatives, a map of which we are not aware. Through our everyday interactions, we trace the moral geography of our lives."[16] The idea that our lives have a "moral geography" is quite suggestive—even though left here at the metaphorical level. We advocate instead a literal interpretation of the idea that the moral dimension of our lives superimposes itself on the spatial dimension.

Morality is primarily about the interactions among beings whose existence, well-being and/or interests are deemed significant to consider, and also about how we ought to live, taking these things into account. The moral life is not something that unfolds only in our minds or in our own private space, but in the much greater expanse that we call "the world." The world itself is not merely physical space but equally phenomenological space—the locale in which experiences happen and which is shaped by experience in turn. Nor is "experience" purely subjective: it is also interactive. When we envision forms of action and ways of being, it is with a view to their enactment in space and time. It is because of this that some acts are selected as appropriate or desirable, others suppressed and still others, left merely imaginary. William S. Lynn remarks, "All human activity, including moral conflict, occurs at *sites* embedded in *situations*, making geographic context a constituent element of all ethical problems."[17] His point is that human doing is situated in the dual respects that *it happens somewhere but also within existing or created circumstances involving others.* Just as no action occurs in a purely subjective realm, so likewise none lacks context or a structural nexus that gives it both a history and a social and personal meaning.

Space is (among other things) where relationships among people, functioning as rather inconsistent and imperfect rational and moral agents, get worked out in whatever ways they do. Moreover, as Henri Lefèbvre points out, "Space has been shaped and moulded from historical and natural elements, but this has been a political process. Space is political and ideological."[18] That is, space is not a neutral or innocent "container," but is *both* the arena for human action and animal and other natural behaviours *and* the medium constructed by its various inhabitants and users—human and nonhuman—by virtue of their distinctive modes of impact and transformation. Of course, the many (mostly adverse) ways in which humans have historically related to animals in space are also politically and ideologically loaded. Klaus Elder remarks, "Nature does not separate people and turn them against one another. Rather, people separate themselves according to culturally determined forms of interaction with nature."[19] Just as humans have stratified their social order in the space of the natural world, and in relation to its available resources, so too have they organized themselves in relation to animals. Simply put, humans have enforced their (self-assigned and largely mythical) "mastery" or dominion" over nature in general, and animals in particular, and have made up stories and created value systems so as to rationalize the power-based hierarchies that always place them "at the top." Animals have been marginalized except insofar as they can be of use to us and serve our needs. Those that aren't, or don't, fail to even show up on the radar screen of human life, or at best appear on the periphery, where they satisfy scientific curiosity. Domesticated animals that have become "part of culture" and wild animals that serve certain human purposes are both defined by the apartheid of inclusion and exclusion. The lives and natural needs of the former are fashioned and controlled; the freedom and unrestrictedness of the latter are soon eradicated by threatened habitats and the struggle for species survival.

Is there a way to reverse these disastrous trends? In order to change behaviour, perceptions and attitudes must first undergo transformation. All animals, in a certain sense, are part of human culture, just because we socially and personally construct their modes of being in relation to our beliefs and desires. Likewise, as many have argued, we also construct "nature," which has no meaning apart from human purposes, values, perspectives and prejudices. If, as we believe, these hypotheses are true, then there is an opportunity to change the constructions we have created—in short, to create new, better ones to substitute for old, discredited and harmful ones. The first step is to reconsider who and what we are, what vision of the moral life we hold and how we think of the world around us within a mutually shared environment of signification and valuation.

Human selves (and we cannot yet speak knowledgeably of any other kind) are relational entities. Each of us exists in space, but we do so in much more interesting and complex ways than may be supposed. Physical objects "are" in space; human beings "emerge" in space. What makes us who we are is not just the body we occupy or what goes on within the space of our heads. As the phenomenologists insist, we all exist "out there." Selves are products of bodies and minds, to be sure; but they are also the sum total of people, places and experiences that have been formative in the lives of each of us. To all of these things we are intimately connected. Now if these relations constitute us, and have physical dimensionalities, then our essential being has spatial extension and complex intersections with other selves.

A large part of what a moral life consists of is the venues and sets of circumstances that participants appropriate or conjointly create. What has escaped notice by and large, in ethical perception and in the ethics literature, is the larger context of configured space within which our lives and plans play out and acquire meaning for us, as we have been arguing. Of course, we all have a working idea of "the world"; many of us have several, according to the project of engagement that occupies us at the moment. It is nearly a cliché that humans are part of nature, not apart from it. (Some assert, paradoxically, that both are true.) We may in fact be part of nature, but it is questionable how many of us really feel a sense of rootedness. Although a sense of place is at the heart of many traditional cultures (and some modern ones), it is being eroded by the present era of mobility, shallow or non-existent ties to the land and global consumerism. For an increasing number, urban centres are the places of self-identification. Disconnection and distancing from nature are tendencies that, while not new, are aggravated by these dynamics.

Most of us are accustomed to thinking of the world as made up of people and places, that is, of humans and the venues in which they do things. But this way of looking at things omits some dimensions that are vital to determining what we are and how we become what we want to be. For starters, the world contains much more than people and places; it is the biosphere in its seamless totality, including its organic and inorganic ingredients, all the animals, all the ecosystems in their interdependency. Next, all the "places" of the world are contiguous; we only separate them artificially (geopolitically, in terms of interests, travel destinations, zones to be avoided, etc.). The world is properly one vast space containing many places, each designated as it is for pragmatic, symbolic, intellectual or other purposes. Furthermore, some authors demonstrate the extent to which nonhumans transform humans and the conditions of their lives, and the reverse is also true, of course.[20] But this is not all, for as Lynn rightly comments, the "shared contexts of all life-forms ... inform our moral understanding and relationship to animals."[21] These contexts too are spatial and meaning-giving aspects of the world.

The question of who, or what, belongs to the moral community has always been a vexed one. Membership and non-membership are functions of inclusion and exclusion respectively, of recognition and non-recognition, validation and denial and so on. As Michel Foucault has so carefully demonstrated, such choices and decisions are made at the conceptual level and reinforced at the social and political level; but in either case they are expressions of power relationships. The dominant group determines who is "in" and who is "out" (or "other"). But for our purposes here, what is interesting to note is that such determinations have operational significance in the ways they are carried out, that is, they become more loaded with meaning as they are applied in the physical space of the lived world. Thus, in addition to the penal institutions and mental hospitals of which Foucault wrote, ghettos, reservations, affluent suburbs and the like are created and maintained. The same dynamics apply in general in our dealings with animals. In the more apparent sense, we have created zoos, laboratories, factory farms, aquariums, circuses, hunting and fishing zones, wildlife refuges and other forms of confinement and separation; but we have also created natural history museums in which animals are safe, but dead and statically on display.

On the more positive side, humans have domesticated animals for several thousands of years and have lived with them in the role of husbanders and companions. These contacts, and the experiences they give rise to, although often more or less benign, have nonetheless firmly established in our minds the instrumentality of certain species (i.e., their status as property) and isolated them from the larger natural world (just as, in a sense, we have done to ourselves). Domesticated animals exist, at our pleasure, within the spatial boundaries of the moral community, yet they are not *of* it, except in the very weak sense that there are anti-cruelty or humane laws in effect in most jurisdictions. Hence, we have a communal life with (selected) animals, but it is a life whose quality is one-sidedly determined and very seldom influenced by reciprocal considerations.

The fact that moral life in general is situated in the real physical space of the world, and that our formative interactions with animals are likewise, indicates clearly enough that any change in our relationship with other species[22] is also going to be a process, a series of events, stretching out in space. Therefore, when we call for radical change in human attitudes, values and behaviours vis-à-vis animals, this entails wholesale alterations in the ways in which the earth's space is to be utilized. At this point, it is useful to return to the concept of "the world" in order to lay some groundwork for talking about the shift in outlook that will facilitate the emergence of a different moral community and a transformed use of the terrestrial surface. In the world at this moment, we already have in common with animals many biological, psychological and cultural similarities that are complex and have a long evolutionary history. Each of us exists in a symbiotic relationship with countless micro-organisms that inhabit our bodies.[23] Our lives depend crucially upon the external activities of micro-organisms, insects, birds and other organisms that preserve nutrient and other forms of equilibrium in nature. It would be somewhat facetious to assert that we "share" ecosystems with animals—though in one sense, of course, we do. More accurately stated, we have used ecosystems as the theatres in which we strive to enact our domination of nature, and have changed them accordingly. Whatever the quality of our species' interactions with animals has been, they have contributed materially to our evolution and character as a life form.

If there is an intimate connection between moral space and physical space, as we have been suggesting, then how is this to be characterized? We are inclined towards the opinion that it is best described as a "homologue." A homologous relationship holds between things that are "corresponding or similar in position, value, structure, or function."[24] (By contrast, an analogue relationship betokens "similarity in some respects between things that are otherwise dissimilar.")[25] Thus, relationships of a hierarchical sort, such as we find everywhere today, are instantiated and reinforced by the utilization of space and socio-political arrangements that are situated in defined locations (such as government ministries, palaces, prime real estate, corporate head offices, gay bars, slums, refugee camps, animal shelters and charities serving the homeless). Hierarchies start off as beliefs and belief systems, then proceed to expressions in interactions among people (and between people and animals). The values embedded in hierarchical mindsets are expressed in the physical structures of human life— ways of doing things, acting (or being acted upon), moving about in the world (or not moving), institutional frameworks—and the positions and functions people (and animals) have are in large measure constructed (and often constricted) in "reality" by these mindsets.

It follows that if hierarchical arrangements and ways of being and doing are to be changed (or eliminated in favour of something different), the corresponding modes of thinking must be altered. But it follows as well that space allocations and the structure and everyday use of space must likewise be transformed, so as to reflect new values and ideas about relationships. Since our concern here is with nonhuman animals, we will confine our attention to the implications for our treatment of, and interaction with, them. A decade ago, an inspiring document known as the "Declaration on Great Apes" was the subject of extensive discussion.[26] According to this manifesto, great apes (chimpanzees, bonobos, gorillas and orangutans) should be guaranteed the minimal moral rights of life, liberty and freedom from torture. We do not necessarily endorse here a rights approach to animals; but it is instructive to consider how human duties correlated with the above rights might be understood. Clearly, the declaration would require that we redefine (or reassign) moral considerability, so that great apes are acknowledged to possess it. Doing so does not require that we see them as autonomous beings or persons, though they may very well be.[27] What it does entail is that we (1) recognize that apes have a life of their own to live and (2) apply to apes the principle of non-maleficence (avoidance of harm), construed as respecting the inviolability of their bodies. To make good on our obligations mandated by this new morality, we would need (among other things) to refrain from experimenting on apes, from keeping them in confinement and to insure the preservation of their habitats. Each of these obligations can be met only by redesigning, reallocating, rechristening or legally redefining various spatial locations. And from the observance of these obligations there would arise new practices and behaviours. It is not just that humans would avoid repeating the damaging conduct of the past towards these animals; in addition, an opening would be created for unprecedented forms of interaction with them. We see this as an invitation to other species to take a role in creating a different kind of relationship with us. Animals may not all be able to respond actively to this invitation, though some can; but we must find the opportunity to learn what they can nevertheless teach us about themselves.

Karla Armbruster acutely remarks that "in her relationship of kinship with the gorillas, [Dian] Fossey reached across the boundary of difference and superiority that Western culture had constructed between itself and the rest of nature."[28] When Fossey "reached across the boundary of difference and superiority," she did so by placing herself in physical proximity to the gorillas, so that she was no longer "objectively studying" them but immersing herself in their world to the best of her ability. To accomplish this, she had to create *an authentic shared space*—a locus of interaction that offered occasions for friendship and understanding, a space not defined by traditional hierarchical thinking but rather *by fresh perceptions*. We do not all have to love apes or seek their companionship, however. No one can dictate the details of an evolved moral life. But what we do need is to accept the obligation to reform the spaces of inclusion, exclusion and interaction and to allow ourselves to remain open to the possibilities of cross-species intersubjectivity that may be encouraged to develop thereby.

PERCEIVING OTHER ANIMALS IN MORAL SPACE

At the outset of this chapter we proposed that a radical shift in the way we reflect on our relationship with other animals is required in order to resituate them in moral space. Furthermore, we suggested that this shift is perceptual: that a complex kind of seeing with feeling is necessary as an opening into the real world of human/animal interactions. We now need to develop further the notion of affective perception in relation to other animals, of seeing them and their distinctive experience in a "highly lucid and richly responsive way."[29] One procedure for doing this is to focus on particular examples, which requires discussion of individual situations involving nonhuman animals; the affective states they can give rise to; and how these feelings as perceptions can contribute to moral deliberations on the circumstances being reported or depicted. Specifically, we will take a closer look at two situations that are told about in uniquely different ways: the first, a poem describing the experience of a young girl and the owl whose life she takes; and the second, a scientific account of an experiment involving the electric shocking of dogs.

There are a number of philosophers whose work on moral perception would be useful here, but given the constraints of space, the work of one in particular will suffice as a prompt to generate discussion.[30] On moral perception, Martha Nussbaum writes, quoting Henry James:

> Moral knowledge ... is not simply intellectual grasp of propositions, it is not even simply intellectual grasp of particular facts; it is perception. It is seeing a complex concrete reality in a highly lucid and richly responsive way; it is taking in what is there with imagination and feeling.[31]

What might "taking in what is there" in these descriptions "with imagination and feeling" amount to, and how does this compare with what constitutes the merely "intellectual grasp" of the particular facts? Further, what might this moral knowledge as affective perception tell us about our relationship with nonhuman animals, particularly in terms of moral space? With these questions in mind, we will take a closer look at part one of Gwen Harwood's poem "Father and Child"[32] and at Martin Seligman's experiments on dogs.[33]

Situation 1

In her poem, Harwood beautifully captures the real-life encounter of a child with an animal, an encounter in which affective perception is crucial.

Father and Child

1. Barn Owl

Daybreak: the household slept.
I rose, blessed by the sun.
A horny fiend, I crept
out with my father's gun.
Let him dream of a child
obedient, angel-mild—

old No-Sayer, robbed of power
by sleep. I knew my prize
who swooped home at this hour
with daylight-riddled eyes
to his place on a high beam
in our old stables, to dream

light's useless time away.
I stood, holding my breath,
in urine-scented hay,
master of life and death,
a wisp-haired judge whose law
would punish beak and claw.

My first shot struck. He swayed,
ruined, beating his only
wing, as I watched, afraid
by the fallen gun, a lonely
child who believed death clean
and final, not this obscene

bundle of stuff that dropped,
and dribbled through loose straw
tangling in bowels, and hopped
blindly closer. I saw
those eyes that did not see
mirror my cruelty

> while the wrecked thing that could
> not bear the light nor hide
> hobbled in its own blood.
> My father reached my side,
> gave me the fallen gun.
> "End what you have begun."
>
> I fired. The blank eyes shone
> once into mine, and slept.
> I leaned my head upon
> my father's arm, and wept,
> owl-blind in early sun
> for what I had begun.

The poem begins with her eager and insolent: eager to kill the owl, and insolent of her father and his rules. Her enthusiasm draws her to the barn, to the place where her quarry sleeps. He is most vulnerable at this time and she is most powerful, for he is blinded by daylight, while she is enlivened by it. (According to *moral* perception, it is at this time that she is also most blind.)

> I stood, holding my breath, / in urine scented hay, / master of life and death, / a wisp-haired judge whose law / would punish beak and claw. /

She shoots the owl, but it does not die instantly. The great bird drops to the ground mangled and maimed by the bullet she fired into its body. It is at this point in the poem where the heart of our interest lies, for it is in her fully seeing and representing the situation—that is, taking in what is there with imagination and feeling—that we are concerned: specifically, her complete recognition of the suffering of the owl, of the cruelty of her actions and finally her full remorse and contrition.

> My first shot struck. He swayed, / ruined, beating his only / wing, as I watched, afraid / by the fallen gun, a lonely / child who believed death clean / and final, not this obscene
>
> bundle of stuff that dropped, / and dribbled through loose straw / tangling in bowels, and hopped / blindly closer. I saw / those eyes that did not see / mirror my cruelty
>
> while the wrecked thing that could / not bear the light nor hide / hobbled in its own blood.

In this part of the poem, to what does the child attend and what is the nature of her attending? A response to the first question might shed some light on the second. Her attention is drawn to the owl, but there is something different in how she now sees it compared with when she initially imagined it. Prior to the shooting she described it as a prize—something of value because she must compete to win it—but subsequent to the shooting the image changes, and it is this latter image, this vision that is crucial to her knowing the owl's suffering; and as such it is of profound moral significance.

Again the animal is referred to as something other than "owl": it is an "obscene / bundle of stuff that dropped, / and dribbled through loose straw / tangling in bowels, and hopped / blindly closer." In perceiving the owl in precisely this way the full horror of the animal's suffering is revealed to her. No longer does she see it as some animate trophy, something that can be won with the right skill and cunning, but as something that can experience pain, that can be maimed and tortured, that struggles in the face of this, that can have its deepest, innermost core exposed yet keep trying, that bleeds, that can hurt and that can feel, that wants life. The child bears witness to all of this in its fullness. She does not turn away, she does not hide her eyes nor cover her ears. In attending with such lucidity to the owl and what it is experiencing at that exact moment, she comprehends its suffering. From this point on, her acknowledgment of her cruelty is assured.

In another extraordinary image the horror of her cruelty is plainly revealed: "I saw / those eyes that did not see / mirror my cruelty / while the wrecked thing that could / not bear the light nor hide / hobbled in its own blood." Why a mirror? Why the owl's eyes? This image of seeing her cruelty in the owl's eyes is absolutely crucial. It is important because it emphasizes the role of perception in her encounter—not so much ordinary perception but *moral perception*. She can, morally speaking, see her act of cruelty because she is attending to the animal, she is not looking away but rather looking directly at its eyes; and these eyes reflect something important, for a mirror rarely lies, it reflects clearly that which is before it. Yet the owl's eyes represent more than a simple mirror image; they belong to a conscious, sentient being that gives a mode of recognition by means of its look. It is because of this that the child sees, in all its ugliness, the cruelty of her actions: that it was *she* that inflicted the pain and suffering on the animal, that *she* was responsible for its hobbling in its own blood, responsible for its being there suffering the daylight, and for its maimed and mangled body. In a sense she, like the owl, cannot bear the light nor hide, for the light reveals to her what she has done, and she cannot hide from it. It is there, right in front of her, and she sees it. The full knowledge of her cruelty is upon her and she is blinded by it. But her blindness is not merely one of insight; it also results from tears, tears of remorse and contrition.

> My father reached my side, / gave me the fallen gun. / "End what you have begun."
>
> I fired. The blank eyes shone / once into mine, and slept. / I leaned my head upon / my father's arm, and wept, / owl-blind in early sun / for what I had begun.

In this moment her full contrition is revealed. She has acknowledged fully the owl's suffering; she has acknowledged fully the cruelty that was of her doing, and now experiences fully her regret and her compassion. Her father, in making her shoot the owl so as to end its suffering, teaches her to bear the full weight of her actions and responsibilities, and comforts her during her expressions of guilt and grief and remorse. Her tears are not false tears, but those which are heavy and thick and blinding; they are real tears, and now, like the owl, she is blind and vulnerable. Her connection to the owl, to its suffering and to her deep feelings of regret, guilt, shame and indeed compassion are complete. What has sealed this connection is her perception of her encounter, her attention to what was there in all its specificity. The nature of this attention is that to which we now turn.

At the centre of the child's moral encounter are her emotions. They reveal to her the suffering and cruelty she has inflicted and so they are central to her expressions of remorse and contrition. She does not just see the events before her, she sees them *with her feelings*. This is best brought out if we think about what it might mean to grasp the reality before her with only her intellect. In contrast to the sort of "connected" thinking that the commentary of the poem has pointed to, we might think of this as a sort of "detached" thinking. Imagine a child who has similarly shot an owl and maimed it, who sees intellectually that the owl suffers, and that she has been cruel in causing the owl to suffer, but who shows no remorse, no guilt, no anguish, no contrition over her actions. We would want to say that there is something missing in this child's perception of the situation, that she hasn't seen it in the right way; she just hasn't gotten it.[34] Her recognition is lacking in some fundamental respect, namely, the emotional part of her cognition.[35] In contrast, for the child of the poem, an emotional response to the reality before her is what guides her recognition rather than her mere intellect. Her emotions are affective perceptions of what is there to be seen, and as such are a necessary part of full acknowledgment and recognition. The child who only knows intellectually that what she has done is cruel and says, "I have been cruel because of this, this and this," but shows no emotional response, is avoiding something crucial to proper moral understanding. The recognition of an act as cruel is not merely the engagement of the reasoning mind, it is awareness based on emotional discernment; it is seeing a reality with one's heart and reacting to it completely and suitably.[36] It is taking in what is there with some combination of compassion, love, sympathy, tenderness and empathy.

In Harwood's poem we have an account of the changing nature of a child's feelings and awareness of a situation, where her emotions have shown her, her cruelty towards the owl and the depth of its suffering. In effect the child has taken in a concrete reality in a "highly lucid and richly responsive way," and as such the poem is a paradigm example of moral perception understood in this manner. That she sees the cruelty of her actions, and that it was her emotions that showed her the cruelty of her actions, are what is crucial to grasp here. The perceptual account of her experience puts her emotional reactions at the centre of her experience, and so her claim to being cruel makes sense to us. To say that the child has grasped the cruelty of her actions towards the owl without offering some account of the role the emotions have played is to miss the point of the poem and its moral force. At the beginning of the poem the girl was not a child of moral insight; her way of seeing her impending actions was emotionally naive and self-interested. She did not fully comprehend the nature of cruelty. If she had shot the owl a second time, but her choice to shoot had been made in the absence of feelings, we would view it as merely a perfunctory act done without due sadness or remorse. Choice such as this, made in the absence of feelings, clouds moral perceptions and stunts moral development. As readers we can learn from the fictional character's experience of seeing cruelty towards animals for what it is and of what it means to acknowledge fully why it is wrong. Her contrition amounts to responding with the right feelings at the right time and in the right way.[37] The poem is an example of what we might see in turning back from theory to the particulars of a reality and understanding the wrongness of certain choices made and actions taken.

Situation 2

When we read a description of an experiment where an animal—who, prior to the experiment was fit and healthy—is maimed, burnt, electrically shocked, dissected, poisoned, isolated, infected or rendered helpless, there is an expectation upon us to turn away from this reality, and indeed the affective states that it gives rise to, towards moral theories for justification of its warrant. Seligman, for example—the person responsible for the experiments we are about to encounter—turns towards utilitarianism to justify his actions: human benefit outweighs the misery of the animals, and consequently this experiment is justified. However, *we* may turn in a different direction. Given what we have learned above from the child's experience, we might describe this as turning away with a deeper conscience. Nussbaum writes that "[Seligman's] work remains morally controversial for its treatment of subject animals [and] I do not conceal the moral unease it causes me to describe these experiments."[38] The unease caused by describing and indeed reading these experiments is important, for the feelings elicited by the experiments are modes of affective perception. To look away from the suffering of the dogs, to turn off our perceptual capacities and in essence our feelings is to get only half the moral story, but worse still, to get that half which further serves to cloud our moral (in)sight and numb our sensibilities. To read scientific experiments intellectually is to take on board a demand to switch off certain kinds of emotions, like fear, disgust, loathing, but also those of sympathy, empathy and compassion. But as we've seen in the previous discussion of Harwood's poem, these emotions are modes of perceiving the suffering and cruelty inflicted on the animals. To bracket off or shut down our emotions is to close down our perceptual apparatus such that we no longer see, or refuse to acknowledge, the animals' pain and suffering. We are asked to neutralize our moral sensibility, to become, in some sense, like moral psychopaths. The act of attending to what is there with our feelings is important, not only for appropriate moral choices and actions but for appropriate responses as well. Whether the decision concerns what is to be done, or deciding on the morality of what has already been done, to the animals, the more carefully or sensitively constituted our discernment of a particular situation is, the more wholesome our moral choices and actions can be. In the following discussion we will compare what "taking in what is there" in the descriptions "with imagination and feeling" amounts to, and compare it to a purely "intellectual grasp" of the particular facts.

The first extract below is taken from a journal article by Seligman and Maier, which cites experimental work in alleviating "learned helplessness" in dogs; and the second comes from Seligman's subsequent book, which develops in more detail his general thesis on learned helplessness.

Extract 1

> When a normal, naïve dog receives escape/avoidance training in a shuttle box, the following behaviour typically occurs: At the onset of electric shock, the dog runs frantically about, defecating, urinating, and howling, until it scrambles over the barrier and so escapes from shock. On the next trial, the dog, running and howling, crosses the barrier more quickly, and so on until efficient avoidance emerges.[39]

Extract 2

> Here is the typical procedure that we used to produce and detect learned helplessness in dogs: On the first day, the subject was strapped into the hammock and given 64 inescapable electric shocks, each 5.0 seconds long and of 6.0 milliamperes (moderately painful) intensity. The shocks were not preceded by any signal and they occurred randomly in time. Twenty-four hours later, the subject was given 10 trials of signaled escape-avoidance training in a two-way shuttle box: the dog had to jump over the barrier from one compartment into the other to escape or avoid shock. Shocks could occur in either compartment, so there was no place that was always safe, but the response of shuttling or jumping always led to safety.... From 1965 through 1969 we studied the behaviour of about 150 dogs who had received inescapable shock. Of these, two-thirds (about 100) were helpless. These animals went through the striking giving-up sequence that I have described.... Since helpless dogs were physically capable of jumping the barrier, their problem must have been psychological.[40]

The intellectual approach to these descriptions is the easier of the two accounts of moral knowledge to discuss initially, for this is the one most valued by moral theorists and experimenters alike. In terms of the latter, attending to the suffering of the dogs is paramount to interpreting the experimental results. They monitor and measure, test and confirm, attend to and record the movements and responses of their experimental subjects. Look at precisely what they write about: when a *naive* dog is shocked it runs about frantically, it pisses and shits itself, it howls, and finally it *scrambles* over the barrier. They shock it again, and while it doesn't, or may not, piss or shit itself it continues to howl, but importantly for the experiment, it crosses the barrier more quickly this time. Look at precisely what goes on in the second experiment: naive dogs are now strapped to hammocks so that they cannot avoid electric shocks. Here, then, we have dogs that will piss and shit themselves, howl and struggle, but they cannot get away from being shocked. This happens over and over again, for what is important for the experiment is the helplessness generated in the experimental subjects. It is a good result according to the experimenters, for some sort of useful, repeatable, measurable knowledge is obtained. This is not simply unqualified knowledge about the experience of the dogs generally, but knowledge of the kind conditional to the greater aims of the experiment.

In terms of many moral theorists who read these experiments, the focus of attention, like that of the experimenters, is the animal's pain, but pain in relation to how it might be used in various philosophical arguments as to the permissibility of the experiments. So, for example (and following Seligman's lead), a utilitarian might represent the situation outlined in the descriptions as the experimenters' having acted cruelly because they caused the animal to suffer. And according to the principle of equality, the interests of any being that suffers ought to be taken into consideration: its suffering should be counted equally with like suffering. In this mode of assessment, attention is paid to an animal's capacity to suffer, which is subsequently measured against the suffering of the humans involved. While well meaning, the theorist's attention slips ever further away from the experience of the animals themselves and moves towards thinking abstractly and argumentatively about the ethical problems they pose. According to the model we are trying to develop of moral knowledge as perception, what has happened to these theorists (and the experimenters) is that they have lost sight of what is ethically important; their perceptions have become shallow and faint; they don't see what is there to be seen because they ignore their emotional and imaginative responses and what these responses should reveal to them. What might be revealed to us when we attend to our emotions and imaginings in relation to these descriptions?

If we use our hearts as well as our minds we are able to see and represent more fully what is there before us, and importantly, we connect more fully to what our affective perceptions reveal. Often in the process of learning what we might call the "desensitized reading process" we are taught to curb our imagination and to limit our vision to the facts before us and only the facts. What of course is inherent in this demand, which isn't always stated explicitly, is the way in which we *attend* to the facts: our grasp of them should be intellectual, that is, free, as much as possible, of our imaginative and emotional responses (in short, it must be "objective"). But these responses, these very ways of seeing the reality before us, are constitutive of how the morally good person sees such a reality, as the discussion of Harwood's poem has shown us. Let's take a closer look at the descriptions again, but this time making the effort to really see and represent what is going on, that is, to take in what is there with imagination and feeling.

What do the experimenters mean by a "naive" dog? A naive dog in the context of the experiment identifies one that has not been conditioned or introduced to the experimental procedures or the equipment or indeed electroshocking procedures. But to be naive is also to have a simple or trusting view of the world, to lack a certain sort of critical and analytic sophistication, to be in many ways vulnerable to those who aren't naive in those situations. Imagine then what it is like for these dogs to be naive of what is to come, to be placed in a space that is entirely unfamiliar to them, to then experience pain that is so intense and so unprovoked that they piss and shit themselves uncontrollably and howl in fear and make every effort to escape this suffering. Imagine then what it's like for them to be placed in another confined space, but this time where there is no means of escape and then to be given shocks of the same intensity as before. Imagine a dog strapped down to the hammock, unable to move save its eyes and perhaps its mouth, being subjected to an intrusive and painful force that in other circumstances drives it to seek refuge anywhere but there. Here we have a dog rendered helpless, unable to escape what causes it to suffer, and it suffers over and over again. We can imagine it, we can see its terror, hear its howling in fear and pain, we can see its feces and urine spilling to the floor. Our horror, our disgust, our grief and our empathy show us the suffering and cruelty inflicted on these dogs, and it is empathy and compassion towards them which for many demand that such forms of cruelty be stopped.

In reading the experiments in a desensitized way we are ironically (given that Seligman's book is all about learned helplessness) being trained in a form of helplessness ourselves—a learned helplessness that teaches us that we are unable to do anything to prevent the experiments from happening because our emotional response, which is a richer way of seeing, is something to be overcome, suppressed, ignored or downplayed. Those who read these descriptions and understand moral knowledge as merely an intellectual exercise, lack the connection with the reality before them to really see what is unjust or cruel about it. This connection is what attending to what is there provides, what our emotional attitudes when understood as modes of perception provide. As moral beings we value those who care rather than those who merely say they do but don't show it in the appropriate ways. It is not enough to say that these experiments are cruel, without responding to this acknowledgement in a decisive way and with engaged feelings.

A NEW PICTURE OF MORAL SPACE

We have sought to illustrate in the foregoing sections that affective perception is essential to ethical deliberations about how we treat animals. If humans' conception of the moral community is evolving (and we think it is), then this evolution amounts to more than an abstract extension to nonhumans of ethical theories, principles and rules. While we acknowledge the importance of this sort of extension in reinforcing good practices, we argue that more basic still is the understanding and development of empathy and compassion towards members of other species. The extensionist model of the human/nonhuman relationship fails to capture certain aspects of immediate moral experience that allow us to see clearly why certain choices and actions involving other animals are cruel and unjust. These aspects are indeed our feelings and emotions. For this reason, we oppose a theoretical extensionism, the effect of which is to distance humans from other animals both conceptually and emotionally, and endorse instead a more phenomenological, experiential and revisionist approach to reconceiving the moral community.

All space in which human beings live and act, we have argued, is moral space. This is because human existence unfolds in a seamless dimension of ethical evaluation. Things, situations, people are good, bad or indifferent to us; behaviour may be designated as morally neutral or morally charged, but in either case it takes place within a sphere of evaluation that determines which of these classifications is appropriate. This sphere is the space of the real world everyone inhabits, which we call "moral space." Conduct (behaviour that is morally charged), therefore, comprises the actions of real persons doing what they do in the space of the real world, where it is subject to critical assessment along ethical lines.

As a consequence, the space within which we interact with animals can no longer be that abstract space where boundaries are shifted or extended to beings on the basis of their having certain characteristics or capacities considered morally relevant. (So, for example, if rationality is the trait deemed morally relevant, all and only those beings that are rational have moral standing.) Rather, we must reorient our discussions about humans and animals to a different kind of space and a different sense of what counts in moral deliberations—a space where feelings and emotions, as well as reasonings, are honoured and carry weight.

We do not claim to have provided here a complete picture of that moral space in which the mental life of animals and their needs and interests acquire positive value and significance. Nor are we taking a stand on the vexing and much debated question of equality between humans and animals or on that of humans' relationship to nature as a whole. Rather, we have tried to open discussion concerning how humans can think more constructively and fairly about the presence of animals in the moral domain. It has also been our aim to sketch an approach to evaluating the ways in which we treat animals that is imaginative, respectful and caring. Whether such a new conception of moral space can be more fully worked out, time will tell. On it will depend our species' success in taking responsibility for integrating animals into a shared and compassionate moral life.

NOTES

1. Tom Regan first introduced this phrase with the following explanation: "Individuals are subjects-of-a-life if they have beliefs and desires; perception, memory, and a sense of the future, including their own future; an emotional life together with feelings of pleasure and pain; preference- and welfare-interests; the ability to initiate action in pursuit of their desires and goals; a psychophysical identity over time; and an individual welfare in the sense that their experiential life fares well or ill for them, logically independently of their utility for others and logically independently of their being the object of anyone else's interests." See *The Case for Animal Rights* (Berkeley: University of California Press, 1983), 243. Regan adds that this criterion is satisfied by members of the class of "normal mammalian animals aged one or more." We make no assumptions in advance, however, about the scope of application of Regan's criterion. Some animals clearly appear to be subjects-of-a-life in the fullest sense; but others may be subjects-of-a-life just in the (more limited) sense that they have a welfare that matters to them and that they care to preserve.
2. James D. Proctor, "A Moral Earth: Facts and Values in Global Environmental Change," in James D. Proctor and David M. Smith, eds., *Geography and Ethics: Journeys in a Moral Terrain* (London: Routledge, 1999), 151.
3. Michael R. Curry, "'Hereness' and the Normativity of Place," in Proctor and Smith, eds., *Geography and Ethics*, 96.

4   Dennis Shepard, in Moises Kaufman and the Members of the Tectonic Theater Project, *The Laramie Project* (New York: Vintage Books, 2001), 95.
5   Alan Goldman, "The Source and Extent of a Patient's Right to the Truth," *Queen's Quarterly* 91 (1984): 126.
6   Nicholas Low and Brendan Gleeson, "Geography, Injustice and the Limits of Rights," in Proctor and Smith, eds., *Geography and Ethics*, 30, 31.
7   Margaret Urban Walker, "Keeping Moral Space Open: New Images of Ethics Consulting," *Hastings Center Report* 23, no. 2 (March–April 1993): 33.
8   B.R. Tilghman, "Picture Space and Moral Space," *British Journal of Aesthetics* 28 (1988): 320.
9   Ibid., 322.
10 Ludwig Wittgenstein, *Philosophical Investigations*, trans. G.E.M. Anscombe (Oxford: Blackwell, 1976), sec. 539.
11 Jim Cheney, "Postmodern Environmental Ethics: Ethics as Bioregional Narrative," *Environmental Ethics* 11 (1989): 129. Emphases in original.
12 Anthony Weston, "Before Environmental Ethics," *Environmental Ethics* 14 (1992): 335, 336. Emphasis in original.
13 Laurence Bove, personal communication to Michael Allen Fox, October 1991.
14 For some details, see Jennifer Wolch and Jody Emel, eds., *Animal Geographies: Place, Politics, and Identity in the Nature–Culture Borderlands* (London: Verso, 1998), "Preface" and chap. 1, "Witnessing the Animal Moment," both by the editors.
15 Steve Nadis, "Look Who's Talking," *New Scientist* 179, no. 2403 (12 July 2003): 39.
16 Stephen S. Birdsall, "Regard, Respect, and Responsibility: Sketches for a Moral Geography of the Everyday," *Annals of the Association of American Geographers* 86 (1996): 620. Birdsall adds, rather unilluminatingly, that "'Moral Geography'... refers to the patterns resulting from everyday expressions of good and evil" (627n3).
17 William S. Lynn, "Animals, Ethics, and Geography," in Wolch and Emel, eds., *Animal Geographies*, 283. Emphases in original.
18 Henri Lefèvbre, "Reflections on the Politics of Space," in R. Peet, ed., *Radical Geography* (London: Methuen, 1978), 341.
19 Klaus Elder, *The Social Construction of Nature: A Sociology of Ecological Enlightenment*, trans. Mark Ritter (London: Sage Publications, 1996), 21.
20 For example, Paul Shepard, *The Others: How Animals Made Us Human* (Washington, DC: Island, 1995); Jennifer Wolch, "Zoöpolis," in Wolch and Emel, eds., *Animal Geographies*, 119–38; Ralph R. Acampora, "Bodily Being and Animal World: Toward a Somatology of Cross-Species Community," in H. Peter Steeves, ed., *Animal Others: On Ethics, Ontology, and Animal Life* (Albany, NY: SUNY Press, 1999), 117–31.

21 Lynn, "Animals, Ethics, and Geography," 282.
22 More precisely, our relationship is with *members* of other species, on either an individual or a collective basis.
23 "Deadly clean [before birth], the child must immediately acquire the thousands of bacteria that will make outer life possible. This he does as he slides through the vaginal canal, passes near the mother's anus at birth, and is handled by those awaiting his emergence. The mouth first, gasping for air, is colonized. Hours later, the nose and throat and armpits are infected. The bacteria consume the child, stabilizing their growth to live comfortably on his skin secretions. A few days later, the mother will be able to recognize her baby by smell—the consequence of the feast of micro-animals." H. Peter Steeves, "They Say Animals Can Smell Fear," in Steeves, ed., *Animal Others*, 173-74.
24 William Morris, *Heritage Illustrated Dictionary of the English Language*, International Edition (Boston: Houghton Mifflin, 1973). "The corresponding sides, etc., of similar polygons are homologues of each other; ... one of the bones in the hand of man is the homologue of that in the paddle of a whale." *Webster's Revised Unabridged Dictionary*, online edition, http://machaut.uchicago.edu.cgi-bin/WEBSTER.sh?WORD=homologue.
25 *American Heritage Dictionary of the English Language*, 4th online ed., 2000, http://www.bartleby.com/61/78/H0257800.html.
26 Paola Cavalieri and Peter Singer, eds., *The Great Ape Project: Equality beyond Humanity* (London: Fourth Estate, 1993); see also *Etica & Animali* 8 (1996), Special Issue Devoted to The Great Ape Project.
27 On chimpanzees and bonobos as autonomous beings, see Steven M. Wise, *Rattling the Cage: Toward Legal Rights for Animals* (Cambridge, MA: Perseus Publishing, 2000), chap. 10; on orangutans and gorillas as autonomous beings, see Steven M. Wise, *Drawing the Line: Science and the Case for Animal Rights* (Cambridge, MA: Perseus Publishing, 2002), chaps. 10 and 11. See also David DeGrazia, "Great Apes, Dolphins, and the Concept of Personhood," *Southern Journal of Philosophy* 35 (1997): 301-20; and Juan Carlos Gomez, "Are Apes Persons? The Case for Primate Intersubjectivity," *Etica & Animali* 9 (1998): 51-63.
28 Karla Armbruster, "'Surely, God, These Are My Kin': The Dynamics of Identity and Advocacy in the Life and Works of Dian Fossey," in Jennifer Ham and Matthew Senior, eds., *Animal Acts: Configuring the Human in Western History* (London: Routledge, 1997), 214.
29 Martha Nussbaum, "'Finely Aware and Richly Responsible': Literature and the Moral Imagination," in *Love's Knowledge: Essays on Philosophy and Literature* (Oxford: Oxford University Press, 1990), 152.
30 That moral perception exists and that it is important isn't in dispute; what account one gives of it certainly is, but that is not the main concern of this

essay. What *is* central here is moral perception in relation to our moral deliberations over situations involving other animals, and so we've chosen an account—not necessarily the only or the best account—to generate discussion in an area of ethics that hasn't thus far taken on board the importance of moral perception.

31 Nussbaum, "'Finely Aware and Richly Responsible,'" 152.
32 Gwen Harwood, *Selected Poems* (Pymble, New South Wales: HarperCollins, 1990), 113-14. We would like to thank Fiona Utley for bringing this poem to our attention.
33 Martin Seligman, *Learned Helplessness: On Development, Depression and Death* (New York: W.H. Freeman, 1992).
34 Martha Nussbaum, "The Discernment of Perception: An Aristotelian Conception of Private and Public Rationality," in *Love's Knowledge*, 79.
35 Ibid.
36 Ibid.
37 Ibid. Nussbaum cites Aristotle here: "To respond 'at the right times, with reference to the right objects, toward the right people, with the right aim, and in the right way, is what is appropriate and best, and this is characteristic of excellence.'" Aristotle, *Nicomachean Ethics*, Book II, 1106b21-23.
38 Martha Nussbaum, *Upheavals of Thought: The Intelligence of Emotions* (Cambridge: Cambridge University Press, 2001), 101.
39 M.E.P. Seligman and S.F. Maier, "Alleviation of Learned Helplessness in the Dog," *Journal of Abnormal Psychology* 73 (1968): 256-62.
40 Seligman, *Learned Helplessness*, 23.

WORKS CITED

Acampora, Ralph R. "Bodily Being and Animal World: Toward a Somatology of Cross-Species Community." In H. Peter Steeves, ed., *Animal Others: On Ethics, Ontology, and Animal Life*. Albany, NY: SUNY Press, 1999.

Aristotle. *Nicomachean Ethics*, Book II.

Armbruster, Karla. "'Surely, God, These Are My Kin': The Dynamics of Identity and Advocacy in the Life and Works of Dian Fossey." In Jennifer Ham and Matthew Senior, eds., *Animal Acts: Configuring the Human in Western History*. London: Routledge, 1997.

Birdsall, Stephen S. "Regard, Respect, and Responsibility: Sketches for a Moral Geography of the Everyday." *Annals of the Association of American Geographers* 86 (1996): 619-29.

Cavalieri, Paola, and Peter Singer, eds. *The Great Ape Project: Equality beyond Humanity*. London: Fourth Estate, 1993.

Cheney, Jim. "Postmodern Environmental Ethics: Ethics as Bioregional Narrative." *Environmental Ethics* 11 (1989): 117–34.

Curry, Michael R. "'Hereness' and the Normativity of Place." In James D. Proctor and David M. Smith, eds., *Geography and Ethics: Journeys in a Moral Terrain*. London: Routledge, 1999.

DeGrazia, David. "Great Apes, Dolphins, and the Concept of Personhood." *Southern Journal of Philosophy* 35 (1997): 301–20.

Elder, Klaus. *The Social Construction of Nature: A Sociology of Ecological Enlightenment*. Translated by Mark Ritter. London: Sage Publications, 1996.

Goldman, Alan. "The Source and Extent of a Patient's Right to the Truth." *Queen's Quarterly* 91 (1984): 124–38.

Gomez, Juan Carlos. "Are Apes Persons? The Case for Primate Intersubjectivity." *Etica & Animali* 9 (1998): 51–63.

Harwood, Gwen. *Selected Poems*. Pymble, New South Wales: HarperCollins, 1990.

Kaufmann, Moises, and the Members of the Tectonic Theatre Project. *The Laramie Project*. New York: Vintage Books, 2001.

Lefèbvre, Henri. "Reflections on the Politics of Space." In R. Peet, ed., *Radical Geography*. London: Methuen, 1978.

Low, Nicholas, and Brendan Gleeson. "Geography, Injustice and the Limits of Rights." In James D. Proctor and David M. Smith, eds., *Geography and Ethics: Journeys in a Moral Terrain*. London: Routledge, 1999.

Lynn, William S. "Animals, Ethics, and Geography." In Jennifer Wolch and Jody Emel, eds., *Animal Geographies: Place, Politics, and Identity in the Nature-Culture Borderlands*. London: Verso, 1998.

Nadis, Steve. "Look Who's Talking." *New Scientist* 179, no. 2403 (12 July 2003): 36–39.

Nussbaum, Martha. *Love's Knowledge: Essays on Philosophy and Literature*. Oxford: Oxford University Press, 1990.

———. *Upheavals of Thought: The Intelligence of Emotions*. Cambridge: Cambridge University Press, 2001.

Proctor, James D. "A Moral Earth: Facts and Values in Global Environmental Change." In James D. Proctor and David M. Smith, eds., *Geography and Ethics: Journeys in a Moral Terrain*. London: Routledge, 1999.

Regan, Tom. *The Case for Animal Rights*. Berkeley: University of California Press, 1983.

Seligman, Martin. *Learned Helplessness: On Development, Depression and Death*. New York: W.H. Freeman, 1992.

Seligman, Martin, and S.F. Maier. "Alleviation of Learned Helplessness in the Dog." *Journal of Abnormal Psychology* 73 (1968): 256–62.

Shepard, Paul. *The Others: How Animals Made Us Human*. Washington, DC: Island, 1995.
Steeves, H. Peter. "They Say Animals Can Smell Fear." In H. Peter Steeves, ed., *Animal Others: On Ethics, Ontology, and Animal Life*. Albany, NY: SUNY Press, 1999.
Tilghman, B.R. "Picture Space and Moral Space." *British Journal of Aesthetics* 28 (1988): 317–26.
Walker, Margaret Urban. "Keeping Moral Space Open: New Images of Ethics Consulting." *Hastings Center Report* 23, no. 2 (March–April 1993): 33–44.
Weston, Anthony. "Before Environmental Ethics." *Environmental Ethics* 14 (1992): 321–38.
Wise, Steven M. *Drawing the Line: Science and the Case for Animal Rights*. Cambridge, MA: Perseus Publishing, 2002.
———. *Rattling the Cage: Toward Legal Rights for Animals*. Cambridge, MA: Perseus Publishing, 2000.
Wittgenstein, Ludwig. *Philosophical Investigations*. Translated by G.E.M. Anscombe. Oxford: Blackwell, 1976.
Wolch, Jennifer. "Zoöpolis." In Jennifer Wolch and Jody Emel, eds., *Animal Geographies: Place, Politics, and Identity in the Nature–Culture Borderlands*. London: Verso, 1998.

8

Electric Sheep and the New Argument from Nature

ANGUS TAYLOR

During the past three decades, as part of the burgeoning field of environmental ethics, there has been a remarkable upsurge of interest among philosophers in the moral status of (nonhuman) animals. The dominant perception of animals as fundamentally *other* than humans has been strongly challenged by those who would admit many nonhumans into the moral community. Yet this project faces formidable obstacles. Philosophically, it is doubted by many that the individualistic orientation of animal liberation is compatible with the holistic orientation of much environmental thought. Practically, the capitalist mode of production militates against viewing the nonhuman world as anything other than a storehouse of exploitable resources. In their own ways, these obstacles reflect the idea that the project of animal liberation is contrary to the natural order of things.

The movement for animal liberation involves the attempt to break down the traditional conceptual boundaries between human beings and animals, in order to include the latter within the moral community. But this breaking down of boundaries is a double-edged sword that is simultaneously being wielded by opponents of animal liberation to uphold the notion of human domination over other species. I want to use the fiction of Philip K. Dick—in particular the novel *Do Androids Dream of Electric Sheep?*—as illustrative material for discussing what is probably the most influential grounds for rejecting animal liberation: what I call *the new argument from nature*. Like the teleological argument for the existence of God, the new argument from nature against animal liberation derives its force as much from intuition as from reason. That it is natural and therefore right that we dominate and exploit animals seems so obvious to many as hardly needing to be rationally defended. Bolstered by pre-reflective intuition, the argument from nature provides a neat way of side-stepping the rigorous philosophical arguments mounted on utilitarian, deontological and other grounds by Peter Singer, Tom Regan and all those who have followed in their wake. On inspection, however, it may be seen that the animating force of the new argument from nature is less science than ideology.

I am not suggesting that at any given time there is only one way in which nature is invoked to explain and justify our interactions with animals. For their part, animal liberationists make their own appeal to nature in presenting their cases—typically arguing that humans and nonhumans have much in common. And as Rod Preece has shown, the overall history of Western thought about animals is complex and very far from the onesided denigration of animals that we may be tempted to assume it is.[1] My focus is on particular ongoing positions within academic philosophy. Lest that focus seem too narrow, it should be pointed out that the arguments of philosophers from Aristotle to Descartes and beyond have not been without influence (as well as being influenced in turn by their times and cultures) and that, especially today, the role of professional philosophers in the public debate about animals is a significant one.

Among the pronouncements that ushered in the modern age of science and industry was Descartes's notorious claim that animals are literally and simply machines. Dogs and cats, parrots and sheep are "natural automata"—robots made by God. Cartesian dualism radically divided the realm of consciousness from the realm of matter and separated humans (allegedly the only earthly beings possessing minds) from all other living creatures. Out was the organic vision of the world as a unified hierarchy of beings, reflecting in varying degrees the perfection of God. Nature, according to the radical new view, was the realm of the mechanical. Already in the seventeenth century, Descartes presented us with a picture of human beings as minds temporarily encased in machine bodies. His consignment of animals to the purely mechanical was part of the project to make humans "masters and possessors of nature" and a portent of the industrial age.

The changed view of nature may have been expressed in its starkest form in the mechanism of Descartes, but the absence of teleology and intrinsic value from the physical world was a foundational principle of the new science. Galileo proclaimed that the domain of science was restricted to what could be measured quantitatively, and excluded the "secondary" qualities (like colour and sound) experienced by the human mind. Newton, who believed that the gravitational attraction of bodies was ultimately caused by God, vehemently rejected the idea that "inanimate brute matter" had any *innate* power to affect other matter except by contact. Matter, significantly, is brute: literally, stupid and animal-like. In its own manner, the emergent scientific view of nature reinforced and even exaggerated the older, organic view's claim that human beings are superior to nonhuman beings in a morally important way. Saint Thomas Aquinas's thirteenth-century claim that God does not care about animals for their own sakes because they are not rational was quite compatible with the new science.

David Hume pointed out the logical truth that *is* by itself cannot generate *ought*. Nevertheless, if we judge, as we commonly do, that human well-being is an end we ought to pursue, and if we believe that our well-being is inextricably bound up with our biological and psychological natures, then a bridge between *is* and *ought* cannot be dismissed. We are led towards Aristotle's position, that only by manifesting the potentiality inherent in our human nature will we achieve true well being (*eudaimonia*). What our nature is becomes a vital matter for deciding how we ought to act and for understanding what the limits of our obligations are. So, for example, Kathryn Paxton George has argued that the physiology of girls and women makes it unhealthy for most of them to adhere to a strict vegetarian (in particular, vegan) diet. At the same time, to excuse them, on this ground, from a standard that is more readily attainable by men, says George, is to relegate girls and women to the status of a moral underclass, unable because of their physical natures to live a truly ethical life.[2] I am not concerned here with the veracity of George's claim (which has not gone unchallenged) about the effect of a strict vegetarian diet on female health. What is pertinent is her point that we must recognize that our nature does circumscribe our ethical responsibilities.

In the version of the argument from nature that reflected the dominant philosophical position of the post-seventeenth-century world, the natural world and culture are distinct. As uniquely rational beings, humans have unique moral worth. We have few, if any, obligations to nature itself, though we should recognize its instrumental value. Animals are excluded from the moral community. They are by nature radically *other*, and therefore legitimate objects of exploitation by us. By contrast, the new argument from nature insists on an overlap between nature and culture. As natural beings we retain our prerogatives as top predators, even while culture supervenes to limit the morally acceptable ways we can treat each other. We respect and have obligations to nature in terms of preserving and enhancing ecosystemic values. Animals are excluded from the moral community. Perversely, it is now our intimate natural connectedness with nonhumans that renders them legitimate objects of exploitation.

Sartre remarks briefly that animals are a philosophical problem.[3] Why this should be so from his point of view is not hard to see. In a Cartesian mould, Sartre divides the world into *être pour soi* (being for itself) and *être en soi* (being in itself). The realm of human consciousness (*être pour soi*) is the realm of autonomy and perpetual self-creation, while the rest of the world is what is in essence given, inert, uncreative and what is thus alien to humanity. However, not only common sense but, increasingly, scientific evidence tells against the Cartesian divorce between humans and animals. Animals, it is true, do not possess the reasoning powers of human beings, yet many of them fit poorly into Sartre's dualistic schema, for they are sentient and possess a degree of autonomy in conducting their lives.

Historically, even those philosophers, like Locke and Hume, who were prepared to say that animals exhibit a degree of reason, balked when it came to admitting nonhumans to the moral community. Today, however, the traditional consensus has broken down and a vigorous philosophical debate rages over the claim that the principle of equal consideration of interests should not be limited in its application to human beings. Unfortunately for those who wish to maintain the divide between humans and animals, almost all the good philosophical arguments come down on the side of full-out animal liberation, or at a minimum on the side of drastic reform to current practices. In particular, the *argument from marginal cases* is devastating to nearly all traditional positions. The argument from marginal cases rests on the observation that there exists an overlap between humans and nonhumans with regard to mental attributes that are typically invoked to include humans in the moral community and exclude animals from it. Not all humans can reason better than animals; not all humans are moral agents; not all humans can imagine an extended future for themselves or have a sophisticated conception of self. Many animals exhibit more autonomy than many humans do, in the sense that they are better able to care for themselves and to navigate successfully through their natural and social environments.

Since Darwin, and with recent findings in ethology and cognitive science, insistence on an essential difference between human and other animals is increasingly untenable. Darwin had no doubt that all the higher mental faculties found in humans could be found in at least incipient form in animals. Of humans and the other mammals, especially the primates, he wrote:

> All have the same senses, intuitions, and sensations,—similar passions, affections, and emotions, even the more complex ones, such as jealousy, suspicion, emulation, gratitude, and magnanimity; they practise deceit and are revengeful; they are sometimes susceptible to ridicule, and even have a sense of humour; they feel wonder and curiosity; they possess the same faculties of imitation, attention, deliberation, choice, memory, imagination, the association of ideas, and reason, though in very different degrees.[4]

Darwin mentioned the use and making of simple tools by nonhumans, and believed that some animals could appreciate beauty and might even—as in the case of dogs' interaction with their human masters—display an incipient form of religious devotion. The point here, however, is not that humans typically exhibit significant superiority in such areas; it is that some humans do not. Hence any attempt to exclude all nonhumans from the moral community would seem to require that many humans—infants and those who suffer from significant mental illness or handicap—likewise be excluded, while any claim that all humans must be included in the moral community would seem to require that many animals also be included. Attempts to evade the argument from marginal cases and to exclude nonhumans from the moral community on the grounds that humans per se constitute a unique natural kind appear arbitrary and inconsistent.[5] Philosophers who would deny nonhumans entry into the moral community based on their alleged radical *otherness* from humans must therefore resort to Hobbes's contract theory of morality, which has potentially dire implications for at least some humans, or must contort themselves mightily in order to draw a convoluted line in the sand between all humans and all nonhumans.

The new argument from nature, on the other hand, offers a possible escape from the looming spectre of moral inclusiveness. It denies that the intrinsic qualities of those outside the human community can give them any claim to equal moral standing with us. What counts is not the capacity to suffer or even, in the last analysis, the capacity to reason, but rather the ecological niche of one's species. It is right that we hunt, kill, eat, exploit and experiment upon members of other species for the simple reason that that's how nature works: it's us against them, and luckily for us, in a world of predators and prey, we are the top predators. The strategy here is not to draw a line in the sand between human and nonhuman qualities, but to erase or blur the line in order all the better to let loose the beast in the human. At the same time, this letting loose is presented as virtuous—as facilitating the development of those positive traits of character that, paradoxically perhaps, make us truly human.

The new argument from nature differs from social Darwinism in that it is not about competition within human society or about progress; its focus is ecological process and balance. Its common refrain is that moral rights have no ecological meaning or applicability. Animals can have no moral claims against each other, and insofar as our interactions with animals (such as hunting and eating) are *natural*, no claims can be made against us. At the same time, proponents of the new argument are likely to lament industrial society's tendency to view the natural world as having value only instrumentally: as simply raw material for the production process.

J. Baird Callicott, the prominent advocate of Aldo Leopold's land ethic, has condemned animal liberation, as well as factory farming, on ecological grounds. Though he subsequently tempered his criticism, he originally accused animal liberation of being a "life-loathing" philosophy, one that if pursued in practice would entail "ruinous consequences" for the environment because its concern for the welfare of individual sentient creatures made it incompatible with promoting the flourishing of ecosystems.[6] In this charge he was joined by an array of writers. The title of an essay by Mark Sagoff put it bluntly: "Animal Liberation and Environmental Ethics: Bad Marriage, Quick Divorce."[7] (For his part, Regan described Leopold's holistic ethic as "ecological fascism.")[8]

Holmes Rolston III provides us with a fine example of the new argument. He makes an eloquent case for ascribing intrinsic value to more than just sentient life, on the grounds that every organism has its own *telos* and pursues its own good: "An organism is a spontaneous, self-maintaining system, sustaining and reproducing itself, executing its program, making a way through the world, checking against performance by means of responsive capacities with which to measure success."[9] So the organism is an evaluative system, even if it is not yet a moral system. If we are to have a *vital* ethic, one that respects life, we must take into account how our behaviour affects these amoral evaluative systems. Even the species has its own *telos*, and an ecosystem *produces* value, though it has no value *for* itself. To believe that morality is purely a matter of interpersonal relations and has nothing to do with our place in the web of nature is to be blind to the way that value is embedded in natural processes.

But Rolston is no egalitarian when it comes to moral standing. Though good and value are embedded in nature, he says, only humans are moral beings. This, it turns out, makes all the difference. "The question, Can they suffer? is not as simple as Bentham thought. What we *ought* to do depends on what *is*. The *is* of nature differs significantly from the *is* of culture, even when similar suffering is present in both."[10] But what *is* the *is* of nature? Rolston wants to have his steak and eat it too. Humans, he says, live both in the realm of culture and in the realm of nature. Our interpersonal relations are cultural and hence bound by moral rules not applicable to the realm of nature: we are bound to assist each other in emergencies and to refrain from eating each other. At the same time, the standards for our dealings with nonhumans are quite different and arise from ecosystemic processes of predation and natural selection. We have evolved as omnivores and may rightly eat animals, since, in effect, the law of the jungle applies to our dealings with them—a law that would be inexcusable to apply to our interpersonal behaviour. "The boundary between animals and humans has not been rubbed out after all; only what was a boundary line has been smeared into a boundary zone."[11] And a most convenient boundary zone it is from our point of view, one into which we may conduct frequent and well-armed raids in search of food and resources. Hobbes reached a similar conclusion in the seventeenth century by arguing that the social contract is not applicable to our dealings with animals, with whom we remain in a state of perpetual war. The realm of nature is nasty, brutish and short, at least for the brutes. If *ought* follows from *is*, our dealings with animals are rightly brutish.

Throughout history, eating (not "feeding") in human communities has been heavy with ritual and symbolism. How and what and whom we eat is of prime cultural significance. Sartre recognized this, and, with his somewhat bizarre rejection of the natural world, wanted his food to be as unnatural as possible, to appear on his plate as the pure manifestation of a human project—like a nicely shaped chocolate éclair.[12] This may be carrying things rather far, but to pretend that while war, murder, slavery and sexism cannot be justified by appeal to nature, our eating habits can be, is disingenuous.

Laura Westra is another who deplores the lack of ecological awareness in animal-liberation philosophy.[13] Like Rolston, she reminds us that we must eat to live, and from this fact infers a moral license to eat animals. Relations between members of different species in the wild, she tells us, are characterized by "hostility and indifference," and nature teaches that we may use animals insofar as this is required for our survival. Hence an appropriate attitude of "respectful hostility" condones our killing animals for food and using them for "unavoidable" medical research. But neither Westra nor Rolston explains how respect for the life or *telos* of sentient beings is manifested by *unnecessary* killing—a notable omission, given that killing animals for food is seldom necessary for our survival. And given that animals do not perform medical experimentation (even of the "unavoidable" variety) on each other, it seems a bit odd to invoke the ecological facts of life in defense of this uniquely human practice—though perhaps a smeared boundary zone will do the trick.

The persistent argument that animal liberation is incompatible with the flourishing of ecosystems—since to admit animals to the moral community allegedly would require massive interference with wild nature to protect them from harm—attacks a straw man. Regan and other liberationists do not maintain that wild animals have moral claims against each other or against the forces of nature; the ethical obligation here is that moral agents not inflict unnecessary harm upon sentient beings, human or not. The general animal-rights position, explicit in Regan's case, is to leave wild animals and their habitats alone.

When liberationists are not being excoriated for failing to recognize ecological realities, they are liable to be attacked for reducing humans to the level of mere animals. For James Reichmann, Regan's attempt to ascribe inherent value to animals runs aground on the impossibility of finding absolute moral values in a Darwinian universe.[14] Reichmann, a Jesuit, argues that we can make sense of inherent moral worth in humans only by recognizing that humans have a distinctive, God-given essence that separates them from the rest of creation. To deny the essential boundaries between human and nonhuman, he claims, has the consequence of denying inherent value to all. While his target is Regan and other liberationists, Reichmann's point—that on the basis of an appeal to nature conceived not in the Aristotelian but in the Darwinian mould, one can justify just about any conduct towards others that one wishes—is at least equally applicable to the new argument from nature. I say "at least" because liberationist arguments have the advantage of consistency: *if* we believe that human individuals do indeed have intrinsic moral worth of some kind, then consistency demands that we ascribe the same worth to all those who possess similar, relevant characteristics. By contrast, anti-liberationists, faced with the (literally and figuratively) unpalatable conclusions of a consistent moral individualism, resort to the moral flexibility of their ecological argument.

I want to turn now to Philip K. Dick's work, for the way it casts into sharp relief the double-edged aspect inherent in the breaking down of boundaries between human and nonhuman. Dick is a writer whose philosophical sophistication is simultaneously masked and manifested in his exuberant and idiosyncratic use of the clichés of pulp science fiction. His subject matter is typically said to be "the nature of reality" or "reality and illusion," but this is facile. The focus of Dick's work is the question: what does it mean to be authentically human? He approaches this question within the context of humanity's encounter with the "other," whether machine, extraterrestrial alien or animal.

In his fiction, Dick erases boundaries so that the artificial and the natural, the human and the nonhuman, the mechanical and the organic, overlap and partially merge. The universe becomes a chain of being, illuminated from the top down by spirit and the possibility of life-enhancing relatedness, so that every individual being can struggle up into the greater light to fulfill its potential. At the same time, he shows us the dark side of this erasure: the potential movement in the other direction, toward entropy and loss of empathic relatedness. Schizophrenia and autism figure prominently in Dick's stories. At the political level, *The Man in the High Castle*, a brilliant alternative-history novel of a world in which the Axis powers won the Second World War, shows us the Nazis bent on further megalomaniacal conquests, identifying with the forces of nature in order to justify dominating and exploiting everything weaker than they are.

> It is their sense of space and time. They see through the here, the now, into the vast black deep beyond, the unchanging. And that is fatal to life. Because eventually there will be no life; there was once only the dust particles in space, the hot hydrogen gases, nothing more, and it will come again. This is an interval, *ein Augenblick*. The cosmic process is hurrying on, crushing life back into the granite and methane; the wheel turns for all life. It is all temporary. And these—these madmen—respond to the granite, the dust, the longing of the inanimate; they want to aid *Natur*.[15]

Nature here threatens us with more than thermodynamic entropy. What Dick fears is moral entropy: the tendency towards a state without the life force that arises only out of the will to relatedness. All beings, great or small, in the chain of life can struggle upward, but always there is the danger of regression. And this regression is alluring, not unlike Sartre's *en soi*, with its illusory possibility of abandoning the burden of moral responsibility. In Dick's fiction, mechanical reflex behaviour presents itself enticingly in the guise of life. What rational measure can we use to tell the difference between life and pseudo-life, between right and wrong? Time and again the inanimate masquerades as the animate, tempting us to mistake the pursuit of power over others for authentic human identity.

The Nazi world view masqueraded as a return to life-affirming nature. If one reads *Meditations on Hunting* by José Ortega y Gasset[16] and examines the arguments of his followers in the hunting community, or the related arguments of other philosophers, like Rolston, who endorse hunting, it is hard not to be struck by the fascist overtones: the notion that modern civilization has made us effete, divorced us from our true nature; the idea that in order to live fully, to reclaim our authentic being, we must return, if only on weekends, to the ways of our paleolithic ancestors, immersing ourselves once more in the struggle for existence by manifesting our animal nature—in our case as top predators, who by right of nature hunt and kill and dominate others not of our kind.

I am not claiming an exact parallel between the Nazi world view and the new argument from nature. The Nazis rejected *humanity* as any basis for social solidarity; the basis for them was the racial nation as embodied in the state. Many leading Nazis opposed hunting, as part of their avowed love for animals. (Hermann Goering was a notable exception on the hunting issue.) What is relevant here is that the Nazis combined a rejection of traditional conceptual boundaries with adherence to a hierarchical scale of moral worth and a belief in nature as an arena of eternal struggle. They insisted that to attempt, as modern civilization had, to transcend the harsh laws of living nature was to court disaster. At the same time, their attitudes towards animals were flexible and inconsistent. They frequently exalted animals (particularly beasts of prey) and identified with them, while also denigrating non-Aryan humans as being no better than animals.[17] They perceived the human in the beast or the beast in the human, as called for by the occasion. As fascists, they violently repudiated the values of liberty, equality and historical progress—values that figure prominently in the animal liberation movement.

Do Androids Dream of Electric Sheep?—not to be confused with the movie *Blade Runner*, which is superficially based on it—plunges us into a world of predator and prey, rich with metaphor. It is also a world where nuclear radiation has left few animals alive and where people keep robotic imitations. The novel's anti-hero, Rick Deckard, is a cop who hunts down and kills androids. Now, the term "android" can itself be confusing. Traditionally in science fiction it has designated an artificially created, but nonetheless flesh-and-blood, human. As such, the android is distinct from the robot, the mechanical being that imitates sentient behaviour and may even outwardly appear to be human. Descartes thought he had discovered tests that could with certainty differentiate real humans from humanoid robots and from animals. These tests (having to do with language and with behaviour) aimed to reveal whether a being could think or was merely programmed, and thus to mark an unbridgeable chasm between human and machine. Thumbing their noses at Descartes, Isaac Asimov's robots passed the Turing test and, despite much resistance from bigoted humans, claimed entry for machines into the moral community. Androids, by contrast, were a metaphor for humans suffering from racial discrimination: after all, they are really just like us, wherever they may come from. More recently, however, the term "android" has tended to be conflated with "humanoid robot."

Dick's androids are flesh-and-blood beings, but not exactly traditional victims of prejudice, since they represent a real threat to human society. For Dick, the android represents the human who is alienated from others and is mechanical in thought and behaviour, while the humanoid robot—the complex system with powers of self-maintenance and self-direction that is constituted originally from simple, inanimate parts—represents the potentiality inherent in all beings to attain authentic existence through relatedness. There is a crossover zone here, and it is probably no coincidence that the artificial humans in *Do Androids Dream of Electric Sheep?* are Nexus models. Further, Dick deliberately obscures identities by having the androids casually referred to as "humanoid robots," though at points in the novel it is made clear that these are organic, flesh-and-blood—not (physically) mechanical—beings. The question for bounty hunter Rick Deckard is how to distinguish the authentic human from dangerous, flesh-and-blood imitations, those who are sinking into a psychic state of mechanism and entropy. The answer: to administer the Voigt-Kampff Empathy Test, centrally involving how one responds emotionally to the idea of animals being harmed. No Cartesian test for rational thought here, but rather an appeal to Darwin.

Darwin argued that nature is not simply an arena of dog-eat-dog competition; mutual aid gives social animals a survival advantage. Because it is naturally selected for, the moral sense as manifest in caring for others can be found in incipient form among many animals. Along this line, Dick's protagonist links the capacity for empathy with a switch away from meat-eating:

> Empathy, he once had decided, must be limited to herbivores or anyhow omnivores, who could depart from a meat diet. Because, ultimately, the empathic gift blurred the boundaries between hunter and victim, between the successful and the defeated.... A herd animal such as man would acquire a higher survival factor through this; an owl or a cobra would be destroyed.[18]

Even language can betray the android: "It, he thought. *She keeps calling the owl it.* Not her."[19]

In Dick's stories, nothing is ever as straightforward as it appears, and at one point Deckard is faced with the possibility that he himself may be an android, given the lack of compassion he displays for those he hunts. The novel is not only an implied critique of hunting, and of our treatment of animals in general, but an admonition that none of us has clean hands when it comes to our treatment of others, human or nonhuman. By the end of the story Deckard has not rid the world of corruption and illusion; he has recognized the value of compassion and he has managed to survive, in order to resume his personal struggle. He realizes that even a robotic animal is worth caring for. "The electric things have their lives, too. Paltry as those lives are."[20]

In Dick's vision, the moral imperative calls on us to care for all sentient beings, human or nonhuman, natural or artificial, regardless of their place in the order of things. And Dick makes clear that this imperative is grounded in empathy, not reason, whatever subsequent role reason may play. Throughout his fiction, the virtue of empathy is contrasted with the dangers of untempered intellect. In the case of philosophers or the person on the street, it is apparent that without the empathic intuition that animals count, reason—even reasoning about the imperative to care—will not ensure that we extend the boundaries of the moral community. A prime example: the ethic of care articulated by Nel Noddings denies animals equal consideration of their interests, on the basis of what is alleged to be *naturally* possible.[21] That animals are limited by nature in their capacity to respond to our caring is said to circumscribe severely our moral obligations to them, in contrast to the inescapable obligation to care that arises whenever we find ourselves in the presence of another human being. That a feminist (or at least "feminine," as Noddings characterizes it) ethic is exercised by its author to exclude the sentient "other" from consideration shows how entrenched is the resistance to admitting nonhumans to the moral community, and that the issue cuts across many lines.

Ecofeminists, aware that culturally dominant conceptions of the natural are to a considerable degree socially constructed, and that rationalizations for moral hierarchy in society typically mirror rationalizations for moral hierarchy in nature at large, urge a more generous notion of caring—one based on a broader appreciation of how our identities are constituted largely through our relations with others, including nonhuman others. Philip Dick shares this relational understanding of identity—appropriate enough for someone whose middle name is Kindred—but places it within his own evolutionary framework. Humans, animals and plants are not ultimately discrete but are overlapping and interacting fields of energy forming not just an ecosphere but a collective *noosphere* of mind and intention. Understood correctly, he says, the term "human being" applies "not to origin or to any ontology but to a way of being in the world."[22] To manifest this human *being-in-the-world* is to display a compassion that recognizes the oneness of all life. Despite the very real danger of regression, there is a *telos* in evolution, towards higher levels of relatedness and potentiality, and although humans possess greater individuality than members of other species, "Still, this is the language of the universe that the ant hears; we thrill with a common joy."[23]

Here something ought to be said about the economic context of the argument from nature against animal liberation. The new version of the argument has not entirely superseded the old. As outmoded, or outrageous, as Descartes' mechanistic view may appear at first glance, it lives on in altered form, in the tendency to interpret living organisms as cybernetic information systems to be exploited for our benefit and profit. The global triumph of capitalism means that the entire world, both natural and artificial, becomes material for the process of capital accumulation. This exerts powerful pressure against the claim that animals have intrinsic value—never mind the claim that many merit inclusion in the moral community. Simultaneously, the common identity of everything as potential capital furthers the breakdown of the distinction between natural and artificial. This breakdown of boundaries, combined with the apprehension of living organisms as mere instruments in the service of capital, is strikingly apparent in genetic engineering. Dolly the clone, created as part of a project to turn sheep into living drug factories for private profit, is the exemplar. The android mentality dreams of making sheep into machines.

Jeremy Rifkin has argued that Darwin's work was crucial in establishing living organisms has having purely instrumental value, by picturing them as assemblages of interchangeable machine parts.[24] This may be simplistic, since natural selection tended to be personified in the public mind as a guiding agent of progress, something of which Darwin was aware, and to which his own manner of writing had contributed. (He was prompted to adopt Herbert Spencer's phrase "survival of the fittest," but this failed to eliminate teleological readings.) What is of note is precisely that key scientific theories tend to escape the control of their creators and to be adapted by society to fit political and economic purposes. Evolution by natural selection was seized on from the start to promote extra-scientific positions. Marx and Engels, though receiving the theory favourably, were among the first to note both the influence of political economy on the theory's formulation, and its subsequent circular use to justify social-Darwinist conclusions about the naturalness of struggle and competition in society. Interpretations of his own ideas in his lifetime led Marx to declare that he was not a Marxist. And the name of Newton, who believed that his theory of gravitation entailed the existence of a divine Creator, could readily be invoked by those who reduced the world in thought to mere clockwork. Today a political struggle is being waged over the implications of the intimate relation between humans and nonhumans revealed by ecology and other sciences.

Rather than being excluded from the moral community by the drawing of a clear boundary signifying rationality, animals are now frequently excluded through a blurring or erasure of boundaries and by manipulations of the category of "nature." What we find, then, in reflecting on current claims and practices about the natural and the artificial, about the human and the nonhuman, about boundaries and the breakdown of boundaries, is a recurring historical theme: ideology masquerading as fresh insight into objective reality.

The struggle over the moral status of animals cannot be understood in isolation from its wider context. Ecological and economic crises are interwoven with moral conundrums and confront us with both danger and opportunity. *The Communist Manifesto* is hardly a fashionable document these days, yet its summary of capitalism's virtues and faults remains relevant: capitalism creates an integrated world and unleashes hitherto undreamt-of technological powers, but this positive development is bought at the price of the destruction of traditional values (whether these be idealistic, familial, or religious), which are drowned "in the icy water of egotistical calculation." What is left to connect individuals is only monetary value—the bottom line. Human beings, now elevated to Descartes's exalted status of "masters and possessors of nature," are simultaneously alienated both from nature and each other.

The present century is bound to confront us urgently with this contradiction between our domination of the natural world, a domination driven by a triumphant capitalism, and the growing movement to re-establish spiritual values and a sense of harmony with nature. But there are different ways of trying to achieve that harmony. At the nexus of the biosphere and the realm of consciousness are the nonhuman beings-in-the-world. Whether we choose to see them as kindred spirits or as prey says everything about how we choose to be human.

NOTES

1 Rod Preece, *Animals and Nature: Cultural Myths, Cultural Realities* (Vancouver: UBC Press, 1999); Rod Preece, *Awe for the Tiger, Love for the Lamb: A Chronicle of Sensibility to Animals* (Vancouver: UBC Press, 2002); Rod Preece, *Brute Souls, Happy Beasts, and Evolution: The Historical Status of Animals* (Vancouver: UBC Press, 2005).
2 Kathryn Paxton George, *Animal, Vegetable, or Woman? A Feminist Critique of Ethical Vegetarianism* (Albany, NY: SUNY Press, 2000).
3 Simone de Beauvoir, *Adieux: A Farewell to Sartre* (New York: Pantheon Books, 1984), 316.
4 Charles Darwin, *The Descent of Man, and Selection in Relation to Sex*, 2nd ed. (London: John Murray, 1890), 79.
5 Nathan Nobis, "Carl Cohen's 'Kind' Arguments *For* Animal Rights and *Against* Human Rights," *Journal of Applied Philosophy* 21 (2004): 43–59.
6 J. Baird Callicott, "Animal Liberation: A Triangular Affair," *Environmental Ethics* 2 (1980): 311–38.
7 Mark Sagoff, "Animal Liberation and Environmental Ethics: Bad Marriage, Quick Divorce," *Osgoode Hall Law Journal* 22 (1984): 297–307.
8 Tom Regan, *The Case for Animal Rights* (Berkeley: University of California Press, 1983), 362.
9 Holmes Rolston III, "Challenges in Environmental Ethics," in Michael Zimmerman et al., eds., *Environmental Philosophy: From Animal Rights to Radical*

Ecology (Englewood Cliffs, NJ: Prentice Hall, 1993), 142. See also Holmes Rolston III, *Environmental Ethics: Duties to and Values in the Natural World* (Philadelphia: Temple University Press, 1988).
10 Rolston, "Challenges in Environmental Ethics," 140.
11 Ibid.
12 de Beauvoir, *Adieux: A Farewell to Sartre*, 333.
13 Laura Westra, "Ecology and Animals: Is There a Joint Ethic of Respect?" *Environmental Ethics* 11 (1989): 215–30.
14 James B. Reichmann, S.J., *Evolution, Animal "Rights," and the Environment* (Washington, DC: Catholic University of America Press, 2000).
15 Philip K. Dick, *The Man in the High Castle* (New York: G.P. Putnam's Sons, 1962), 42–43.
16 José Ortega y Gasset, *Meditations on Hunting* (New York: Charles Scribner's Sons, 1972).
17 See Arnold Arluke and Clinton R. Sanders, *Regarding Animals* (Philadelphia: Temple University Press, 1996), chap. 6, "Boundary Work in Nazi Germany."
18 Philip K. Dick, *Do Androids Dream of Electric Sheep?* (Garden City, NY: Doubleday, 1968), 27–28.
19 Ibid., 51.
20 Ibid., 208.
21 Nel Noddings, *Caring: A Feminine Approach to Ethics and Moral Education* (Berkeley: University of California Press, 1984).
22 Philip K. Dick, *The Shifting Realities of Philip K. Dick: Selected Literary and Philosophical Writings*, ed. Lawrence Sutin (New York: Vintage, 1995), 212.
23 Ibid., 224.
24 Jeremy Rifkin, *Algeny* (New York: Viking Press, 1983).

BIBLIOGRAPHY

Arluke, Arnold, and Clinton R. Sanders. *Regarding Animals*. Philadelphia: Temple University Press, 1996.

Beauvoir, Simone de. *Adieux: A Farewell to Sartre*. New York: Pantheon Books, 1984.

Callicott, J. Baird. "Animal Liberation: A Triangular Affair." *Environmental Ethics* 2 (1980): 311–38.

Darwin, Charles. *The Descent of Man, and Selection in Relation to Sex*. 2nd edition. London: John Murray, 1890.

Dick, Philip K. *The Shifting Realities of Philip K. Dick: Selected Literary and Philosophical Writings*. Edited by Lawrence Sutin. New York: Vintage, 1995.

———. *Do Androids Dream of Electric Sheep?* Garden City, NJ: Doubleday, 1968.

———. *The Man in the High Castle*. New York: G.P. Putnam's Sons, 1962.
George, Kathryn Paxton. *Animal, Vegetable, or Woman? A Feminist Critique of Ethical Vegetarianism*. Albany, NY: SUNY Press, 2000.
Nobis, Nathan. "Carl Cohen's 'Kind' Arguments For Animal Rights and Against Human Rights." *Journal of Applied Philosophy* 21 (2004): 43-59.
Noddings, Nel. *Caring: A Feminine Approach to Ethics and Moral Education*. Berkeley: University of California Press, 1984.
Ortega y Gasset, José. *Meditations on Hunting*. New York: Charles Scribner's Sons, 1972.
Preece, Rod. *Brute Souls, Happy Beasts, and Evolution: The Historical Status of Animals*. Vancouver: UBC Press, 2005.
———. *Awe for the Tiger, Love for the Lamb: A Chronicle of Sensibility to Animals*. Vancouver: UBC Press, 2002.
———. *Animals and Nature: Cultural Myths, Cultural Realities*. Vancouver: UBC Press, 1999.
Regan, Tom. *The Case for Animal Rights*. Berkeley: University of California Press, 1983.
Reichmann, James B. *Evolution, Animal "Rights," and the Environment*. Washington, DC: Catholic University of America Press, 2000.
Rifkin, Jeremy. *Algeny*. New York: Viking Press, 1983.
Rolston III, Holmes. "Challenges in Environmental Ethics." In Michael Zimmerman et al., eds., *Environmental Philosophy: From Animal Rights to Radical Ecology*. Englewood Cliffs, NJ: Prentice Hall, 1993.
———. *Environmental Ethics: Duties to and Values in the Natural World*. Philadelphia: Temple University Press, 1988.
Sagoff, Mark. "Animal Liberation and Environmental Ethics: Bad Marriage, Quick Divorce." *Osgoode Hall Law Journal* 22 (1984): 297-307.
Westra, Laura. "Ecology and Animals: Is There a Joint Ethic of Respect?" *Environmental Ethics* 11 (1989): 215-30.
Zimmerman, Michael et al., eds. *Environmental Philosophy: From Animal Rights to Radical Ecology*. Englewood Cliffs, NJ: Prentice Hall, 1993.

9

Monsters
The Case of Marineland

JOHN SORENSON

DISPLAYING SLAVES, FREAKS AND MONSTERS

In 1861, P.T. Barnum was the first to put a captive whale on public display for profit. As an ambitious and crafty entrepreneur who became famous for his promotion of carnival sideshows and for his ability to dupe the public, Barnum was always on the lookout for new "curiosities" that would attract paying customers. Barnum made his start by purchasing an enslaved African-American woman, Joice Heth, and putting her on display as "the world's oldest woman" until her death in 1836 (Barnum also turned her death to commercial advantage, arranging for a public autopsy to determine her age). In his sideshows and at his American Museum in New York, he made a lucrative business from exhibiting various human "freaks" as well as exotic nonhuman animals. These human "freaks" included the midget Charles Sherwood Stratton ("General Tom Thumb"), hirsute individuals such as Josephine Fortune Clofullia ("the Bearded Lady"), Feodor Jeftichew ("Jojo the Dog-Faced Boy") and the conjoined "Siamese Twins" Eng and Chen Bunker; William Henry Johnson, an African-American man with an oddly shaped skull (sometimes reported to be microcephalic or mentally disabled) was displayed, sometimes in a fur costume, as the "Missing Link," the "What-Is-It?" and as "Zip the Pinhead."

In addition to the commercial gains to be had from placing human freaks on display, Barnum also recognized that he could turn a tidy profit from the public's appetite for viewing large, unusual nonhuman animals. Having learned that Québécois fishermen had captured beluga whales at

Isle aux Coudres at the mouth of the St. Lawrence River, Barnum determined that these "monsters of the deep" would serve to profitably augment his existing attractions. A trap was built and two whales were penned in until the receding tide allowed the fishermen to capture them. The whales were taken by railway to New York. An early master of advertising, Barnum ensured that large, excited crowds met the train at its every station-stop. When the "marine monsters" finally arrived, "anxious thousands literally rushed to see the strangest curiosities ever exhibited in New York."[1] Their captors had no idea of the animals' needs. There was no supply of ocean water for the whales in the small tank constructed for them in the museum's poorly ventilated basement; Barnum's crew used fresh water, to which they added some quantity of salt in an effort to duplicate ocean water. Both whales were dead within a week. Not wanting to allow the death of these individuals to interfere with a profitable idea, Barnum tried again. He captured a second pair of whales and installed them in the basement tank, this time using a steam engine to pump in water from New York's bay. Although this second pair of whales also died soon after their capture, Barnum was not deterred and captured a third pair. Recognizing the probability that his new prisoners faced a similar fate, Barnum turned this liability into a marketing strategy: "As it is very doubtful whether these wonderful creatures can be kept alive more than a few days, the public will see the importance of seizing the first moment to see them."[2]

Today, Barnum's activities seem alternately amusing and appalling. While we may laugh at the gullibility of those who flocked to view the "Feejee Mermaid," which combined the shrivelled head of a baboon and an orangutan's body, attached to the tail of a large fish, many of Barnum's other activities strike us as being cruel, exploitative and racist. Of course, Barnum was not alone in exploiting the idea of monstrous human "others" and playing on images of savagery and primitivism. For example, Carl Hagenbeck, one of the key figures in the development of modern zoos, organized anthropological-zoological exhibitions in Germany in the late nineteenth century to show Africans, Indians, Lapps and assorted "wild men" from various parts of the colonized world, while in 1906 William T. Hornaday, director of the Bronx Zoo, arranged for a "pygmy" from Congo named Ota Benga to be placed on public display in one of the cages. We now reject the idea that people of "inferior races" would be suitable subjects for public exhibition, and we find the connections between such displays and the institution of slavery as clear as they are morally wrong and reprehensible. We now believe that it is ugly and mean to place on public exhibition individuals with various genetic disorders or physical abnormalities. It is difficult to say which we find more distasteful today: the eager voyeurism of the crowd or Barnum's manipulation of their vulgar curiosity. Even as we recognize that these attitudes emerged in a specific historical context, that of institutionalized racism and slavery and public anxiety about identity in light of emerging discoveries on human origins and evolution, Barnum's displaying of "freaks" now seems repugnant to us. Similarly, we are distressed by Barnum's crass attitudes and casual violence towards the nonhuman animals he captured, putting them on commercial display in the full knowledge that they were unlikely to survive their imprisonment and, as he had done with Joice Heth, even turning their grim fate into a marketing strategy, emphasizing the danger to them and encouraging the public to pay to see them before they died. To us, now, it is not the whales who are the "monsters" in this story. But in the century and a half since Barnum displayed his captive whale, how much has changed?

CONTINUITIES

A sobering answer to this question can be found at Marineland, the theme park in Niagara Falls, Ontario, that uses captive marine mammals as its key attractions to bring in over a million visitors a year. Rather than seeing the development over time of more progressive ethical principles concerning our relationship with other animals, we find that many of the same cruel and exploitive attitudes persist. Marineland (along with other similar institutions that imprison nonhuman animals for commercial purposes) demonstrates that little moral progress has been made in so-called mainstream society since Barnum put captured whales on display at his American Museum. Although animal protection groups have proliferated, the exploitation of animals has actually intensified in factory farms and the animal exploitation industries have mobilized to prevent even modest changes to anti-cruelty laws;[3] the continued existence of zoos and aquaria embody

> the commodification, fragmentation, and technification of living processes—biodiversity reduced to artificially sustained "exhibits"... perfect symbol[s] then for the entombment of the planet, for the sarcophagus of animal species, and for a human power pathology spiraling out of control. Zoos are first and foremost about power relations; they are both a cause and a symptom of the human will to mastery over the natural world.[4]

Established in the 1960s, Marineland seems like a relic from a more distant past, with its sad displays of imprisoned animals. Marineland has been widely criticized by international animal protection groups. For example, in a September 1996 report, the San Francisco–based animal protection group No Compromise described marine mammals at Marineland being kept in conditions little better than a "warehouse": a windowless, shallow pool next to the performance tank and noted that animals were kept "totally alone, with no stimulation, daylight or companions, and died there"; No Compromise stated that Marineland is "considered by experts to be one of the worst marine mammal theme parks in North America."[5] This view was echoed by a posting by William Rossiter to *Whales Alive!* the journal of the Cetacean Society International, in which he suggested that Marineland "may be the worst marine park in Canada, a place to make you cry and then angry enough to act."[6]

The idea of moral progress may be questionable among those of a postmodernist inclination, but it is safe to say that many do regard the recognition that racism, slavery and genocide are undesirable things as an ethical step forward. Adding the protection of animals to these concerns represents another advance. Just as doctrines of racism once operated to legitimize human slavery, supplying arguments that it was acceptable to enslave black people on the grounds that they were inherently inferior to their captors, ideologies of speciesism serve similar purposes today, legitimizing the exploitation of nonhuman animals. Zoos and aquaria are prisons for animals where the public can visit and observe the suffering of the inmates, just as the circus sideshow allowed paying customers the opportunity to derive pleasure from viewing the misfortunes of the disabled. Just as in earlier centuries the display of individual humans from "primitive cultures" provided spectators a sense of racial hierarchy and confirmed the legitimacy of imperial conquest, these animal prisons demonstrated the power of empire. Rooted in philosophical traditions that elevate human beings in general over the rest of the natural world and separate them from it, the zoo came to function as one important sign of the superiority of particular human beings. As Randy Malamud has observed, the zoo is a fundamental construct of imperialism: "The zoo itself acts as both a model of empire (where humanity holds domination over lesser species arrayed for our pleasure, our betterment, our use) and simultaneously as a metaphor for the larger, more important imperial enterprises in the sociopolitical hierarchy in which it flourishes."[7] In these institutions, animals are used as specimens that demonstrate the imperial power to penetrate and control the world, to collect and to order. As Mullan and Marvin state, zoos are fundamentally institutions of power, demonstrating the human ability to capture large numbers of other animals and put them on display for human enjoyment:

> The zoo constitutes a gallery of images constructed by man. The fact that he is able to arrange around him living creatures from all parts of the world, to make decisions with regard to the quality and conditions of their lives and to give shape to the world for them in terms of his imagination and desire is, in the end, an expression of power.[8]

Barnum's enduring fame is that of an energetic and effective huckster, who pandered to the gullibility of the public and used imaginative means to exploit it. His name is linked to the widely quoted observation that "there's a sucker born every minute" (although this particular insight appears to have been that of one of Barnum's competitors, David Hannum, exhibitor of the "Cardiff Giant" advertised as an enormous fossilized human being and later revealed as a hoax). Today, animal exploitation industries have access to more advanced technology but they play on many of the same desires and appear to operate with much the same dismal assessment of human nature. Marineland conducts an extensive television advertising campaign and maintains its own website, but the world constructed in these advertising campaigns is just as much an illusion as that created by Barnum or any of his competitors.

Marineland is located in Niagara Falls, a city which has managed to surround the impressive natural features of the area with an equally memorable display of bad taste embodied in its honeymoon motels, souvenir shops, casinos and wax museums, which emphasize the exploits of serial killers. Advertising material on Marineland's website[9] indicates that a similar aesthetic permeates the attractions at that institution, where killer whales perform every other hour at "King Waldorf's Theatre" and the "hilarious antics" of captive animals are supplemented by those of King Waldorf's sidekick, Chester the Jester. Marineland's website promotes a visit to the amusement park as a chance to experience a "unique thrill." It may be the case that having dominion over animals, forcing them to behave in grotesque and unnatural ways in order to obtain food, actually does provide some people with a sense of singular excitement that cannot be obtained in other ways. However, it is worth asking whether this psychological state is one that should be cultivated, especially among children, who will be encouraged to believe that such an approach to the world is acceptable and healthy. The "thrill" is clearly a managed one that promises safe entertainment and proximity to animals in a controlled environment. The animals imprisoned in the park are advertised as being "affectionate, as well as incredibly intelligent," and the website repeatedly refers to their "playful, friendly" qualities. The animals' apparent eagerness to entertain can be witnessed in "fun-filled shows" where their "high-flying bows, spectacular breaches and amazing flips... will have you saying 'wow'.... Adorable walruses will make you smile and the hilarious antics of the sea lions, as they outwit their human companions, will have you laughing right out loud." Visitors will also "be amused by black bears." Marineland promises its customers the "unique opportunity to feed and touch" them and to "make friends with killer whales." Although the marine mammals are penned into concrete tanks, their prisons are given softer names. "Friendship Cove" is described as "the largest whale habitat in the world." This is clearly misleading, since the normal habitats of whales are huge, open bodies of water such as oceans, seas and rivers that cannot be duplicated by artificial structures like cement tanks. In "Arctic Cove" the "naturalistic rockwork" is supposedly "designed to reflect the whale's ocean environment," although the accompanying photograph depicts children leaning over a concrete wall to feed a beluga whale in a swimming pool. For those who tire of observing captive animals, Marineland offers a number of mechanical rides such as the Sky Screamer where participants "will be launched up and down at speeds up to 96 km/h," the Space Avenger or the Viking Boat Carousel. Marineland's website presents these mechanical devices in such a way as to suggest that, through some unexplained process, the excitement they provide is imbued with the essence of the captive animals caged nearby: Kandu's Twister is a "teacup style ride" where "each gondola features the image of a killer whale" while the Magic ride is "themed to honour our black bears." Animals and machinery seem interchangeable, existing only to service the entertainment needs of paying customers who seek "fun" and "thrill[s]."

    These sorts of magical exchanges are continued within the gift shop, where customers can purchase orca beach towels, killer whale mugs, whale tail earrings, belugas, dolphins and killer whales in plush toy or inflatable versions, or the cuddly mascot himself, King Waldorf. Through the processes of juvenilization and commodification, customers feel a sense of control over these animals. At Marineland, customers are given the chance to purchase that which is normally unknown and unseen, albeit in a domesticated version that bears only superficial resemblance to the animals as they would be in their own environment. That which is strange and wild is trivialized and made familiar, manageable and clownish. Referring to Elizabeth Lawrence's work on neotony, Mullan and Marvin argue that the juvenilization of fantasy animals at sites such as Disneyland and processes of neotonization provide us with a sense of power over other animals and relieve us of any sense of understanding and respect for the inherent qualities of those animals: "what is important for the public is what they can draw out of the animal, especially in terms of affection."[10] Just as visitors to Barnum's sideshows were reassured of their own normalcy and of their place in hierarchies established by racism and imperialism by viewing those who were excluded from and subjugated to those systems, so are visitors to Marineland reassured of their mastery over other animals and persuaded that those animals love them for it.

Marineland's website and television commercials market a trip to the institution as a family outing. They depict the process of observing imprisoned animals who are forced to serve as clowns as a suitable activity for children. Many parents feel that taking their children to an institution that puts captive animals on public display is a worthwhile and morally commendable practice. They believe that by visiting such institutions children will learn about nature and develop an appreciation for animals. Indeed, Marineland's owner, John Holer, argues that Marineland serves such a purpose: "I really believe the only way for people to really develop an understanding and appreciation for animals is for them to be able to get close to these wonderful creatures."[11] These are admirable goals but it is highly unlikely that they will be achieved by visiting what are essentially prisons for animals. Rather than learning about the natural needs and behaviour of nonhuman animals, children will see those animals transformed into cartoonish creatures and gazing on their plight in captivity to learn about nature is like attending Barnum's carnival sideshows to develop sensitivity for the needs of disabled people. What children will see in zoos and aquaria are sad and lonely captives. These imprisoned individuals are beings who have been, in many cases, abducted from their families and societies through violence, subjected to various forms of abuse and deprivation as they have been transported over long distances and finally confined in severely restricted cages where they cannot escape the gaze of human spectators and often must perform on command in order to receive food. A visit to these animal prisons offers all the moral benefits of a trip to the freak show.

EDUCATION

Marineland, like other commercial aquaria and zoos around the world, argues that it is doing more than simply providing entertainment to the public. Typically, animal prisons do argue that they play an educational role, disseminating information about the natural world that will encourage public efforts to conserve it. While Marineland emphasizes the entertainment value of keeping animals in captivity, its advertising also suggests that there is some educational aspect to these activities. As noted, many parents and schools send children to Marineland believing they will learn something about animals and develop an appreciation for nature. However, Marineland's actual contribution to education appears very limited. The corporation's website contains an "Educational Manual," but this offers only superficial information. Based on the assessments made by recognized experts, Marineland does not seem to be meeting any significant educational goals. For example, Dr. Naomi A. Rose, marine mammal scientist and co-ordinator of marine mammal programs for the Humane Society of the United States, describes the dolphin show as "almost devoid of biological information" and notes that the performance "would not meet the minimum professional educational standards required under the (American) Marine Mammal Protection Act." Rose judged Marineland to be "a sub-standard facility," based on the small tanks to hold animals and the lack of educational content in the staged performances. Discussing the killer whale and sea lion performances, she stated:

> Both performances at this theater were almost completely devoid of informational content—the difference from even the limited amount provided in the dolphin show was marked. I recall the announcer stating two or three facts about these whales, such as their size, weight, and birth date of the calf. However, no information about general anatomy, social, foraging, or other natural behaviors, general ecology, or even husbandry was imparted. The sea lion show was clownish (at one point, a trainer "boxed" with the male sea lion, complete with comical sound effects) and high energy. One part of the whale performance emphasized splashing the audience; another had a trainer in the water with Kiska performing a "whale ballet." The announcer's primary function was clearly to excite and energize the audience. This performance most certainly did not satisfy recognized professional educational standards. The killer whale theater did not have any graphics of any kind that I could see posted inside or outside.[12]

In this regard Marineland is not exceptional. For example, Susan G. Davis, author of a book on Sea World in California, described that institution's educational achievements in an interview on PBS television's *Frontline* program:

> I think you can get about the same level of education from a reasonably good library book aimed at a third grader at your public library, okay. I think the kinds of amount of information and the sophistication of the information maybe even is not as good as that third grade level library book.[13]

It is possible for aquaria to conduct educational programs and to promote an interest in conservation and protection of animals. However, it is widely agreed that the educational services currently provided by these institutions typically remain superficial, offering approximately the same level of information that might be gained from browsing through any popular book on animals. In the case of Marineland, the educational material provided on its website is very limited and only geared to young children. Of course, there is great value to educating young children about animals and the environment, but questions can be raised about what they are learning at institutions such as Marineland. Watching the animals perform tricks encourages children to believe that this is normal behaviour for them and that it is proper for them to carry out the "hilarious antics" devised for them at King Waldorf's Theatre. Even if these institutions were to offer more detailed information and to present some of this at a more sophisticated level, it is not clear that this would have much effect. In fact, visitors to zoos seem to have very little interest in learning about animals. Noting that formal instruction is not likely to attract or hold people's interest, Mullan and Marvin observe that visitors want to know the names of animals and some basic points about behaviour: "beyond this they are not much interested."[14]

It is often suggested that the experience of seeing animals in itself is educational. However, a visit to the zoo is likely to be short and superficial: "unless there is some particular activity in a cage or enclosure, or unless the animal is a special favorite, it seems that, for the majority of people, watching consists of merely registering that they have seen something as they move quickly past it."[15] Lien notes that "the average visitor to a zoo or aquarium spends 30 seconds to two minutes at a typical exhibit" and points out that shows and demonstrations at aquaria will hold people's attention sometimes for as long as a half-hour.[16] Recognizing that people are likely to be bored by the sight of animals at rest, commercial institutions such as Marineland attempt to produce "thrills" and create a sense of "fun" by forcing the animals to perform tricks, to allow people to interact with them and to intersperse mechanical rides among the animal attractions.

Another argument about educational benefits made by many aquaria and zoos is that they are engaged in research that will add to scientific knowledge of the animals they imprison. However, many experts believe that research based on animals held in these institutions may be irrelevant or misleading because captivity alters behaviour. Aquaria and zoos generally offer only a distorted picture of life for the animals on display. In most cases, the conditions of captivity are far removed from those of the animals' natural habitat and this is certainly true in the case of the large marine mammals imprisoned at Marineland. These animals would normally travel great distances and spend their lives interacting with their families and social groups while at Marineland they are confined to small concrete pools and are held individually or penned in together with other animals who are not part of their own group. Furthermore, the lessons conveyed to the public by the confinement of animals are negative ones: they normalize imprisonment and domination. Instead of being seen as individuals with their own subjectivity and viewed within their natural ecosystems, they are turned into mere objects or presented as performing clowns, anxious to please their human masters.

Lien has argued that the line between education and entertainment is not so clearly defined and that injecting a sense of fun into the educational process can aid learning.[17] However, all this is beside the point. No matter what benefits we derive from viewing animals in captivity and whether we seek to justify them on the grounds of education or scientific research, the fact remains that these are speciesist arguments. We would not condone forcing people of African descent to perform tricks for food nor would we allow the public exhibition of disabled people, even if these activities provided some educational value.

Any educational benefits derived from visits to Marineland and other aquaria seem minimal. Those with an interest in learning about cetaceans likely would obtain more detailed information by reading about their lives in their natural habitat than from briefly seeing them confined in a small tank. Any information about animals that people do obtain from observations at Marineland and other such commercial institutions is likely to be misleading since it is based on abnormal circumstances. Although seeing these impressive animals may create further interest in them and inspire a commitment to preserving them, it is just as likely to contribute to an idea that animals are cartoon-like creatures who exist to make us laugh and whose interests can be disregarded as long as we derive some amusement from their suffering. However, even if Marineland and other commercial institutions based on exploitation of animals were to convert their activities to provide some more serious level of education, this would still not justify the imprisonment of sentient beings. We would no longer condone the imprisonment of people such as Ota Benga in a cage in the zoo for educational purposes and it is only speciesist prejudices that allow us to think it is acceptable to confine nonhuman animals for these ends. As People for the Ethical Treatment of Animals (PETA) notes:

> animals deserve the most basic rights—consideration of their own best interests regardless of whether they are useful to humans. Like you, they are capable of suffering and have interests in leading their own lives; therefore, they are not ours to use—for food, clothing, entertainment, or experimentation, or for any other reason.[18]

CAPTIVITY

There is no doubt that human beings are interested in other animals and the large marine mammals kept at Marineland and in other aquaria exert a special fascination. Whales and dolphins are particularly attractive because most humans rarely see these animals in their natural conditions, so a visit to aquaria where they are held provides people with a glimpse of something exotic and mysterious. Commercial whale watching operations are extremely popular but often do not guarantee a sighting and even when animals are located, viewers may see only parts of their bodies. In Canada, Marineland and the Vancouver Aquarium are the only institutions that have whales on display and that offer easy viewing access. However, a shopping centre in Alberta, known as the West Edmonton Mall, did keep captive dolphins until 2004. Biologist Dr. Toni Frohoff called the display the worst example of dolphin welfare she had seen in North America and in July 2002, shoppers complained that a dead baby dolphin floating in the tank was an inappropriate part of their entertainment experience. After the other prisoners died, the sole survivor, Howard, became the subject of a campaign to obtain his release from the shopping mall and he was eventually transferred to Florida's Theatre of the Sea, where he was also required to perform but at least had the company of some other dolphins. Undeterred by the death of the dolphins, West Edmonton Mall replaced them with sea lions it obtained from a "safari park" in Scotland and announced plans to create a zoo with lions, elephants, zebras and bears.

In 1967, Vancouver was the world's first aquarium to put captive orcas on display and while that institution seems to provide slightly more information about the animals it imprisons, it does offer some activities similar to those at Marineland, although at a more expensive rate: the "Beluga Encounters" program offers interaction with the whales for $150 per person. Many cetaceans have died in captivity in Vancouver and, after a long public campaign, the institution finally agreed that it would no longer capture whales or import any whales captured after September 1996, although it would still trade with other institutions for whales born in captivity and continue to keep dolphins on display.

The opportunity to observe these large marine animals at close range through underwater windows does, in fact, offer many Marineland customers an experience they would not have otherwise. However, it is necessary to question the nature of this experience and to ask if the costs to the animals justify the benefits to human curiosity. Certainly, the whales at Marineland are not being observed in anything that remotely resembles their normal habitats. Behind the insistent appeals to fun, affectionate relationships, appreciation and education for children, is the harsh reality of captivity for these animals. In their natural habitat, whales dive deep beneath the surface of the ocean and can travel over a hundred kilometres a day at rapid speed. No concrete pool can offer anything that remotely "reflect[s] the whale's ocean environment." Barnum's first pair of captive whales died because the American Museum did not provide them with the salt water they needed to live; today, captive marine mammals are confined in small concrete pools full of what marine mammologist Naomi Rose refers to as a "toxic soup" that is treated with chlorine and other chemicals that irritates their eyes and skin.[19] Confined in this chemically-treated water and fed according to the institution's entertainment schedule rather than through their own predatory activities, the whales exist in a sterile, featureless world that thwarts their instincts, impairs their health and shortens their lives. Captivity means boredom, deprivation and stress. Not surprisingly, the lifespan of captive animals is significantly shorter than those who live normally in the ocean.

One typical consequence of captivity for orcas is the collapsing of the dorsal fin. Forced to spend much of their time on the surface of the water due to the shallowness of the tanks, the dorsal fin is not supported by water as it would normally be and is pulled down by gravity; some suggest that this condition is caused by nutritional deficiencies or by physiological stress. Most captive orcas exhibit this condition, although it is rare in ocean-dwelling animals. Certainly, the drastically confined environment, chemically treated water, the individual's removal from her or his social group and the artificial conditions that are characteristic of confinement contribute to the stresses that lead to this.

In their natural habitat, whales live in pods, which are family units characterized by close bonds and co-operative behaviour. Captive animals are either isolated or forced into proximity with animals from different pods or of different species in conditions that would never occur naturally. The consequences range from depression to aggression. Normally, whales manoeuvre through their world largely through echolocation, high frequency sounds emitted over great distances to explore the surrounding environment; sound is also used to communicate with family members. In a small, concrete pool this ability becomes worse than useless since it is not needed to navigate and the signals bounce back to create an effect that many have likened to what a human being would experience in being confined to a lifetime inside a house of mirrors. Environmentalist and filmmaker Jean-Michel Cousteau describes these concrete pools as "acoustic jails"—echo chambers that completely disorient the animals, who must learn to stop using their natural senses or be driven insane.[20]

CAPTURE OF CETACEANS

In general, the practices of capturing and displaying marine mammals have been extensively criticized. Dolphins and whales are intelligent, sensitive animals that live within complex societies. Methods of capture are often violent and many animals are accidentally killed in the process or die in transport. Removing individuals from their families and social groups is stressful for the captured individuals as well as for those who manage to escape. Captivity has a radical effect on these animals. In their natural environment they dive deeply and travel vast distances. No tank in an amusement park can duplicate these conditions. Removed from their rich ecosystem and complex social world, captive dolphins and whales are imprisoned in a miniscule alien environment, bombarded with strange sounds, fed an artificial diet, forced to perform unnatural activities and subjected to the stressful proximity of hordes of shouting, gesticulating tourists who are eager to see the animals do something to entertain them. Trapped in these conditions, most animals live drastically shortened lives. It is impossible to imagine anything remotely attractive or entertaining in all of this.

Many aquaria and zoos present themselves as institutions that are engaged in the conservation of endangered species. However, in most cases captive animals do not constitute sufficient breeding populations, which means that these institutions continue to capture animals from their natural habitats and thus contribute to the depletion of these populations rather than to their conservation. Zoocheck and other groups such as the International Fund for Animal Welfare also have criticized Marineland's importation of Russian beluga whales and bottlenose dolphins, after the Canadian government prohibited them from capturing these animals in Canadian waters. For example, in 1999 Marineland applied to the Department of Fisheries and Oceans to capture six beluga whales from Manitoba's Churchill River. The whales were to be chased down by speedboats, subjecting them to stress and possible injury from the propellers or the ropes that would be used to restrain them. The town of Churchill opposed the capture, arguing that it would seriously damage their ecotourism industry. While the federal government delayed its consideration of new rules, Marineland was able to use Canada's existing lax regulations (requiring only an export permit from the source country) to import beluga whales from Russia. Commenting on this in the *Whales Alive!* newsletter in 2000, William Rossiter, president of the Cetacean Society International, noted that "many people in the Canadian zoo/aquarium industry and government feel Marineland is an embarrassment."[21] Speaking in the House of Commons on 2 April 2001, MP Libby Davis stated that Canada's lack of policy and regulation on capturing marine mammals had allowed unscrupulous operators to bypass stricter regulations in their own countries and that there was "no question" that Marineland had played a role in this, helping to undermine international protection.[22]

The capture of marine mammals is not a pleasant experience for the animals. For example, dolphin trainer Richard O'Barry described his experiences for PBS *Frontline*:

> It's violent, it's kind of like rape and I've captured many, many dolphins. That's how I started, capturing dolphins for the ... Aquarium. You chase them down to exhaustion. You separate mothers and babies. You take the young. We take the very best, incidentally. 80% of the captures are

young females taken away from their mothers. How this affects the gene pool nobody will ever know. I mean the science of that is very, very questionable. The word science doesn't even come up when they're doing that and the National Marine Fishery Service doesn't ask them to prove that this is not having a detrimental impact on the environment—the captive industry and the National Marine Fishery Service. It's only when you want to put them back do they question the science.[23]

In fact, as O'Barry suggest, Marineland does "question the science" of releasing captive animals:

Many animal rights groups have been advocating for the release of long term aquarium residents. However, the majority of marine mammal veterinarians and scientists are against the release of long-term aquarium residents. No killer whales held for more than one year have ever been successfully released to the wild. Released cetaceans would face a significant health risk. Wild cetaceans typically carry a variety of internal parasites which are absent in captive killer whales and dolphins. When exposed to this, a released cetacean would be faced with a sudden influx of parasitism which could greatly weaken the animal's immune system. Conversely, a whale or dolphin that has been an aquarium resident for many years may have been exposed to viruses or pathogens to which wild populations would have no or little resistance. Much more research needs to be done on the viability of cetacean release programs.[24]

While Marineland defends keeping animals in captivity on the basis of the entertainment or educational value we will derive from them, it characterizes its opposition to release in terms of concern for the animals. However, it is evident that Marineland derives its profits from keeping marine mammals in captivity. Dr. John Hall, a marine biologist who was a senior researcher at Sea World and who has been involved in rehabilitation and reintroduction programs, argues:

In my opinion, based on something over thirty years of working with cetaceans in captivity and the wild, there should be no place for a discussion of the "value of keeping small cetaceans in captivity. To a very great degree it is done only for the profits displaying cetaceans for entertainment produces.[25]

DISTORTED NATURE

Marineland depends on the presence of large marine mammals to attract the public and its money. Every business will seek to protect its investments but Marineland claims to be concerned for the inherent well-being of the animals. As Marineland's owner, John Holer, states on the corporation's website: "I will spare no expense when it comes to the health and well-being of the animals in my care." However, according to a review of Marineland's facilities by a number of internationally recognized experts on marine mammals and on zoos and aquaria, Marineland does not meet accepted standards.

In 1998 the Toronto-based animal protection group Zoocheck Canada issued the comprehensive report *Distorted Nature: Exposing the Myth of Marineland*, which outlines many of the problems with Marineland. The document was based on investigations carried out by thirteen internationally recognized scientific experts in a variety of disciplines such as aquarium animal husbandry, biology, conservation, ethology, marine mammal science, veterinary science, wildlife rehabilitation and zoology. The report expressed concerns about the well-being of the various animals held at the facility, dismissed the suggestion that Marineland played a valid role in conservation activities, assessed the institution's educational activities in negative terms, noted deficiencies in terms of ensuring public health and safety and pointed out the inadequate legislation that applied to the capture, sale and display of animals.

While some claim that captivity is justified on the grounds that animals will benefit in the long run due to increased support for conservation generated by viewing animals in aquaria and zoos, Zoocheck rejected this idea, arguing instead that these institutions constructed artificial, commercialized images of nature in settings that were little more than amusement parks and that the results actually undermined conservation goals. Zoocheck concluded that inadequate facilities and care led to abnormal behaviour, so that visitors to these institutions did not see nature but rather a distorted version of it and called for an end to the display of animals in facilities where their physical, psychological and social needs could not be met.

Reviewing Marineland's care of animals, Dr. Naomi Rose found that enclosures for animals did not meet minimum standards for size and noted rust and chipping paint that affected water quality. Similarly, Dr. John Gripper, a veterinarian with over thirty years of international experience, an appointed zoo inspector in the UK, and Advisory Director of the World

Society for the Protection of Animals, also found the animal enclosures too small and advised that Marineland "would fail an inspection under the standards of the UK Zoo Licensing Act." Other scientists who contributed to the Zoocheck report came to similar conclusions. Clearly, then, one of the strongest messages that children will derive from a visit to Marineland is that it is ethically acceptable to imprison animals in unacceptable conditions and force them to do pathetic tricks for our entertainment.

Doug Cartlidge, a trainer of dolphins and killer whales for commercial zoos and consultant and researcher for government reviews of zoo facilities in the United Kingdom, described the cramped conditions at Marineland and their effects on the killer whales:

> The main show tank housing 2 adult females, 1 calf and an adult male was clearly not adequate for the number of animals being held. The adult male, Kandu, was maintained in isolation and was clearly exhibiting prolonged and severe stereotypical behaviour. On both visits, he was held and filmed for prolonged periods in the right hand pool that was only slightly larger than he is. While in there, he remained in the same location for most of the time. Lethargy and lack of normal movement was clear to see. He lay in the exact same position virtually all of the time. His head was rubbing in the same position, and there appeared to be a mark on the pool wall from his constant rubbing. He was not observed to swim or engage in any normal movement.[26]

Cartlidge likened conditions at Marineland to those found in Victorian-era zoos and noted that the institution was failing to provide adequate facilities for the animals or to address the abnormal behaviour of the animals held there. He stated that the first show he observed contained "NO educational content whatsoever. It was simply a 1960s circus performance," although he noted that some educational information was included in a subsequent show. Cartlidge also found the dolphin pool to be too small and restrictive and to contain nothing that would provide any stimulation for the animals:

> Stereotypic swimming patterns were filmed in all the bottlenose dolphins within this pool. The dolphins as observed in the underwater viewing area were swimming anti-clockwise all of the time, like robots with no variation in pattern whatsoever. They even breathed in the same location virtually every time. It was also very disturbing to note that while the pool was barren and sterile, containing NOTHING to stimulate the animals, a rock pool with vegetation, waterfalls etc. had been constructed

just a few feet away from the dolphins, simply for the benefit and aesthetic amusement of visitors. I viewed this with deep concern.[27]

Marine mammals are not the only animals imprisoned at Marineland. In 1998, the animal protection groups Animal Alliance, Bear Alliance and Zoocheck had to threaten a lawsuit against John Snobelin, then minister of natural resources, in order to have two bear cubs released from Marineland. In a 2002 report for the World Society for the Protection of Animals and Zoocheck, Rob Laidlaw described how bears and deer are confined in wholly artificial, featureless environments that provide no stimulation, privacy or shelter and that do not allow them to exercise their full range of natural behaviour and movement. The bears, normally solitary in their natural environment and sensitive to auditory stimulation, are crowded together directly opposite what Marineland touts as the world's largest steel roller coaster. Given these conditions, it is very difficult to accept the arguments made by Marineland's owner, John Holer, that a visit to his theme park will promote the public's understanding of animals; it is clear the institution itself has little regard for the animals' needs. There has been widespread criticism of the safety and health conditions at Marineland and many animals do not survive their captivity there. Zoocheck and the World Society for the Protection of Animals have noted that there is a high cetacean mortality rate at Marineland compared with other such institutions. According to a local animal protection group, Niagara Action for Animals (NAFA), twenty-three dolphins and ten orcas had died at Marineland as of 2003.

Despite the criticism it has received, Marineland continues to be profitable. The corporation's website announces plans to expand with a new $160 million complex to become the world's largest aquarium, covering twenty acres. Four domed aquaria will be constructed. The largest and most central dome will be called "Friends of the Sea" and will feature an interactive dolphin show. "Terrors of the Sea" will contain different types of sharks, "Discovery Reef" will hold Caribbean species and "Rainforest Lagoon" will contain freshwater fish. In addition to peering through underwater viewing panels, customers will be able to "personally interact with some of the sea life such as: dolphins, stingrays, starfish, etc."

What "interactive" will actually mean in these domes is yet to be seen, but it is likely to include feeding and handling sessions and possibly a swim-with-the-dolphins arrangement. These arrangements reflect the unnatural conditions of life in aquaria. Whereas dolphins typically spend most of their time underwater when they are in their natural environment, in captivity they are seen spending much of their time at the surface, seeking food. These swim-with-the-dolphins programs have become increasingly popular and are undoubtedly linked with the popular image of the dolphin as a friendly, always-smiling animal. In reality, this expression has nothing to do with the dolphins' emotional state. No doubt, people make such assumptions about the animals' eagerness to share human company partly on the basis of the dolphin's facial structure, which makes it seem as though the animal is continuously smiling. The structures of dolphins' faces suggest that they are happy to interact with people, even when they are not and even when human contact disturbs them. Frohoff suggests that such appearances can be very deceiving and that people who are "interacting" with dolphins may misread signs of agitation and stress as signs of fun. Pointing out that people on commercial dolphin-watching boats misinterpret signs of disturbance as signs that dolphins are happy to see them or that the dolphins are "giving us a show," she notes that "a commercial-driven ecotour industry (with notable exceptions) and overzealous desire to be near dolphins can certainly contribute to such errors in judgment and sensitivity."[28]

In many marine parks, dolphins and, in the case of Marineland, even whales are trained to beach themselves on platforms, another behaviour that goes against their instincts and can injure them. Commercial institutions may misrepresent dolphins' behaviour, claiming that the animals are happy to see people or that they are voluntarily putting on a performance to please the onlookers when their behaviour actually may represent anxiety and a desire to escape their circumstances. Again, the educational benefits of commercialized "interaction" are dubious ones. Instead of learning about the normal behaviour of these animals, the public may be presented with distorted ideas about them. Seeing animals in concrete tanks provides false images, presenting the animals as divorced from their environment. In addition to these unreal images that are created in these commercial contexts, institutions such as Marineland convey beliefs that should be seen as political and ideological: ideas that animals are commodities, clowns and conveniences for public curiosity.

When these messages are conveyed to children, they learn that it is acceptable to imprison animals and to harass them. These messages are conveyed in the guise of fun and family entertainment, presenting domination as entertainment, slavery as fun. Putting dolphins and whales on display conveys all the wrong messages about animals, the environment and human relationships with the world. Captivity teaches that animals are toys that exist for our amusement, not individual beings who have their own vital concerns and interests. Jane Goodall has remarked on how she was criticized for giving human names to chimpanzees in her studies of those animals, engaging in anthropomorphism and thus distorting any data she obtained.[29] In reality, it is the marine parks that project human characteristics onto their captives, asserting that they are happy performers who wish to entertain the paying audiences. In doing so, they transform marine mammals into cartoonish versions of themselves whose strongest desire is to do tricks for the human crowds surrounding their tanks. Since those crowds have paid the price of admission to the show, they will not want to be disappointed by animals who do not perform those tricks, and it is reasonable to think that profit-seeking commercial institutions will find ways to guarantee that the animals do indeed carry out their entertainment duties, whether they want to or not.

Frohoff also points out the lack of any scientific research that demonstrates the educational benefits of swim-with-dolphin programs or of captive dolphins generally. She suggests that "a false and potentially harmful message is imparted to the public by displaying wild animals, especially marine mammals, in captivity. It teaches people by example that they are not inextricably linked to their natural environment, where they have evolved and to which they belong."[30] Shows such as those that will be given at "Friends of the Sea" are likely to convince the public that "interaction" is benign when in fact it may be very harmful to the animals. As with its whale performances, Marineland emphasizes the opportunity to interact with the animals, playing on assumptions that the animals want to interact with people on a regular basis. The "interaction" offered by commercial organizations such as Marineland basically can be placed in the same category as that of the common petting zoo, where children are allowed to grope at various animals who are unable to escape their attention. If the "friends of the sea" are not feeling interactive, it is unlikely that they will be allowed to retreat from the paying customers.

FIGHTING MONSTERS

The crowds who paid to see Barnum's human "freaks" and nonhuman animal "monsters" have their contemporary counterpart in those who visit Marineland. However, not everyone finds it amusing to watch slaves perform tricks for food. The "deep concerns" that dolphin trainer Doug Cartlidge expressed about the conditions for animals at Marineland are shared by others. Animal protection groups consider Marineland a monstrous institution that should stop exploiting animals for commercial purposes. In addition to Zoocheck, NAFA has spoken out against what it considers to be abuse of animals at Marineland. Over the past few years, NAFA has organized protests in front of Marineland. On 1 September 1996, hundreds of international marine mammal experts and animal advocates gathered for the third annual Gadfly Conference and joined a protest at Marineland. Although the protest was non-violent, police arrested several of those who had come to defend the animals, while overlooking the threatening actions of the Marineland staff, including the owner, John Holer. The animal protection group No Compromise reported on the protest on their website and indicated that Marineland's owners were ready to use violence to silence their critics:

> Near the end of the day's protest, an act of violence which has been played down by both the police and the media occurred. A local protester—known by sight to John Holer, the owner of Marineland—was leaving the protest site with other activists. Holer, known for his acts of violence against animal rights activists (and who was, in the past, filmed punching a member of the crew from Australia's *60 Minutes*), was seen by numerous witnesses hitting the woman with his truck, knocking her to the ground. The woman had only just managed to jump out of the way and was fortunately hit only on the shoulder; however, she spent three hours in the hospital suffering from shock and minor injuries. Even though Holer left the scene (i.e.: a hit and run), he has not yet been charged with any offence by Niagara Region Police, despite evidence (skid marks, the damaged side mirror to the truck, the injuries done to the protester) and pressure from witnesses and the victim.[31]

No Compromise suggested that police did not lay charges against Holer because of the economic benefits accruing to Niagara Falls from Marineland: "if you're a millionaire responsible for bringing in hundreds of thousands of dollars in tourist money to the region, you can run people down with impunity and expect to never be charged."[32]

More recently, Marineland has turned to other methods to attempt to silence its critics. On 27 July 2003, Marineland served NAFA with notice of a libel suit claiming $250,000 in punitive damages and seeking an injunction that would stop NAFA from publishing statements against Marineland. Marineland based its claim on a letter sent by NAFA to a Niagara Falls car dealership, Autoland Chrysler, requesting a meeting so that NAFA could explain its case against the dealership's plan to stage a Christmas party at Marineland. Apparently, many corporations were finding animal prisons attractive sites for their business-related socializing. For example, writing in the *Vancouver Sun* on 12 December 2003, Jennifer Blain reported that corporations were increasingly using locations such as aquaria for these events in order to make a "lasting impression" on their clients and noted that "part of the appeal lies in giving partygoers something to do besides toss back drinks."[33] Recognizing that partygoers "toss[ing] back drinks" would be unlikely to derive much educational benefit from their visits, Vancouver animal advocacy groups responded to Blain's promotional piece by protesting the further exploitation of captive animals for commercial purposes. In the case of its Marineland bash, Autoland Chrysler ignored NAFA's letter and went on with the festivities. Responding to the suit, NAFA argued that no libel was committed since the statements made about conditions at the amusement park were true and Marineland suffered no economic loss since Autoland went ahead with its party.

NAFA viewed Marineland's legal action as an attempt to use the courts to limit freedom of speech. In the *St. Catharines Standard* and the *Niagara Falls Review* on 27 May 2004, John Law of the Osprey News Network quoted NAFA spokesperson Dan Wilson: "We all believe in standing up and speaking out for the animals. NAFA has done just that and now a big corporation is trying to silence us through bankruptcy."[34] This is a tactic that has been widely used by large corporate polluters against environmentalist groups; Pring and Canan have coined a term for this: Strategic Lawsuits Against Public Participation (SLAPP). They suggest that SLAPPs are not usually intended to reach the courts (where they typically lose) but are designed to silence criticism through legal intimidation.[35] The goal is to limit public debate and to allow corporations to continue their activities without restriction. Rowell has noted that corporations have launched thousands of SLAPPs, targeting people for attending meetings, signing petitions, reporting violations of pollution laws, writing letters to local newspapers, testifying in public hearings or supporting boycotts.[36]

One famous case was that of the Texas billionaire Paul Engler, owner of Cactus Feeders, Inc., who sued Howard Lyman, vegetarian activist, former rancher, employee of the US Humane Society and television talk-show host, for making "disparaging comments" about the cattle-flesh industry on *The Oprah Winfrey Show* of 16 April 1996; the charges were dismissed after a six-year legal battle. The most famous case, of course, is the "McLibel" trial in which McDonald's fast-food corporation sued a postal worker and a gardener in London (Helen Steel and Dave Morris, respectively). The two-and-a-half-year case became the longest trial in England. In 1997, the judge ruled that McDonald's "exploits children" with "misleading" advertising, were "culpably responsible" for cruelty to animals, were "antipathetic" to unionization and paid their workers low wages. Although the judge ruled that the two activists had not proved all their points and should pay damages, they refused to do so and, reeling from the negative publicity, McDonald's did not pursue it. In 1999 the Court of Appeal made further rulings against McDonald's concerning heart disease and employment. Due to the publicity surrounding the court case, the anti-McDonald's campaign became an international movement, resulting in books and a documentary film. Steel and Morris have continued their campaign and have taken the British government to the European Court of Human Rights to defend the public's right to criticize multinationals, claiming British libel laws are unfair. Those who make valid criticisms of powerful corporations should not have to fear retaliation in court. This is one reason why Marineland's efforts to silence NAFA should be of concern to all Canadians, even those who are not distressed about mistreatment of nonhuman animals. These tactics used by large corporations to stifle criticisms from grassroots activists obviously pose a serious danger to democratic freedoms, such as the right to express our opinions and to speak out against injustices.

Clearly, the case raises important ethical and political questions. Those who are concerned about freedom of speech and civil liberties in general and those who care about animals will be watching the case closely. Although Marineland has been able to characterize itself as an institution that provides healthy fun for families rather than as a monstrous prison for animals, the decision to launch a lawsuit against NAFA actually may lead to changes in public opinion. Public sympathy is more likely to be with a small group of volunteers who care deeply about animal welfare than with a large corporation that looks like it is trying to crush those same volunteers when they speak out against what they see as cruelty and injustice. Certainly, the controversy will raise public awareness of what actually happens inside Marineland and, if the case does proceed to court, a great deal of previously unattainable information will be exposed about Marineland's operations, such as the number and causes of animal deaths and conditions inside the park. In attempting to silence its critics, Marineland may be opening doors on secrets it has tried to hide for years.

CONCLUSION

While large numbers of people still visit aquaria and zoos for entertainment, seeking the same thrills that once drew crowds to gaze upon the human freaks and nonhuman animal monsters displayed in Barnum's American Museum and carnival sideshows, we are now beginning to recognize aquaria and zoos as manifestations of power, as institutions that demonstrate human dominance over other animals. The lives of the animals confined in these prisons are shortened and deformed. These institutions do not only exploit the animals they imprison but also cause detrimental effects on those who visit them, reinforcing the idea of a qualitative division between us and other forms of life and convincing us to act in monstrous ways as we come to see animals as objects and resources that exist only for us, in this case as entertainers. As Steven Best notes:

> Zoos speak simultaneously about the animal objects they dominate, and the human dominating subjects. The abomination of zoos is a projection of the horror that haunts the human spirit, its utter revulsion from its own psychic roots and animalic origins. When we stare through the bars at confined animals, at the hirsute commodities imprisoned for entertainment value, we peer into the face of our own alienation.[37]

In the case of Marineland, we see something more: the ability of a commercial institution to draw on the power of the police and the legal system to maintain this dominion and to silence those who advocate for better treatment of nonhuman animals. The struggle for moral progress will be opposed by those commercial institutions that benefit from a system of oppression not unlike the earlier system of human slavery. Just as the owners of human slaves used the power of the state to crush dissent, so have the owners of Marineland and other corporations that exploit nonhuman animals turned to the legal system to silence their critics. It is our decision whether we wish to allow these forms of exploitation to continue or to join those who seek to create a better and more just world, not only for ourselves but for those other living creatures with whom we share it.

NOTES

1. Joel Benton, *Life of Phineas T. Barnum* (1891), retrieved 21 December 2007 from http://etext.lib.virginia.edu.toc/modeng/public/BenLife.html.
2. Ibid., p. 465.

3 John Sorenson, "'Some Strange Things Happening in Our Country': Opposing Proposed Changes in Anti-Cruelty Laws in Canada," *Social and Legal Studies* 12, no. 3 (2003): 377–402.
4 Steven Best, "Zoos and the End of Nature" (n.d.), retrieved 21 December 2007 from http://www.drstevebest.org/Essays/ZoosAndTheEnd.htm.
5 "6 Arrested at Marineland," *No Compromise* website, retrieved 21 December 2007, from www.nocompromise.org/news/960902a.html.
6 William Rossiter, "Marineland of Canada: GET INVOLVED, PLEASE!" *Whales Alive!* (Cetacean Society International) 6, no. 1 (1997), retrieved 21 December 2007 from http://csiwhalesalive.org/csi97108.html.
7 Randy Malamud, *Reading Zoos* (New York: New York University Press, 1998), 59.
8 Bob Mullan and Garry Marvin, *Zoo Culture* (Urbana: University of Illinois Press, 1999), 160.
9 See http://www.marinelandcanada.com.
10 Mullan and Marvin, *Zoo Culture*, 25.
11 See http://www.marinelandcanada.com.
12 Naomi Rose, in "Distorted Nature: Exposing the Myth of Marineland," ed. Holly Perfound and Brian McHattie, retrieved 21 December 2007 from www.zoocheck.com/Reports%20pdf's/Distorted%20Nature.pdf.
13 See http://www.pbs.org/wgbh/pages/frontline/shows/whales/interviews/davis.html.
14 Mullan and Marvin, *Zoo Culture*, 127.
15 Ibid., 133.
16 Jon Lien, "Lien Report: A Review of Live-Capture and Captivity of Marine Animals in Canada" (Ottawa: Department of Fisheries and Oceans). Retrieved 21 December 2007 from http://www.dfo-mpo.gc.ca/communic/lien/lien_e.htm.
17 Ibid.
18 "Frequently Asked Questions about Animal Rights," People for the Ethical Treatment of Animals (PETA). Retrieved 21 December 2007 from www.peta.org/mc/factsheet_display.asp?ID=129.
19 Naomi Rose, "Interview." Frontline Online (1998). Retrieved 21 December 2007, from www.pbs.org/wgbh/pages/frontline/shows/whales/interviews/rose1.html.
20 Brenda Peterson, "'Necessary Kindness': An Interview with Jean-Michel Cousteau," in Toni Frohoff and Brenda Peterson, eds., *Between Species* (San Francisco: Sierra Books, 2003), 324.
21 William Rossiter, "Canada's Captive Cetaceans," *Whales Alive!* 9, no. 4 (October 2000), retrieved 21 December 2007 from http://csiwhalesalive.org/csi00404.html.

22 William Rossiter, "Captivity Gets Uglier," *Whales Alive!* 10, no. 2 (2001), retrieved 21 December 2007 from http://csiwhalesalive.org/csio1205.html.
23 "Marine Mammal Care," Marineland website. Retrieved 21 December 2007 from www.marinelandcanada.com/educational/caregivers/care.
24 Ibid.
25 Ibid.
26 Ibid.
27 Ibid.
28 Toni Frohoff, "The Kindred Wild," in Frohoff and Peterson, eds., *Between Species*, 64–67.
29 Jane Goodall, *Through a Window: My Thirty Years with the Chimpanzees of Gombe* (Boston: Houghton Miflin, 1990).
30 Frohoff, "The Kindred Wild," 67.
31 See www.nocompromise.org/news/960902a.html.
32 Ibid.
33 See www.whaleprotection.org/articles/canada/031212.htm.
34 John Law, "Marineland Suing Animal Rights Group," *St. Catharines Standard*, March 27, 2004.
35 George Pring and Penelope Canan, *SLAPPs: Getting Sued for Speaking Out* (Philadelphia: Temple University Press, 1996).
36 Andrew Rowell, *Green Backlash* (New York: Routledge, 1996).
37 Best, "Zoos and the End of Nature."

BIBLIOGRAPHY

Benton, Joel. *Life of Phineas T. Barnum*. 1891. Retrieved 21 December 2007 from http://etext.lib.virginia.edu/toc/modeng/public/BenLife.html.
Best, Steven. "Zoos and the End of Nature." n.d. Retrieved 21 December 2007 from http://www.drstevebest.org/Essays/ZoosAndTheEnd.htm.
Frohoff, Toni. "The Kindred Wild." In Toni Frohoff and Brenda Peterson, eds., *Between Species*. San Francisco: Sierra Books, 2003.
Goodall, Jane. *Through a Window: My Thirty Years with the Chimpanzees of Gombe*. Boston: Houghton Mifflin, 1990.
Laidlaw, Rob. "Commentary on the Canadian Association of Zoos and Aquariums (CAZA) accreditation process: Marineland of Canada." Toronto: Zoocheck and World Society for the Protection of Animals (Canada), 2002.
Lien, John. "Lien Report: A Review of Live-Capture and Captivity of Marine Animals in Canada." Ottawa: Department of Fisheries and Oceans. Retrieved 21 December 2007 from www.dfo-mpo.gc.ca/communic/lien/lien_e.htm.

Malamud, Randy. *Reading Zoos*. New York: New York University, 1998.
Mullan, Bob, and Garry Marvin. *Zoo Culture*. Urbana: University of Illinois, 1999.
Peterson, Brenda. "'Necessary Kindness': An Interview with Jean-Michel Cousteau." In Toni Frohoff and Brenda Peterson, eds., *Between Species*. San Francisco: Sierra Books, 2003.
Pring, George, and Penelope Canan. *SLAPPs: Getting Sued for Speaking Out*. Philadelphia: Temple University Press, 1996.
Rose, Naomi. In "Distorted Nature: Exposing the Myth of Marineland." Ed. Holly Perfound and Brian McHattie. Retrieved 21 December 2007 from www.zoocheck.com/Reports%20pdf'sDistorted%20Nature.pdf.
Rose, Naomi. In "Distorted Nature: Exposing the Myth of Marineland." Ed. Holly Perfound and Brian McHattie. Retrieved 21 December 2007 from www.zoocheck.com/Reports%20pdf'sDistorted%20Nature.pdf.
———. "Interview." Frontline Online (1998). Retrieved 21 December 2007 from www.pbs.org/wgbh/pages/frontline/shows/whales/interviews/rose1.html.
Rossiter, William. "Marineland of Canada: GET INVOLVED, PLEASE!" *Whales Alive!* 6, no. 1 (1997). Retrieved 21 December 2007 from http://csiwhalesalive.org/csi00404.html.
———. "Canada's Captive Cetaceans." *Whales Alive!* (Cetacean Society International) 9, no. 4 (October 2000). Retrieved 21 December 2007 from http://csiwhalesalive.org/csi00404.html.
Rowell, Andrew. *Green Backlash*. New York: Routledge, 1996.
Sorenson, John. "'Some Strange Things Happening in Our Country': Opposing Proposed Changes in Anti-Cruelty Laws in Canada." *Social and Legal Studies* 12, no. 3 (2003): 377–402.
Zoocheck Canada. "Distorted Nature: Exposing the Myth of Marineland" (1998). Retrieved 21 December 2007 from www.zoocheck.com/Reports%20pdf's/Distorted%20Nature.pdf.

10

"I sympathize in their pains and pleasures"
Women and Animals in Mary Wollstonecraft

BARBARA K. SEEBER

In the *Memoirs of the Author of a Vindication of the Rights of Woman*, William Godwin describes his wife's childhood in a violent home:

> The conduct ... [her father] held toward the members of his family, was of the same kind as that he observed towards animals. He was for the most part extravagantly fond of them; but, when he was displeased, and this frequently happened, and for very trivial reasons, his anger was alarming.... In some instance of passion exercised by her father to one of his dogs, she was accustomed to speak of her emotions of abhorrence, as having risen to agony.[1]

Sympathy for the suffering of animals and its connection to domestic tyranny is a recurrent pattern in Mary Wollstonecraft's writings and appears to be grounded in the author's lived experience. While critics have characterized her attitudes towards animals as conventional, I re-examine Wollstonecraft's view of animals, and argue for her place in the history of ecofeminism. As defined by Karen Warren, ecofeminism investigates "the connections—historical, empirical, conceptual, theoretical, symbolic, and experiential—between the domination of women and the domination of nature."[2] Throughout her work, Wollstonecraft is concerned with the ethical treatment of animals, and develops a political critique that is rooted in the perceived interconnectedness of structures of domination. This essay reads her texts in the context of eighteenth-century discourses of animal welfare and rights, and demonstrates that she puts sentience at the centre of ethics. Secondly, Wollstonecraft explores the intersections between gender, class and species in all of her fiction and educational writings, and in her *Letters Written during a Short Residence in Sweden, Norway, and Denmark*, she develops an ecological vision that transforms the human/animal divide.

In a 1990 article entitled "Animal Rights and Feminist Theory," Josephine Donovan cited Wollstonecraft as one in "a long list of first-wave feminists who advocated vegetarian or animal welfare reform," and listed *Vindication of the Rights of Woman* and *Original Stories from Real Life* in the attendant footnote. Donovan's suggestion has not been developed by other critics. Mary Mellor, for example, argues that "in common with Enlightenment thinking of the time,... [she] framed her claim for a common humanity in terms of the distinctiveness of human beings from 'brute nature.'"[3] "Despite her insistence of the kindness to animals, the gulf she describes between humans and animals is far greater than any we find expressed by the Romantic poets," states Rod Preece, as does Christine Kenyon-Jones: "human beings' place in the chain of being" as superior "is stressed time and time again"; hence Wollstonecraft's attitudes to animals are akin to those of "political conservatives." Similarly, David Perkins, while acknowledging that Wollstonecraft is "strongly in favor of kindness to animals," sees her ultimately as "quite traditional" since she "maintained" that animal "behaviour is merely instinctive."[4]

Wollstonecraft's reputation as politically conservative in terms of animals seems to be based more on the *Vindication of the Rights of Woman* than her other texts. Certainly, Wollstonecraft's argument for the education of women takes as its starting point the human/animal divide: "In what does man's pre-eminence over the brute creation consist? The answer is as clear as that a half is less than the whole; in Reason."[5] Women, like men, are rational beings, not animals, even though they are treated as such. Yet, this categorical division becomes problematized by the fact that often Wollstonecraft compares women's social condition to that of caged and domesticated birds and dogs. For instance: "Confined then in cages like the feathered race, they have nothing to do but to plume themselves, and stalk with mock majesty from perch to perch."[6] Or, "Considering the length of time that women have been dependent, is it surprising that some of them hug their chains, and fawn like the spaniel? 'These dogs,' observes a naturalist, 'at first kept their ears erect; but custom has superseded nature, and a token of fear is become a beauty.'"[7] These examples reveal the domination of both women *and* animals, in fact drawing a structural parallel between the two forms of domination. The animals in the *Vindication* tend to be pets, not animals in their habitat, which suggests that Wollstonecraft comments on the function of animals within the ideology of domesticity. That is, she draws attention to how "nature" is constructed to naturalize female subordination.

In the *Letters Written during a Short Residence in Sweden, Norway, and Denmark*, Wollstonecraft's descriptions turn to animals in their natural habitat and there, animals' alleged inferiority is treated very differently, as we shall see. Nor are the animals in the *Letters* suffering; they are not objects of pity; and some evade her observation. It is also worth pointing out that Wollstonecraft's political tracts do admit ambivalence about animal souls and reason. For example, in a footnote in *Vindication of the Rights of Men*, Wollstonecraft qualifies the absoluteness of the human/animal distinction: "I do not now mean to discuss the intricate subject of their [animals'] mortality; reason may, perhaps, be given to them in the next stage of existence, if they are to mount in the scale of life, like men, by the medium of death."[8] The occasion and genre of the political tracts must be kept in mind before labelling Wollstonecraft's position on the animal question as conservative.[9] If we shift the focus from the famous polemical works to other genres, a different Wollstonecraft begins to emerge.

The early educationalist writings all emphasize kindness to animals. In *Thoughts on the Education of Daughters* (1787), Wollstonecraft suggests that if children "were told stories" of animals and "led to take an interest in their welfare and occupations, they would be tender to them; as it is, they think man the only thing of consequence in the creation."[10] In *Original Stories from Real Life; With Conversations, Calculated to Regulate the Affections, and Form the Mind to Truth and Goodness* (1788), Mrs. Mason explains "Goodness" to her female pupils: "It is, first, to avoid hurting any thing; and then, to contrive to give as much pleasure as you can." This moral schema includes nonhuman animals. The first three chapters are titled "The Treatment of Animals"; in chapter 1, Mary and Caroline progress from running "eagerly after some insects to destroy them" to nursing wounded birds who had been shot at by an "idle boy."[11] Kindness is due to animals, explains Mrs. Mason, not only because they are part of God's Creation but also because of their sentience: "Look at it [a wounded bird] ... do you not see [that] it suffers as much, and more than you did when you had the small-pox, [when] you were so tenderly nursed."[12] Animals also are attributed emotional lives; they are capable of "strong parental affection": "if you take away their young, it almost kills them."[13] While *Original Stories* does not challenge the chain of being—men are superior to animals just "as men are inferior to angels"[14]—the text nevertheless fosters an ethical awareness. As Sylvia Bowerbank explains, it "is designed to stimulate relational ways of thinking even as the child learns the facts of natural history" and "the animal is granted status as a feeling subject requiring ethical consideration."[15] Wollstonecraft's argument for ethical treatment is based on not only the principle of sentience but also the similarities between children and animals.

The educational writings frequently suggest that human/animal relations ought to be governed by the same principle governing adult–child relations. For example, in *Original Stories*, Mrs. Mason retorts to Mary's statement that "worms are of little consequence in the world": "Yet... God cares for them, and gives them every thing that is necessary to render their existence comfortable. You are often troublesome—I am stronger than you—yet I do not kill you."[16] While the comparisons between animals and children can be seen as inscribing human dominance and stewardship of the animal world, they simultaneously destabilize the hierarchical power relations of the human/animal divide. If animals and children are comparable, then animals' ethical status is surely increased in significant ways. This is especially the case in the light of Alan Richardson's insightful argument that Wollstonecraft "reject[s] the 'arbitrary principle' of parental authority and the 'blind obedience' that renders children 'slavish' in character."[17] In *Lessons*, a fragment on the education of infants and children published posthumously by William Godwin, the mother explains to her child:

> Oh! the poor puppy has tumbled off the stool. Run and stroke him. Put a little milk in a saucer to comfort him.... You are wiser than the dog, you must help him. The dog will love you for it, and run after you. I feed you and take care of you: you love me and follow me for it. When the book fell down on your foot, it gave you great pain. The poor dog felt the same pain just now.[18]

While the child is "wiser than the dog," the ability to feel "the same pain" and "love" complicates and mitigates the distinction between child and dog, human and nonhuman animals.

Nor is the topic of kindness to animals relegated to Wollstonecraft's writings for children. In *Vindication of the Rights of Woman*, her most famous political tract, she argues that "humanity to animals should be particularly inculcated as a part of national education":

habitual cruelty is first caught at school, where it is one of the rare sports of the boys to torment the miserable brutes that fall in their way. The transition, as they grow up, from barbarity to brutes to domestic tyranny over wives, children, and servants, is very easy. Justice, or even benevolence, will not be a powerful spring of action unless it extend to the whole creation; nay, I believe that it may be delivered as an axiom, that those who can see pain, unmoved, will soon learn to inflict it.[19]

The repeated emphasis on animals' ability to feel pain situates Wollstonecraft in discourses of animal welfare and rights.

Eighteenth-century arguments for the ethical treatment of animals centre on sentience. Richard Dean's *An Essay on the Future Life of Brutes* (1768) "attempts ... to confute the Doctrine of De Carte [sic]" and insists that "the Brute is sensible of Pain" and was not "created only for the present Purposes of Man": they "feel every Bang and Cut, and Stab, as much as" humans, "some of them perhaps more."[20] Similarly, Thomas Young's *An Essay on Humanity to Animals* (1798) emphasizes that "animals are endued with a capability of perceiving pleasure and pain."[21] Humphrey Primatt is concerned with the lives of animals in their own right—not just because animal cruelty might later lead to cruelty towards humans. Aaron Garrett and Andreas Holger Maehle both argue that Primatt is "one of the most important figures in the development of a notion of animal rights" and as one of the first to present an "alternative to the concept of a merely indirect obligation towards animals." Dethroning reason as the determinant of human obligation towards animals in *A Dissertation on the Duty of Mercy and Sin of Cruelty to Brute Animals* (1776), Primatt argues that "a man can have no natural right to abuse and torment a beast, merely because a beast has not the mental powers of man." Instead, he posits the commonality of sentience as the central determinant of human/animal relations: "Pain is pain, whether it be inflicted on man or on beast." Animals, according to Primatt, have a right to "Ease," "Comfort," and "Happiness." There are many parallels between Wollstonecraft and these texts, and her work, in turn, was quoted by George Nicholson as support for his vegetarian argument in *On the Primeval Diet of Man* (1801).[22]

There has been a tendency to discount discourses of animal welfare as "really" being about something other than animals. For example, Robert Malcolmson writes that "the concern for cruelty and its consequences was strongly reinforced by the solicitude for public order and for labour discipline" and that the anti-cruelty movement "betrayed a pronounced class bias," more concerned with the activities of the lower classes than the fashionable rural sports of the upper classes. G.J. Barker-Benfield claims that eighteenth-century women writers sympathizing with animals were "concerned first and foremost with women's brutalization," their protest about the plight for animals functioning as "a kind of surrogate feminism." While this is true in some cases, it is not true in others. Harriet Ritvo's caution about the nineteenth-century equally applies to the eighteenth century: "Wherever we look... the role of animals appears not only multiple but contested... the search for a single generalization or a single unfolding narrative may be intrinsically misguided—not only doomed to failure, but likely to mislead us."[23] In the specific case of Mary Wollstonecraft, I argue, the treatment of animals *is* a morally significant and political issue in its own right. Animal suffering matters in and of itself and it intersects with other forms of oppression. In this, she shares some of the fundamental assumptions of ecofeminism. While varied, ecofeminism's main elements have been effectively summarized by Mary Mellor in *Feminism & Ecology*:

> A critique of the dualism of (western) patriarchal society that makes a distinction between humanity (man) and the natural world; the subordinate position of women in that dualism, so that women are associated with, and materially experience, a relationship with the natural world; the necessity of creating a non-destructive connectedness between humanity (man) and the natural world; the centrality of women to creating that connectedness.[24]

As Carol J. Adams, Josephine Donovan and Karen Davis have cogently argued, ecologists and ecofeminists alike frequently marginalize the lives of individual animals in their concern for nature and species preservation. It is important to recognize that Wollstonecraft's ecofeminist analysis includes animals.[25]

Wollstonecraft's fiction explores the interconnections between gender, class and species oppression. In *Mary*, the heroine's father is an avid hunter *and* a domestic tyrant: "He hunted in the morning, and after eating an immoderate dinner, generally fell asleep." Mary "was continually in dread lest he should frighten her mother to death"; in anger, he "had a dog hung" and, in a turn of poetic justice, meets his death by being thrown from his horse.[26] Similarly, in *The Wrongs of Woman*, the heroine's brother "from tormenting insects and animals... became the despot of his brothers, and still more of his sisters."[27] Animal cruelty not only happens from the top down; as Wollstonecraft explains in *Vindication of the Rights of Woman*, it also is perpetrated as a compensation by those who "are trodden under foot by the rich": they "domineer over ... [animals] to revenge the insults that they are obliged to bear from their superiours."[28] Wollstonecraft's focus then is systemic violence and domination, for she distinguishes between kindness to animals as a fashion of sensibility and the inclusion of animals in an ethical framework. The description of the heroine's mother in *Mary* is a case in point:

> two most beautiful dogs ... shared her bed, and reclined on cushions near her all the day. These she watched with the most assiduous care, and bestowed on them the warmest caresses. This fondness for animals was not that kind of *attendrissement* which makes a person take pleasure in providing for the subsistence and comfort of a living creature; but it proceeded from vanity, it gave her an opportunity of lisping out the prettiest French expressions of ecstatic fondness, in accents that had never been attuned by tenderness.[29]

The passage contrasts the ethical treatment of animals given their sentience and the fashion of pets: hers was not "pleasure in providing for the subsistence and comfort of a living creature." A similar attack on the affected affection for animals is found in the *Letters Written during a Short Residence in Sweden, Norway, and Denmark*: "ladies of the most exquisite sensibility, who were continually exclaiming against the cruelty of the vulgar to the brute creation, have in my presence forgot that their attendant had human feelings, as well as forms."[30] Wollstonecraft attacks those ladies whose sensibility to animals is a display of emotion as empty as the other feminine accomplishments, and, instead, puts forward concern for animals as an ethical position that is linked to class and gender politics.

Animals repeatedly figure as tropes for the suffering of women and the lower classes in *The Wrongs of Woman*. In chapter 5, Jemima tells the story of her life. Illegitimate, orphaned and poor, she endured a childhood of abuse: "It seemed indeed the privilege of their superior nature to kick me about, like the dog or cat. If I were attentive, I was called fawning, if refractory, an obstinate mule, and like a mule I received their censure on my loaded back ... I was the filching cat, the ravenous dog, the dumb brute, who must bear all."[31] Jemima repeatedly expresses that she was "treated like a creature of another species." This is repeated three times in her narration. "I had not even the chance of being considered a fellow-creature"; "They had been accustomed to view me as a creature of another species"; "Who ever acknowledged me to be a fellow-creature?"[32] (Jemima internalizes the ideology that animalizes her: "Whither could I creep for shelter?" and "I hurried back to my hole."[33] Maria, too, uses these tropes to describe her experience: "I could not sometimes help regretting an early marriage; and that, in my haste to escape from a temporary dependence, and expand my newly fledged wings, in an unknown sky, I had been caught in a trap, and caged for life."[34]

Wollstonecraft also employs the hunting trope with striking repetition in her novel. Jemima was "hunted from family to family" and "hunted almost into a fever."[35] Maria, attempting to leave her abusive husband, "was hunted" and this is repeated three times.[36] It should be noted that while Wollstonecraft protests the Game Laws which restrict shooting to the land-owning class in *The Rights of Men*, her depictions of rural sports in general are negative. *The Female Reader* includes passages from William Cowper's *The Task* which denounce hunting, and in *The Rights of Woman*, she "inveigh[s] against ... ardour in hunting, shooting, and gaming."[37] The hunting trope connects the plight of the working-class woman and the upper-class woman, reflecting the novel's intent "to show the wrongs of different classes of women, equally oppressive, though, from the difference of education, necessarily various."[38] These tropes not only capture gender and class oppression but also suggest that since cruel treatment of animals paves the way for the cruel treatment of humans (a point repeatedly made in the early educational writings), animals should not be treated cruelly. That is, the tropes call into question the logic of domination, the "perversions of the understanding, which systematize oppression"[39] and reveal the interconnectedness of structures of domination: gender, class and species.

In her fiction, as we have seen, Wollstonecraft explores how the human/animal divide serves to naturalize social distinctions; that is, rather than positing an essentialist connection between women and animals (which, as she was powerfully aware, potentially disenfranchises women from public life), she demonstrates an ideological connection. In *Letters Written during a Short Residence in Sweden, Norway, and Denmark*, Wollstonecraft moves beyond depicting animals' suffering at the hands of humans, and instead encounters animals in their habitat. She attempts to relate to them outside the socially constructed human/animal divide and, in certain passages, reimagines human/animal relations. *Letters*, composed during the summer of 1795 on a business trip to Scandinavia that Wollstonecraft took on behalf of her lover, Gilbert Imlay, crosses many generic boundaries and covers a wide range of topics: capital punishment, the treatment of servants, mortality, theatre, education, trade and prison reform. The text's depiction of nature has been celebrated since its publication. Robert Southey wrote that Wollstonecraft "has made me in love with a cold climate, and frost and snow, with a northern moonlight."[40] Several readings have focused on the ways in which Wollstonecraft's nature descriptions significantly rework eighteenth-century aesthetic theories. For example, Elizabeth Bohls states that *Letters* is a "politically motivated" critique of "disinterested contemplation by destroying the distance between a perceiver and a statically framed scene." Jeanne Moskal explains that "the roles of affectionate mother and picturesque traveler do not conflict but combine." Similarly, Beth Dolan Kautz argues that the speaker "presents herself as a whole person moving through landscapes, rather than as the conventional disembodied and distanced aesthetic eye."[41]

Bohls, Moskal and Kautz hence address how Wollstonecraft subverts the convention of the masculine, detached observer of a feminine landscape, and a number of critics also have extended this to make a claim for the *Letters* as an ecofeminist text. Karen Hust suggests that the text "rewrit[es] ... the nature-culture dualism" by entering into a "dialogue with nature." Wollstonecraft "connects ... deeply to the land while maintaining the difference between them," and as such, "her journey can guide us ... to a new synthesis of feminist and ecological criticism."[42] Lila Marz Harper identifies ecological consciousness in the scenes where Wollstonecraft records the destruction of nature due to mining, canal-building and glue manufacturing. Sylvia Bowerbank argues that *Letters* is a "significant text in the history of ecological feminism": "in her observations on the Scandinavian environment, she comes to understand the ongoing reciprocal relationships between human settlements and nonhuman life."[43] What is missing in all of these accounts, however, is the animal world. Wollstonecraft's descriptions of the natural world go beyond climate, frost, snow and moonlight to include bears, seals, starfish, cows, goats, eagles, vultures, seagulls, foxes, hares, crows, bittern and wild geese.

Wollstonecraft rewrites eighteenth-century aesthetics by situating herself in the landscape rather than remaining a detached observer, hence disrupting subject–object relations. This has important ramifications for human-animal relations, as in the following passage:

> A slow fever preyed on me every night, during my residence in Sweden, and after I arrived at Tonsberg. By chance I found a fine rivulet filtered

> through the rocks, and confined in a bason for the cattle. It tasted to me like a chalybeat; at any rate it was pure; and the good effect of the various waters which invalids are sent to drink, depends, I believe, more on the air, exercise and change of scene, than on their medicinal qualities. I therefore determined to turn my morning walks towards it, and seek for health from the nymph of the fountain; partaking of the beverage offered to the tenants of the shade.[44]

Nature here is not a static object; rather, the scene emphasizes reciprocity between Wollstonecraft and the environment. Moreover, Wollstonecraft here becomes one with the animal world; "partaking" of the same spring of water as the cows, she dissolves the human/animal divide. Animals—human and nonhuman alike—are embodied beings situated in a shared ecological space.

In Letter Eight, Wollstonecraft records her observation of jellyfish and seals during a rowing expedition near Tonsberg:

> Sometimes, to take up my oar, once more, when the sea was calm, I was amused by disturbing the innumerable young starfish which floated just below the surface: I had never observed them before; for they have not a hard shell, like those which I have seen on the sea-shore. They look like thickened water, with a white edge; and four purple circles, of different forms, were in the middle, over an incredible number of fibers, or white lines. Touching them, the cloudy substance would turn or close, first on one side, then on the other, very gracefully; but when I took one of them up in the ladle with which I heaved the water out of the boat, it appeared only a colourless jelly.
>
> I did not see any of the seals, numbers of which followed our boat when we landed in Sweden; for though I like to sport in the water, I should have had no desire to join in their gambols.
>
> Enough, you will say, of inanimate nature, and of brutes, to use the lordly phrase of man; let me hear something of the inhabitants.[45]

Harper comments that

> [Wollstonecraft's] observation points to a major weakness in a study of nature that is limited to the results of measurement and collection. The glob of colorless jelly in Wollstonecraft's ladle bears no resemblance to the graceful moving creature in the water. Only subjective and immediate observation could provide such information.[46]

Moreover, this passage is important in its rendering of human/animal relations. Wollstonecraft attributes animals with a degree of agency; the fish are shown as withholding something from the observer and they do so gracefully—which elevates the action above mere instinct. They are not an open book—they remain outside the full comprehension and assimilation on the part of the human observer. Wollstonecraft appears to enjoy the sight of the playing seals, but acknowledges her position as an outsider, granting the seals a right to "their gambols" free from human intervention, like the starfish who lose their colour and texture when taken out of their element. Similarly, Wollstonecraft wishes to see a bear in its natural habitat, rather than one confined in an exhibit: "I heard of the bears, but never saw them stalk forth, which I was sorry for; I wished to have seen one in its wild state."[47] While Bohls argues that "her irrepressible wish to see a real, live bear reduces to absurdity the aesthetics of the sublime and its fashionable obsession with the 'savage' and 'wild,'" the passage relates to the ecological concern of the *Letters*, and it again disrupts the authority of the human observer: the bear is not available to her view as a object of study.[48]

At the conclusion of the passage, Wollstonecraft distances herself from the language of human supremacy: "Enough, you will say, of inanimate nature, and of brutes, to use the lordly phrase of man; let me hear something of the inhabitants."[49] She implies that the animal/human divide serves the "lordly" view of "man," and she draws into question the "proper" focus of the travel narrative by framing it as an apprehended interruption from another point of view: "you will say... let me hear something of the inhabitants." Clearly, the "I" considers the starfish and seals as inhabitants of the landscape, while the "you" does not. In this passage, Wollstonecraft is aware of how the culture/nature opposition is a construction that reinforces male domination, the "lordly" view of "man," and she distances herself from masculine "culture" here in a way that does not reinforce a female "essentialist" closeness to nature but rather subverts the constructed division of culture and nature. This revisioning of "culture" is also evident in the passages that lament and critique the destruction of nature for profit and economic development. A similar splitting of "you" and "I" occurs in the following quotation:

> At Gothenburg I shall embrace my *Fannikin*; probably she will not know me again—and I shall be hurt if she do not. How childish is this! still it is a natural feeling. I would not permit myself to indulge the "thick

coming fears" of fondness, whilst I was detained by business.—Yet I never saw a calf bounding in a meadow, that did not remind me of my little frolicker. A calf you say. Yes; but a *capital* one, I own.[50]

Maternal affection crosses species lines, in contrast to the masculine "you."

The split between the "I" and "you" also manifests itself in the division between the main body of the text (the letters) and the appendix. The letters describe animals with interest, respect and affection: "I like to see animals sporting, and sympathize in their pains and pleasures."[51] In the appendix, on the other hand, animals are reduced to a strictly instrumental role. The first note, providing factual information on Norway's geography, political organization, military and economy, lists animals as a natural resource no different from inanimate matter: "Its natural products are wood, silver, copper, and iron, a little gold has been found, fish, marble, and the skins of several animals." And after detailing the profits accrued through copper and iron production, she states: "The exportation of salted and dried fish is very considerable. In the year 1786 the returns for its exportation amounted to 749,200 rixdollars, £169,840."[52] While earlier she lamented the destruction of nature—"to commerce every thing must give way; profit and profit are the only speculations"[53]—here the cost is evaded. The "pains and pleasures" of animals are erased as they are reduced to their function of food and export value. The internal contradiction between main text and appendix is reflected also in other passages. At the beginning of her journey, Wollstonecraft's view of animals is in keeping with conventional Enlightenment views; man, endowed with the power of "mind," is the "lord of the creation." Wollstonecraft's disdain for the local residents in Letter One is framed as their closeness to the "brute creation."[54] In Letter Sixteen, she records with disapproval the drunken revelers who "though the evening was fresh ... were stretched on the grass like weary cattle." Later that evening, she enters a local inn and "was almost driven back by the stench—a softer phrase would not have conveyed an idea of the hot vapour that issued from an apartment, in which some eight or ten people were sleeping, not to reckon the cats and dogs stretched on the floor"; when leaving in the morning, she "hastened through the apartment ... not wishing to associate the idea of a pigstye with that of a human dwelling."[55] These depictions obviously are troubling as Wollstonecraft's class prejudice is revealed by lowering the inhabitants to the bestial level; here, proximity to animals only degrades humans.

The shifting positions in the *Letters* speak of the difficulties faced by an eighteenth-century feminist writer questioning the human/animal divide at a time when the political struggle to include women in the category of the "human" was far from over. Today's ecofeminists continue the careful negotiation of the "danger of returning to the essentialist arguments that denied women's equality in the first place."[56] We should not underestimate Wollstonecraft's achievement; in all her works, she includes animals in ethical considerations and links structures of domination. Her place in ecofeminism is an important one—both for what she achieves and for what her contradictions reveal about eighteenth-century conceptions about women and nature, and the legacy of those ideas.

NOTES

1. William Godwin, *Memoirs of the Author of a Vindication of the Rights of Woman*, ed. Pamela Clemit and Gina Luria Walker (Peterborough, ON: Broadview Literary Texts, 2001), 46.
2. Karen Warren, "Introduction," *Hypatia: A Journal of Feminist Philosophy* 6, no. 1 (1991): 1.
3. Josephine Donovan, "Animal Rights and Feminist Theory," *Signs: Journal of Women in Culture and Society* 15, no. 2 (1990): 359; Mary Mellor, *Feminism and Ecology* (New York: New York University Press, 1997), 72.
4. Rod Preece, *Awe for the Tiger, Love for the Lamb: A Chronicle of Sensibility to Animals* (Vancouver: UBC Press, 2002), 203; Christine Kenyon-Jones, *Kindred Brutes: Animals in Romantic-Period Writing* (Aldershot: Ashgate, 2001), 63, 64; David Perkins, *Romanticism and Animal Rights* (Cambridge: Cambridge University Press, 2003), 26.
5. Mary Wollstonecraft, *The Works of Mary Wollstonecraft*, ed. Marilyn Butler and Janet Todd, vol. 5 (London: Pickering and Chatto, 1989), 81.
6. Ibid., vol. 5, 125.
7. Ibid., vol. 5, 152.
8. Ibid., vol. 5, 31.
9. Drawing a parallel to the nineteenth-century "woman question" and its debates about women's status, the "animal question" refers to the debate about the moral status of animals. It is also the title of Paolo Cavalieri's book, *The Animal Question: Why Nonhuman Animals Deserve Human Rights*, trans. Catherine Woollard (Oxford: Oxford University Press, 2001).
10. Wollstonecraft, *The Works of Mary Wollstonecraft*, vol. 4, 44.
11. Ibid., vol. 4, 367–68.
12. Ibid., vol. 4, 369.
13. Ibid., vol. 4, 373.
14. Ibid., vol. 4, 371.
15. Sylvia Bowerbank, *Speaking for Nature: Women and Ecologies of Early Modern England* (Baltimore: Johns Hopkins University Press, 2004), 152, 149–50.

16 Wollstonecraft, *The Works of Mary Wollstonecraft*, vol. 4, 368.
17 Alan Richardson, "Mary Wollstonecraft on Education," in Claudia Johnson, ed., *The Cambridge Companion to Mary Wollstonecraft* (Cambridge: Cambridge University Press, 2002), 37.
18 Wollstonecraft, *The Works of Mary Wollstonecraft*, vol. 4, 473.
19 Ibid., vol. 5, 244.
20 Richard Dean, *Animal Rights and Souls in the Eighteenth Century*, vol. 2, *An Essay on the Future Life of Brutes*, ed. Aaron Garrett (Bristol: Thoemmes Press, 2000), xix, 51, 68, 104.
21 Thomas Young, *Animal Rights and Souls in the Eighteenth Century*, vol. 5, *An Essay on the Humanity to Animals*, ed., Garrett, 8.
22 Aaron Garrett, Introduction, *Animal Rights and Souls in the Eighteenth Century*, 6 vols. (Bristol: Thoemmes, 2000), xix; Andreas Holger Maehle, "Cruelty and Kindness to the 'Brute Creation': Stability and Change in the Ethics of the Man-Animal Relationship, 1600-1850," in Aubrey Manning and James Serpell, eds., *Animals and Human Society: Changing Perspectives* (London: Routledge, 1994), 94; Humphrey Primatt, *A Dissertation on the Duty of Mercy and Sin of Cruelty to Brute Animals*, vol. 3 of *Animal Rights and Souls in the Eighteenth Century*, 12, 7, 202; George Nicholson, *On the Primeval Diet of Man*, ed. Rod Preece (Lewiston, NY: Edwin Mellen Press, 1999), 209.
23 Robert W. Malcolmson, *Popular Recreations in English Society, 1700-1850* (Cambridge: Cambridge University Press, 1973), 138, 152; G.J. Barker-Benfield, *The Culture of Sensibility: Sex and Society in Eighteenth-Century Britain* (Chicago: University of Chicago Press, 1992), 231, 237; Harriet Ritvo, "Animals in Nineteenth-Century Britain: Complicated Attitudes and Competing Categories," in Manning and Serpell, eds., *Animals and Human Society*, 122.
24 Mellor, *Feminism and Ecology*, 59-60.
25 Carol J. Adams, *The Sexual Politics of Meat: A Feminist-Vegetarian Critical Theory* (New York: Continuum Press, 1990); Josephine Donovan and Carol J. Adams, eds., *Animals & Women: Feminist Theoretical Explorations* (Durham: Duke University Press, 1995); Karen Davis, "Thinking Like a Chicken: Farm Animals and the Feminine Connection," in Donovan and Adams, eds., *Animals & Women*, 192-212.
26 Wollstonecraft, *The Works of Mary Wollstonecraft*, vol. 1, 7-11.
27 Ibid., vol. 1, 124.
28 Ibid., vol. 5, 244.
29 Ibid., vol. 1, 8.
30 Ibid., vol. 6, 254.
31 Ibid., vol. 1, 109-10.
32 Ibid., vol. 1, 110, 111, 119.
33 Ibid., vol. 1, 111, 112.
34 Ibid., vol. 1, 138.

35　Ibid., vol. 1, 110, 112.
36　Ibid., vol. 1, 160, 165, 168, 179.
37　Ibid., vol. 5, 74.
38　Ibid., vol. 1, 84.
39　Ibid., vol. 1, 88.
40　Robert Southey's Letter to Joseph Cottle, quoted in "Introduction" by Richard Holmes, *Mary Wollstonecraft's A Short Residence in Sweden, Norway and Denmark and William Godwin's Memoirs of the Author of the Rights of Woman* (London: Penguin, 1987), 17.
41　Elizabeth A. Bohls, *Women Travel Writers and the Language of Aesthetics, 1716–1818* (Cambridge: Cambridge University Press, 1995), 141, 151; Jeanne Moskal, "The Picturesque and the Affectionate in Wollstonecraft's *Letters from Norway*," *Modern Language Quarterly: A Journal of Literary History* 52, no. 3 (1991): 269; Beth Dolan Kautz, "Mary Wollstonecraft's Salutary Picturesque: Curing Melancholia in the Landscape," *European Romantic Review* 13, no. 1 (2002): 42.
42　Karen Hust, "In Suspect Terrain: Mary Wollstonecraft Confronts Mother Nature in *Letters from Norway*," *Women's Studies* 25, no. 5 (1996): 498, 497; Karen Hust, "Facing the Maternal Sublime: Mary Wollstonecraft in Sweden," in Anka Ryall and Catherine Sandbach-Dahlstrom, eds., *Mary Wollstonecraft's Journey to Scandinavia: Essays* (Stockholm: Almquiest and Wiksell International, 2003), 141.
43　Lila Marz Harper, *Solitary Travelers: Nineteenth Century Women's Travel Narratives and the Scientific Vocation* (Madison, NJ: Fairleigh Dickinson University Press, 2001); Sylvia Bowerbank, "The Bastille of Nature: Mary Wollstonecraft and Ecological Feminism," in Ryall and Sandbach-Dahlstrom, eds., *Mary Wollstonecraft's Journey to Scandinavia*, 181; Bowerbank, *Speaking for Nature*, 211.
44　Wollstonecraft, *The Works of Mary Wollstonecraft*, vol. 6, 280–81.
45　Ibid., vol. 6, 281.
46　Harper, *Solitary Travelers*, 45.
47　Wollstonecraft, *The Works of Mary Wollstonecraft*, vol. 6, 263.
48　Bohls, *Women Travel Writers and the Language of Aesthetics*, 156.
49　Wollstonecraft, *The Works of Mary Wollstonecraft*, vol. 6, 281.
50　Ibid., vol. 6, 299.
51　Ibid., vol. 6, 259.
52　Ibid., vol. 6, 347.
53　Ibid., vol. 6, 343.
54　Ibid., vol. 6, 245.
55　Ibid., vol. 6, 314.
56　Mellor, *Feminism and Ecology*, 70.

BIBLIOGRAPHY

Adams, Carol J. *The Sexual Politics of Meat: A Feminist-Vegetarian Critical Theory.* New York: Continuum Press, 1990.
Barker-Benfield, G.J. *The Culture of Sensibility: Sex and Society in Eighteenth-Century Britain.* Chicago: University of Chicago Press, 1992.
Bohls, Elizabeth A. *Women Travel Writers and the Language of Aesthetics, 1716–1818.* Cambridge: Cambridge University Press, 1995.
Bowerbank, Sylvia. *Speaking for Nature: Women and Ecologies of Early Modern England.* Baltimore: Johns Hopkins University Press, 2004.
———. "The Bastille of Nature: Mary Wollstonecraft and Ecological Feminism." In Anka Ryall and Catherine Sandbach-Dahlstrom, eds., *Mary Wollstonecraft's Journey to Scandinavia: Essays.* Stockholm: Almquiest and Wiksell International, 2003.
Cavalieri, Paolo. *The Animal Question: Why Nonhuman Animals Deserve Human Rights.* Translated by Catherine Woollard. Oxford: Oxford University Press, 2001.
Davis, Karen. "Thinking Like a Chicken: Farm Animals and the Feminine Connection." In Josephine Donovan and Carol J. Adams, eds., *Animals & Women: Feminist Theoretical Explorations.* Durham, NC: Duke University Press, 1995.
Dean, Richard. *Animal Rights and Souls in the Eighteenth Century.* Vol. 2, *An Essay on the Future Life of Brutes.* Edited by Aaron Garrett. Bristol: Thoemmes Press, 2000.
Donovan, Josephine. "Animal Rights and Feminist Theory." *Signs: Journal of Women in Culture and Society* 15, no. 2 (1990): 359.
Donovan, Josephine, and Carol J. Adams, eds. *Animals & Women: Feminist Theoretical Explorations.* Durham, NC: Duke University Press, 1995.
Garrett, Aaron. "Introduction." *Animal Rights and Souls in the Eighteenth Century,* 6 vols. Bristol: Thoemmes, 2000.
Godwin, William. *Memoirs of the Author of a Vindication of the Rights of Woman.* Edited by Pamela Clemit and Gina Luria Walker. Peterborough, ON: Broadview Literary Texts, 2001.
Harper, Lila Marz. *Solitary Travelers: Nineteenth Century Women's Travel Narratives and the Scientific Vocation.* Madison, NJ: Fairleigh Dickinson University Press, 2001.
Holmes, Richard. *Mary Wollstonecraft's A Short Residence in Sweden, Norway and Denmark and William Godwin's Memoirs of the Author of the Rights of Woman.* London: Penguin, 1987.
Hust, Karen. "Facing the Maternal Sublime: Mary Wollstonecraft in Sweden." In Anka Ryall and Catherine Sandbach-Dahlstrom, eds., *Mary*

Wollstonecraft's Journey to Scandinavia: Essays. Stockholm: Almquiest and Wiksell International, 2003.

———. "In Suspect Terrain: Mary Wollstonecraft Confronts Mother Nature in *Letters from Norway*." In *Women's Studies* 25, no. 5 (1996): 498.

Kautz, Beth Dolan. "Mary Wollstonecraft's Salutary Picturesque: Curing Melancholia in the Landscape." *European Romantic Review* 13, no. 1 (2002): 42.

Kenyon-Jones, Christine. *Kindred Brutes: Animals in Romantic-Period Writing*. Aldershot: Ashgate, 2001.

Maehle, Andreas Holger. "Cruelty and Kindness to the 'Brute Creation': Stability and Change in the Ethics of the Man-Animal Relationship, 1600–1850." In Aubrey Manning and James Serpell, eds., *Animals and Human Society: Changing Perspectives*. London: Routledge, 1994.

Malcolmson, Robert W. *Popular Recreations in English Society, 1700–1850*. Cambridge: Cambridge University Press, 1973.

Mellor, Mary. *Feminism and Ecology*. New York: New York University Press, 1997.

Moskal, Jeanne. "The Picturesque and the Affectionate in Wollstonecraft's *Letters from Norway*." *Modern Language Quarterly: A Journal of Literary History* 52, no. 3 (1991): 269.

Nicholson, George. *On the Primeval Diet of Man*. Edited by Rod Preece. Lewiston, NY: Edwin Mellen Press, 1999.

Perkins, David. *Romanticism and Animal Rights*. Cambridge: Cambridge University Press, 2003.

Preece, Rod. *Awe for the Tiger, Love for the Lamb: A Chronicle of Sensibility to Animals*. Vancouver: UBC Press, 2002.

Primatt, Humphrey. *A Dissertation on the Duty of Mercy and Sin of Cruelty to Brute Animals*, vol. 3 of *Animal Rights and Souls in the Eighteenth Century*. Edited by Aaron Garrett. Bristol: Thoemmes, 2000.

Richardson, Alan. "Mary Wollstonecraft on Education." In Claudia Johnson, ed., *The Cambridge Companion to Mary Wollstonecraft*. Cambridge: Cambridge University Press, 2002.

Ritvo, Harriet. "Animals in Nineteenth-Century Britain: Complicated Attitudes and Competing Categories." In Aubrey Manning and James Serpell, eds., *Animals and Human Society: Changing Perspectives*. London: Routledge, 1994.

Warren, Karen. "Introduction." *Hypatia: A Journal of Feminist Philosophy* 6, no. 1 (1991): 1.

Wollstonecraft, Mary. *The Works of Mary Wollstonecraft*. Edited by Marilyn Butler and Janet Todd. 7 vols. London: Pickering and Chatto, 1989.

Young, Thomas. *Animal Rights and Souls in the Eighteenth Century*. Vol. 5, *An Essay on the Humanity to Animals*. Edited by Aaron Garrett. Bristol: Thoemmes, 2000.

11

Animals as Persons

DAVID SZTYBEL

THE ROLE OF PERSONHOOD IN ETHICS

Can nonhuman animals legitimately be construed as *persons*? Extending personhood to all sentient beings may seem absurd at first. For example, *The Oxford English Dictionary* defines a "person" in human-centred terms as "a man or a woman," or "a human being in general," and the term can also be used "emphatically" to distinguish a person from a thing "or from the lower animals." The *Oxford Dictionary* also provides philosophical definitions of a person as a self-conscious or rational being, an individual personality and a being having legal rights. The *Funk and Wagnall's Standard College Dictionary* defines a "person" as "any human being considered as a distinct entity." However, as I wish to maintain, the traditional definition of "person" is unacceptably anthropomorphic. In this essay, I will show that it is indefensible to identify persons with humanity and to centre personhood on rationality is also unacceptably contrary to the ways in which we think about our own personhood.

I propose that a better test of who is a person may be found through a thought experiment. Very briefly, if you were suddenly to experience the experiences of another conscious being such as a chicken's experience of pain, you would count that as *a personal experience*, and you would count the experience of pain as a personal experience whether or not the being were capable of reasoning (either wholly, or at a particular time). I will elaborate and defend this controversial idea.

The concept of the *person* has a central pride of place in ethics, political philosophy and philosophy of law. In the words of philosopher Jonathan Jacobs:

> There is nothing magical about the concept person, and it is not simple or obvious. But it is the focal concept to which and through which concepts of moral goods and harms, needs, responsibilities, respect, friendship, virtue, happiness, agency, and so forth are connected.[1]

Historically, there has been a certain stinginess about recognizing personhood. The denial of personhood seems to have something to do with being oppressed. Women, for instance, and blacks have historically suffered a denial of their status as persons, resulting in a concomitant denial of rights.

An individual is likely not to be equally respected if he or she is not considered to be essentially the same kind of being as those who are substantially respected in the moral community. For example, the Barabaig, a North African tribe, although they considered the killing of fellow Barabaigians to be murder, used to consider the killing of members of neighbouring tribes not to be murder: killing non-Barabaigians was less like the killing of persons and more like the killing of animals.[2]

R.S. Downie argues in *Respect for Persons* that persons are "formal objects of *agape*" (i.e., love of one's neighbour), by which he means that we are inclined to follow moral rules when we have an active sympathy for the purposes of persons.[3] He does not consider "children, the senile, lunatics and animals" to be persons, since he claims that such beings lack personality to a lesser or greater extent.[4] Downie's conceptualization hardly does justice, for example, to the fact that so-called lunatics often go through long phases in which they are lucid. Downie, however, holds that "congenital idiots," although they will never be persons in the full sense, still have sufficient resemblances to persons "to justify extending the language of *agape* to them."[5] He characterizes nonhuman animals as having "minimal personality" in the form of sentience. However, are the conscious experiences of nonhuman animals only "minimally" personal? Or are they full persons in their own right?

HOW NOT TO ARGUE THAT ANIMALS ARE PERSONS

Whether or not nonhuman animals qualify as persons is—for animals—a highly important conceptual question. A number of thinkers have urged that nonhuman animals are persons. Joan Dunayer makes a grammatically based argument that "animal" is a noun and a noun is a person, a place or a thing. She observes that animals are not places, and since they have minds, they are not mere things, thus by a process of elimination animals must be persons.[6] This argument while suggestive is not conclusive because nouns are merely conventional categories that do not pretend to be logically exhaustive. What if animals are "sentient beings" that are neither things nor persons? We cannot settle the philosophical question of nonhuman personhood merely by linguistic or social fiat. Similarly, animals "populate" various lands and although the root of "populate" is "people," the linguistic derivation alone does not entail that animals are persons. Or, although we use the pronoun "who" to refer to humans who, for example, are in a coma and have only brain-stem functioning,[7] our use of "who" in this context does not entail that these humans are persons, although they may be called that in some honorary sense.

Another moral philosophical tactic is to define "person" in keeping with the *Oxford English Dictionary* as a rights-holder. In Gary Francione's opinion, an animal is a person because "to say that a being is a person is merely to say that the being has morally significant interests, that the principle of equal consideration applies to that being, and that the being is not a thing."[8] However, if I were to assume from the outset that animals have rights, I would merely be begging the question. It is similarly unilluminating to say that a person *is* a being that is morally significant. The *Mona Lisa* may be morally significant in different ways, in that people arguably have a duty to preserve it from harm, but it is not a person. Perhaps sentient beings are morally significant in that we ought not to be cruel to them, but perhaps they are not all persons.

None of these moral arguments says anything about what persons are or could be, but only that they must be morally respected. Since these concepts do not truly explore the concept of what is a person, nothing in these sorts of accounts identifies that which is distinctive to a person that entitles her or him to moral respect. Such arguments are both circular and superficial.

Francione also notes that "there is no characteristic or set of characteristics that is possessed by all humans (whom we regard as persons) that is not possessed by at least some animals."[9] However, this begs the question, are some humans and nonhumans *not* persons because they lack rationality and self-consciousness to any substantial extent? He points out that many animals possess beliefs, desires, memory, perception, intention, self-consciousness and a sense of the future.[10] Again, are these *sufficient* for personhood when they—or their manifestation in animals—do not match the traditional definition? We need, rather, a *reason* to favour a revisionist definition of personhood and a reason to reject the traditional definition of personhood.

Evelyn B. Pluhar argues that children are often referred to as "little persons," even though they may lack rationality, autonomy and language abilities.[11] However, it is not clear whether children are in such cases merely being referred to affectionately or whether the reference suggests that the children will in most cases develop advanced capacities in the future. Pluhar agrees with Regan that a person must be able to initiate actions in pursuit of goals,[12] but perhaps this is discriminatory against the disabled. Do we really wish to say that a dying man, paralyzed and unable to speak is not a person because he will never again be a full agent? Is one *less* of a person when idle or resting? Is there then an *interruption* in being a person when sleeping? Pluhar frankly confesses that she wavers about how high standards for personhood should be,[13] and so uses the idea of "full personhood" when discussing the traditional view of persons as rational, autonomous and so forth.

Certainly, it would be a poor strategy to argue—as some have argued[14]—that nonhuman animals are persons because they are rational beings, for nonhuman animals do not reason in the same ways that most humans can. Even if some animals are said to reason in their own ways, they may not reason to the same degree as most humans, and so if reasoning is the crucial attribute, animals may not be respected to the same degree as humans. It is also inadequate to point out that humans are animals too, since, again, that begs the issue: are we the *only* animals who qualify as persons?

While it is true that linguistic conventions cannot be used to prove that nonhuman animals are persons, neither can linguistic usage settle the issue that they are *not* persons. Dictionary definitions of persons may focus on human beings, but such definitions are merely conventional records of traditional thinking. For example, an old dictionary may offer a definition of "phlogiston" as though it were a real substance, as scientists once believed, even though present-day physicists and chemists now deny that phlogiston exists.[15] If critical analysis can reveal inconsistencies in our traditional idea that personhood is an attribute restricted to humans, then we may be forced to rethink just what "person" really means to us. A social ethic may rely on socially popular definitions, but a philosophically justified ethic cannot afford to take the meaning of terms for granted.

Most animal rights philosophers specifically reject invoking the language of personhood on behalf of nonhuman animals. Tom Regan stipulates that in his understanding of animal rights, he takes the term "animal" to mean "normal" adult mammals who are more than one year old.[16] He tailors the concept of "animal" to fit his notion of a "subject of a life." According to Regan, a subject of a life has:

> beliefs and desires, perception, memory, and a sense of the future, including their own future; an emotional life together with feelings of pleasure and pain; preference- and welfare-interests; the ability to initiate action in pursuit of their desires and goals; a psychophysical identity over time; and an individual welfare in the sense that their experiential life fares well or ill for them, logically independently of their utility for others and logically independently of their being the object of anyone else's interests.[17]

"Preference-interests" are those things that beings are consciously *interested in*, or at least are *disposed* to be consciously interested in.[18] "Welfare-interests" are those things that are *in a being's interest*, including biological needs such as adequate nourishment, shelter, water and rest,[19] and psychological needs such as companionship, security and liberty.[20]

Regan views having an individual welfare as the key aspect of being a subject of a life and, he argues, having a welfare entitles a being to an equal share of justice: "A sufficient condition of being owed such duties [of justice] is that one have a welfare—that one be the experiencing subject of a life that fares well or ill for one as an individual."[21] In his book, *Animal Rights, Human Wrongs*, Regan opines that "person" covers too few individuals, including humans who lack rational capacities.[22] In *Empty Cages*, Regan indicates that there is no universal agreement as to who qualifies as a person, but one popular definition he cites is one who is morally responsible.[23] I propose that much more sweeping consideration can be offered to sentient beings, some of whom may not qualify as "subjects of a life," although all of whom are persons.

Peter Singer, S.F. Sapontzis and Bernard Rollin speak of animals as sentient beings. Singer defines persons as "rational and self-conscious beings, aware of themselves as distinct entities with a past and a future"[24]—a definition that excludes many animals. While this is a definition in keeping with the *Oxford English Dictionary*, it is not an account that is very critical about what capacities someone must have to generate "personal experiences." Singer further writes that "fish appear to be the clearest case of animals who are conscious but not persons... for they are not autonomous."[25]

Evelyn Pluhar, as we have noted above, is ambivalent about whether or not, or how, to consider animals as persons. Gary Francione refers to animals as persons, but according to a merely stipulative definition that is powerless to convince anyone who does not already agree with him. Most animal advocacy organizations do not speak of animals as persons, which is not surprising, given both that it is not conventional to do so and there is a lack of forceful argumentation in favour of such an idea.

The crux of the issue of what a person is lies in what we consider to be the core of our own personhood: our capacity for conscious experience, and this is a capacity we share with any number of nonhuman animals. I hope that once we have understood this we will eventually adopt the proposal that many nonhuman animals are persons.

PERSONHOOD ACROSS SPECIES

I now return to our earlier thought experiment in which we were asked to imagine experiencing the experience of another conscious being such as, in my example, a chicken. In the thought experiment we came to the idea of *personal experience*. I shall here elaborate what I mean by personal experience.

We identify ourselves not just with a living body but with a continuity of consciousness.[26] Indeed, if I somehow managed to switch bodies with somebody else, it would still be "myself" that is "in" the other body, as endless stories and philosophical thought experiments suggest. Similarly, if I were to lose an arm or a leg I might have different personal attributes, but I would still be the same person. The conscious point of view is so central that many thinkers would accept a definition of death as the "permanent loss of all consciousness," implying that the essence of life as a person is being conscious. If someone's body lives on as something that merely breathes or circulates blood—in the sense of being maintained by a brain stem—such a body would not obviously be a person because it lacks personality. A corpse may also be said to be devoid of personality, implying that personality is essentially psychological in nature. I am speaking of consciousness itself as something that occurs in the world, regardless of whether anyone is aware of it or not. We are the ones who have our experiences. Even though we cannot experience our conscious point of view as an object, we experience a conscious standpoint through the act of experiencing. A person is that-which-experiences.[27] There is no "impersonal" combination of conscious states that could occur anywhere.[28] They all must pertain to some specific and unique point of view.

Granted that a person must have consciousness, are there some kinds of experience that it would be necessary to have to qualify as a person? Is reasoning necessary to have the kind of consciousness necessary for personhood? We do not employ reasoning in all of our conscious states, nor do we always act rationally. Yet we would say that such non-rational experiences are a part of our personal experiences. In fact, the type of experiences that a person could have must be very broad—going beyond just experiences of reasoning—if it is to encompass the wide variety of experiences that we, as persons, do have. Otherwise, we may find that we lose our continuity of personal experience, and become persons only part of the time, even though we remain alive throughout—a patently absurd result.

No one would deny that an experience of extreme agony is a personal experience. Indeed, it is one of the forms of suffering that we dread most. You would call the feeling of pain that you experience a personal experience, or a part of your own personal time, without hesitation. You would not have to wait for it to be redeemed as a personal experience later on, say, by reflecting on it rationally or analytically. Pain would become a part of your personal biography as soon as it occurs. By parity of logic, we should call the same experience of pain that occurs in an animal, such as the pain experience of the chicken in my example, "personal" as well, since it is the same general sort of experience as the human type of experience. Conversely, if the bird could experience our own human kind of non-rational pain, or at least the aspect of our experience that involves agony, that would also be "personal."

We cannot confirm directly whether animals have personal experiences by asking them. The best we can do is ascertain whether they have them by evaluating whether, if we had their experiences, we would call them personal experiences. The answer is clearly in the affirmative. Any entity that has personal experiences must be a person, since no non-personal thing logically could have personal experiences.

This argument is not an argument from analogy, in which similar but somewhat different things are compared, but is a logically compelling argument from *identity*. We cannot logically affirm personhood in the one case and deny it in the other. Thus, it is no leap of logic to call nonhuman animals "persons." On the contrary, refusing to acknowledge animals as persons is condemned here as illogical. The argument may be formalized as follows:

1. If we had an animal's experience of pleasure or pain, we would immediately call that a "personal experience."
2. Since our experience would be generically identical with that of the animal, the animal's own experience has sufficient characteristics to be considered a "personal experience" as well.
3. Therefore animals have personal experiences.
4. Personal experiences can only be attributed to persons, not things.
5. Therefore animals are persons.

I argue that we ought to embrace rational and self-consistent definitions and usages or at least to recognize all cases to which our existing concepts apply, given the ways that we actually use these concepts. To acknowledge animals as persons may be at odds with the current dictionary definitions, but that is better than being at odds with our deepest and most honest thinking.

IMPLICATIONS OF THE THOUGHT EXPERIMENT

Thus, I need not be human to have a personal experience.[29] If I assert that one kind of experience in humans is personal and hold at the same time that the same kind of experience when it occurs in nonhumans is not personal then I violate the principle of sufficient reason. If something has characteristics sufficient for it to be called "personal" in one case, then the same characteristics are enough reason to label it "personal" in another case. Differences exist only between species: a bird's and my own. One does not require a special kind of body to qualify as a person. An extraterrestrial with a very different kind of body but with a mind known to be very similar to a human's would be deemed a person without much controversy. As well, a human who is paralyzed from the neck down would still be considered a person. And if nonhuman animals are not persons because they are not rational, then, impossibly, neither are human persons during the times that they experience non-rational states such as states of pain. At most, humans in pain would be "waiting" to be persons once again, which is an unacceptable result and contrary to how we actually think of ourselves.

It follows from this thought experiment that if sensations of pleasure and pain are called personal experiences in our own lives then sentience is sufficient for personhood. There is no doubt that personal experience can be much more elaborate than pain and pleasure states. Personal experience can include reasoning, remembering, decision-making, finding events to be meaningful in various ways and language-wielding abilities. It makes sense to refer specifically to *rational persons* when contemplating moral agency, or issues of trust, competence, consent or responsibility. But persons need not have complex inner states to be persons. Persons do not even have to *do* anything, but only to experience, if the experience is personal, and indeed we do not cease to be persons when we cease to be active ourselves. When we dream we also continue to have personal experiences. If one can continue to be a person while merely feeling something, then one can be a person if that is the only kind of psychological state of which one is capable. It is just a matter of extending, across a lifetime, what is already conceded to be a personal experience in a given moment of time. Many nonhuman animals appear to be capable of thoughts and beliefs as well. Yet a viable definition of "person" must embrace even the most unreasoning of animals, as long as they are capable of feeling.

This thought experiment reveals the ways in which we think of personal experience without any religious connotations, but even the idea of a soul that survives death is essentially a vehicle for continued consciousness or experience of one kind or another. Also, the notion of an angel as a person already pushes personhood beyond the biological species of humanity.

Investigating the problem of personal identity helps to reveal what a person essentially *is*, even after all manner of transformations.[30] Thus, the problem of personal identity is relevant to whether nonhuman animals are or can be persons. Mentally disadvantaged humans too have personal experiences, for we would call their experiences personal if we had them. Peter Singer denies that human newborns are persons[31] because they lack capacities for rationality, self-consciousness and having a sense of a past and a future, although if he were to experience what a newborn does, he would no doubt classify that as a personal sort of experience. We do not need rationality to have personal experiences, but we need to have personal experiences—be they cognitive or emotional—to continue to be a person.

Evelyn Pluhar, in *Beyond Prejudice*, uses the term "full personhood" to refer to the full range of traditional characteristics associated with persons: rationality, autonomy, human-like language and so on. However, I object to this usage, because it implies that (merely) sentient beings are not fully persons but only partly persons. The same can be said of the term "minimal persons," derived from Downie's above-mentioned concept of "minimal personality," which implies that some individuals are merely percentages of normal persons. *In fact, merely sentient persons are whole and complete as they are.* Furthermore what counts as a "normal" person is what is normal for the kind of person under consideration, not only what is normal for a privileged adult white male *Homo sapiens*, especially given the implication of this argument, that there is a very wide variety of persons, and many humans who have been oppressed have often, in history, suffered a denial of their personhood. It does not make sense to state that one is only partially a person because one is merely unlike another person.

One human being is not less of a person, by degrees, if he or she is less intelligent than another, so it would be arbitrary to deny personhood, absolutely or by degrees, to nonhuman animals just because they are less intelligent than humans. It is purely anthropomorphic to think of personhood in exclusively human terms, projecting human traits onto the concept of "person" unnecessarily. It is also ableist to require a variety of special abilities to be a person at all, arbitrarily discriminating against the disabled. There is such a variety of personhood, in fact, that every person is unique and has a distinctive personality, quite noticeably in the case of many animals, including birds and reptiles.

Traits that are not *necessary* for being a person cannot be part of the essence of what it is to be a person. Rationality is not necessary for having personal experiences. Thus, human and nonhuman persons do have enough in common to call both "persons," if they have what is common to all known forms of personal experience (and therefore perhaps essential to personal experience): sentience.

I will now abandon Regan's term "subject of a life" in favour of the term "person." A sentient being need not have all of Regan's criteria[32] in order to count as a subject of a life. For instance, it is not clear that a person need have a memory or a sense of the future, nor the ability to initiate action in pursuit of desires and goals. An elderly person who suffers from acute dementia, lacks memory, is too disoriented to have a sense of the future, is unable to initiate action in pursuit of desires or goals, and perhaps is even unable to communicate or think in problem-solving ways may lack self-consciousness in one sense. Such a being may have no *concept* of "self" and "other." However, such a person may have self-consciousness in another sense. He or she may be aware of his or her time in the moment and would be aware of his or her own body. These personal times and the body would be a part of that person's "self," and so he or she would have self-consciousness in that sense. Consciousness may mean self-consciousness in certain cases. After all, being aware of one's own mind and body is not consciousness of any entity other than oneself. Such a person would still find things significant to him or her in the here and now, although such significance may not be recalled later or anticipated for the future. It cannot be said of this person that nothing is of significance but only that the world does not mean what it used to mean to her or him. However, I would not wish to compare animals to demented humans overmuch, since many animals exhibit profound evidence of memory, reflection and anticipation, which afford them not only learning but also a continuity of life in their own minds.

Ethics is an attempt to re-examine the normal. One of the aims of ethics is to determine the destiny of cultural norms. A contemplation of our understanding of personhood shows that we are often unwilling to admit what we can grasp only too well: that many nonhuman animals are indeed persons. Given the tyranny of corporations that dominates today's global market, where it is corporations that "take risks" (speaking anthropomorphically about a legal fiction) and primarily rich individuals who reap benefits, we should question overextending personhood to mere legal fictions (which is what corporations are) more than we should worry about overextending the concept to animals. The alternative to my account is either the familiar idea that nonhuman animals are mere things, as Descartes asserted, or at best sentient beings that are little more than things with feelings.

If you were to spend the rest of your life experiencing only a nonhuman animal's experiences, you would still be a person. So what of the nonhuman animals themselves? All experience is personal. We need to say this because, very often, the experiences of nonhuman animals are somehow considered "not personal enough," except when their like occurs in us. If nonhuman animals are treated totally impersonally, they become, or are conceived to be, things to be managed. Even calling a sentient being a "being" uses a term that is indifferently applied to mere things as well. If nonhuman animals are ambiguously regarded as persons or things, then they will be abused as supposed things.

Is all experience and preference personal? Certainly insofar as these are had by actual persons they are paradigmatically personal. However, experience discussed abstractly, as a philosophical concept, although it may apply to persons, is not personal in the same way. Also, if I speculate about someone else's experiences, or predict what experiences I will have, my discussion of a set of experiences will also not be "personal" in the sense that they may not ever be had by any real person. Preferences are not always paradigmatically personal either. We can form preferences on the basis of conceding to a democratic majority, as representatives of a company, or simply on the basis of what is most effective, what has the lowest price, or what is in fact possible. Those preferences are not as "personal" perhaps if they are not formed solely with reference to the person. None of this terminological pondering, however, affects my argument that animals have personal experiences and therefore are persons.

As the foregoing arguments suggest, the concept of person logically extends more widely than most would think. Thus, we should understand "persons" differently. At the very least, my definition of "person" must be accepted for the sake of understanding how I use the term. However, I have argued that this understanding of persons is accurate philosophical terminology, and thus should eventually become a part of linguistic usage more generally. "Person" is interchangeable with humans in most dictionaries, but we need to update our lexicon in order to overcome speciesist thinking. We already grant in common usage that a person does not have to be human, since an angel or an extraterrestrial might be considered a person. An analytic approach that emphasizes ordinary usage is conservative and reflects merely social ethics; an approach that clarifies the way the concept in fact applies is more consonant with the best philosophical ethics we can offer. If it now sounds strange to say that nonhuman animals can be persons, it is mostly because this usage is a novelty. There is a close relationship between being considered a "person" and being given respect in ethics. If a language lacks a term for personhood, it might be inspirational to adopt either it or some suitable equivalent. We cannot regard animals respectfully if we continue to call ourselves "persons" while denying the same status to other animals. We face a logical choice: either deny that our sentient experience is a part of our personhood or accept that other sentient beings are persons. There is no other choice and no more reasonable choice than the former.[33] Do we depersonalize ourselves in order to deny that animals are persons? It is true that terms are defined not only philosophically but also in terms of common usage. However ideally, our widely understood definitions will eventually come to reflect the best results of our most honest inquiries.

I am not redefining personhood, here, but merely employing the term as it is used, but with more clarity, consistency and justice than is usually the case. People had long denied that slaves were persons so long as they were enslaved, and animals were and are still no exception. The Great Ape Project[34] invests in an anthropocentric idea of personhood, elevating apes and dolphins to this coveted status, while implicitly denying that other nonhuman animals can be persons in an otherwise very significant legal, cultural and political initiative. Steve Wise argues in favour of granting dignity rights only to those creatures whom he conservatively claims have "practical autonomy"—chimpanzees and bonobos[35]—although many creatures have not only their own preferences but also their own independent ways of seeking to satisfy their desires. He does not defend rights for sentient beings, although he indicates that "if I were Chief Justice of the Universe, I might make the simpler capacity to suffer ... sufficient for personhood."[36] However, he notes that the capacity to suffer "appears irrelevant to common-law judges."[37] We must, however, anticipate—and seek to help to formulate and justify—the opinions of revisionist judges of the future, who may need to adjudicate anew in light of enlightened animal rights legislation which may yet appear on the law books of tomorrow. This is not as far-fetched as it may superficially appear. A poll by the Associated Press and the *Los Angeles Times* found that fully two-thirds of adult Americans agree that "an animal's right to live free from suffering should be just as important as a person's."[38]

Wise makes it seem that whether or not animals are persons is a matter of arbitrary choice on the part of humans. However, I hold that it is logically undeniable that sentient animals are the sorts of beings with personal experiences: that is, persons.

In these uncivilized days, even full persons who are human are often treated impersonally or with hostility or indifference, but we must continue to make the world more civilized as best we can. Although nonhuman animals cannot be subject to "dehumanization," which humans who are treated like commodities can experience, nonhuman animals are currently, more often than not, subject to "depersonalization." "Us versus them" attitudes can be notoriously oppressive, and perhaps the ultimate "us" is the class of persons who think of animals contemptuously as "them" and treat them like mere things or impersonal entities. If animals' experiences are only called personal experiences when they occur in beings of a certain species, namely humans, and denied to be personal when they occur in any other species, that would seem to be simple speciesism, or arbitrary and prejudicial discrimination on the basis of species membership.

Arguably, persons as such do not universally have rights so long as nonhuman animals lack them. Only those persons who are powerful enough to command a share of resources, or who are admired by others who are powerful, currently enjoy significant respect. If animals are best conceived as having equal inherent value, as Tom Regan argues, then respect for persons, in this world, continues to hover at a relatively primitive stage compared with what may be conceived as both possible and desirable.

NOTES

1 Jonathan Jacobs, "Moral Imagination, Objectivity, and Practical Wisdom," *International Philosophical Quarterly* 31 (March 1991): 27.
2 George Klima, *The Barabaig* (Long Grove, IL: Waveland Press, 1970), 60.
3 R.S. Downie, *Respect for Persons* (London: George Allen and Unwin, 1969), 29.
4 Ibid., 34.
5 Ibid., 35.
6 Joan Dunayer, *Animal Equality: Language and Liberation* (Derwood, MD: Ryce Publishing, 2001), 7.
7 Ibid., 153. Brain-stem functioning only manages physiological functions such as breathing.
8 Gary L. Francione, *Introduction to Animal Rights: Your Child or the Dog?* (Philadelphia: Temple University Press), 100-101.
9 Gary L. Francione, "Animal Rights Theory and Utilitarianism: Relative Normative Guidance," *Between the Species* 3 (August 2003), retrieved 10 December 2007 from http://cla.calpoly.edu/~jlynch/issueIII.html. Derek W. St. Pierre, "The Transition from Property to People: The Road to the Recognition of Rights for Non-Human Animals," *Hastings Women's Law Journal* 9 (Summer 1998): 255-71, actually does not map out any original territory in how animals are to be conceived as persons, but mainly cites the analysis of Francione. In terms of animal rights, St. Pierre merely cites Tom Regan's *The Case for Animal Rights*, but incorrectly also refers to Peter Singer's *Animal Liberation*, which is not a defence of rights at all.
10 Ibid.
11 Evelyn B. Pluhar, *Beyond Prejudice: The Moral Significance of Human and Nonhuman Animals* (Durham: Duke University Press, 1995), 2-4.
12 Ibid., 5.
13 Ibid., 4.
14 For example, those who support the Great Ape Project often defend the assertion that great apes deserve rights because they can function rationally.
15 Phlogiston theory originated in the late seventeenth century, and was widely believed through most of the eighteenth century, until it was refuted by Lavoisier. It was thought to be a substance without odour, colour, taste or weight present in combustible materials and given off when burning. The ash was thought to be the true material without the phlogiston.

16 Tom Regan, *The Case for Animal Rights* (Los Angeles: University of California Press, 1983), 239.
17 Ibid., 243.
18 Ibid., 87.
19 Ibid., 88.
20 Ibid., 90.
21 Ibid., 171.
22 Tom Regan, *Animal Rights, Human Wrongs: An Introduction to Moral Philosophy* (Lanham, MD: Rowman and Littlefield, 2003), 80.
23 Tom Regan, *Empty Cages: Facing the Challenge of Animal Rights* (Lanham, MD: Rowman and Littlefield, 2004), 45.
24 Peter Singer, *Practical Ethics*, 2nd ed. (Cambridge: Cambridge University Press, 1993), 110–11. Does this imply that fish are not self-managing or do not look after themselves? Who does look after wild fish, then?
25 Ibid., 119.
26 I speak of continuity of consciousness, but I do not mean that we always have to *recall* our conscious states to be the same person we once were, any more than we need to anticipate our conscious states to be the same person that we will be in the future. Rather, consciousness flows on in a continuous stream from moment to moment, whether or not, at any given time, we happen to be aware of much of this stream. Others may be able to verify that continuity of consciousness in ourselves, or it may be that no one can verify it. I am not, then, necessarily speaking of a continuity of consciousness of consciousness, nor self-consciousness, nor indeed of anyone's awareness of others' consciousness. Beings such as those with senile dementia with only momentary or restricted awareness can still be affected for better or worse in ways that their caregivers can understand, even if these disabled persons cannot.
27 Some philosophers allege they can make sense of experiences without an experiencer, or one who experiences, but I admit that I cannot understand such an idea beyond some philosophers refusing to consider real anything that we cannot examine as an object, and thus dismissing out of hand the idea of an entity that is a subject of experience, because we cannot experience such a being as an object.
28 Buddhists dispute this idea, and maintain that people are merely a conglomerate of "five aggregates," namely, body, sensation, perception, mental phenomena and consciousness. I do not understand how consciousness and what we are conscious of can so easily be separated. See Hans Wolfgang Schuman, *Buddhism: An Outline of Its Teachings and Schools* (Wheaton, IL: Quest, 1974), 42–43.
29 Note: Personal experiences can also refer to private experiences of one's own, and while this is not what is under discussion, there is no reason to doubt that nonhuman animals can have personal experiences in this sense, as well.

30 *Human* transformations, in the way the problem is typically contemplated.
31 Singer spoke on a documentary devoted to his controversial views which permit infanticide, *A Dangerous Mind*, broadcast in January 2004 on *CBC Newsworld*.
32 Regan's criteria of counting as a subject of a life, I remind the reader, are as he writes in *The Case for Animal Rights*: "Beliefs and desires, perception, memory, and a sense of the future, including their own future; an emotional life together with feelings of pleasure and pain; preference- and welfare-interests; the ability to initiate action in pursuit of their desires and goals; a psychophysical identity over time; and an individual welfare in the sense that their experiential life fares well or ill for them, logically independently of their utility for others and logically independently of their being the object of anyone else's interests" (243).
33 If animals are persons, then their species are peoples, and many animals are deeply social with their fellows in ways that we can scarcely grasp. Supposing for a moment that Regan is correct in finding that animals have rights, he is mistaken in stating, in *The Case for Animal Rights*, 359–61, that the protection of individuals is sufficient to account for the moral imperative of species-protection, although this would be an important component of any such imperative. Many animals may in some sense identify with their own peoples, and they may have a psychological need to associate with others of their kind. Individuals exist, but so do relationships, as ethics of care theorists never tire of emphasizing. Such social considerations may help to lend a special urgency to species-preservation.
34 See Paola Cavalieri and Peter Singer, eds., *The Great Ape Project: Equality beyond Humanity* (New York: St. Martin's Press, 1993).
35 Steven M. Wise, *Drawing the Line: Science and the Case for Animal Rights* (Cambridge: Perseus Books, 2002), 33.
36 Ibid., 34.
37 Ibid.
38 Regan, *Animal Rights, Human Wrongs*, 121.

BIBLIOGRAPHY

Cavalieri, Paola, and Peter Singer, eds. *The Great Ape Project: Equality beyond Humanity*. New York: St. Martin's Press, 1993.
Downie, R.S. *Respect for Persons*. London: George Allen and Unwin, 1969.
Dunayer, Joan. *Animal Equality: Language and Liberation*. Derwood, MD: Ryce Publishing, 2001.
Francione, Gary L. *Introduction to Animal Rights: Your Child or the Dog?* Philadelphia: Temple University Press, 2000.

———. "Animal Rights Theory and Utilitarianism: Relative Normative Guidance." *Between the Species* 3 (2003). Retrieved 10 December 2007 from http://cla.calpoly.edu/~jlynch/issueIII.html.

Jacobs, Jonathan. "Moral Imagination, Objectivity, and Practical Wisdom." *International Philosophical Quarterly* 31 (1991): 23–37.

Klima, George. *The Barabaig.* Long Grove, IL: Waveland Press, 1970.

Pluhar, Evelyn B. *Beyond Prejudice: The Moral Significance of Human and Nonhuman Animals.* Durham, NC: Duke University Press, 1995.

Regan, Tom. *Empty Cages: Facing the Challenge of Animal Rights.* Lanham, MD: Rowman and Littlefield, 2004.

———. *Animal Rights, Human Wrongs: An Introduction to Moral Philosophy.* Lanham, MD: Rowman and Littlefield, 2003.

———. *The Case for Animal Rights.* Los Angeles: University of California Press, 1983.

Schuman, Hans Wolfgang. *Buddhism: An Outline of Its Teachings and Schools.* Wheaton, IL: Quest, 1974.

Singer, Peter. *Practical Ethics.* 2nd ed. Cambridge: Cambridge University Press, 1993.

St. Pierre, Derek W. "The Transition from Property to People: The Road to the Recognition of Rights for Non-Human Animals." *Hastings Women's Law Journal* 9 (1998): 255–71.

Wise, Steven M. *Drawing the Line: Science and the Case for Animal Rights.* Cambridge: Perseus Books, 2002.

12

Power and Irony
One Tortured Cat and Many Twisted Angles to Our Moral Schizophrenia about Animals

LESLI BISGOULD

Our relationship with the others in the animal kingdom is confused indeed. On the one hand, there are some animals whom we love quite personally: we give them names, bring them into our homes and spend billions of dollars treating them to such luxuries as booties, yoga and daycare. On the other hand, there are many more animals to whom, instead of giving such care, we cause tremendous harm—on a daily, institutionalized and very profitable basis. Gary Francione has called this our "moral schizophrenia" regarding animals.[1]

If this seems strange, we should recall the inter-human moral schizophrenia with which we somehow also manage to live. For example, while in North America we also spend a lot of money on booties, yoga and daycare for our human children, we spend a far greater portion of our collective resources developing and dropping bombs on other people's children, George Bush's adventures in Iraq being just the most recent example.[2]

We have tried so hard for so long to identify the magic feature that qualitatively distinguishes the human from the nonhuman animals so as to justify the treatment we accord them. While the old favourites have been dismissed by science in the many decades since Darwin first said "evolution" (they can't reason, they don't think, they can't communicate, they don't feel pain...) perhaps we have found one after all: let us never underestimate the unique power of the human mind to rationalize—and even make ourselves feel good about—behaviour that is harmful to others.

Nowhere was our inter-species moral schizophrenia more apparent than in a criminal law case every Torontonian knows well.

JESSE POWER MAKES A STATEMENT

The sobs of the men and women watching made it almost impossible to hear the sound on the videotape being played in the courtroom at Toronto's Old City Hall in early 2002. But every now and then an audible cry made it through, or a voice: "That's good stuff, man." A cat was being tortured by three men who had first set up a tripod and camera to record the seventeen-minute episode.[3]

By the end, Kensington (the nickname given posthumously to the cat, after the neighbourhood in which she was killed) had been hung from a noose, beaten, stabbed and thrown against the wall. Her ear had been removed with pliers, her eye had been removed with dental tools, she had been disembowelled. Jesse Power, who had the idea to arrange and film the event, is seen near the end of the tape, while Kensington still lives, spreading her slit skin and inhaling deeply.

Power later hung Kensington's carcass in his freezer and encouraged his roommate to go and see what he had done, thinking she would be impressed. She called the police.

The detectives who investigated this crime work in the downtown area of a big city, yet some expressed that they had never seen anything so gruesome and that they had to leave the room before the tape ended. They were motivated to find the three men and lay the appropriate criminal charges.

They got creative and laid two: one charge of animal cruelty and one charge of mischief.

The first irony presented itself as these charges were laid. Animal cruelty is a summary conviction offence, the least serious kind of criminal offence in Canada, with a maximum penalty of six months imprisonment and a $2,000 fine in this case. Mischief can be treated either as a summary conviction or a more serious indictable offence, with a maximum penalty, in this case, of two years' imprisonment.

The animal cruelty offence is an offence against the animal herself. Mischief, however, is a property offence. It prohibits people from interfering with other people's things. The basis of this charge, then, was that a crime had been committed, not against Kensington, but against the family who lost its cat.[4]

Simply by virtue of the different penalties we ascribe to these offences, we see that Canadian criminal law is much more concerned with protecting one's rights over one's property—generally inanimate things, like sport utility vehicles and lawnmowers—than with the agony of a sentient animal. That might offend one's sense of values, yet the fact is that Power and his partners were exposed to considerably greater punishment because the police treated Kensington as an object and laid the mischief charge.

This is a strange situation in which the law finds itself, where we purport to care about other animals, but still hold fast to the idea that if they are not human, they are objects we own and may use for our own purposes. Even an animal cruelty charge—the one that is supposed to be about the animal herself—requires a court to determine whether the suffering inflicted on the animal was "unnecessary"—meaning some pain and suffering is "necessary" and perfectly fine—meaning that even when actual crimes are committed against them, we still regard animals as things whose fate we are entitled to decide.[5]

This characterization seems to conflict with the overwhelming public outrage regarding this offence. The sentencing hearing proceeded in a courtroom overflowing with media, interested police officers and members of the public. Those who couldn't get a seat held vigil outside the courthouse over the three-day hearing. And everybody, everywhere talked about the case with disgust. They were not upset because somebody's cat had been hurt, they were upset for the cat, that such pain and suffering was caused to a sentient individual.

And it was indefensible, as far as everybody was concerned. When Power's relatively minor sentence was read aloud in court, someone called out, "Why don't you throw in a bouquet of flowers?" No punishment was great enough for what these people had seen and learned.

The second irony emerged in the courtroom. Power's explanation for his act was given by his lawyer. This is permitted in a sentencing matter, but it is strange for the person being sentenced not to take the stand and subject himself to cross-examination when offering such a challenging explanation for his behaviour.[6]

In 2001 when this incident took place, Power was a student at the Ontario College of Art and Design. He claimed—through his lawyer—that he was a vegetarian and that he was trying to make a statement about cruelty to animals.[7] Power contended that this video was the second installment of a piece he did for a school project, in which he filmed himself decapitating a chicken. For his work in that course, he had received an "A." Power said he was trying to make people think about why they don't mind a chicken dying, but they are upset when it's a cat. He wanted people to see that an animal's life is sacrificed when we eat meat, and he chose an animal that is consumed in some places but revered here. He hadn't intended for the cat to suffer but the blade wasn't sharp enough.

Ironic. Or perhaps just ridiculous, in the face of his behaviour on the tape. Three grown men who want a cat to die need no blade. ("Killing a raccoon would be a helluva lot more exciting," whispered one of the men on the tape. "Pillowcase," suggests another. "No, we won't be needing that.")[8] What if Power had chosen to explore the theme of child abuse in the same manner? Would the word "art" have been part of the debate?

Power's explanation was that he believes in "animal rights" and that it is not wrong to end an animal's life, only to do so in such a prolonged fashion. But if the dullness of the blade was the only problem, what rights does Power—or a good part of our society that seems to agree with him in principle—say an animal ought to have? Where do other rights find their premise if one has no basic claim over her or his own existence? And does not the right to live preclude having one's life sacrificed in the name of art, or any idea, or anybody else's purpose?

When it comes to our own species we have, at least ostensibly, rejected the idea that it is acceptable to own others and use them as means to our own ends. We aspire to equality, not because people are actually equal (some are taller than others, smarter, more patient, some have better hearing than others, some are better at math, some can write symphonies, paint masterpieces or run marathons) but because we have come to understand that the differences are not morally relevant when it comes to deciding about fundamental rights. A blind person may not get a driver's license, a child may not vote or see restricted movies. That doesn't mean that it's all right to kill them when it seems that their population has grown too much.[9] But for animals, that kind of discrimination is still the rule.

Irony doesn't get any more poignant than it does here: a sadistic act causing profound pain in the name of objecting to pain; a psychopath claiming to be an advocate for animals, in the face of a courtroom full of animal advocates in tears.[10]

CRIME AND PUNISHMENT

Power's sentence included ninety days to be served on weekends (per his own request, so as not to interfere with his plan to take summer courses in pursuit of the very artistic studies that, at least by his lawyer's account, led him to this act in the first place). Judge Ormston said that the maximum sentence was not warranted here—there were worse ways the cat could have died; if the men had intended to torture her, it would have gone on longer.

This part—the sentence, the judge's characterization—is revealing. An otherwise respected judge—perhaps afraid of being seen as too emotional in a highly publicized case (he began reading his sentence by mentioning that he had lived with cats for thirty years) or of giving in to animal rights militants (he also mentioned having received many letters from people expressing their desire that Power and his partners receive the maximum sentence) seemed to have bought into the perception that Power really was some kind of animal activist, those *unusual* people being a *very misguided* bunch.

It is indeed remarkable that the corporate media and other social institutions represent those who advocate for animal rights as emotionally soft bunny-huggers and militant extremists in the same breath. One might wonder how a person could be both, if one ever had cause to wonder, but there is no impetus to do so in a society that has already been trained to disregard other kinds of beings and to avoid critical thought altogether.

So the irony here, somewhat twisted by now, lay in how a violent and dangerous man helped to show the animal-friendly public that, in the end, animals have no rights at all.

In May 2003, the Crown's appeal of Power's sentence was heard in another packed courtroom by Ontario's Court of Appeal. This collision of ideas was not lost on that court.

Mr. Justice Doherty got directly to the point when he asked the Crown Attorney why there was a mischief charge being pursued at all; wasn't the real crime the cruelty to the animal? And should it make a difference that the cat belonged to somebody? The Crown was asking that there be an additional two years added for mischief, to a six-month sentence being sought for animal cruelty. Does that mean, wondered Justice Doherty aloud, that Power should get two and a half years for doing this to somebody else's cat but six months if the cat were his own?

The Crown struggled silently to find the right response. And the animal-friendly spectators in the public gallery struggled too, craving the toughest possible sentence but trapped themselves now in the awkward dilemma. In the end, the appeal was dismissed.[11]

Let's be clear that whether Power and his associates were to spend six months or two and a half years in jail, neither experience could be expected to produce a more humane man at the end nor to bring any justice to hundreds of millions of animals living in Canada who are regularly scared and hurt. A compelling query at this point is why we think jails are a solution to our social problems—what benefits can such captivity really offer anyway? But these questions are not for this essay. One conclusion we should be able to make as we begin to untwist some of the ironies of this case is that, to the extent that our existing laws are our way of expressing our collective values, our laws do not reflect the modern public sentiment about violence against animals.

This, as we recall our schizophrenic meanderings, is not to say that most people are prepared to agree that we must never cause animals to suffer. As noted above, our laws prohibit "unnecessary" suffering, meaning we have granted ourselves permission to hurt other animals when "necessary" to serve our various purposes. Since we are the ones who write the laws, it is perhaps not surprising that the word "unnecessary" has been defined in a perfectly circular, self-serving manner.

For example, eating animals is generally unnecessary. It may be one's custom, habit or preference. It may be tasty. But it is not *necessary* for our health; quite the contrary, as mounting evidence confirms the links between cancer, heart disease, stroke, diabetes and animal products.[12] And as the case becomes ever clearer that our consumption of animal products is making us sick, the harm caused by intensive agriculture to the environment and to the other animals who try to live there is epidemic.

Quite apart from the criminal laws of the country, the agriculture industry is governed by elaborately detailed regulations and legislation that similarly purports to prohibit the causing of "unnecessary" (or "undue" or "prolonged" or "avoidable") suffering. However, the interpretation that the courts have applied to date does not question the validity of the use to which an animal is put. The status quo is assumed to be acceptable and the "unnecessary" qualification is applied only in the context of particular practices that occur in the course of the activity. While from this one might expect that some of the particularly problematic practices of modern agriculture would be rendered unlawful, that is not the way courts have chosen to interpret the term.

When Pacific Meat Company was charged with a criminal offence for causing pain to pigs it "shackled" by a hind leg, "swung against" a metal wall "with some force" and then thrust a knife into their throats whether unconscious or not, the question in the case was not whether this caused the animals pain, which was admitted and obvious, but whether the pain was "necessary." The court dismissed the charge, noting:

> Hogs fulfill a purpose of providing food for human beings. Before the hogs can be eaten by mankind they must of necessity be killed, so that the fatal injury that is administered to each hog by the "sticker" is a necessity and therefore not "unnecessary."[13]

Most of us, albeit sometimes unwittingly, are the consumers of animals who have been terribly hurt, or of products that have been developed and tested on animals who were terribly hurt, and so on. These animals rarely have names like "Kensington"; they have numbers, lest we dare confront their individuality. Old MacDonald's farm is hard to find these days. There are still some family farms standing in Canada, but they are few in number and they may be compared to the belugas of the St. Lawrence: polluted by the effluent of megacorporations and destined for a painful death.

More than 650 million animals—some twenty times the human population of the country—are raised and killed every year for the agriculture industry in Canada alone.[14] Of these, several million individuals are so depleted or diseased that they arrive at the slaughterhouse already dead.[15] In the agricultural context where some amount of beating, mutilation, intensive confinement, sickness, injury, fatigue, pain, fear and suffering are both predicted and permitted, where the premature death of many animals is expected, even the few regulations that do purport to address their welfare cannot reasonably be expected to be broadly interpreted or enforced in their favour.[16]

And so it goes for all the animals who seem handy to us. Millions more are used as subjects in macabre experiments in secretive laboratories across the country. These animals couldn't have names either, or we could not burn, starve, isolate or electrocute them; they are usually called B-42 or C1373. Countless millions of wild animals are shot or trapped for their fur, their flesh, for being pests or just for kicks. Others die more slowly in the entertainment industry and the trafficking that supports it. And most of us prefer to look away when someone tries to show us the photographs; while we care on the one hand, we prefer to be oblivious on the other and, as a whole, we are prepared to grab on to the first available excuse in order to protect our turkey dinners, our annual hunting trips, our fur-trimmed jackets, our nice day at the zoo.

POWER'S FINAL IRONY?

This paradox may be the most difficult one to confront. The overwhelming revulsion the broad public felt to the treatment Kensington received was visceral; nobody needed a moral theory to propound, everybody just knew it was wrong. And yet, we avoid realizing that animals (including cats, who are popular in neurological experiments, for example)[17] are (often without anaesthetic) mutilated, beaten, brutalized and killed every day in this country for somebody's purpose, be it in the course of producing food, household products, clothing, entertainment or whatever. Should we not finally confront Orwell's observation literally and ask, why are some animals more equal than others?

Christie Blatchford, a reporter writing for the *National Post* at the time, observed that when he inhaled the cat as she was dying, "Jesse Power probably thought he was smelling death; he was smelling moral decay, and it was his own." That Power's morality had decayed, if it ever existed, is self-evident. But what about our own morality, those who cry for a tortured cat and go home to eat other animals whose lives certainly included much more than seventeen minutes of excruciating pain and fear?

We may have the power to hurt others for our own reasons, but it seems we do realize, at least in some contexts, that "because I can" is not a good enough excuse. Jesse's exercise of his power was an extreme example that brings our own ostensibly legitimate behaviour into question. In the end, the greatest irony may be the one we all live with ourselves, to varying degrees: is there really a difference between the animals that we call "pets" and the animals we call "dinner" or does the difference reside in the comfort of our own imagination?

POSTSCRIPT: ONE MORE IRONY AFTER ALL

In September 2004, the Toronto International Film Festival entered the fray by screening the premiere of a $500 documentary entitled, *Casuistry: The Art of Killing a Cat*. Produced by two independent filmmakers, *Casuistry* considered the actions of Jesse Power and his friends as well as others who have used animals and their dead parts in making allegedly artistic statements.

Whether the film endorsed the activities of these men or whether it exposed them and their behaviour for the pathetic reality they embody, it raised yet another troubling angle to this act. Some people denounced the film and the film festival for airing it; protests were organized, banning of the film was called for and a new media controversy was sparked. This was before anybody even saw it and could say whether the film promoted the idea that what the men did was a valid artistic endeavour, or whether it tried—even badly—to challenge it.

Was this then the ultimate irony of the ordeal? The struggle of animal advocates consists not only of political battles to change laws and practices but also, and *first*, of intellectual battles to encourage people to try on new ideas, to confront the inconsistencies in old ideas that seem normal to them. It seems normal to pamper some animals and eat others, to lock humans in cages for punishment and lock animals up because we "love" them. It seems normal to dress up in their skins and to assume that other animals are lesser creatures than ourselves: who is not insulted when referred to as a pig? an ape? a snake? an *animal*?

Animal advocates must search constantly for ways into minds that have been closed by a culture that increasingly favours corporate messaging over thinking and worships profit-making ideals above almost everything else. The fear of ideas, or of having ideas that seem ugly to some people up for discussion, has never served us well. The reaction against an unseen film was very dangerous behaviour on the part of people who themselves promote ideas that the mainstream would prefer to silence.

These comments should not be mistaken for a suggestion that it might be justifiable to be violent in the name of art. Nor are they intended to be critical of people who were affected by what happened to Kensington and who were understandably distressed by the thought that Power's demented ego had found its way to the big screen after all. They are expressed in the hope of cultivating ideas over ideology and in praise of constant questions, the answers to which must place all of us face to face with our own inconsistencies and may lead some of us to evolve.

NOTES

1. See chapter 1 in Gary L. Francione, *Introduction to Animal Rights—Your Child or the Dog?* (Philadelphia: Temple University Press, 2000). Francione is an American animal rights lawyer and law professor. He is the first modern scholar to articulate a thoughtful philosophical theory of animal rights.
2. The bumper sticker that reads "The day will come when public schools have all the funding they need and the air force has to hold a bake sale to buy a bomber" comes to mind.

3 The entire film was seventeen minutes long, including several minutes when the men teased the cat with a mouse, hoping the cat would attack; the active torture lasted approximately six minutes.
4 Nobody ever claimed Kensington and it is impossible to know whether she was lost and how far from home she might have been when she was captured, but her condition suggested that she was not a stray.
5 For a detailed and enlightening discussion on the property status of animals in the legal system of the United States, which is remarkably analogous to Canada, see Gary L. Francione, *Animals, Property and the Law* (Philadelphia: Temple University Press, 1995).
6 Power and the other men pleaded guilty to the charges so there were no trials, only sentencing hearings.
7 Anecdotal accounts from people who claimed to know Power refuted these claims.
8 Christie Blatchford, "Torture for Torture's Sake," *National Post*, 14 June 2003, A1.
9 Describing the problem this way is something I have learned from Gary Francione, who has used this characterization in several of his works.
10 The word "psychopath" seems fitting when one considers the approximately eighty hours of videotape found by the police in Power's apartment in which he is seen dancing and otherwise interacting with what turned out to be animal corpses, though the police were not sure at first. Power had worked in the taxidermy department of the Royal Ontario Museum and in a slaughterhouse. This was not the first indication of his fascination with death, and particularly the deaths of those with no voice and with much less power than he.
11 It is a principle of Canadian sentencing law that the maximum sentence is applicable only in circumstances where the offence is the worst offence and it is committed by the worst offender. Judge Ormston had found that neither condition applied in this case; the Court of Appeal found that while Power was not the worst offender (he had no criminal record, a favourable psychiatric report and the support of family, friends and a teacher from his art school), this was indeed the worst offence.
12 For example, T. Colin Campbell with Thomas M. Campbell, *The China Study* (Dallas: Benbella Books, 2005).
13 *R. v. Pacific Meat Company Limited* (1950), 27 C.R. 128 (B.C.Co.Ct.) at 130.
14 In the United States, the number is somewhere around ten billion.
15 Charlotte Montgomery, *Blood Relations — Animals, Humans and Politics* (Toronto: Between the Lines, 2000), 153.
16 This last sentence was borrowed from a report by Lesli Bisgould, Wendy King and Jennifer Stopford, *Anything Goes: An Overview of Canada's Legal Approach to Animals on Factory Farms* (Toronto: Animal Alliance of Canada, 2001). Available online at www.animalalliance.ca/article.phtml?article=anythinggoes&dir=projects.

17 As another example, the University of Toronto's dentistry school was the subject of criticism by animal advocates several years ago when information leaked out about the pain experiments it was conducting on cats.

BIBLIOGRAPHY

Bisgould, Lesli, Wendy King, and Jennifer Stopford. *Anything Goes: An Overview of Canada's Legal Approach to Animals on Factory Farms.* Toronto: Animal Alliance of Canada, 2001. Available online at www.animal alliance.ca/article.phtml?article=anythinggoes&dir=projects.

Blatchford, Christie. "Torture for Torture's Sake." *National Post*, 14 June 2003, A1.

Campbell, T. Colin with Thomas M. Campbell. *The China Study.* Dallas: Benbella Books, 2005.

Francione, Gary L. *Introduction to Animal Rights—Your Child or the Dog?* Philadelphia: Temple University Press, 2000.

———. *Animals, Property and the Law.* Philadelphia: Temple University Press, 1995.

Montgomery, Charlotte. *Blood Relations—Animals, Humans and Politics.* Toronto: Between the Lines, 2000.

R. v. Pacific Meat Company Limited (1950), 27 C.R. 128 (B.C.Co.Ct.) at 130.

13

Blame and Shame?
How Can We Reduce Unproductive Animal Experimentation?

ANNE INNIS DAGG

Biomedical scientists continue to insist that animal experimentation is essential to progress in combating illness.[1] Yet each year, as many millions of animals suffer and die around the world in biomedical experimentation,[2] there are only a few important medical discoveries: most experiments have minimal effect in improving human health. It is, therefore, worthwhile to examine how the number of animals can be reduced without reducing important biomedical findings.

We should note first that thousands of experiments involving myriad animals will certainly be of no use to science, since the experimental results have never been published (nor will anyone beyond the small research community even know that such animals have died in the name of science) for the following reasons:

a. Some experiments go so badly that they are not written up—the animals escape, the chemicals are mislabelled, the equipment malfunctions, et cetera.
b. Some experiments produce negative results (such as animals being given cancer lesions only to be treated with chemicals that do not affect the lesions) and for this reason the researcher cannot find a publisher.
c. Some small journals, especially new ones that have not yet "proved" themselves, may not be surveyed for the *Web of Science* so that few scientists know they exist.
d. Many articles are deemed unacceptable for publication; some biological journals have refused half of all submitted articles.[3]

Of published research, some papers receive many citations by other scientists and influence future research, but others which garner few or no citations do not. This latter group is the focus of this essay.

Whether a research paper is valuable or not can be roughly measured by the number of citations it receives in the years following its publication, indicating that subsequent scientists found the work useful for their own future research. The electronic database *Web of Science*, available at large universities, documents bibliographic references from articles published in over 8,700 academic journals that can be searched online.

Many papers are judged to be of no scientific worth because no subsequent scientist has cited them, but how does one make scientists in general care about this? They can argue that no one knows in advance how an experiment will turn out, so each one is justified just in case it produces something worthwhile. Some research is carried out without any real theory to guide it—for example, simply injecting carcinogens into mice to produce cancerous lesions and then experimenting with other chemical injections to see if any of them reduce the size of the lesions.

My weapon of choice to fight such waste of animal lives has been to carry out four research projects on citation analysis to try to shame scientists, as this article will detail. My first two papers were about experiments/papers published in psychological and behavioural/neurological journals because I felt that it was especially bad to harm and kill animals in a discipline that was often peripheral to human health.[4] My third study was about cancer research; cancer experiments tend to be exceptionally invasive and painful, involving giving animals cancer before trying to eradicate the cancer by various invasive means, so I hoped that scientists might be willing to take action on my findings on compassionate grounds. As well, huge amounts of money are collected from the public and spent on cancer research—$2 billion a year in the United States and many millions in Canada. My fourth study was about researchers at a large research hospital—the Hospital for Sick Children in Toronto—in the hope that the institution would be too embarrassed to continue supporting the research of scientists with little competence.

In the first study, completed in 1998, I read and analyzed 115 articles in five psychological or neurological journals published in 1989 and 1990.[5] First, I checked the *Web of Science* for seven years following the date of publication to determine the number of subsequent articles that cited each of these papers. (This database is now online, but then I had to pay a librarian a dollar for each datum to collect the information.) Citations tend to peak in the second and third years following publication, although they may continue to be notable for six years[6] and in a few rare cases may continue strongly for decades.[7]

(Citation numbers are important but not perfect. Some citations for a paper may have far greater importance than others, or be cited for methodology rather than the results obtained. Other citations may be negative: made in order to criticize the paper; included for the sake of friendship for a fellow researcher; or self-cited with little reference to the topic at hand as a way to increase the author's profile.)

Second, I counted the number of animals used for the research, although this was often difficult to do because the number was not clearly stated, as if the authors did not want the number to be known.

Third, although these journals had policies in place to encourage the humane treatment of animal subjects, a definition of what is "humane" is subjective and only insists that animals be handled as humanely as possible, given the parameters of each experimental protocol. The procedures can range from "minor stress or pain" to "severe pain near, at, or above the pain tolerance threshold of unanaesthetized conscious animals,"[8] so I noted four categories of invasiveness used on the animals:

N — Animals were subject to little trauma beyond their *normal* captivity.

D — Animals were *deprived* of some necessity, usually food and/or water, to force them to take part in experiments during which food or water were offered as rewards.

C — Animals were subject to invasive procedures, usually by surgery or injection, and then allowed to recover enough so that they could be further tested in some way. They thus spent days or weeks in pain. The range of *cruelty* experienced by animals varied from modest to extreme.

K — Animals were *killed* at the start of an experiment or anaesthetized and later killed without regaining consciousness.

To correlate the number of animals used for a research paper with the number of citations that the paper elicited in subsequent years, an Animal Number/Citation Number Index (AN/CN) was calculated for each paper and for each journal by dividing the number of animals by the number of citations. Although this index gives only a rough approximation of actual harm to animals, it does illustrate, in an objective manner, a useful cost-benefit balance. Those with few animals and many citations were most worthwhile, while those with many animals and few citations were the least valuable. In addition, as I would do in all four papers, I included recommendations (available from adagg@uwaterloo.ca) on how to reduce the number of animals used in experimentation. (See the conclusion of this paper.)

My results showed that:

a. Some journals were far more influential than others, the average number of citations for their articles ranging from 8 to 27.
b. Within each journal there was also a large variation of citation numbers; all had articles that were seldom cited (23 percent had five or fewer citations) and the maximum citation numbers ranged from 24 to 102.
c. The variation in the AN/CN Index was also great, ranging from 0.5 (meaning that for each animal used, an average of two citations were generated) to a troubling 117, meaning that this many animals were used for each citation received.
d. Journals also varied in the number of papers they published which described experiments that were cruel and invasive to animals.

The major conclusions for my paper "Citations Dearth: Another Reason to Reduce Animal Experimentation" were first, that many animals suffered and died in experiments that subsequently elicited few or no citations, indicating a huge waste of both animal life and money. Second, it is possible to pinpoint many experiments and the journals that published them as especially wasteful by calculating an AN/CN value. The higher the number, the more effort should be spent in trying to prevent similar experiments from being funded and performed. I hoped that the researchers and journals which I had shown to be especially at fault would be shamed into changing their behaviour.

In "Citations Dearth" I also discussed not only the ethics of using animals in research but also the culture that makes it acceptable. The very existence of research institutes often depends on animal experimentation, as does the careers of thousands of research scientists. The more papers they publish, even if they receive no citations, tends to mean the more likely they will be to gain promotion, win tenure and receive large funding grants.

Dreaming happily of the positive repercussion for animals that my paper would have once it was published—now that there was solid proof with verifiable numbers that some animal research at least was of no value—

I prepared three copies and sent them to the Ottawa contact person of the British *ATLA (Alternatives to Lab Animals)* journal as it requested, the journal's name itself giving me hope. This contact was a member of the Canadian Council on Animal Care (CCAC), so I felt she would appreciate its importance. Silly me. I waited and waited for months without hearing from her. When I wrote to her again, I received no answer. When I wrote to *ATLA*, I was informed that it had never received my paper; the contact had taken it upon herself to "disappear" it. This woman remains highly regarded by the CCAC.

While I was waiting eagerly for the publication of this first paper, I decided to do a second, more comprehensive one based on the analysis of 155 articles in fourteen similar psychological and behavioural/neurological journals. Again, I concentrated on the three traits that I had rated before, subtitling my final draft "Responsible Animal-Based Research: Three Flags to Consider." These traits were the number of animals used in a paper's experiment(s), the number of citations received by the paper and the level of invasiveness experienced by the animals. I also analyzed the citation data for authors from Canadian universities and for sources (especially Canadian) of funding.

Of the fourteen journals, the "best" one was *Brain Research*, which had on average a total of forty-six citations for invasive experiments; this is a huge Elsevier Science publication comprising sixteen volumes a year that, in 1990, reached 5,770 pages. The "worst" journal was *Behavioural Brain Research* with an average of ten citations per paper. Some journals carried various articles not involved with invasive animal experimentation that were well cited, showing that painful experiments need not be carried out for the authors to have considerable influence.

Based on the three characteristics detailed above, I found that the "best" research came from the University of Montreal (39 citations on average for invasive experiments) and the University of British Columbia (34 citations). The "worst" came from Memorial University (9 citations), Carleton University (13 citations) and the University of Toronto (14 citations).

In total, the papers acknowledged forty sources for financial help that allowed the experiments to be carried out. Strikingly, invasive experiments funded by both the Medical Research Council of Canada (MRC, now the Canadian Institutes of Health Research) and the Natural Sciences and Engineering Research Council of Canada (NSERC) garnered far fewer citations on average (20 and 19) than those funded by other sources (37) or than those that acknowledged no funding source at all (30).

After "Three Flags" was published in 1999 by the *Journal of Applied Animal Welfare Science* (JAAWS), I highlighted the research results specific to the journals I reviewed and sent a copy along with a personal note to each journal, to each university represented and to the major funding agencies as well as to many animal welfare and animal rights groups. The latter groups were supportive, some included reference to my paper in subsequent newsletters. I never heard from the journals, universities or funding groups. I like to think of these recipients as bustling around worriedly, urging researchers to be more conscientious in their future experiments. In reality, they more likely rolled their eyes and dumped my paper in the garbage.

For the third study I decided to tackle cancer research, a vast enterprise involving each year the lives and health of millions of animals and billions of dollars in public funds. It wasn't hard to find suitable journals to search; although the University of Waterloo does not have a medical faculty, its library holdings include forty-eight journals devoted to cancer.

My paper was titled "Animal Experimentation in Cancer Research" in which I analyzed in detail 186 articles involving animals and cancer research from nine general cancer journals. In addition to tabulating the citations of papers in journals, I tabulated the affiliation of the author(s) and funding agencies as I had done before, as well as the nationality of the authors.

Even reading these articles was horrific because of both the suffering of the animals in the experiments and the frequent stupidity of the experiments themselves. As an example, for a study into the dangers of tobacco, forty healthy male golden hamsters were divided into four groups of ten each.[9] The inner cheek pouches of the groups were painted three times a week with sesame oil (the control group), with nicotine dissolved in the oil (the second group), with a carcinogen dissolved in the oil (the third group) and with both the nicotine and the carcinogen solutions (the fourth group).

After twelve weeks of probable pain for the hamsters as they tried to eat, they were killed and their cheek pouches cut out and examined. The hamsters of the last group had significantly larger and a greater number of tumours than those of the third group, indicating that the presence of nicotine increased "tumorigenesis." This experiment was silly because it was already well known that the chewing of tobacco increased the risk of a person developing oral cancer by up to fifty times.[10] The money needed to carry out this research (hamsters, cages, animal workers, laboratory space, feed for the animals, etc.) would have been far better spent on educating tobacco chewers about the dangers of their habit. Other scientists obviously agreed with this conclusion, since only four of their papers have cited this work in the fifteen years since its publication.

In general, the authors of cancer articles were dismissive of animals in their write-ups. Usually, the number of animals was not explicitly given and they were treated with no more sensitivity than if they were test tubes, which also can be purchased in quantity from supply houses. Sometimes the animals were not even mentioned in the "Material and Methods" section. Yet researchers argue that animals are both an essential and an integral part of endeavours to solve problems of cancer.

For my analysis I again ranked the AN/CN values for the four entities to obtain "best" and "worst" groups, so I would know which group deserved the most blame for its ineptitude. For journals, the "best" were *Cancer* and *Journal of the National Cancer Institute*, two of the largest and most well-known publications with an average of two and three animals used for every citation garnered. The "worst" was *Nutrition and Cancer* with an average of sixteen animals used for each citation received. The *Japanese Journal of Cancer Research* stood out in that more than half the articles received fewer than four citations in the next nine years.

To determine if some nations were more cavalier than others in their use of animals in experiments, I tabulated the authors' nationalities along with their AN/CN values. The most effective research was carried out by Norway, Canada, the United States and the Netherlands with values of 2, 4, 6 and 6, respectively (= 2, 4, 6 and 6 animals used for each citation garnered). The least effective were France (value 32), Italy (24), Japan (12) and the United Kingdom (10). There was a huge discrepancy, therefore, between the experimentation carried out in these two groups of nations. Logically, it would be wise for Italy and France to give up their animal experimentation because their results are so pitiful.

For the authors' affiliations, I examined the relative effectiveness of foundations, governments, commercial businesses and universities, calculating the average AN/CN value for each group. Foundations did the "best" research (AN/CN average value of 5), followed by governments (6), businesses and universities (both 8). The values for foundations may be the best because they have very focused research, whereas those for the less-effective universities are more likely to be high risk. Thousands of graduate students and postdoctoral fellows flock to do cancer research at universities because the stakes are so high; they may perform "do and see" research without theoretical basis, which is all right for the researchers but devastating for the animals. It may be that animal care committees of universities, although functioning as they must by law, are unable or unwilling to forbid experiments that seem likely to be unproductive. If one researcher votes against a colleague's proposal, he or she might fear retaliation in the future.

There was more variation when AN/CN values were tabulated for acknowledged funding agencies. Again foundations and governments financed the "best" experiments (AN/CN values 6 and 7). The "worst" were funded by universities (17), with non-governmental groups and commercial businesses in between (13 and 14).

When I had written up my results I sent "Animal Experimentation" to *Cancer*, the journal of the American Cancer Society, because it had a "best" record it could be proud of and I thought this group would be influential in spreading my message. Instead, my paper was returned immediately without any explanatory letter. Was this the society's way of expressing contempt for someone interested in animal welfare? At least it allowed me to send the paper to a second journal, *Journal of Applied Animal Welfare Science*, which was pleased to publish it.

Only once during these studies did I receive a response from a journal to whom I had sent a copy of the paper. It came from Leonard Cohen, editor of *Nutrition and Cancer*, who wrote me (7 December 2000) to say that he agreed there was an unnecessary use of animal models in cancer research that should be addressed, but that he felt it was unfair to compare his small focused journal with larger journals covering broader areas.

In general, there was more interest in "Animal Experimentation" than in the earlier published one because the group Animal Alliance printed my précis of the work and I presented my results at two small non-mainstream conferences in Toronto and Ottawa. An academic responded by noting, as Cohen had, that large journals are more often cited than smaller ones, giving them an advantage I hadn't taken into account. Several women asked for copies of my paper, one for a course she was teaching in Illinois called "Human/Animal Interactions."

More recently, in 2004 during Cancer Month in April, I wrote up a popular account of my cancer findings, which I sent to four large newspapers. I hoped that if they didn't want to use it as news, they might still print it to show they had open minds. Alas, no. The *Globe and Mail*, the *National Post*, the *Toronto Star* and the *Ottawa Citizen* all refused it, as did a popular columnist on health issues known for his non-mainstream ideas.

For the final study, fellow scientist Troy Seidle and I analyzed the citations received for the work of researchers at the Hospital for Sick Children in Toronto.[11] We chose this teaching institution because it is well known, has a huge and increasing investment in animal research (although this is not evident on its website where the fact might alienate some donors) and receives many millions of dollars for such research each year in government and charity funds. We felt that if the public knew how many animal lives and how much of their money was wasted, it might force the hospital to become more responsible.

This time, instead of reading through scores of sickening journal articles, we collected our data from the database Medline using the name of the hospital and the terms "Toronto," "animal" and "1990." For each of the 594 published papers, we then recorded the number of citations each paper had received in the next ten years: 174 papers (29 percent) had fewer than ten citations, a depressing finding.

By analyzing the number of citations that full-time hospital researchers had each received for their publications, we calculated who were the best and who the worst at their work. The thirteen "best" researchers had an average of sixty-five citations per paper while the thirteen "worst" averaged only eleven citations, a huge difference.

To determine if the same researchers retained their superior or inferior effort through time, we did a second search on Medline using the dates 1998–2002. Again, the same "best" scientists did the "best" work and the same "worst" scientists continued to do poorly cited research. Obviously, the hospital continues to employ and fund researchers of little competence who harm many animals in their many little-cited experiments. Because there are large numbers of summer students, graduate students and postdoctoral fellows working at the hospital, these inferior scientists continue to "teach" incompetence to the young scientists of the future who work with them.

DISCUSSION

It seems that the vast majority of animal researchers do not care if many animals suffer and die in experiments that are often obviously flawed. As an example of the attitude of scientists, Weinberg wrote that in the early days of cancer research on animals, the work "seemed to be going nowhere, a research field littered with the bodies of thousands of scientists who had spent their lives fruitlessly trying to figure out what cancer was all about."[12] Yet in reality, it was the millions of mice and rats who suffered and died—a point Weinberg ignored—while the researchers had well-paid careers.

Although research is generally considered to be "a forward-looking, progressive activity," science has been unwilling to recognize the need to save money and animal lives by reducing where possible the large number of animal-based experiments that science itself (by lack of citations) has indicated are worthless.[13] Many millions of animals have died just because scientists have delayed implementing new and improved techniques in their laboratories.[14] Researchers too often suffer from complacency, failure of imagination, orthodoxy and inertia, while governments have been slow to update regulations and push for the use of alternative methods of research where feasible.[15]

Wasteful animal research, given the status quo, seems indestructible for four reasons:

1. Career researchers have persuaded the government, charities and most of the public that animal experimentation is so essential to conquer illnesses that they provide vast amounts of money for it.
2. The career of researchers depends largely on the number, not quality, of their publications.
3. The raison d'être of research institutions is often biomedical research and no institution wants its activities curtailed. Commercial publishers make a great deal of money on thousands of biomedical journals, some of them published biweekly.
4. The sale of animals, animal food, equipment and cages is big business.

The public would surely object to the current waste of money and animal lives in biomedical research if they knew about it. But how can they be made aware when research scientists are so vehemently opposed to change in the status quo? As far as I know, my extensive documentation of pointless research has not resulted in a reduction of animal experiments. What else can one do?

RECOMMENDATIONS TO MINIMIZE WASTEFUL ANIMAL EXPERIMENTATION

From 25 percent to 50 percent of animal experimentation has been shown to be not worth doing, judging from the few citations received. Although it is impossible to know how successful any proposed experiment using animals will be, it is possible to reduce the number of animals experimented upon and minimize their pain and suffering by using the following recommendations.

For Researchers

1. Researchers should use animals in experiments only if no alternative feasible methods are available to test a theory.
2. Researchers using animals should undertake small pilot studies first to ensure that a large investigation is worth conducting.
3. Well-considered theoretical experiments, not the need to have laboratory animals earning their keep, should drive research.
4. Experiments involving exotic species or wild-born animals (with unknown genetic history) are infrequently cited, so these should be performed with even greater reluctance than usual.
5. If feasible, experiments should have more rather than fewer researchers involved, because those with many authors apparently garner most citations.

For Animal Care Committees and Research Institutions

1. At least two non-scientists, and optimally more, should be present on animal care committees to prevent unnecessary and poorly thought out experimentation. As well, each committee should include a statistician and an ethicist.
2. Approval for experiments should be decided by secret committee ballot; it is difficult for researchers on a committee to veto the work of a colleague who might, in retaliation, later veto their own proposals.
3. Researchers and laboratories that routinely produce papers that are seldom cited, especially if they use many animals, should have their funding cut and not be allowed to teach or mentor young scientists.
4. Researchers should receive funding, promotion and honours only for carrying out quality research that is frequently cited.

5. Institutions should provide public information on experiments they carry out: the number of animals involved, the pain the animals suffered and the citations the research later received.

For Funding Agencies

1. In addition to rules already in effect, applications for funding should require researchers to list for each past research publication the number of animals used and the citations subsequently received.
2. Applications should require researchers to list their research papers that remain unpublished, along with the number of animals involved in the experiment.
3. Research proposals from researchers or laboratories, or both, that routinely produce seldom-cited articles yet use many animals should not receive funding.

For Research Journals

1. Each submitted paper should state the number of animals used in each experiment and the procedures involved, indicating how pain-producing procedures were minimized for the animal subjects.
2. Journals should be more selective in their acceptance of papers, because in four surveys all the journals published many papers that were rarely cited.
3. Published papers should all include acceptable statistical analyses showing that an excessive number of animals was not used in the experiments.

NOTES

1. See Jeffrey Paul, *Why Animal Experimentation Matters: The Use of Animals in Medical Research* (Somerset, NJ: Transaction, 2001).
2. It is impossible to know this number accurately. The web indicates that the United States Department of Agriculture used about 1.4 million animals in 2000, but this number excludes mice, rats and birds that comprise about 85 percent to 90 percent of all individuals involved in experimentation. The European Community used about 11.6 million animals in 1996, and Canada used about 1.7 million in 2001 including rats, mice and birds. See Canadian Council on Animal Care, "CCAC Survey of Animal Use—2001," *Resource* 27, no. 1 (2003-2004): 11-12. Asian countries such as Japan and China also have extensive research programs.

3 J. Rotton and M. Levitt, "Citation Impact, Rejection Rates, and Journal Value," *American Psychologist* 48 (1993): 911-12.
4 See Alan D. Bowd and Kenneth J. Shapiro, "The Case against Laboratory Animal Research in Psychology," *Journal of Social Issues* 49, no. 1 (1993): 133-42.
5 A.I. Dagg, "Citations Dearth: Another Reason to Reduce Animal Experimentation. A Report" (Waterloo, ON, unpublished, 1998).
6 J.A. Stewart, "Achievement and Ascriptive Processes in the Recognition of Scientific Articles," *Social Forces* 62 (1983): 166-89.
7 R.J. Sternberg, "*Psychological Bulletin's* Top 10 Hit Parade," *Psychological Bulletin* 112 (1992): 387-88.
8 Canadian Council on Animal Care, *Animal Utilization Study, 1996* (Ottawa: CCAC, 1998). The "Categories of Invasiveness" noted in this report are available on the CCAC website.
9 Yi-Ping Chen and Christopher A. Squier, "Effect of Nicotine on 7,12-Dimethylbenz[a]anthracene Carcinogenesis in Hamster Cheek Pouch," *Journal of the National Cancer Institute* 82, no. 10 (1990): 861-64.
10 Ibid.
11 A.I. Daigg and T. Seidle, "Levels of Citation of Animal Studies Conducted at a Canadian Research Hospital," *Journal of Applied Animal Welfare Science* 7, no. 3 (2004): 205-13.
12 R.A. Weinberg, *Racing to the Beginning of the Road* (New York: Harmony Books, 1996), 20-21.
13 G. Langley, "Establishment Reactions to Alternatives," in D. Paterson and M. Palmer, eds., *The Status of Animals: Ethics, Education and Welfare* (Wallingford Oxon, UK: CAB International, 1989), 136-53.
14 Ibid.
15 Ibid.

BIBLIOGRAPHY

Bowd, Alan D., and Kenneth J. Shapiro. "The Case against Laboratory Animal Research in Psychology." *Journal of Social Issues* 49, no. 1 (1993): 133-42.
Canadian Council on Animal Care. *Animal Utilization Study, 1996.* Ottawa: CCAC, 1998.
———. "CCAC Survey of Animal Use—2001." *Resource* 27, no. 1 (2003-2004): 11-12.
Chen, Yi-Ping, and Christopher A. Squier. "Effect of Nicotine on 7,12-Dimethylbenz[a]anthracene Carcinogenesis in Hamster Cheek Pouch." *Journal of the National Cancer Institute* 82, no. 10 (1990): 861-64.

Dagg, A.I. "Citations Dearth: Another Reason to Reduce Animal Experimentation. A Report." Waterloo, ON, unpublished, 1998.

———. "Responsible Animal-Based Research: Three Flags to Consider." *Journal of Applied Animal Welfare Science* 2, no. 4 (1999): 337–46.

———. "Animal Experimentation in Cancer Research: A Citation Analysis." *Journal of Applied Animal Welfare Science* 3, no. 3 (2000): 239–51.

Dagg, A.I., and T. Seidle. "Levels of Citation of Animal Studies Conducted at a Canadian Research Hospital." *Journal of Applied Animal Welfare Science* 7, no. 3 (2004): 205–13.

Langley, G. 1989. "Establishment Reactions to Alternatives." In D. Paterson and M. Palmer, eds. *The Status of Animals: Ethics, Education and Welfare.* Wallingford Oxon, UK: CAB International.

Paul, Jeffrey. 2001. *Why Animal Experimentation Matters: The Use of Animals in Medical Research.* Somerset, NJ: Transaction.

Rotton, J., and M. Levitt. "Citation Impact, Rejection Rates, and Journal Value." *American Psychologist* 48 (1993): 911–12.

Sternberg, R.J. "*Psychological Bulletin's* Top 10 Hit Parade." *Psychological Bulletin* 112 (1992): 387–88.

Stewart, J.A. "Achievement and Ascriptive Processes in the Recognition of Scientific Articles." *Social Forces* 62 (1983): 166–89.

Weinberg, R.A. *Racing to the Beginning of the Road.* New York: Harmony Books, 1996.

14

On Animal Immortality
An Argument for the Possibility of Animal Immortality in Light of the History of Philosophy

JOHANNA TITO

Had a dog named Blue...
Come on Blue, you good dog you...
When I get to heaven first thing I'll do,
is shake off my bones and whistle for Blue,
together we'll run in fields of air,
but I don't want to go if Blue's not there...
—from the ASPCA humane education video
Throwaways

THE ISSUE

Had a dog named Blue...

Broadly speaking, the collection of essays in this volume deals with the moral and ethical treatment of nonhuman animals as a cultural studies issue. "To my mind," writes the editor of the series in a call for papers, "these concerns [of the ethical treatment of animals] are germane to cultural studies with its focus on other aspects of culture such as racism, sexism, ageism, etc." The editor implies that in certain respects our relation to animals may have something in common with racism, sexism and ageism. The latter are all instances of prejudices, of overgeneralizations, pejorative in nature, often produced and sustained by uncritically accepted platitudes. The editor is correct in her implication: as a culture, much of our behaviour towards nonhuman animals is the result of uncritically accepted, commonly held beliefs, many pejorative, about the nature of animals. "They aren't aware of death the way humans are" and "They don't experience pain the way humans do" are just two examples of such platitudes. It cannot be denied that as a society we show a great deal of insensitivity to nonhuman animals: factory farming, commercial slaughter of seals, our unwillingness to control pet overpopulation resulting in the killing of millions of unwanted cats and dogs every year, the failure of our legal system to protect nonhuman animals from even the most horrendous instances of torture, are all cases in point. Part of our insensitivity towards animals is undoubtedly based on prejudices such as those listed above.

Another commonly held prejudice concerning nonhuman animals is the belief that they are excluded from the possibility of immortality. While at face value this belief seems innocuous enough—after all, many humans do not believe in *human* immortality either—when we examine more closely the position that denies nonhuman animals the very possibility of immortality, we find that it consists not only of a number of sub-beliefs expressive of human chauvinism, but that it also reflects prejudices concerning *human* nature as well, prejudices well worth challenging.

ON KNOWING

When I get to heaven...

The belief that attributes immortality exclusively to the human soul, and more specifically to only the rational part of the human soul, is a long-standing one in the history of Western thought. It is part of a philosophy or culture of *knowing* that harks back to Plato, the father of philosophy. Plato observed that the soul perceives Ideas. In order to perceive them, he concluded, the soul must be *like* the Ideas: immaterial and simple. Because it is simple and immaterial, the soul can never be broken down or destroyed the way composite material things can be. Hence, the soul's immortality. But the Ideas the soul perceives stand in relation to each other—they are related hierarchically, logically or rationally. (The paradigm of this would be the science of mathematics in which all truths are derived from basic axioms.) The soul is at home with Ideas, and with their logical, rational relation, so much so, according to Plato, that prior to birth the soul lived in the realm of Ideas and knew the Ideas. But birth is a fall through forgetfulness and the soul's task in this earthly life, Plato maintains, is to recollect the Ideas and relate them back to the highest Idea, that of the Good. In short, the soul's task is to be *rational*. The more rational the soul is, the more it expresses its immortal nature. The highest expression of this rationality would be philosophy, according to Plato.

It has been said that all philosophy is but a footnote to Plato, and it certainly is true that some version or other of Plato's theory of the immortal soul has informed not only Western philosophy but also Western culture in general. The tradition *has*, by and large, stressed a philosophy of knowing or science and has, by and large, ignored the warning by Plato's teacher, Socrates, that until we embrace the fact that all we know is that we know nothing, we will remain fools.

Since animals are not capable of high-minded rational thinking, that is, they are not capable of science and philosophy, their souls cannot share in immortality, according to this theory. Denying immortality to animals is, in other words, a corollary of the view that humans differ from animals by being rational: man is a *rational* animal, says Plato.

Plato's view that only the rational part of the soul is immortal was not only incorporated into the Western philosophical tradition but was also somewhat influential upon Christian thinkers for whom the question of immortality was, of course, central. St. Augustine and St. Thomas, for example, were influenced by Plato's thought, even though, unlike Plato, they believed in the resurrection of the *body*.

ON NOT KNOWING

I'll whistle for Blue...

From the beginning, however, there has been another, less dominant strain of thought in both the philosophical and the Christian tradition, one that values aspects of the soul other than its rational prowess. This strain of thought consequently presents a different understanding of the immortal soul, one that, in principle at least, gives animals a chance at immortality. In the Christian tradition there have always been those who give special prominence not to rationality or knowledge but to faith and to love, the latter being instances of non-rational acts of the soul. "Credo quia absurdam est," asserts Tertullian, the early Christian theologian reacting against the ancient Hellenic philosophy, "I believe because it is *absurd*." And for St. Augustine, who reconciles Platonic doctrine with Christianity, both faith and love figure prominently. Reason does not stand alone, according to Augustine, for, although it is not the final step, faith is the first step in the full realization of human rationality. "Credo ut intelligam," "I believe in order that I might understand," says St. Augustine. In other words, understanding needs faith, according to St. Augustine, and so the rational is intimately linked with loving faith, which, in effect, is "absurd."[1] Furthermore, "I love" is one of the three certainties upon which St. Augustine builds his philosophy, so influential on Christian thought after him, "I am" and "I know" being the other two certainties.

In the philosophical tradition also there have always been those who were much closer to the Socratic position of ignorance—"All that I know is that I know nothing," declares Socrates—than the Platonic position of philosopher king. Nineteenth- and twentieth-century philosophy has seen the emergence of existential and phenomenological positions critical, if not of the very idea of a philosophy of knowing, then at least of a narrowly construed rationality. Their changing "definition" of what it is to be human impacts our understanding of animals, and the twentieth-century postmodern philosophies to which they gave rise do so even further.

Standing out especially in this regard is Kierkegaard, the nineteenth-century Danish existential philosopher whose definition of truth in his *Postscript* ("An objective uncertainty held fast in an appropriation-process of the most passionate inwardness") is a full-blown critique of philosophies of knowing. According to Kierkegaard, the truths that matter most to the individual in his or her life—answers to such questions as, what must I do? what is death? is there a God? can I love?—cannot be found by the objective certainty of reason and science, but only by a subjective faith, the intensity of the latter being inversely proportionate to the degree of objective uncertainty one feels. What this does, for our purposes, is shift the framework of our self-understanding and with it the parameters of the immortality debate. If faith, not science, becomes all-important to us and becomes the bearer of truth, then what is immortal in the human soul cannot be merely the rational as Plato held.

The twentieth-century phenomenologist Edmund Husserl, while not fully critical of a philosophy of knowing, was critical of a narrow understanding of knowing, of rationality and science. While science can help us in our lives, Husserl argues, it cannot give us *values*.[2] Writing in Europe in the turbulent years leading up to the Second World War, Husserl laments: "in our vital need ... science has nothing to say to us ... Science," he goes on to say, "excludes in principle precisely the questions which man, given over in our unhappy times subject to the most portentous upheavals, finds the most burning: questions of the meaning or the meaninglessness of the whole of this human existence."[3]

Science may be able to treat or cure our disease, for example, but ultimately how we cope with a given disease or with the death that we all must ultimately face and from which no science can save us, is not a matter of science, but a matter of value. So too is how we *use* science. Whether or not we permit genetic engineering, cloning or the use of our nuclear science to create weapons of war is determined not by science but by our system of values. Husserl was not disparaging science; rather, he was urging that it is important to be aware of the *limits* of objective science. Science is a human creation, an abstraction from our living experience, and it is vital, Husserl maintained, to be aware of the living experience from which objective science springs and against which it must ultimately be verified and justified. An objective science unaware of its ground in subjective, living experience Husserl called an "objectivistic science." Such a science has a blind spot, according to him: it ignores anything subjective that does not fit into its objective framework, something that occurs at a cost to human self-understanding, responsibility and even happiness. Husserl's phenomenology, which we might call a "subjective science," explores this living ground of objective science as well as of objective thought in general. It explores the living ground in all its richness, complexities and paradoxes. Phenomenology, in seeing the limits of objective science, is itself, then, paradoxically, a product of reason, but a reason beyond or broader than the reason of objective science, a reason that sees more deeply into the human subject.

Not surprisingly, phenomenology constitutes a critique of objective psychology since the latter too purports to deal with the subject. But the human subject, Husserl argued, cannot be treated by the methods of the objective sciences since these deal with *abstractions* from the world we live in, from the life-world, sacrificing all impurities, roughness and inexactness of the world we experience and live in to the mathematical approach of exact measurement. The subject, claims Husserl, cannot fundamentally be understood by measurement or quantification and any psychology that tries to do so essentially destroys the subject. What developed from this critique was a phenomenological psychology; a psychology marked by interpretation rather than measurement; an interpretation informed by an appreciation of the life-world, by an appreciation of or feel for how humans are situated in the world. In other words, methodologically, phenomenological psychology relies heavily on empathy rather than measurement.

What is important for this paper is that Husserl's critique of objective psychology as a method of studying *human* subjectivity applies equally to nonhuman animal subjects. As we will see below, in *The Lives of Animals* both novelist J.M. Coetzee and anthropologist-psychologist Barbara Smuts argue for what amounts to a phenomenological-psychological, rather than an objectivistic-psychological, approach to nonhuman animals.

But let us be more specific about how phenomenology begins to level the playing field for human and nonhuman animals. Whereas Plato speaks of the rational *soul*, Husserl speaks of intentional *consciousness*. The definition of consciousness as "*intentional*," a definition that in effect embodies the argument against a narrowly construed rationality, means to express the fact that consciousness is a *relation*, that consciousness is always conscious of *something* at the same time that it is conscious of itself. Consciousness gives us "objects" in the broadest sense of the term; it gives us not only ideas but emotions, feelings, material objects, a world, many worlds, other people, other animals. The essence of consciousness, says Husserl, is not just rationality as expressed in concepts and ideas and their relation, as Plato had it, but also *seeing* or *witnessing*. Seeing/witnessing is a much broader notion than rationality or rational thinking as understood by Plato, because it literally thrusts us into a *living context*. Consciousness, after all, can present us with a world only via a living body[4]—it always operates in and through a living body, which, in turn, presents us with, opens us to, the world we live in, the life-world.[5]

But a living body is a *feeling* body, and so consciousness is also *feeling*, for when we see what we see we cannot help but feel and, correlatively, when we feel, we are seeing something, though we may not initially know, that is, be able to articulate, what it is we are seeing in our feeling. In the words of the painter Paul Klee, "One eye sees, the other feels." Good thinking, then, may also be feeling and feeling may also be good thinking. Since all thinking is embodied, rational thought is essentially bound up with elements of the living body such as desire, instinct and the unconscious, elements that have irrational and opaque aspects to them. All thinking, in other words, will have its rootedness in the opaqueness of the living body.

This insight of Husserl, that the rational is grounded in life, begins to challenge our traditional way of thinking of the rational and irrational. It opens the way to the postmodern insight that not only can we no longer think in terms of rational *versus* irrational, but also no longer in terms of man *versus* woman, animal *versus* human. With its emphasis on the life-world (the world we experience and live in, rather than the abstracted world presented by science) phenomenology offers a philosophical framework for the equalization of human and nonhuman animal subjects. Nonhuman animals no less than human animals have an intentional consciousness, an embodied consciousness situated in a life-world shared by human and nonhuman animals alike.[6]

The postmodern thinker who unflinchingly follows Husserl's insight of a return to pure, concrete living experience even further than Husserl himself is the twentieth-century philosopher Georges Bataille. Bataille's philosophy too brings us closer to animals. Whereas Husserl, after critiquing objectivistic science, will still speak of a science of phenomenology (albeit science in a new, broader sense), Bataille speaks only of a philosophy of non-knowledge, even though for him too, of course, it is not that knowledge no longer exists but rather that it has become senseless. "Non-knowledge does not abolish particular knowledge, but [abolishes] its sense—removes from it all sense," writes Bataille.[7] Indeed, as stated previously, what *sense* has knowledge when it comes to things that matter most to us, when, to borrow Husserl's words, it is a question "of the meaning or the meaninglessness of the whole of this human existence"? Combining Kierkegaard's notion of truth as the passion of the single individual and Husserl's notion of a return to concrete living experience, to radical subjectivity in other words (i.e., to the pre-objective subject that informs the objective), Bataille's turn to inner experience requires that we *continually* keep before us the awareness that we ultimately dwell in non-knowledge. And non-knowledge is suffering, for we *desire* to know; we *need* to know. Only a suffering awareness of our non-knowledge will keep us focused on our own inner experience, on our *living* experience, for any *knowledge* (i.e., discursive thought) will always pull us away from the living moment into the abstraction of concepts. "Discursive thought ... *is the putting off of existence to a later point*," writes Bataille.[8]

For Bataille the "disgrace" of perpetual suffering becomes the grace of communication, for it is the *feeling* of utter intellectual impotence, the *passion* suffered by us, that compels us to turn our face to the "Other" in order to reach out to him or her in genuine communication. Anguish, torment, leads one to appeal to the "Other" in a supplicating communication. "Like laughter, it [anguish] breaks down the barriers of isolation,"[9] writes Bataille. It leads us to that "rupture in the very centre, in the heart of humanity."[10]

In refusing to turn experience into a narrow knowledge—something animals are not in danger of doing—we remain aware of inner *experience*, which, although potentially opened up and enriched by concepts, is always something more and other than concepts. Whereas concepts (objectifications) are always generalities—abstractions from reality—experience puts us directly in touch with existents, with singularities rather than generalities or objectifications, it puts us in touch with the individual or ipse, to use Bataille's term.[11] That is, underlying objectification and conceptualization is the experience of that which we objectify or conceptualize, the singularity, this "x." In other words, we are confronted by *something* (an x) that is subsequently objectified as blue or noisy or frightening. This something is the singularity, the individual ipse. These singularities meet us with the full intensity of concrete life—we immediately feel them, are attracted to or repulsed by them.

It is between singularities, between ipseities, that genuine communication occurs, according to Bataille.[12] While *knowing* the "Other" involves objectifying the "Other," which is but an attempt to appropriate or possess the "Other"—something, Bataille maintains, that stems from the self's desire to be everything[13]—genuine communication avoids objectification of the "Other," according to Bataille. Genuine communication neither limits nor appropriates the "Other" but relates to the "Other" as open, as infinite, as a mystery. As the existentialists have long urged, as persons we are never "fixed" or "completed," but are always growing, changing, developing, are always in process.[14] In genuine communication this infinity is respected. But how is this done?

The existential-phenomenologist Jacques Maritain calls the way in which we encounter singularities "poetic intuition."[15] "Poetic intuition," he writes, "tends and extends to the infinite, it tends toward all the reality, the infinite reality which is engaged in any singular existing thing."[16] This is so, according to Maritain, because poetic intuition has no conceptualized object. That is, poetry is not literal but is *excessive*, overflowing its own boundaries. In this way it respects the infinity and, indeed the *mystery* of the "Other." This, in part,[17] is why Bataille says that "*poetry leads from the known to the unknown*" (i.e., the mystery).[18]

But what does that mean, "poetic intuition"? Maritain maintains that the intentionality of consciousness, which he calls a spirituality, is on a fundamental level unconscious or pre-conscious, so that rather than primarily *think* the world, we see, feel and intuit relations and situations at once, in a flash, non-discursively. Fundamentally and primarily, experience operates by means of images rather than concepts and it does so in a highly creative way, leading Maritain to term our primary relation to the world "poetic." "Poetry has its source in the pre-conceptual life of the intellect," he writes.[19]

> By poetry I mean, not the particular art which consists in writing verses, but a process both more general and more primary: that intercommunication between the inner being of things and the inner being of the human Self which is a kind of divination (as was realized in ancient times; the Latin *vates* was both a poet and a diviner).[20]

Whereas concepts and universal ideas are disengaged from concrete, living, flowing reality and are scrutinized by reason, says Maritain, "poetic intuition is directed toward some singular existent."[21]

Though intuitive and non-conceptual, Maritain, unlike Bataille, still calls this type of experience a *kind* of knowledge because it reveals the world, because it is intentional in the Husserlian sense of the term,[22] in other words. Poetic intuition is, to repeat, the manner in which we are initially and primarily in touch with the world. At this level, consciousness, full of intensity and feeling, is *immediately* attracted by form, shape and colour, by similarity and contrast, by mood, by what matters. Marked by associative thinking, poetic intuition joins things that discursive thought would not. "*The lion's ferocious chrysanthemum head,*" an example that Maritain uses, illustrates how poetic intuition has produced the truly *new* in a way that a strictly logical or rational, that is, discursive mode of thought, which is literal, would not, for in the cold light of reality what could be further apart than a chrysanthemum and a lion's head? Yet the images so combined are clear and powerful; they work.

THE LIVES OF ANIMALS

You good dog, you...

Finally, this brings us to J.M. Coetzee's novel *The Lives of Animals*, in which protagonist Elizabeth Costello, speaking about the psychologist Wolfgang Kohler's well-known laboratory experiments on the great ape, Sultan, appeals to the need to cultivate a *poetic feel* for Sultan's experience. "Wolfgang Kohler was probably a good man. A good man but not a poet.... This is as far as Kohler, for all his sympathy and insight, is able to go; this is where a poet might have commenced, with a *feel* for the ape's experience."[23]

Having been captured from the wild after his mother was shot, having suffered mistreatment at the hands of his captors, Sultan's final destination is Kohler's lab. There, Sultan has been fed bananas that were placed on the cage floor at a regular time each day. As part of his experiment, Kohler increases Sultan's hunger by delaying feeding time and makes the bananas less accessible to Sultan, requiring the great ape to engage in problem-solving skills in order to obtain them. Costello argues that throughout the experiments Kohler *assumes* that the single most important thought and perhaps even the *only* thought Sultan is thinking is: "I am hungry. How can I reach the bananas?" But as Elizabeth Costello cautions, Kohler's scientific approach to the ape may well have led him to misrepresent the ape. Is this really what Sultan primarily thinks? Might Sultan have other thoughts, thoughts such as "Why is he starving me?" or "What have I done? Why has he stopped liking me?" or "What is wrong with him, what misconception does he have of me, that leads him to believe it is easier for me to reach a banana hanging from a wire than to pick up a banana from the floor?"[24]

Sultan's problem-solving skills are good so he is successful in obtaining the bananas, but Kohler continues to make the conditions under which Sultan must get the bananas increasingly challenging. All the while Kohler is convinced that the primary thought in Sultan's mind is how to obtain the bananas and, by starving Sultan, Kohler in effect ensures that it *does* become Sultan's preoccupation. As Costello goes on to say:

> At every turn Sultan is *driven* to think the less interesting thought. From the purity of speculation (Why do men behave like this?) he is relentlessly propelled toward lower, practical, instrumental reason (How does one use this to get that?) and thus toward acceptance of himself as primarily an organism with an appetite that needs to be satisfied...[25]

In other words, Kohler's narrowly construed scientific or rationalistic world view (exactly the world view critiqued by Husserl), which represents an animal as being primarily "an organism with an appetite that needs to be satisfied," closes the door to any other way of relating to Sultan. It precludes, as Costello puts it, a *feel* for Sultan's experience. This, as she says, is where a poet might have commenced.

To the possible objection that a *feel* for the animal is no better than Kohler's approach, in that it is mere subjective emotion that might lead one to read *anything* into the animal, we repeat that the emotion or feel, no less than the concept of thought, is intentional, is a means or vehicle whereby reality is grasped. "At first glance," writes Maritain, "one believes, and often the poet him [or her] self believes, that he [or she]... never thinks...[but] only feels, feels, feels.... Well," he adds, "the poet also thinks. And poetic knowledge proceeds from the intellect in its most genuine and essential capacity as intellect, though through the indispensable instrumentality of feeling, feeling, feeling."[26]

The following passage by Barbara Smuts, professor of psychology and anthropology, in which she speaks of her fieldwork with baboons, provides a moving illustration of having a *feel* for the animal's experience:

> Friendship requires some degree of mutuality, some give-and-take. Because it was important, scientifically, for me to minimize my interactions with the baboon, I had few opportunities to explore the possibilities of such give-and-take with them. But occasional events hinted that such relations might be possible, were I encountering them first and foremost as fellow social beings, rather than as subjects of scientific inquiry. For example, one day...I came upon a "nursery" group of mothers and infants...I sat near them and watched the mothers eating and the babies playing...my eyes met the warm gaze of an adolescent female, Pandora. I continued to look at her, silently sending friendliness her way. Unexpectedly, she stood and moved closer. Stopping right in front of me, with her face at eye level, she leaned forward and pushed her large, flat, wrinkled nose against mine...Her warm, sweet breath fogged up my glasses, blinding me. I felt no fear for her. Perhaps she sensed my attitude, because in the next moment I felt her impossibly long ape arms wrap around me, and for a few precious seconds, she held me in her embrace. Then she released me, gazed once more into my eyes, and returned to munching on leaves.[27]

Smuts, who goes so far as to call the animals she relates to "persons,"[28] speaks here as a poet rather than a scientist, for the truth of the experiences are presented to her not in concepts of discursive thought but in stunning images and feelings which *are* her experience of the baboon. Interesting too is Smut's emphasis on the individual (i.e., the singularity) in experiencing animals as "persons":

> ...relating to other beings as persons has nothing to do with whether or not we attribute human characteristics to them. It has to do, instead, with recognizing that they are social subjects, like us, whose idiosyncratic, subjective experience of us plays the same role in their relations with us that our subjective experience of them plays in our relations with them. If they relate to us as individuals, and we relate to them as individuals, it is possible for us to have a personal relationship.[29]

We are persons to one another, human to human as well as human to animal, in poetic intuition, in the wisdom of emotion and feeling that reveals our singularity.

PHILOSOPHY AGAIN

Together we will run in fields of air...

As we move from Plato's definition of the rational as ideal to Husserl's grounding of meaning or the rational in concrete life (in the living body in the life-world), we move away from human chauvinism to embrace our common bond with animals. The transformation of a scientific psychology into a phenomenological psychology in which the subject is treated, not by number and abstraction, but by empathy, of which Bataille's emphasis on communication in suffering is an extension, brings us yet closer to animals.[30] The suffering of non-knowledge opens us to the encounter with singularities—to our own and that of others, including that of nonhuman animals. How often have we communicated with animals in agony, we in *our* agony with them and they in *theirs* with us? Who of us, when ill or lonely, has not been comforted by an animal companion? And who has not unmistakably understood the pleas of the hungry, cold stray asking to come in? Was it not *impossible* to refuse?

With the emphasis on communication between singularities in suffering, gone is the human chauvinistic emphasis on rationality, on science and rationalistic philosophy. Gone too is the human's exclusive claim to immortality. If anything is immortal, it is not merely or even especially the rational part of the soul, but that which we *love*: the singular existence. It is the singular that is important to us, that touches us, whom we love. It is *Blue* for whom the person in the ASPCA song is willing to sacrifice his own immortality. What we love is the singular existent, not some shadow of the existent, not some abstract, rational or otherwise, of the existent. I love this particular human being or this particular animal. Is this not what St. Augustine means when he writes, "God loves each of us as if there were only one of us to love"? It is the death of a singular particularity I mourn, and it is the life of this actual singular particularity that is celebrated and given tribute to in the eulogy. But this singularity will always be more and other than any *description* or eulogy can capture. Directly, in poetic intuition, we experience and love, but do not know, the mystery that is this singularity. We experience and love this singularity, whether human or animal, and they us.

NOTES

1. The most "radical" form of Christian love is asymmetrical love, love of enemy. As William James argues in the *Varieties of Religious Experience* (Lectures xi, xii and xiii on "Saintliness"), the command to "love your enemies, your positive and active enemies ... if radically followed ... would involve such a breach with our instinctive springs of action as a whole, and with the present world's arrangements, that a critical point would practically be passed, and we should be born into another kingdom of being." It is this "breach with our instinctive springs of action" that made Freud dismiss this commandment. In its "breach with our instinctive springs of action," then, asymmetrical love, the extreme most statement of Christian love, can be said to be irrational, absurd. In a way, then, one might say love is irrational.
2. E. Husserl, *The Crisis of European Sciences and Transcendental Phenomenology: An Introduction to Phenomenological Philosophy*, trans. with an introduction by David Carr (Evanston, IL: Northwestern University Press, 1970.)
3. Ibid., 6.
4. E. Husserl, *Ideas: General Introduction to Pure Phenomenology* (London: George Allen and Unwin, 1969), 164. "Only through the empirical relation to the body does consciousness become real in a human and animal sense, and only thereby does it win a place in Nature's space and time-the time which is physically measured."
5. Husserl, *The Crisis of European Sciences and Transcendental Phenomenology*, 106.
6. "We recollect that it is only through the connecting of consciousness and body into a natural unity that can be empirically united that such a thing as mutual understanding between the animal natures that belong to one world is possible, and that only thereby can every subject that knows find before it a full world containing itself and other subjects, and at the same time know it for one and the same world about us belonging in common to itself and all other subjects." Husserl, *Ideas*, 164–65.
7. G. Bataille, *Inner Experience* (Albany, NY: SUNY Press, 1988), 53.
8. Ibid., 46. Emphasis added.
9. Ibid., 192.
10. Ibid., 195.
11. Ibid., 54.
12. Ibid.
13. Ibid., 153.
14. Sartre's famous expression for this in *Being and Nothingness: An Essay on Phenomenological Ontology* (New York: Routledge, 2003), chap. 2, sec. ii, is "human reality, in its most immediate being ... must be what it is not and not what it is."

15 J. Maritain, *Creative Intuition in Art and Poetry* (New York: World Publishing Company, 1961), 91.
16 Ibid.
17 I say "in part" because I do not want to imply that Bataille's notion of poetry is identical to that of Maritain. There, are, however, points of intersection.
18 Bataille, *Inner Experience*, 136.
19 Maritain, *Creative Intuition in Art and Poetry*, 3.
20 Ibid.
21 Ibid.
22 Maritain, *Creative Intuition in Art and Poetry*, 87.
23 J.M. Coetzee, *The Lives of Animals* (Princeton, NJ: Princeton University Press, 1999), 29–30. Emphasis added.
24 Ibid., 28. For those who find it hard to believe that an ape might have such thoughts, let me recount an experience I had just recently with one of my cats, Francis. Francis, who was orphaned when just three weeks old, was brought to me, along with his siblings, as a rescue kitten. (Since the tiny Francis was very ill, I thought that naming him after St. Francis might charm the saint into exercising his healing powers on the little orphan. It seems to have worked because Francis is now a robust one-and-a-half-year-old.) One day, just recently, I had just placed a bowl of food in front of Chomsky, another feline member of my household, when Francis came storming into the room, pushed Chomsky aside, and began to devour the latter's food. To give Chomsky the opportunity to eat his meal in peace I temporarily put Francis in a large cage standing near by, one used for cat rescue. About three minutes later Chomsky, having finished his meal, walked away, leaving, however, a little bit of food in his bowl. I opened Francis's cage and, to my surprise, instead of racing to the bowl with the remaining food, as Francis slowly walked out of the cage he locked his golden eyes onto mine, stood on his hind legs, and stretched his front paws up on me. Clearly Francis was less concerned with the remaining food and more concerned with whether everything was still right between us, having never been put in the cage before. I petted him to assure him everything was fine, at which point he made a dash for the bowl and vigorously consumed the remaining morsel.
25 Coetzee, *The Lives of Animals*, 29. Emphasis added.
26 Ibid., 86–87.
27 Coetzee, *The Lives of Animals*, 114.
28 Ibid., 118.
29 Ibid.
30 One might object that Barbara Smuts's example of Pandora wrapping her impossibly long ape arms around her is not one of communication in suffering but in sheer love. To this I would reply that all love is a type of suffering—a passion.

BIBLIOGRAPHY

Bataille, G. *Inner Experience*. Albany, NY: SUNY Press, 1988.
Coetzee, J.M. *The Lives of Animals*. Princeton, NJ: Princeton University Press, 1999.
Husserl, E. *Ideas General Introduction to Pure Phenomenology*. London: George Allen and Unwin, 1969.
———. *The Crisis of European Sciences and Transcendental Phenomenology: An Introduction to Phenomenological Philosophy*. Translated and with an introduction by David Carr. Evanston, IL: Northwestern University Press, 1970.
Maritain, J. *Creative Intuition in Art and Poetry*. New York: World Publishing Company, 1961.
Sartre, Jean-Paul. *Being and Nothingness: An Essay on Phenomenological Ontology*. New York: Routledge, 2003.

Contributors

LESLI BISGOULD has worked as a lawyer in Ontario since 1992. She practised civil litigation at a Toronto boutique firm before establishing her own practice in animal rights law in 1995. Bisgould was Canada's only animal rights lawyer for ten years. Currently she is Legal Aid Ontario's Barrister in Residence, assisting legal clinics in their work on behalf of Ontario's poorest residents.

JODEY CASTRICANO is an Associate Professor in the Department of Critical Studies at the University of British Columbia, Okanagan, where she teaches critical theory and Cultural Studies. Her interests lie in posthumanism and animal studies, and she has also published on the philosopher Jacques Derrida and is working on an SSHRC-supported book-length study, under contract with the University of Wales Press, on the influence of 19th-century spiritualism on the rise and practice of psychoanalysis. Recently she was appointed as a Fellow of the Oxford Centre for Animal Ethics in the UK.

PAOLA CAVALIERI, whose research interests include ethics, bioethics and political philosophy, is the editor of the international philosophy journal *Etica & Animali*. She is the co-editor, with Peter Singer, of *The Great Ape Project* (London: Fourth Estate, 1993) and the author of *The Animal Question* (New York: Oxford University Press, 2001).

Biologist ANNE INNIS DAGG, PhD, teaches in the Independent Studies program of the University of Waterloo. Her academic research articles and books have focused on mammals (especially giraffe and camels), feminism (particularly as it affects academic women), evolutionary psychology and, most recently, animal rights. Her most recent publications include *The Feminine Gaze, Love of Shopping Is Not a Gene* and *Pursuing Giraffe*.

MICHAEL ALLEN FOX is Emeritus Professor of Philosophy, Queen's University, and Adjunct Professor of Social Science, University of New England (Australia). He has written, lectured and consulted extensively on animal ethics issues and is the author of *The Case for Animal Experimentation, Deep Vegetarianism* and *The Accessible Hegel*. His current writing project is *A Student's Guide to Existentialism*. He lives in Armidale, New South Wales, Australia.

DONNA HARAWAY earned a PhD from the Biology Department at Yale in 1972 for an interdisciplinary dissertation on the functions of metaphor in shaping research in developmental biology in the twentieth century. She is now professor and former chair of the History of Consciousness Program at University of California, Santa Cruz. Her many publications include *The Companion Species Manifesto: Dogs, People, and Significant Otherness, Primate Visions: Gender, Race, and Nature in the World of Modern Science* and the highly influential *Simians, Cyborgs, and Women: The Reinvention of Nature*.

DAWNE MCCANCE is Professor and Head, Department of Religion, University of Manitoba, and Editor of *Mosaic: a journal for the interdisciplinary study of literature*. Her book, *Medusa's Ear: University foundings from Kant to Chora L* (2004), approaches the conflation of "animal" and "woman" (deaf and mute female) in founding texts on the modern research university. She is currently extending this study in a book-length project supported by SSHRC, *A Little History of Hearing*.

LESLEY MCLEAN has recently completed her PhD at the University of New England, Armidale (Australia). Her thesis is entitled "How Should One Live with Nonhuman Animals? An examination of the ways three philosophers have answered this question." Her research interests centre on notions of moral and imaginative attention with respect to nonhuman animals.

ROD PREECE is Professor Emeritus at Wilfrid Laurier University in Waterloo, Ontario, and is the author of numerous volumes, including *Animals and Nature: Cultural Myths, Cultural Realities* (1999), *Awe for the Tiger, Love for the Lamb: A Chronicle of Sensibility to Animals* (2002) and *Brute Souls, Happy Beasts and Evolution: The Historical Status of Animals* (2005).

BARBARA K. SEEBER is an Associate Professor of English at Brock University in St. Catharines, Ontario, specializing in eighteenth- and early-nineteenth-century literature. She is the author of *General Consent in Jane Austen: A Study of Dialogism* (2000).

JOHN SORENSON is a professor in the Department of Sociology at Brock University. His books include *Culture of Prejudice; Ghosts and Shadows; Imaging Ethiopia* and *Disaster and Development in the Horn of Africa*. He is currently working on a study of various "representations of animals" supported by the Social Science and Humanities Research Council of Canada.

DAVID SZTYBEL completed his doctorate at the University of Toronto, Ontario, and also an Advisory Research Committee Post-Doctoral Fellowship, centring on the ethics of vivisection, at Queen's University, Ontario. A Fellow of the Oxford Centre for Animal Ethics, he is an advocate for animal rights, human rights and the environment. He instructs mainly in Critical Animal Studies at Brock University in St. Catharines, Ontario.

ANGUS TAYLOR is the author of *Animals and Ethics: An Overview of the Philosophical Debate*. He teaches philosophy at the University of Victoria. Once upon a time he worked in Toronto at the Spaced Out Library (now the Merril Collection), and wrote *Philip K. Dick and the Umbrella of Light*, one of the first extended critical essays on Dick's work.

JOHANNA TITO was born in the Netherlands and received her early education there. She did undergraduate work in philosophy and psychology at York University and received her MA and PhD in philosophy from McMaster University. She works in the area of phenomenology and is the author of *Logic in the Husserlian Context*.

CARY WOLFE has taught at Indiana, SUNY (Albany), and at Rice, where he currently holds the Bruce and Elizabeth Dunlevie Chair in English. He has published widely on US culture and critical theory in *Diacritics, boundary 2, New Literary History, Cultural Critique, New German Critique*, and many others, and is the author of three books and two edited collections. His book *Animal Rites: American Culture, the Discourse of Species, and Posthumanist Theory* (Chicago, 2003) was nominated for the MLA's James Russell Lowell Prize, and the edited collection *Zoontologies: The Question of the Animal* (Minnesota) also appeared in 2003. His collection *The Other Emerson* (co-edited with Branka Arsic) is forthcoming from Fordham University Press in 2008, and he is currently completing a book called *What Is Posthumanism?*

Index

A

abjecting the animal, 117n38
abyssal rupture. *See* Derrida, Jacques
Adams, Carol: absent referent, 101; *The Sexual Politics of Meat: A Feminist-Vegetarian Critical Theory*, 115n19
aesthetics, 231–33
affective perception, 17, 159–60, 164–65, 167, 169. *See also* moral perception
Alighieri, Dante: *Paradise*, 48
Alternatives to Lab Animals (journal), 275
altruism, 13, 43, 49, 52–53, 57–58; acquisition of, 45; and compassion, 55; in Hobbes's *Leviathan*, 44; as misnomer, 50; as related to kin selection, 46
Anatomy Lesson of Dr. Jan Deyman (Rembrandt), 82
Anatomy Lesson of Dr. Nicolaas Tulp (Rembrandt), 78, 85
anatomy theatre, 14, 65, 75–76, 87n12, 90n59; anatomy lesson, 67–68, 70, 72, 74, 77–78; Cartesian, 80; lector, 68; sector, 68; subject-object dichotomy, 74
android, 187–88, 190
Animal Alliance of Canada, 212, 268n16
animal experimentation, 184, 205, 271; cancer research, 272, 276–77; invasive, 272–75; waste of animal lives, 272; *Web of Science*, 271–72

"Animal Experimentation in Cancer Research" (Dagg), 276, 278
animal liberation, 1, 17, 27n4, 97, 147, 152, 177, 180, 182, 184, 189; -ists, 178; movement, 186; philosophy, 183
Animal Liberation (Singer), 1, 27n4, 254n9
Animal Others: Ethics, Ontology, and Animal Life (Steeves), 115n18, 118n52, 171n20, 172n23
animal question, 2, 97, 98, 114, 235n9; nonhuman- 5, 7, 10; Wollstonecraft's position on, 225
Animal Question: Why Nonhuman Animals Deserve Human Rights (Cavalieri), 120n77
"Animal Rights and Feminist Theory" (Donovan), 224
Animal Rights and Human Obligations (Singer), 27n4
Animal Rights, Human Wrongs (Regan), 245
Animal Rites: American Culture, the Discourse of Species, and Posthumanist Theory (Wolfe), 1, 141n43, 141n46, 304
animal studies, 4, 21, 24, 28n8
"Animal that therefore I Am (More to Follow)," (Derrida), 118n56, 119n58, 119n64, 120n75

Animals and Ethics: An Overview of the Philosophical Debate (Taylor), 17
Animals, Property and the Law (Francione), 268n5
anthropocentrism, 5, 119n64, 151
anthropomorphism, 9, 141n53, 142; charges of, 11, 21; by ethologists, 57
anti-humanism, 15, 97–98, 102, 112–13
anti-humanist, 100, 103, 107, 111; Kantian distinction, 101
aquarium: Vancouver, 205–6
argument: from identity, 247–48; from marginal cases, 109, 119n61, 121, 180–81; from nature, 17, 177–79, 181–82, 184, 186, 189
Aristotle, 40, 59n5, 134, 138, 173n37, 178–79
Aristotle Contemplating the Bust of Homer (Rembrandt), 85
Armbruster, Karla, 158
Augustine, Saint, 287–88, 296
Auschwitz, 11
automata: animals as, 41, 43, 178
avian flu, 12, 36

B

Bacon, Francis, 52
Bakhtin, Mikhail, 4, 28n12
Bal, Mieke: *Double Exposures: The Subject of Cultural Analysis*, 74; *Reading "Rembrandt": Beyond the Word–Image Opposition*, 82
Barker-Benfield, G.J., 228
Barnum, P.T., 18, 195
Bataille, Georges, 291–92, 296, 298n17
Bear Alliance, 212
Beavers, Anthony F., 5
Bentham, Jeremy, 44–45, 49, 52, 58 59n9; Derrida, Peter Singer, and, 138; Holmes Rolston III and, 183
Best, Steven, 218
bête machine, 46
Beyond Prejudice (Pluhar), 249
biomedical, 22, 107, 271, 280
bio-power, 64–66, 74–75, 79–81, 86, 87n16
Birdsall, Stephen S., 153, 171n16
Blatchford, Christie, 266
Bobby (dog), 15, 102–4, 117n45
Bohls, Elizabeth A., 231, 233

Bowerbank, Sylvia, 226, 231
Budiansky, Stephen, 9

C

Calder, Alison, 7
Callicott, J. Baird, 182
Canadian Council on Animal Care (CCAC), 275
Canadian Institutes of Health Research, 275
Canadian sentencing law, 268n11
Cancer (journal), 277–78
capacity to suffer, 167, 180, 253
captivity, 201–2, 204, 206–10, 213–14, 264; bears, 212; dolphins, 212; orcas, 212
capture: human ability to, 199; Kensington the cat, 268n4; methods of, 207–9; Sultan the great ape, 293; of whales, 195–96
Cartesian, 51, 79–81, 83, 85, 91n76, 92n107, 99, 127, 129–31, 133, 137, 139n4, 180, 187; dualism, 178; -ism, 46, 133, 136–37; subject-object division, 67. *See also* anatomy theatre; Dennet, Daniel; Descartes, René; human–animal divide
Cartlidge, Doug, 211, 214–15
Case for Animal Rights (Regan), 170n1, 254n9, 256n32, 256n33
Casuistry: The Art of Killing a Cat (film), 266–67
Cavalieri, Paola: *The Animal Question: Why Nonhuman Animals Deserve Human Rights*, 120n77; *The Great Ape Project: Equality beyond Humanity*, 141n53
Cetacean Society International, 198, 208
chauvinism, 286, 296
Cheney, Jim, 150
Chicken Run (film), 37
"Citations Dearth: Another Reason to Reduce Animal Experimentation" (Dagg), 274
Coetzee, J.M.: *The Lives of Animals*, 290, 293; Sultan the great ape, 293–94
cognition, 7, 128, 147, 165
cognitive endowment 108–10
cognitive science, 125–27, 136, 180
Collini, Stefan, 3

INDEX   307

Communist Manifesto, 190
compassion, 11, 13, 27, 52, 54–56, 58, 108, 112, 163–65, 169–70, 188–89, 272
Comte, Auguste, 42
consciousness, 54, 103, 105, 128–31, 133, 135–36, 138, 148, 178, 191, 231, 246–47, 255n26, 255n28, 273, 291, 293, 297n4, 297n6; ecological, 231; human, 117n38, 137, 145, 180; intentional, 290, 292; self-, 243–44, 249–50
Consciousness Explained (Dennet), 131
Cousteau, Jean-Michel, 207, 219n20
Covance, 23
cruelty, 22–23, 29n22, 152, 160–65, 168, 217, 227–29, 260–61, 263, 273; anti-, 145, 156, 197. *See* Power, Jesse; Kensington
Curry, Michael R., 148–49
"Cyborg Manifesto, A: Science, Technology, and Socialist-Feminism in the Late Twentieth Century" (Haraway), 7, 11

D

Dagg, Anne Innis: "Citations Dearth: Another Reason to Reduce Animal Experimentation," 274; "Animal Experimentation in Cancer Research," 276
Darwin, Charles, 48, 58, 60n17, 60n30, 180–81, 184, 187, 190, 259; post-Darwinian, 108; social Darwinism, 182
Davis, Karen, 228
Davis, Libby (MP), 208
Davis, Susan G., 203
Dawkins, Richard, 13, 40–41, 50–58: altruism, 50; and Democritus, 43; and John Stuart Mill, 45; *River Out of Eden: A Darwinian View of Life*, 40; selfish gene theory, 40–41; *The Selfish Gene*, 40, 51, 59n11, 61; survival machines, 40, 50–51, 56; universal love, 48, 53
De cive (Hobbes), 42
Deacon, Terrance, 127, 135, 139n4
Dean, Richard: *An Essay on the Future Life of Brutes*, 227

"Declaration on Great Apes" (Cavalieri, Singer), 158
deconstruction, 15–16, 97, 107–8, 113, 125–26
dehumanization, 151, 253
Democritus, 42–43, 52, 59n5
Department of Fisheries and Oceans, 208, 219n16
depersonalization, 253
Dennet, Daniel: Cartesian theatre, 129–30; cognition and consciousness, 128; cognitive tasks, 129–30; *Consciousness Explained*, 131; functionalism, 127, 129; *Kinds of Minds*, 129, 131–32; moral standing, 129
Derrida, Jacques, 92n87, 97–98, 116n25, 118n53, 119n65, 119n67, 119n72, 125–26, 129, 132–36, 138, 140n17, 141n44; abyssal rupture, 108, 110, 118n56; "The Animal that therefore I Am (More to Follow)," 118n56, 119n58, 119n64, 120n75; animals and genocide, 107; biologism, 110–11; carno-phallogocentric structure, 107; interest in animals, 106; phonocentrism, 80; *Speech and Phenomena*, 80, 91n81
Descartes, René, 77–78, 85, 87n16, 90n70, 91n81, 108; animals as automata, 41, 43, 178; animals' capacity for speech lacking, 79, 133–34; animal spirits, 81; brutes, 100; Cartesian dualism, 85; cornarium, 81; *Discourse on Method*, 78; "masters and possessors of nature," 191; mechanistic view, 46, 78, 178, 189; pineal gland, 81–82, 93n110; real speech, 74, 79; res cogito, 80–81; res extensa, 80; robots, 187; unreason, 100
determinism, 41–43; materialistic, 52; philosophical, 53
determinist, 41, 43, 45, 49, 58
Dick, Phillip K., 186, 189; *Do Androids Dream of Electric Sheep?* 177, 186–88; *The Man in the High Castle*, 185
Discourse on Method (Descartes), 78, 87n16
dissection, 26–27, 31n45, 68, 70, 72, 74–76, 86, 89n41, 89n45, 90n59, 90n63; barber-surgeons, 67;

308　INDEX

Descartes, 78–80, 82; history of, 63–66; human–animal difference, 65
Dissertation on the Duty of Mercy and Sin of Cruelty to Brute Animals (Primatt), 227
Distorted Nature: Exposing the Myth of Marineland (Zoocheck), 210
Do Androids Dream of Electric Sheep? (Dick), 177, 186–87
Doherty, Mr. Justice, 263
Dolly (sheep), 190
domination, 111, 114n7, 204; as entertainment, 213–14; male, 233; of nature, 157, 191, 223; relationships of, 100–101; structures of, 223–24, 230, 235; systemic, 229
dominion, 99, 154, 199, 218
Dominion: The Power of Man, the Suffering of Animals, and the Call to Mercy (Scully), 9–10, 29n26
Donovan, Josephine, 228; "Animal Rights and Feminist Theory," 224
Double Exposures: The Subject of Cultural Analysis (Bal), 74
Downie, R.S., 242, 249
Dunayer, Joan, 243

E

Economy of Nature and the Evolution of Sex (Ghiselin), 40
Émile (Rousseau), 59n9
empathy, 5, 26, 52, 115n10, 164–65, 168–69, 188, 289, 296
Empty Cages (Regan), 245
Enlightenment, 45, 234
Epicurus, 42–43, 49, 52
epistemological, 98, 125–26, 136, 138
Essay on Humanity to Animals (Young), 227
Essay on the Future Life of Brutes (Dean), 227
essentialism, 99
essentialist, 230, 233, 235
Ethics (Spinoza), 47
ethics, 5, 7, 52, 98, 102, 104–5, 112–14, 146–47, 149–50, 173n30, 223, 251–52, 256n33, 274; animal liberation, 97; concept of *person* in, 242; designer, 35; environmental, 17, 177; perception and literature, 155

Etica & Animali (Cavalieri), 172n26, 172n27
existential, 5, 288, 292

F

factory farming, 34, 107, 111, 152, 156, 182, 197, 286
"Father and Child" (Harwood), 159–64, 168
Female Reader, The (Wollstonecraft), 230
feminism, 228; eco-, 223, 228, 235; socialist-, 21, 30n32
Feminism & Ecology (Mellor), 228
Fossey, Dian, 158
Foucault, Michel, 97–102, 105–6; human subject, 102; *Madness and Civilization*, 102; nonhumans, 100; power, 101; treatment of the other, 112
Francione, Gary, 26, 243, 246, 259; *Animals, Property and the Law*, 268n5; *Introduction to Animal Rights: Your Child or the Dog?* 22, 267n1
Franklin, Sarah, 35
Frohoff, Toni, 205, 213–14
Fuery, Patrick, 6, 28n16

G

Galen, 66–68, 74, 87n16
Galileo, 78, 88n35, 178
Gassendi, Pierre, 43, 49, 53; *The Life, Modes and Doctrines of Epicurus*, 42
genetics, 40, 58n1
genocide, 107, 198
George, Kathryn Paxton, 179
Ghiselin, Michael T., 55; *The Economy of Nature and the Evolution of Sex*, 40
Gleeson, Brendan, 149
globalization, 4, 33
Godwin, William: *Memoirs of the Author of a Vindication of the Rights of Woman*, 223
Goodall, Jane, 56, 214
Great Ape Project (organization), 252, 254n14
Great Ape Project: Equality beyond Humanity (Cavalieri, Singer), 97, 109–10, 141n53
Gripper, John, 210
Guiccardini, Francesco, 42

H

Hall, John, 209
Hall, Stuart, 3–4
Haraway, Donna: "A Cyborg Manifesto: Science, Technology, and Socialist-Feminism in the Late Twentieth Century," 7, 11
Harper, Lila Marz, 231–32
Harwood, Gwen: "Father and Child," 159–64, 168
Heidegger, Martin, 98, 106–7, 112–13, 119n64, 119n72, 133, 138; Heideggerian, 103–4, 110
hierarchy, 2, 178; moral, 189; racial, 198; sociopolitical, 198
Hobbes, Thomas, 41, 49, 54, 181, 183; *De cive*, 42; *Leviathan*, 42
Hornaday, William T., 196
Hugo, Victor, 53; *Les Miserables*, 48–49; *Notre Dame de Paris*, 49
human-animal divide, 74, 224, 226, 230, 232, 234; Cartesian, 79, 85; difference, 67; distinction, 225; division, 72; first-person speech, 74–75; real speech 74, 79, 80
human-animal interactions, 146–47, 159, 178, 182; relations, 226–27, 230, 233
humanism, 97–98 104, 111, 134; anti-, 102–3, 112–13; metaphysical, 109
Hume, David, 44, 179–80
Husserl, Edmund, 288–91, 294, 296
Hust, Karen, 231
hybridity, 3, 28n8

I

immortality, 286–88, 296
interconnectedness, 223, 230
International Fund for Animal Welfare (IFAW), 208
Introduction to Animal Rights: Your Child or the Dog? (Francione), 22, 267n1

J

James, William, 297n1
Journal of Applied Animal Welfare Science (JAAWS), 276, 278
Journal of the National Cancer Institute, 277

K

Kautz, Beth Dolan, 231
Kellert, Stephen R., 56
Kensington (cat), 260–61, 265–68
Kenyon-Jones, Christine, 224
Kierkegaard, Soren, 291; *Postscript*, 288
Kinds of Minds (Dennet), 129, 131–32
Kiska (whale), 202
Klee, Paul, 290
Kohler, Wolfgang, 293–94
Kristeva, Julia, 72–73, 89n42, 89n44

L

La Rochefoucauld, François de: *Maxims*, 48
Laidlaw, Rob, 212
Lawrence, Elizabeth, 201
Lefèbvre, Henri, 153
Lessons (Wollstonecraft), 226
Letters Written during a Short Residence in Sweden, Norway, and Denmark (Wollstonecraft), 224–25, 229–30
Leviathan (Hobbes), 42, 44
Levinas, Emmanuel, 98, 112, 134, 138; Other and Same 103, 104, 105–6; story of Bobby 102–4
Life, Modes and Doctrines of Epicurus (Gassendi), 42
Low, Nicholas, 149
Lynn, William S., 153, 155

M

Machiavelli, Nicolo, 42; *The Prince*, 47
Madness and Civilization (Foucault), 102
Malamud, Randy, 198
Malcolmson, Robert, 227
Man in the High Castle (Dick), 185
Mansfield, Nick, 6, 28n16
Marineland: education/entertainment, 202–5; expansion of, 212; history of, 198; International Fund for Animal Welfare, 208; protest at, 215; website, 200–201; Zoocheck, 208
Maritain, Jacques, 292–94, 298n17; poetic intuition, 292
Marvin, Garry, 199, 201, 203
Marxism, 3, 99
Marx, Karl, 42–43, 190
Mary (Wollstonecraft), 228
Masson, Jeffrey, 10

materialism, 11, 42, 48, 49, 52-54, 129; eliminative, 127, 135
Maxims (La Rochefoucauld), 48
McCarthy, Susan, 10
McDonald's, 30n38, 35, 216-17
Medical Research Council of Canada, 275
Meditations on Hunting (Ortega y Gasset), 186
Medoro, Dana, 7
Mellor, Mary, 224; *Feminism & Ecology*, 228
Memoirs of the Author of a Vindication of the Rights of Woman (Godwin), 223
Mill, John Stuart, 45, 49, 51
Miserables, Les (Hugo), 48-49
moral: agency, 105, 111-12, 249; agent, 98, 102, 105-6, 111, 153; patients, 98, 102, 106, 111; perception, 159, 162, 164, 172n30; psychopaths, 165; schizophrenia, 259; space, 147-50, 152-53, 157, 159, 169-70; status, 108-9, 111, 145-46, 177, 190, 235n9
Moskal, Jeanne, 231
Mullan, Bob, 199, 201, 203

N

Nazi, 186
Newton, Sir Isaac, 190
Niagara Action For Animals (NAFA), 20, 29n22, 212, 215-17
Nicholson, George: *On the Primeval Diet of Man*, 227
Nietzsche, Friedrich, 98-99, 114n5, 115n18; and Foucault, 99; will to power, 99-100
No Compromise, 198, 215
Notre Dame de Paris (Hugo), 49
Nussbaum, Martha, 159, 165, 173n37
Nutrition and Cancer, 277-78

O

Oakeshott, Michael, 40
O'Barry, Richard, 208-9
objectivity, 89n44, 136
Old Woman (Rembrandt), 85
On the Primeval Diet of Man (Nicholson), 227
Ontario College of Art and Design, 261
Ontario Court of Appeal: Jesse Power's sentence, 263
ontology, 109, 189; of nonhuman beings, 127; ontological, 99, 104, 126, 133, 137; post-ontological, 127
Original Stories from Real Life; With Conversations, Calculated to Regulate the Affections, and Form the Mind to Truth and Goodness (Wollstonecraft), 224-26
Ortega y Gasset, José: *Meditations on Hunting*, 186

P

Pacific Meat Company, 264-65
Paradise (Dante), 48
Perkins, David, 224
Person, 138, 244-45, 250; definition of, 241, 243, 249, 252; the Persons Case, 21
personhood, 146, 241, 243-52; denial of, 242, 250; "full personhood," 249
PETA (People for the Ethical Treatment of Animals), 23, 30n36, 30n38, 31n45, 205, 219n18
phenomenology, 131, 290-91; dominion, 154-55; Husserl's, 289; phenomenological psychology, 289, 296; space, 153
Philosophical Investigations (Wittgenstein), 150
phlogiston theory, 244, 254n15
Plato, 286, 296; immortal soul, 287; the rational, 288; rational soul, 290
Pluhar, Evelyn, 244, 246; *Beyond Prejudice*, 249
postcolonial, 34-37
postmodern, 97, 290-91; philosophers, 98
Postscript (Kierkegaard), 288
Power, Jesse, 260-63, 266-67, 268n6, 268n7, 268n10, 268n11
Preece, Rod, 178, 224
Primatt, Humphry: *A Dissertation on the Duty of Mercy and Sin of Cruelty to Brute Animals*, 227
Prince, The (Machiavelli), 47
Proctor, James D., 148
psychopath, 165, 262, 268n10

R

racism, 1-2, 9, 100, 110-11, 113, 197-98, 201
rationalist tradition, 42
Reading "Rembrandt": Beyond the Word–Image Opposition (Bal), 82-83
Regan, Tom, 178, 182, 184, 244-45, 250, 254; *Animal Rights, Human Wrongs*, 245; *The Case for Animal Rights*, 170n1, 254n9, 256n32, 256n33; *Empty Cages*, 245
Reichmann, James, 184
Rembrandt, 78, 83, 85-86, 88n41, 90n71, 92n107, 93n110; *An Old Woman*, 85; *The Anatomy Lesson of Dr. Jan Deyman*, 82; *Anatomy Lesson of Dr. Nicolaas Tulp*, 78; *Aristotle Contemplating the Bust of Homer*, 85; *Slaughtered Ox*, 82
res cogito, 79-80, 129
res extensa, 80
Rifkin, Jeremy, 190
Ritvo, Harriet, 228
River Out of Eden: A Darwinian View of Life (Dawkins), 40
Rolston III, Holmes, 182, 237n40
Rorty, Richard, 135; representationalism, 126
Rose, Naomi A., 202, 206, 210
Rossiter, William, 198, 208
Rousseau, Jean Jacques, 50, 52; *Émile*, 59n9

S

Sabine, George H., 43
Salutati, Caluccio, 42
Sartre, Jean-Paul, 100, 180, 183, 186, 297n14
Schjelderup-Ebbe, Thorleif, 37
Schulman, Norma, 4
Scully, Matthew: *Dominion: The Power of Man, the Suffering of Animals, and the Call to Mercy*, 9-10, 29n26
Sea World, 203, 209
Seidle, Troy, 279
self-interest theory, 43, 45
selfish gene theory, 40-41, 43, 45, 47-49, 51-54, 57, 59n8
Selfish Gene, The (Dawkins), 39-40, 51, 56

Seligman, Martin, 159, 165, 167; learned helplessness, 166, 168
Sexual Politics of Meat: A Feminist-Vegetarian Critical Theory (Adams), 115n19
Singer, Peter, 8-9, 137-38, 141n53, 178, 245, 249, 256n31; *Animal Liberation*, 1, 27n4, 254n9; *Animal Rights and Human Obligations*, 27n4; *The Great Ape Project*, 141n53
Skinner, B.F., 42
Slaughtered Ox (Rembrandt), 83-86
slavery, 6, 183, 196-98, 213, 218
Smith, John Maynard, 51, 170n2
Smuts, Barbara, 290, 295, 298n30
sociobiology, 40, 44-46, 48, 58n1
Sociobiology (Wilson), 41
Southey, Robert, 231
speciesism, 9, 27n4, 111, 113, 198, 253
Speech and Phenomena and Other Essays on Husserl's Theory of Signs (Derrida), 80, 91n81
Spinoza, Baruch: *Ethics*, 47
Steeves, H. Peter: *Animal Others: Ethics, Ontology, and Animal Life*, 115n18, 118n52, 171n20, 172n23
Strategic Lawsuits Against Public Participation (SLAPP), 216
subjectivity, 5, 15-16, 107, 125-26, 137, 204, 291; metaphysics of, 112; nonhuman, 6, 127
survival machines, 40, 50-51, 56

T

technoscience, 33, 35
Tertullian, 287
Thoughts on the Education of Daughters (Wollstonecraft), 225
Three Scientists and Their Gods (Wright), 46-47
Tilghman, Benjamin R., 150
Topia: A Canadian Journal of Cultural Studies, 1, 27n2
Toronto International Film Festival, 266
Treatise of Man (Descartes), 81
Turing test, 187

U

utilitarianism, 59n8, 165

V

vegetarian, 179, 224, 227, 261
vegetarianism, 107, 118n52; *Deep Vegetarianism*, 16
Vesalius, Andreas, 64-67, 70, 72, 74-78, 80, 85, 87n16, 88n35, 88n37, 88n38, 89n45, 90n63, 90n71
Vindication of the Rights of Men, 225, 230
Vindication of the Rights of Women (Wollstonecraft), 224, 226-27, 229

W

Walker, Margaret Urban, 149-50
Warren, Karen, 223
Weinberg, R.A., 279-80
Westra, Laura, 183-84
Weston, Anthony, 150
Whales Alive!, 198, 208
Williams, Raymond, 3
Wilson, Dan, 216
Wilson, Edmond O., 45-46; *Sociobiology*, 41
Wise, Steven M., 172n27, 253
Wittgenstein, Ludwig: *Philosophical Investigations*, 150
Wollstonecraft, Mary, 223-24, 227-28; *The Female Reader*, 230; *Lessons*, 226; *Letters Written during a Short Residence in Sweden, Norway, and Denmark*, 224-25, 229-30; *Mary*, 228; *Original Stories from Real Life; With Conversations, Calculated to Regulate the Affections, and Form the Mind to Truth and Goodness*, 224-26; *Thoughts on the Education of Daughters*, 225; *Vindication of the Rights of Men*, 225, 230; *Vindication of the Rights of Women*, 224, 226-27, 229; *The Wrongs of Woman*, 228-30
woman question, 235n9
World Society for the Protection of Animals, 210-12
Wright, Robert, 48; kin selection, 46; *Three Scientists and Their Gods*, 46-47
Wrongs of Woman, The (Wollstonecraft), 228-30

Y

Young, Thomas: *An Essay on Humanity to Animals*, 227

Z

zoo, 156, 196-99, 201-6, 208, 210-12, 214, 218, 265; West Edmonton Mall, 205

CULTURAL STUDIES SERIES

Cultural Studies is the multi- and interdisciplinary study of culture, defined anthropologically as a "way of life," performatively as symbolic practice, and ideologically as the collective product of media and cultural industries, i.e., pop culture. Although Cultural Studies is a relative newcomer to the humanities and social sciences, in less than half a century it has taken interdisciplinary scholarship to a new level of sophistication, reinvigorating the liberal arts curriculum with new theories, new topics, and new forms of intellectual partnership.

The Cultural Studies series includes topics such as construction of identities; regionalism/nationalism cultural citizenship; migration; popular culture; consume cultures; media and film; the body; postcolonial criticism; cultural policy; sexualities; cultural theory; youth culture; class relations; and gender.

The new Cultural Studies series from Wilfrid Laurier University Press invites submission of manuscripts concerned with critical discussions on power relations concerning gender, class, sexual preference, ethnicity, and other macro and micro sites of political struggle.

For further information, please contact the Series Editor:

> Jodey Castricano
> Department of Critical Studies
> University of British Columbia Okanagan
> 3333 University Way
> Kelowna, BC V1V1V7

ENVIRONMENTAL HUMANITIES SERIES

Environmental thought pursues with renewed urgency the grand concerns of the humanities: who we think we are, how we relate to others, and how we live in the world. Scholarship in the environmental humanities explores these questions by crossing the lines that separate human from animal, social from material, and objects and bodies from techno-ecological networks. Humanistic accounts of political representation and ethical recognition are re-examined in consideration of other species. Social identities are studied in relation to conceptions of the natural, the animal, the bodily, place, space, landscape, risk, and technology, and in relation to the material distribution and contestation of environmental hazards and pleasures.

The Environmental Humanities Series features research that adopts and adapts the methods of the humanities to clarify the cultural meanings associated with environmental debate. The scope of the series is broad. Film, literature, television, Web-based media, visual art, and physical landscape—all are crucial sites for exploring how ecological relationships and identities are lived and imagined. The Environmental Humanities Series publishes scholarly monographs and essay collections in environmental cultural studies, including popular culture, film, media, and visual cultures; environmental literary criticism; cultural geography; environmental philosophy, ethics, and religious studies; and other cross-disciplinary research that probes what it means to be human, animal, and technological in an ecological world.

Gathering research and writing in environmental philosophy, ethics, cultural studies, and literature under a single umbrella, the series aims to make visible the contributions of humanities research to environmental studies, and to foster discussion that challenges and reconceptualizes the humanities.

SERIES EDITOR
Cheryl Lousley, English and Film Studies, Wilfrid Laurier University

EDITORIAL COMMITTEE
Adrian J. Ivakhiv, Environmental Studies, University of Vermont
Catriona Mortimer-Sandilands, Tier 1 CRC in Sustainability and Culture, Environmental Studies, York University
Susie O'Brien, English and Cultural Studies, McMaster University
Laurie Ricou, English, University of British Columbia
Rob Shields, Henry Marshall Tory Chair and Professor, Department of Sociology, University of Alberta

FOR MORE INFORMATION, CONTACT
Lisa Quinn
Acquisitions Editor
Wilfrid Laurier University Press
75 University Avenue West
Waterloo, ON N2L 3C5
(519) 884-0710 ext. 2843
Email: quinn@press.wlu.ca